Mastering Unity 5.x

Create amazing games with solid gameplay features, using a professional-grade workflow inside the Unity engine!

Alan Thorn

BIRMINGHAM - MUMBAI

Mastering Unity 5.x

First published: January 2017

Production reference: 1200117

Published by Packt Publishing Ltd.
Livery Place
35 Livery Street
Birmingham
B3 2PB, UK.

ISBN 978-1-78588-074-2

www.packtpub.com

Credits

Author

Alan Thorn

Reviewer

Francesco Sapio

Commissioning Editor

Amarabha Banerjee

Acquisition Editor

Larissa Pinto

Content Development Editor

Onkar Wani

Technical Editor

Murtaza Tinwala

Copy Editor

Safis Editing

Project Coordinator

Ulhas Kambali

Proofreader

Safis Editing

Indexer

Aishwarya Gangawane

Production Coordinator

Arvindkumar Gupta

Graphics

Abhinash Sahu

About the Author

Alan Thorn is a multidisciplinary game developer, author, and educator with industry experience of 17 years. He makes games for PC desktop, mobile, and VR. He founded *Wax Lyrical Games* and created the award-winning *Baron Wittard: Nemesis of Ragnarok* game, working as designer, programmer, and artist. He has written twenty-three technical books on game development and presented 19 video training courses. These cover game-play programming, Unity development, 3D modeling, and animation. He has worked in games education as a senior lecturer for Teesside University, a lead teacher for Uppingham School, and a visiting lecturer for the London South Bank University. He is currently the head of department for *Games Design and Development* at the National Film and Television School.

Acknowledgment

This book would not have been possible if it hadn't been for the valuable help of many people. I would like to thank all my friends and family, and also the team at Packt. This includes Onkar Wani and Larissa Pinto.

About the Reviewer

Francesco Sapio obtained his computer science and control engineering degree from Sapienza University of Rome, Italy, with a couple of semesters in advance, scoring summa cum laude. He is currently working on a master of science in engineering in artificial intelligence and robotics at the same university.

He is a Unity 3D and Unreal expert, a skilled game designer, and an experienced user of the major graphics programs. He developed *Game@School* (Sapienza University of Rome) an educational game for high school students to learn some concepts of physics, and *Sticker Book* (Dataware Games), a cross-platform series of games for kids. In addition, he worked as a consultant for the (successfully funded by Kickstarter) game *Prosperity – Italy 1434* (Entertainment Game Apps, Inc) and for the open online collaborative ideation system titled *Innovoice* (Sapienza University of Rome). Moreover, he has been involved in different research projects, such as *Belief Driven Pathfinding* (Sapienza University of Rome), which is a new technique of pathfinding in video games that was presented as a paper at the *DiGRA-FDG Conference 2016* and *perfekt.ID* (Royal Melbourne Institute of Technology), which included developing a recommendation system for games.

He is an active writer on the topic of game development. Recently, he authored the book *Unity UI Cookbook, Packt* which teaches readers how to develop exciting and practical user interfaces for games within Unity, and a short e-guide, *What do you need to know about Unity, Packt*. In addition, he co-authored the book *Unity 5.x 2D Game Development Blueprints, Packt*. Furthermore, he has also been a reviewer for the following books: *Game Physics Cookbook, Unity 5.x by Example*, and *Unity Game Development Scripting*, all from Packt.

Finally, Francesco loves math, philosophy, logic, and puzzle solving, but most of all, creating video games, thanks to his passion for game designing and programming.

You can connect with him at www.francescosapio.com.

I'm deeply thankful to my parents for their infinite patience, enthusiasm, and support throughout my life. Moreover, I'm thankful to the rest of my family, in particular to my grandparents, since they have always encouraged me to do better in my life with the Latin expressions "Ad maiora" and "Per aspera ad astra".

Finally, a huge thanks to all the special people around me whom I love, in particular to my girlfriend—I'm grateful for all of your help in everything.

www.PacktPub.com

For support files and downloads related to your book, please visit www.PacktPub.com.

Did you know that Packt offers eBook versions of every book published, with PDF and ePub files available? You can upgrade to the eBook version at www.PacktPub.com and as a print book customer, you are entitled to a discount on the eBook copy. Get in touch with us at service@packtpub.com for more details.

At www.PacktPub.com, you can also read a collection of free technical articles, sign up for a range of free newsletters and receive exclusive discounts and offers on Packt books and eBooks.

https://www.packtpub.com/mapt

Get the most in-demand software skills with Mapt. Mapt gives you full access to all Packt books and video courses, as well as industry-leading tools to help you plan your personal development and advance your career.

Why subscribe?

- Fully searchable across every book published by Packt
- Copy and paste, print, and bookmark content
- On demand and accessible via a web browser

Customer Feedback

Thank you for purchasing this Packt book. We take our commitment to improving our content and products to meet your needs seriously—that's why your feedback is so valuable. Whatever your feelings about your purchase, please consider leaving a review on this book's Amazon page. Not only will this help us, more importantly it will also help others in the community to make an informed decision about the resources that they invest in to learn.

You can also review for us on a regular basis by joining our reviewers' club. **If you're interested in joining, or would like to learn more about the benefits we offer, please contact us**: customerreviews@packtpub.com.

This book is dedicated to Mark Lovering, a gentleman and a scholar.

Table of Contents

Preface

Greetings and welcome to Mastering Unity 5.x! This book teaches Unity initially from a beginner's perspective, and then helps you develop that knowledge in a particular way. Specifically, it develops a general, overarching mastery, in which you'll learn Unity like a seasoned indie developer' capable of turning your hand to pretty much any department and feature set within Unity. The following chapter outline explains, in detail, the full range of features that we'll explore. However, the central aim of this book is to make you versatile and fully competent with Unity, capable of encountering a problem and solving it in the language of Unity's feature set. In this book, we'll concentrate, for the most part, on a practical example; we'll build a first-person combat game across multiple chapters, which will test your typing skills in more ways than one. So, let's go!

What this book covers

Chapter 1, *Preparation and Asset-Configuring*, outlines the project we'll be focusing on in the book. It specifies tips and tricks to import assets optimally, configure assets, and best-practice workflows to keep your project organized.

Chapter 2, *Level Design and Structure*, gets you started with designing and building the main game level inside Unity, exploring interesting level design ideas as well as critically important practical considerations.

Chapter 3, *Player Controls – Movement*, explores player controls, that is, how player input drives and controls the main game camera.

Chapter 4, *Player Controls – Typing and Health*, focuses on creating a combat mechanic that damages enemies; every character that can be damaged needs health, representing the total amount of damage a character may sustain.

Chapter 5, *Enemies and Artificial Intelligence*, looks at how to achieve intelligent and believable enemy behavior using AI. By using AI, enemies will move around the level seeking the player and will attack when in range.

Chapter 6, *Project Management and Version Control*, looks at ways to optimize the game development workflow by using Version Control software. This keeps a record of your project as it moves through all its iterations.

Chapter 7, *Persistent Data – Load and Save Game States*, focuses on the different saving methods available with Unity as players often want their in-game progress saved, allowing them to resume where they left off previously every time they start a new play session.

Chapter 8, *Performance, Optimization, Mobiles, and More*, explores a selection of related topics. Specifically, it will explore how to improve the performance of your games through optimization, how to prepare your games for mobile deployment, and how to prepare generally for VR development.

What you need for this book

To read this book effectively, and to complete the tasks within it, you need only two things: first, the Unity 5 software (which you can get for free from https://unity3d.com) and second, the determination to succeed! Using only these tools, you can learn to produce great games in Unity.

Who this book is for

If you are a Unity developer who now wants to develop and deploy interesting games by leveraging the new features of Unity 5.x, then this is the book for you. A basic knowledge of C# programming is assumed.

Conventions

In this book, you will find a number of text styles that distinguish between different kinds of information. Here are some examples of these styles and an explanation of their meaning.

Code words in text, database table names, folder names, filenames, file extensions, pathnames, dummy URLs, user input, and Twitter handles are shown as follows: "This should be dragged and dropped into the music folder."

A block of code is set as follows:

```
//Collection of combat sounds
public AudioClip[] CombatSounds;
```

New terms and **important words** are shown in bold. Words that you see on the screen, for example, in menus or dialog boxes, appear in the text like this: "From the Command Palette, choose **Change Case Lower**."

Warnings or important notes appear in a box like this.

 Tips and tricks appear like this.

Reader feedback

Feedback from our readers is always welcome. Let us know what you think about this book—what you liked or disliked. Reader feedback is important for us as it helps us develop titles that you will really get the most out of.

To send us general feedback, simply e-mail feedback@packtpub.com, and mention the book's title in the subject of your message.

If there is a topic that you have expertise in and you are interested in either writing or contributing to a book, see our author guide at www.packtpub.com/authors.

Customer support

Now that you are the proud owner of a Packt book, we have a number of things to help you to get the most from your purchase.

Downloading the example code

You can download the example code files for this book from your account at http://www.packtpub.com. If you purchased this book elsewhere, you can visit http://www.packtpub.com/support and register to have the files e-mailed directly to you.

You can download the code files by following these steps:

1. Log in or register to our website using your e-mail address and password.
2. Hover the mouse pointer on the **SUPPORT** tab at the top.
3. Click on **Code Downloads & Errata**.
4. Enter the name of the book in the **Search** box.
5. Select the book for which you're looking to download the code files.
6. Choose from the drop-down menu where you purchased this book from.
7. Click on **Code Download**.

You can also download the code files by clicking on the **Code Files** button on the book's webpage at the Packt Publishing website. This page can be accessed by entering the book's name in the **Search** box. Please note that you need to be logged in to your Packt account.

Once the file is downloaded, please make sure that you unzip or extract the folder using the latest version of:

- WinRAR / 7-Zip for Windows
- Zipeg / iZip / UnRarX for Mac
- 7-Zip / PeaZip for Linux

The code bundle for the book is also hosted on GitHub at `https://github.com/PacktPubl ishing/Mastering-Unity-5x`. We also have other code bundles from our rich catalog of books and videos available at `https://github.com/PacktPublishing/`. Check them out!

Downloading the color images of this book

We also provide you with a PDF file that has color images of the screenshots/diagrams used in this book. The color images will help you better understand the changes in the output. You can download this file from `https://www.packtpub.com/sites/default/files/down loads/MasteringUnity5x_ColorImages.pdf`.

Errata

Although we have taken every care to ensure the accuracy of our content, mistakes do happen. If you find a mistake in one of our books—maybe a mistake in the text or the code—we would be grateful if you could report this to us. By doing so, you can save other readers from frustration and help us improve subsequent versions of this book. If you find any errata, please report them by visiting http://www.packtpub.com/submit-errata, selecting your book, clicking on the **Errata Submission Form** link, and entering the details of your errata. Once your errata are verified, your submission will be accepted and the errata will be uploaded to our website or added to any list of existing errata under the Errata section of that title.

To view the previously submitted errata, go to https://www.packtpub.com/books/content/supportand enter the name of the book in the search field. The required information will appear under the **Errata** section.

Piracy

Piracy of copyrighted material on the Internet is an ongoing problem across all media. At Packt, we take the protection of our copyright and licenses very seriously. If you come across any illegal copies of our works in any form on the Internet, please provide us with the location address or website name immediately so that we can pursue a remedy.

Please contact us at copyright@packtpub.com with a link to the suspected pirated material.

We appreciate your help in protecting our authors and our ability to bring you valuable content.

Questions

If you have a problem with any aspect of this book, you can contact us at questions@packtpub.com, and we will do our best to address the problem.

1
Preparation and Asset-Configuring

Greetings and welcome to this comprehensive and detailed exploration of Unity 5 that examines carefully how we take a game project from conception to completion. Here, we'll pay special attention to the best-practice workflows, design elegance, and technical excellence. The project to be created will be a first-person cinematic shooter game, for desktop computers and mobile devices, inspired by *Typing of the Dead* (`https://en.wikipedia.org/wiki/The_Typing_of_the_Dead`). Our game will be called *Dead Keys* (from here-on, abbreviated *DK*). In DK, the player continually confronts evil flesh-eating zombies, and the only way to eliminate them safely is to complete a set of typing exercises, using either the physical keyboard or a virtual keyboard. Each zombie, when they appear, may attack the player and is associated with a single word or phrase chosen randomly from a dictionary. The chosen phrase is presented clearly as a GUI label above the zombie's head. In response, the player must type the matching word in correct and full words, letter by letter, to eliminate the zombie. If the player completes the word or phrase without error, the zombie is destroyed. If the player makes a mistake, such as pressing the wrong letter in the wrong order, then they must repeat the typing sequence from the beginning.

This challenge may initially sound simple for the player, but longer words and phrases naturally give zombies a longer life span and greater opportunities for attacking. The player inevitably has limited health and will die if their health falls below 0. The objective of the player, therefore, is to defeat all zombies and reach the end of the level.

Dead Keys, the game to be created

Creating the word-shooter project involves many technical challenges, both 3D and 2D, and together, these make extensive use of Unity and its expansive feature set. For this reason, it's worth spending some time exploring what you'll see in this book and why. This book is a *Mastering* title, namely *Mastering Unity 5*, and the word *Mastering* carries important expectations about excellence and complexity. These expectations vary significantly across people, because people hold different ideas about what mastery truly means. Some think mastery is about learning one specific skill and becoming very good at it, such as mastery in scripting, lighting, or animation. These are, of course, legitimate understandings of mastery. However, others see mastery more holistically, and this view is no less legitimate. It's the idea that mastery consists in cultivating a general, overarching knowledge of many different skills and disciplines, but in a special way by seeing a relationship between them and seeing them as complementary parts that work together to produce sophisticated and masterful results. This is a second and equally legitimate understanding of the term, and it's the one that forms the foundation for this book.

This book is about using Unity generally as a holistic tool—seeing its many features come together, as one unit, from level editing and scripting to lighting, design, and animation. For this reason, our journey will inevitably lead us to many areas of development—not just coding. Thus, if you're seeking a book solely about coding, then check out *Packt's* title on *Mastering Unity Scripting*. In any case, this book, being about mastery, will not focus on fundamental concepts and basic operations. It assumes already that you can build basic levels using the level editor and can create basic materials and some basic script files using C#. Though this book may at times include some extra, basic information as a refresher and also to add context, it won't enter into detailed explanations about basic concepts, which are covered amply in other titles. Entry level titles from Packt include *Unity 5.x By Example*, *Learning C# by Developing Games with Unity 5.x*, and *Unity Animation Essentials*. This book, however, assumes you have a basic literacy in Unity and want to push your skills to the next level, developing a masterful hand in building Unity games, across the board.

So, with that said, let's jump in and make our game!

Getting clear on design

To build games professionally and maximize productivity, always develop from a clear design, whether on paper or in digital form. Ensure that the design is stated and expressed in a way that's intelligible to others, and not just to yourself. It's easy for anybody to jump excitedly into Unity without a design plan, assuming you know your own mind best of all, and then to find yourself wandering aimlessly from option to option without any direction. Without a clear plan, your project quickly descends into drift and chaos. Thus, first produce a coherent **game design document** (**GDD**) for a general audience of game designers who may not be familiar with the technicalities of development. In that document, you will get clarity about some very important points before using development software, making assets, or building levels. These points, and a description, are listed in the following sections, along with examples that apply to the project we'll be developing.

 A GDD is a written document created by designers detailing (through words, diagrams, and pictures) a clear outline of a complete game. More information on GDD can be found online at `https://en.wikipedia.org/wiki/Game_design_document`.

Target Platforms

Target Platforms

The Target Platform specifies the device, or range of devices, on which your game runs natively, such as Windows, Mac, Android, iOS, and so on. This is the full range of hardware on which a potential gamer can play your game. The Target Platforms for DK include Windows, Mac, Android, and iOS.

Reaching decisions about which platforms to support is an important logistical and technical as well as political matter. Ideally, a developer wants to support as many platforms as possible, making their game available to the largest customer base. However, whatever the ideals may be, supporting every platform is almost never feasible, and so, practical choices have to be made. Each supported platform involves considerable time, effort, and money of the developer, even though Unity makes multi-platform support easier by doing a lot of low-level work for you. Developing for multiple platforms normally means creating meshes, textures, and audio files of varying sizes and detail levels as well as adapting user interfaces to different screen layouts and aspect ratios, and also being sensitive to the hardware specifics of each platform.

Platform support also influences core game mechanics; for example, touch-screen games behave and feel radically different from keyboard-based games and motion controls behave differently from mouse-based controls. Thus, a platform always constrains and limits the field of possibilities as to what can be achieved, not just technically, but also for content. App Store submission guidelines place strict requirements upon permissible content, language, and representations in games and allowed in-app purchases and access to external, user-created content.

The upshot is that Target Platforms should, for the most part, always be chosen in advance. That decision will heavily influence core game mechanics and how the design is implemented in a playable way. Sometimes, the decision to defer support for a particular platform can, and should, be made for technical or economic reasons. However, when such a decision is made, be aware that it can heavily increase development time further along the cycle, as reasonable adjustment and redevelopment may be needed to properly support the nuances of the platform.

Intended audience

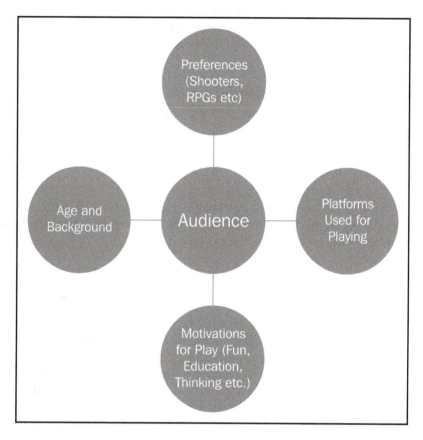

Deciding on an Intended Audience

The intended audience is like a personality profile. It defines in summary who you're making the game for. Using some stereotyping, it specifies who is supposed to play your game: casual gamers, action gamers, or hardcore gamers; children or adults; English speakers or non-English speakers; or someone else. This decision is important especially for establishing the suitability of the game content and characters and difficulty of gameplay. Suitability is not just a matter of hiding nudity, violence, and profanity from younger gamers. It's about engaging your audience with relevant content: issues and stories, ideas that are resonant with them and encourage them to keep playing. Similarly, difficulty is not simply about making games easier for younger gamers. It's about balancing rewards and punishments and timings to match audience expectations, whatever their age.

As with Target Platform, you should have a target audience in mind when designing your game. This matters especially for keeping focused when including new ideas in your game. Coming up with fun ideas is great, but will they actually work for your audience in this case? If your target audience lacks sufficient focus, then some problems such as the following will emerge:

- Your game will feel conceptually messy (a jumble of disconnected ideas)
- You'll struggle to answer how your game is fun or interesting
- You'll keep making big and important changes to the design during its development

For these reasons, and more, narrow your target audience as precisely as possible, as early as possible.

For Dead Keys, the target audience will be over 15 years of age and *Shoot 'Em Up* fans who also enjoy quirky gameplay that deviates from the mainstream. A secondary audience may include casual gamers who enjoy time-critical word games.

Genre

Genre is primarily about the game content: what type of game is it? Is it RPG, first-person shooter, adventure, or any other type? Genres can be even narrower than this, such as fantasy MMORPG and cyberpunk, competitive, deathmatch and first-person-shooter. Sometimes, you'll want the genre to be very specific, and other times you'll not, depending on your aims. Be specific when building a game in the truest and most genuine spirit of a traditional, well-established genre. The idea in this case is to do a *good job* at a tried and tested formula. In contrast, avoid too narrow of a definition when seeking to innovate and push boundaries. Feel free to combine existing genres in new ways or, if you really want a challenge, to invent a completely new genre.

Innovation can be fun and interesting, but it's also risky. It's easy to think your latest idea is clever and compelling, but always try it out on other people to assess their reactions and learn to take constructive criticism from an early stage. Ask them to play what you've made or to play a prototype based on the design. However, avoid relying too heavily on document-based designs when assessing fun and playability, as the experience of playing is radically different from reading and the thoughts it generates.

For Dead Keys, the genre will be a cinematic first-person zombie-typer! Here, our genre takes the existing and well-established first-person shooter tradition, but (in an effort to innovate) replaces the defining element of shooting with *typing*.

Game mode

The term *game mode*, might mean many things, but in this case, we'll focus on the difference between single-player and multi-player game modes. Dead Keys will be single player, but there's nothing intrinsic about its design that indicates it is for a single player only. It could be adapted to both local co-op multiplayer and Internet-based multiplayer (using the Unity networking features). More information on Unity network, for the interested reader, can be found online at `https://docs.unity3d.com/Manual/UNet.html`.

It's important to decide on this technical question very early in development, as it heavily impacts how the game is constructed and the features it supports.

Game objective

Every game (except for experimental and experiential games) need an objective for the player; something they must strive to do, not just within specific levels, but across the game overall. This objective is important not just for the player (to make the game fun), but also for the developer to decide how challenge, diversity, and interest can be added to the mix. Before starting development, have a clearly stated and identified objective in mind.

Challenges are introduced primarily as obstacles to the objective, and bonuses are things that facilitate the objective–that make it possible and easier to achieve. For Dead Keys, the primary objective is to survive and reach the level end. Zombies threaten that objective by attacking and damaging the player, and bonuses exist along the way to make things more interesting.

I highly recommend that you use project management and team collaboration tools to chart, document, and time-track tasks within your project. Also, you can do this for free; some online tools for this include Trello (`https://trello.com`), Bitrix24 (`https://www.bitrix24.com`), Basecamp (`https://basecamp.com`), Freedcamp (`https://freedcamp.com`), Unfuddle TEN (`https://unfuddle.com`), Bitbucket (`https://bitbucket.org`), Microsoft Visual Studio Team Services (`https://www.visualstudio.com/en-us/products/visual-studio-team-services-vs.aspx`), and Concord Contract Management (`http://www.concordnow.com`).

Asset preparation

When you've reached a clear decision on the initial concept and design, you're ready to prototype! This means building a Unity project demonstrating the core mechanic and game rules in action as a playable sample. After this, you typically refine the design more, and repeat prototyping until arriving at an artifact you want to pursue. From here, the art team must produce assets (meshes and textures) based on the concept art, the game design, and photographic references. When producing meshes and textures for Unity, some important guidelines should be followed to achieve optimal graphical performance in-game. This is about structuring and building assets in a smart way so that they export cleanly and easily from their originating software and can then be imported with minimal fuss, performing as best as they can at runtime. Let's take a look at some of these guidelines for meshes and textures.

Meshes – work only with good topology

A good mesh topology consists in all polygons having only three or four sides in the model (not more). Additionally, Edge Loops should flow in an ordered, regular way along the contours of the model, defining its shape and form.

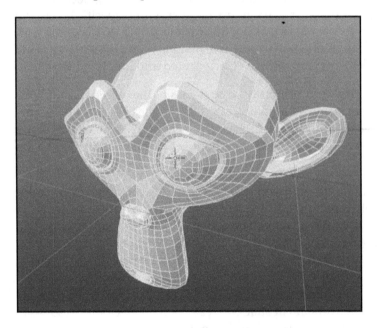

Clean topology

Unity automatically converts, on import, any **NGons** (polygons with more than four sides) into triangles, if the mesh has any. However, it's better to build meshes without NGons as opposed to relying on Unity's automated methods. Not only does this cultivate good habits at the modeling phase, but it avoids any automatic and unpredictable retopology of the mesh, which affects how it's shaded and animated.

Meshes – minimize polygon count

Every polygon in a mesh entails a rendering performance hit insofar as a GPU needs time to process and render each polygon. Consequently, it's sensible to minimize the number of a polygons in a mesh, even though modern graphics hardware is adept at working with many polygons. It's a good practice to minimize polygons wherever possible and to the degree that it doesn't detract from your central artistic vision and style.

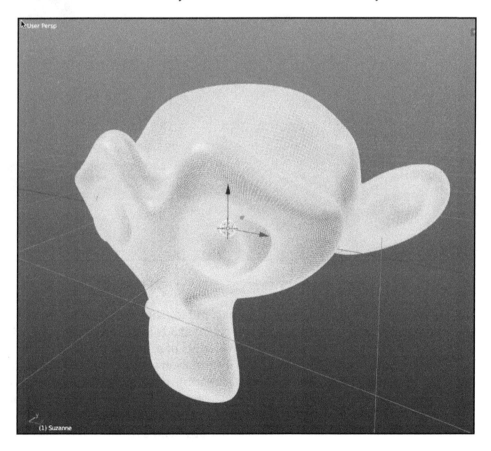

High-poly meshes! (try reducing polygons where possible)

There are many techniques available to reduce polygon counts. Most 3D applications (such as 3ds Max, Maya, and Blender) offer automated tools that decimate polygons in a mesh while retaining its basic shape and outline. However, these methods frequently make a mess of topology, leaving you with faces and edge loops leading in all directions. Even so, this can still be useful for reducing polygons in **static meshes** (meshes that never animate), such as statues, houses, or chairs. However, it's typically bad for animated meshes where topology is especially important.

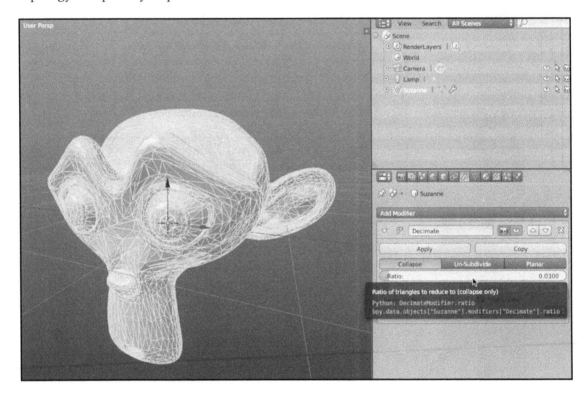

Reducing mesh polygons with automated methods can produce messy topology!

If you want to know the total vertex and face count of a mesh, you can use your 3D software statistics. Blender, Maya, 3ds Max, and most 3D software let you see vertex and face counts of selected meshes directly from the viewport. However, this information should only be considered a rough guide! This is because after importing a mesh into Unity, the vertex count frequently turns out higher than expected! There are many reasons for this, which is explained in more depth online at `http://docs.unity3d` `.com/Manual/OptimizingGraphicsPerformance.html`.

In short, use the Unity vertex count as the final word on the actual vertex count of your mesh. To view the vertex count for an imported mesh in Unity, click on the right-arrow on the mesh thumbnail in the **Project** panel. This shows the internal mesh asset. Select this asset, and then view the vertex count from the preview pane in the **Inspector** object.

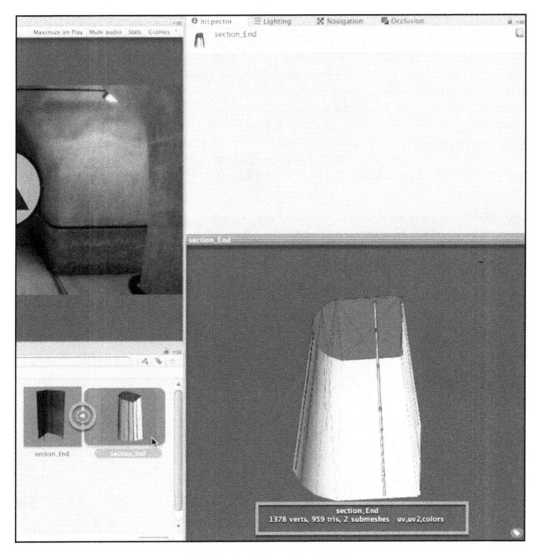

Viewing the vertex and face count for meshes in Unity

Meshes – simulating bump details without geometry

As mentioned, try keeping meshes as low-poly as possible. Low-poly meshes are, however, of lower quality than higher-resolution meshes. They have fewer polygons and thereby hold fewer details. Yet, this need not be problematic. Techniques exist for simulating detail in low-poly meshes, making them appear at a higher resolution than they really are. **Normal Mapping** is one example of this. Normal Maps are special textures that define the orientation and roughness of a mesh surface across its polygons and how those polygons interact with lighting. In short, a Normal Map specifies how lighting interacts over a mesh and ultimately effects how the mesh is shaded. This influences how we perceive the details. You can produce Normal Maps in many ways, for example, typically using 3D modeling software. By producing two mesh versions (namely, a high-poly version containing all the needed details, and a low-poly version to receive the details), you can bake normal information from the high-poly mesh to the low-poly mesh via a texture file. This approach (known as **Normal Map Baking**) can lead to stunningly accurate and believable results, as follows:

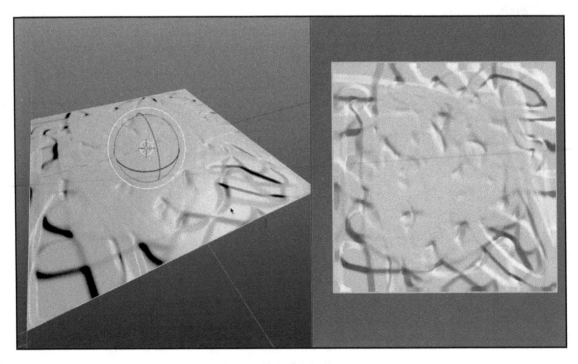

Simulating high-poly detail with Normal Maps

However, if you don't have any Normal Maps for an imported mesh, Unity can generate them from a standard, diffuse texture, via the **Import Settings**. This may not produce the most believable and physically accurate results, like Normal Map Baking, but it's useful to quickly and easily generate displacement details, enhancing the mood and realism of a scene. To create a Normal Map from a diffuse texture, first select the imported texture from the **Project** panel and duplicate it–make sure that the original version is not invalidated or affected. Then, from the object **Inspector**, change the **Texture Type** (for the duplicate texture) from **Texture** to **Normal map**. This changes how Unity understands and works with the texture:

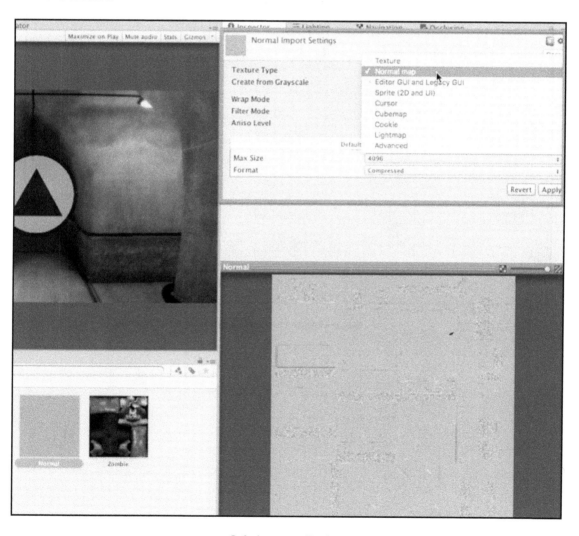

Configuring texture as a Normal map

Specifying Normal Map for a texture configures Unity to use and work with that texture in a specialized, optimized way for generating bump details on your model. However, when creating a Normal Map from a diffuse texture, you'll also need to enable the **Create from Grayscale** checkbox. When enabled, Unity generates a Normal Map from a grayscale version of the diffuse texture, using the **Bumpiness** and **Filtering** settings, as follows:

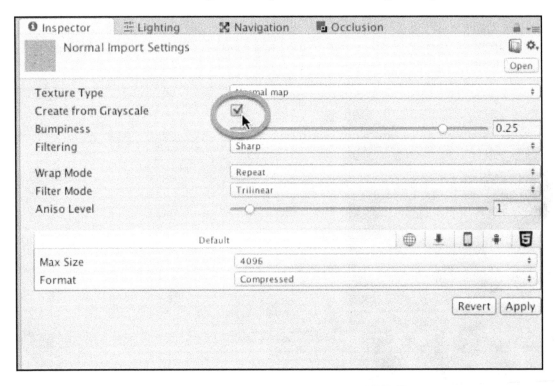

Enable Create from Grayscale for Normal maps

With **Create from** Grayscale enabled, you can use the **Bumpiness** slider to intensify and weaken the bump effect and the **Filtering** setting to control the roughness or smoothness of the bump. When you've adjusted the settings as needed, confirm the changes and preview the result by pressing the **Apply** button from the **Inspector** object:

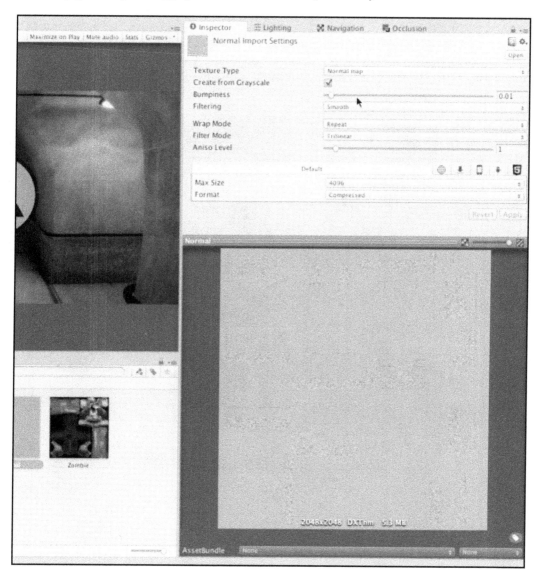

Customizing an imported Normal Map

Meshes – minimize UV seams

Seams are edge cuts inserted into a mesh during UV mapping to help it unfold, flattening out into a 2D space for the purpose of texture assignment. This process is achieved in 3D modeling software, but the cuts it makes are highly important for properly unfolding a model and getting it to look as intended inside Unity. An edge is classified as a seam in UV space when it has only one neighboring face, as opposed to two. Essentially, the seams determine how a mesh's UVs are cut apart into separate UV shells or UV islands, which are arranged into a final UV layout. This layout maps a texture onto the mesh surface, as follows:

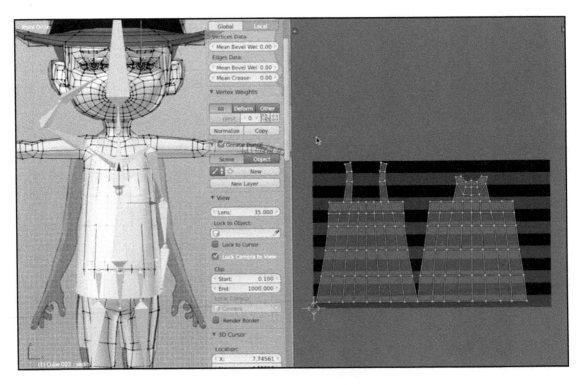

Creating a UV layout

Always minimize UV seams where feasible by joining together disparate edges, shells, or islands, forming larger units. This is not something you do in Unity, but in your 3D modeling software. Even so, by doing this, you potentially reduce the vertex count and complexity of your mesh. This leads to improved runtime performance in Unity. This is because Unity must duplicate all vertices along the seams to accommodate the rendering standards for most real-time graphics hardware. Thus, wherever there are seams, there will be a doubling up of vertices, as shown here:

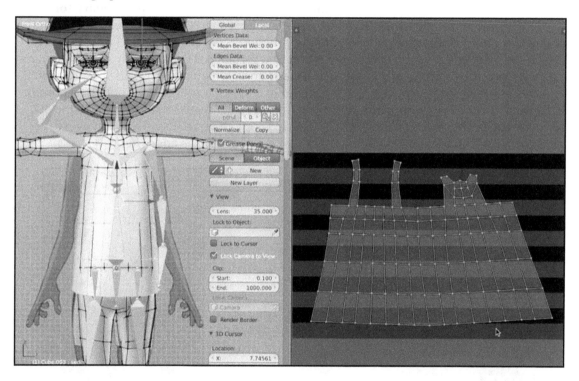

Binding together edges and islands to reduce UV seams

Meshes – export as FBX

Unity officially supports many mesh import formats, including `.ma`, `.mb`, `.max`, `.blend`, and others. Details and comparisons of these are found online at `http://docs.unity3d.co m/Manual/3D-formats.html`. Unity divides mesh formats into two main groups: **exported** and **proprietary**. The **exported formats** include `.fbx` and `.dae`. These are meshes exported manually from 3D modeling software into an independent data-interchange format, which is industry recognized. It's feature limited, but widely supported. The **proprietary formats**, in contrast, are application-specific formats that support a wider range of features but at the cost of compatibility. In short, you should almost always use the exported FBX file format. This is the most widely supported, used and tested format within the Unity community and supports imported meshes of all types, both static and animated. It gives the best results. If you choose a proprietary format, you'll frequently end up importing additional 3D objects that you'll never use in your game, and your Unity project is automatically tied to the 3D software itself. That is, you'll need a fully licensed copy of your 3D software on every machine for which you intend to open your Unity project; this is annoying.

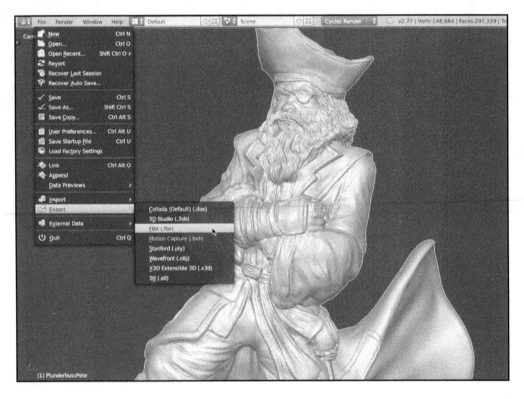

Exporting meshes to an FBX file, works best with Unity

Meshes – use meters scale (metric)

Unity measures 3D space using the metric system, and 1 world unit is understood, by the physics system, to mean 1 meter. Unity is configured to work with models from most 3D applications using their default settings. However, sometimes, your models will appear too big or small when imported. This usually happens when your world units are not configured to metric in your 3D modeling software. The details of how to change units varies for each software, such as Blender, Maya, or 3ds Max. Each program allows unit customization from the **Preferences** menu.

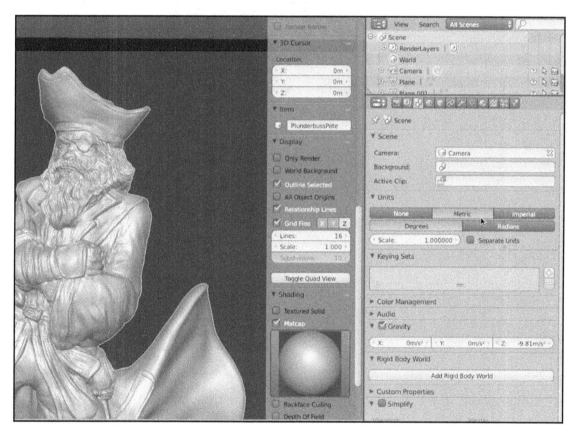

Configuring 3D software to Metric units

Textures – never use lossless compression

Always save your textures in lossless formats, such as PNG, TGA, or PSD. Avoid lossy formats such as JPG, even though they're typically smaller in file size. JPG might be ideal for website images or for sending holiday snaps to your friends and family; but, for creating video game textures, they are problematic–they lose quality exponentially with each successive save operation. By using lossless formats and by removing JPG from every step of your workflow (including intermediary steps), your textures can remain crisp and sharp:

Saving textures to PNG files

Textures – power of 2 sizes

If your textures are for 3D models and meshes (not sprites or GUI elements), then make their dimensions power-2 size for best results. The textures needn't be square (equal in width and height), but each dimension should be from a range of power-2 sizes. Valid sizes include 32, 64, 128, 256, 512, 1024, 2048, 4096, and 8192. Sizing textures to a power-2 dimension helps Unity scale textures up and down, as well as copy pixels between textures as needed, across the widest range of graphical hardware.

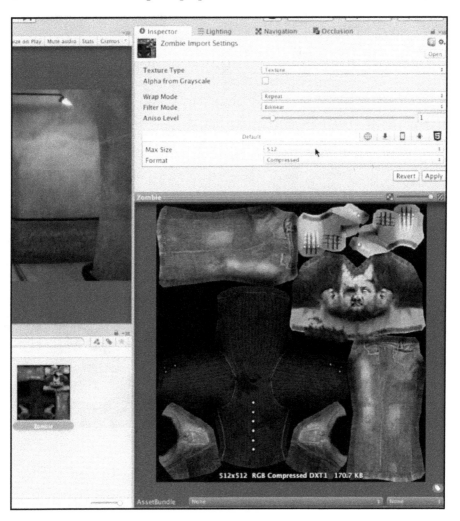

Creating textures at power-2 sizes

When creating textures, it's always best to design for the largest possible power-2 size you'll need (as opposed to the largest possible size allowed), and then to downscale wherever appropriate to smaller power-2 sizes for older hardware and weaker systems, such as mobile devices. For each imported texture, you can use the Unity platform tabs from the **Inspector** object to specify an appropriate maximum size for each texture on a specific platform: one for desktop systems, one for Android, one for iOS, and so on. This caps the maximum size allowed for the selected target on a per-platform basis. This value should be the smallest size that is compatible with your artistic intentions and intended quality.

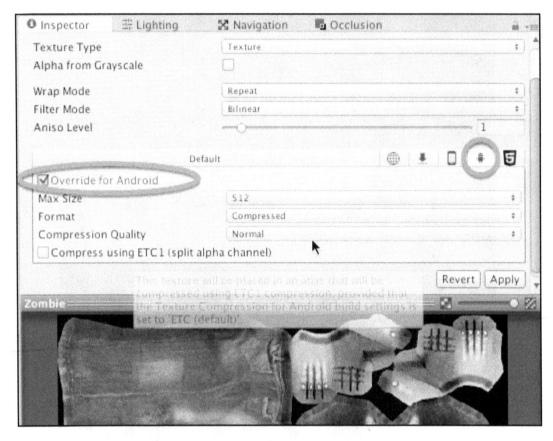

Overriding texture sizes for other platforms

Textures – alpha textures

Alpha textures are textures with transparency. When applied to 3D models, they make areas of the model transparent, allowing objects behind it to show through. Alpha textures can be either TGA files with dedicated alpha channels or PNG files with transparent pixels. In either case, alpha textures can render with artifacts in Unity if they're not created and imported correctly.

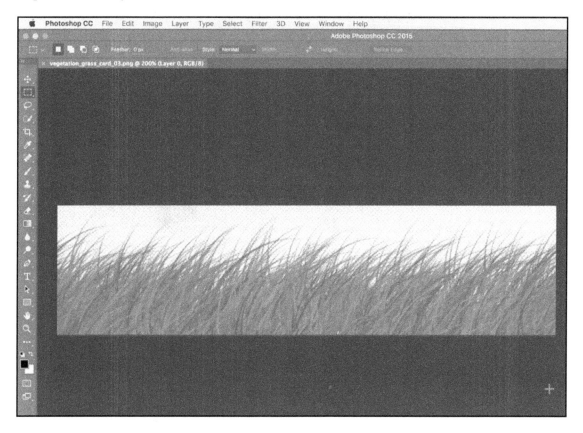

Creating alpha textures

If you need to use alpha textures, ensure that you check out the official Unity documentation on how to export them for optimal results from `http://docs.unity3d.com /Manual/HOWTO-alphamaps.html`.

Asset importing for Dead Keys

The previous section explored some general tips on preparing assets for Unity, with optimal performance in mind. These tips are general insofar as they apply for almost all asset types in almost all cases, including *Dead Keys*. Let's now focus on creating our project, DK, a first-person zombie-typer game. This game relies on many assets, from meshes and textures to animation and sound. Here, we'll import and configure many core assets, considering optimization issues and asset-related subjects. We don't need to import all assets right now; we can and often will import more later in development, integrating them into our existing asset library. This section assumes you've already created a new Unity project. From here on, we can begin our work.

To prepare, let's create a basic folder structure in the **Project** panel to contain all imported assets in a systematic and organized way. The names I've used are self-descriptive and optional. The named folders are animation, audio, audiomixers, Materials, meshes, music, prefabs, Resources, scenes, scripts, and textures. Feel free to add more, or change the names, if it suits your purposes.

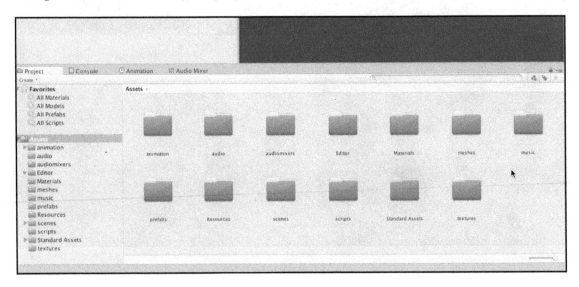

Organizing the Project folder

Importing textures

The textures folder will contain all textures to be used by the project. Most importantly, this includes textures for the NPCs zombie characters (hands, arms, legs, and so on) and the modular environment set. In *Dead Keys*, the environment will be a dark industrial interior, full of dark and moody corridors and cross-sections. This environment will really be composed from many smaller, modular pieces (such as corner sections and straight sections) that are fitted together, used and reused, like building blocks to form larger environment complexes. Each of the pieces in the modular set maps in UV space to the same texture (a Texture Atlas), meaning that the entire environment is actually mapped completely by one texture. Let's quickly take a look at that texture:

Environment Atlas Texture

All textures for the project are included in the book companion files, in the `ProjectAssets/Textures` folder. These should be imported into a Unity project, simply by dragging and dropping them together into the **Project** panel. Using this method, you can import multiple texture files as a single batch, as follows:

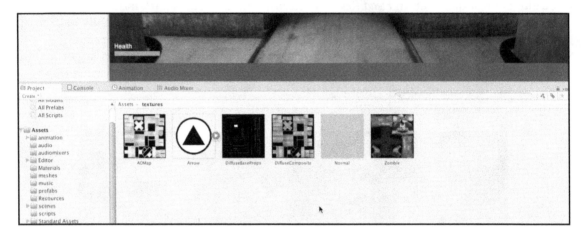

Importing textures into the project

By default, Unity incorrectly configures Normal Map textures as regular textures. It doesn't distinguish the texture type based on image content. Consequently, after importing Normal Maps, you should configure each one properly. Select the **Normal map** from the **Project** panel, and choose **Normal map** from the **Texture Type** dropdown in the object **Inspector;** afterwards, click on **Apply** to accept the change:

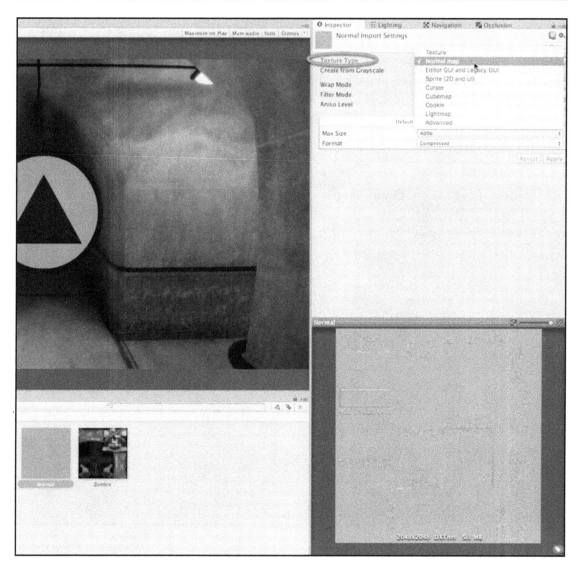

Importing and configuring Normal maps

Since every mesh in the modular environment set maps to the same texture space (corners, straight sections, turns, and so on), we'll need to make some minor tweaks to the Atlas Texture settings, for best results. First, select the **Atlas Texture** in the **Project** panel (DiffuseComposite.png) and change the **Texture Type** to **Advanced**, from the **Inspector** object; this offers us greater control over texture settings:

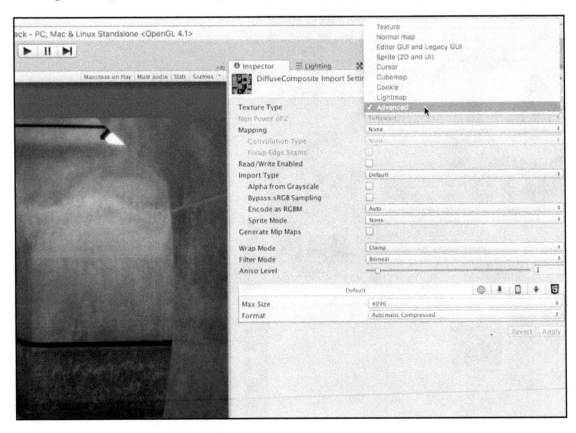

Accessing advanced texture properties

To minimize any texture seams, breaks, and artifacts in the environment texture wherever two mesh pieces meet in the scene, change the texture **Wrap Mode** from **Repeat** to **Clamp**. Clamp mode ensures that edge pixels of a UV island are stretched continuously across the mesh, as opposed to repeated, if needed. This is a useful technique for reducing any seams or artifacts for meshes that map to a Texture Atlas.

In addition, remove the check mark from the **Generate Mip Maps** option. When activated, this useful optimization shows progressively lower quality textures for a mesh as it moves further from the camera. This helps optimize the render performance at runtime. However, for Texture Atlases, this can be problematic, as Unity's texture resizing causes artifacts and seams at the edges of UV islands wherever two mesh modules meet. This produces pixel bleeding and distortions in the textures.

If you want to use Mip Maps with Atlas Textures without risk of artifacts, you can pre-generate your own Mip Map levels. That is, produce lower-quality textures that are calibrated specifically to work with your modular meshes. This may require manual testing and re-testing, until you arrive at textures that work for you. You can generate your own Mip Map levels for Unity by exporting a DDS texture from Photoshop. The DDS format lets you specify custom Mip Map levels directly in the image file. You can download the DDS plugin for Photoshop online at `https://developer.nv idia.com/nvidia-texture-tools-adobe-photoshop`.

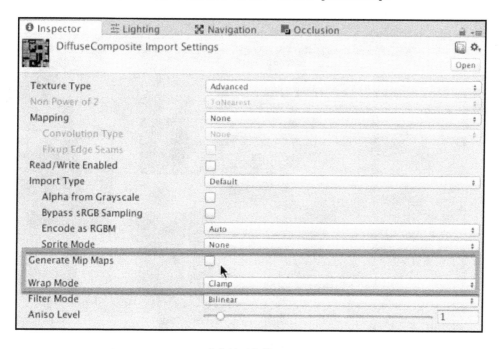

Optimizing Atlas Textures

[35]

Finally, specify the maximum valid power-2 size for the Atlas Texture, which is **4096**. The format can be **Automatic Compressed**. This will choose the best-available compression method for the desktop platform; then, click on **Apply**:

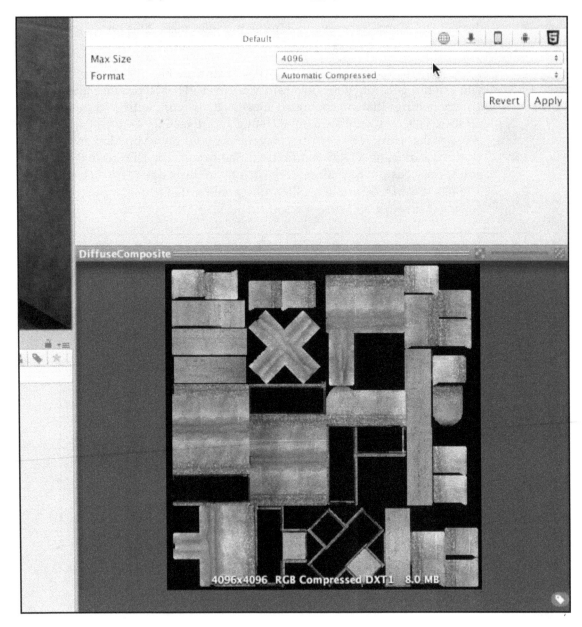

Applying changes to the Texture Atlas

In this chapter, we'll put aside most of the UI concerns. However, all GUI textures should be imported as the **Sprite (2D and UI)** texture type, with Mip Maps disabled. For UI textures, it's not necessary to follow the power-2 size rule (that is, pixel sizes of 2, 4, 8, 16, 32, 64, 128, 256, 512, 1024, 2048, 4096 and so on).

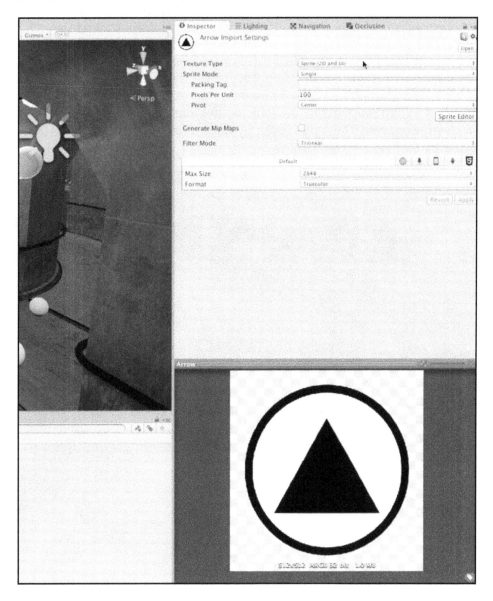

Importing UI textures

Importing meshes

Ideally, you should import textures before meshes, as we've done here. This is because, on mesh import, Unity automatically creates materials and searches the project for all associated textures. On finding suitable textures, it assigns them to the materials before displaying the results on the mesh, even in the **Project** panel thumbnail previews. This makes for a smoother and easier experience. When you're ready to import meshes, just drag and drop them into the **Project** panel to the designated `meshes` folder. By doing this, Unity imports all meshes as a single batch. This project relies heavily on meshes, both animated character meshes for the NPC zombies and static environment meshes for the modular environment–as well as prop meshes and any meshes that you would want to include for your own creative flourish. These files (except your own meshes!) are included in the book's companion files.

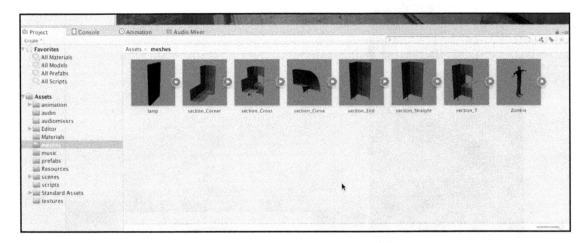

Importing meshes (both environment and character meshes)

Let's now configure the modular environment meshes. Select all meshes for the environment, including `section_Corner`, `section_Cross`, `section_Curve`, `section_End`, `section_Straight`, and `section_T`. With the environment meshes selected, adjust the following settings:

- Set the mesh **Scale Factor** to `1`, creating a 1:1 ratio between the model, as it was made in the modeling software, to how the model appears in Unity.
- Disable **Import BlendShapes**. The environment meshes contain no blended shapes to import, and you can streamline to import and re-import process by disabling unnecessary options.
- Disable **Generate Colliders**. In many cases, we'd have enabled this setting. However, Dead Keys is a first-person shooter with a fixed, AI controlled camera, as opposed to free roam movement. This leaves the player with no possibility of walking through walls or passing through floors.
- Enable **Generate Lightmap UVs**. Enabling this option generates a second UV channel. Unity automatically unwraps your meshes and guarantees no UV island overlap. You can further tweak light map UV generation using the **Hard Angle**, **Pack Margin**, **Angle Error**, and **Area Error** settings. However, the default settings work well for most purposes. The **Pack Margin** can, and perhaps should, be increased if your light map Resolution is low, as we'll see in the next chapter. The angle and error settings should sometimes be increased or decreased to better accommodate light maps for organic and curved surfaces.

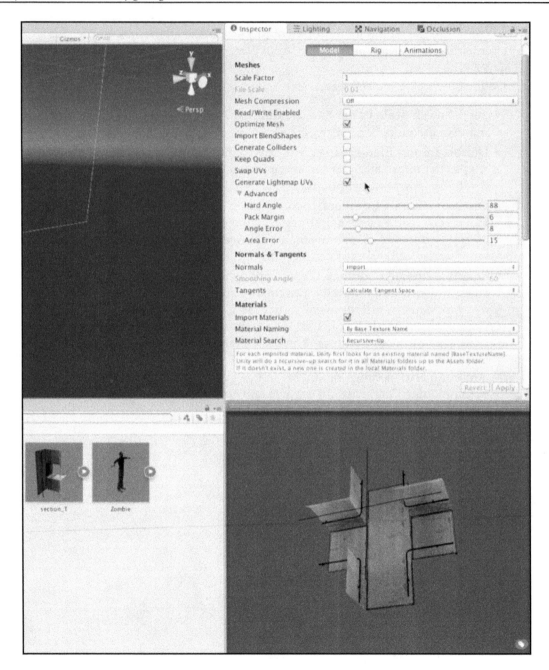

Configuring Environment Meshes

In addition to configuring the primary mesh properties, as we've seen, let's also switch to the **Rig** and **Animations** tab. From the **Rig** tab, specify **None** for the **Animation Type** field, as the meshes don't contain animation data.

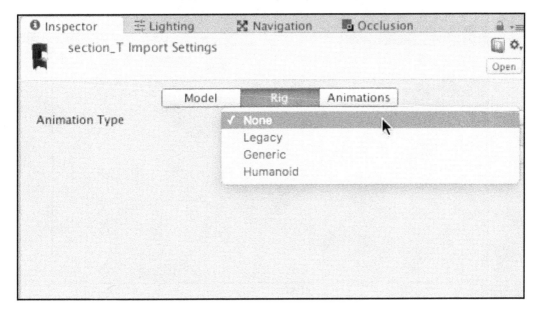

Setting the Rig type for environment meshes

Next, switch to the **Animations** tab. From here, remove the check mark from **Import Animation**. The environment meshes have no animations to import; then, click on **Apply**:

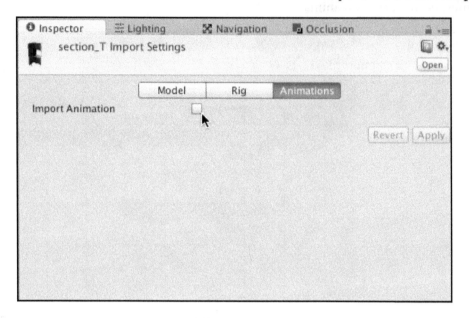

Disabling Import Animation

Of course, *Dead Keys* is about completing typing exercises to destroy zombies. The zombie character for our project is based on the public domain zombie character, available from *Blend Swap* at `http://www.blendswap.com/blends/view/76443`. This character has been rigged and configured in Blender for easy import to Unity. Let's configure this character now. Select the **Zombie** mesh in the **Project** panel; and from the object **Inspector**, adjust the following settings:

- Set the Mesh **Scale Factor** to 1, to retain its original size.
- Enable **Import BlendShapes**, to allow for custom vertex animation.
- Disable **Generate Colliders**, as collision detection is not needed.
- Enable **Swap UVs** if the texture doesn't look correct on the zombie model from the preview panel. If an object has two or more UV channels (and they sometimes do), Unity occasionally selects the wrong channel by default.

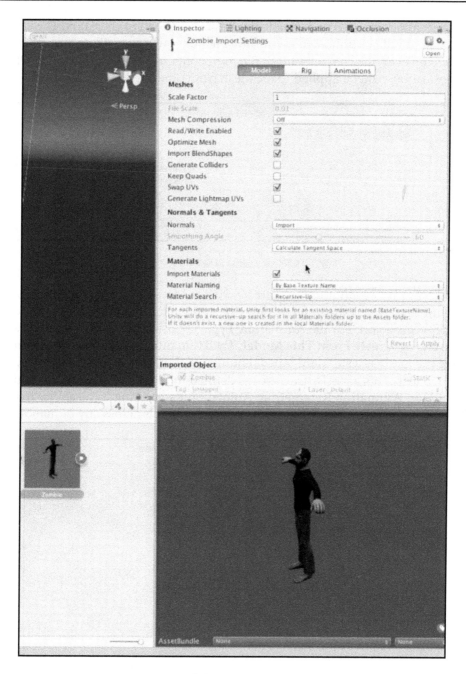

Configuring a zombie NPC

Switch to the Animations tab, and disable the **Import** Animation checkbox. The character mesh should, and will, be animated–performing actions such as walking and attacking animations. However, the character mesh file itself contains no animation data. All character animations will be applied to the mesh from other files.

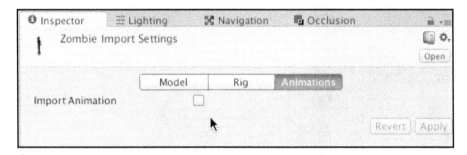

Disable Import Animation for the zombie NPC

That's great! Now, let's configure the character rig for Mecanim. This is about optimizing the underlying skeleton to allow the model to be animated. To do this, select the **Rig** tab from the **Inspector** object. For the **Animation Type**, choose **Humanoid**; and for **Avatar Definition**, choose **Create From This Model**. The **Humanoid** animation type instructs Unity to see the mesh as a standard bipedal human–a character with a head, torso, two arms, and two legs. This generic structure (as defined in the avatar) is mapped to the mesh bones and allows **Animation Retargeting**. Animation Retargeting is the ability to use and reuse character animations from other files and other models across any humanoid.

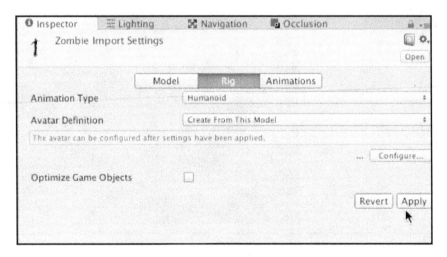

Configuring the zombie rig

After clicking on the Apply button for the zombie character, a check mark icon appears next to the **Configure…** button. For some character meshes, a **X** icon may appear instead. A check mark signifies that Unity has scanned through all bones in the mesh and successfully identified a humanoid rig, which can be mapped easily to the avatar. An **X** icon signifies a problem, which can be either minor or major. A minor case is where a humanoid character rig is imported, but differs in subtle and important ways from what Unity expects. This scenario is often fixed manually in Unity, using the **Rig Configuration Window** (available by clicking on **Configure…**). In contrast, the problem could be major; for example, the imported mesh may not be humanoid at all, or else it differs so dramatically from anything expected that a radical change and overhaul must be made to the character from within the content creation software.

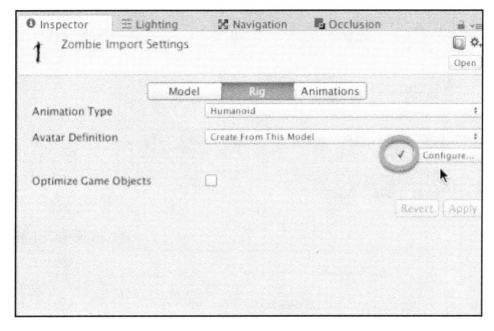

Character rig successfully configured

Even when your character rig is imported successfully, you should still test it inside the **Rig Configuration Editor**. This acts as a *sanity check* and confirms that your rig is working as intended. To do this, click on the **Configure...** button from the **Rig** tab in the object **Inspector;** this displays the Rig Configuration Editor:

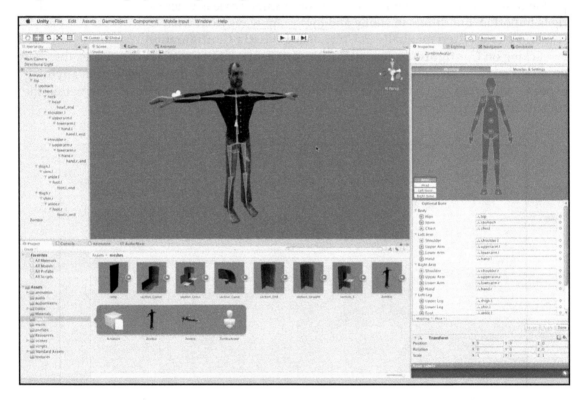

Using the Rig Configuration Editor to examine, test, and repair a skeleton avatar mapping

From the Rig Configuration Editor, you can see how imported bones map to the humanoid avatar definition. Bones highlighted in green are already mapped to the Avatar, as shown in the **Inspector** object. That is, imported bones turn green when Unity, after analysis, finds a match for them in the Avatar. The Avatar is simply a map or chart defined by Unity, namely, a collection of predetermined bones. The aim of the Rig Configuration Editor is to simply map the bones from the mesh to the avatar, allowing the mesh to be animated by any kind of humanoid animation.

For the zombie character, all bones will be successfully auto-mapped to the avatar. You can change this mapping, however, simply by dragging and dropping specific bones from the **Hierarchy** panel to the bone slots in the **Inspector** object.

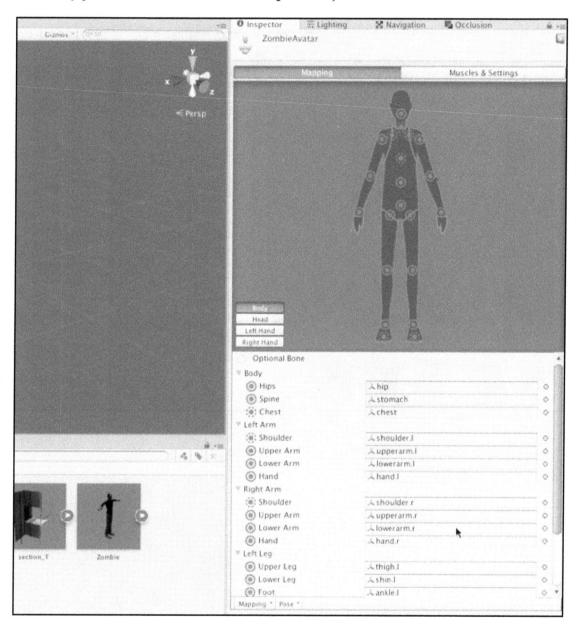

Defining avatar mappings

Now, let's stress test our character mesh, checking its bone and avatar mapping and make sure that the character deforms as intended. To do this, switch to the **Muscles & Settings** tab from the **Inspector** object. When you do this, the character's pose changes immediately inside the viewport, which means it is ready for testing.

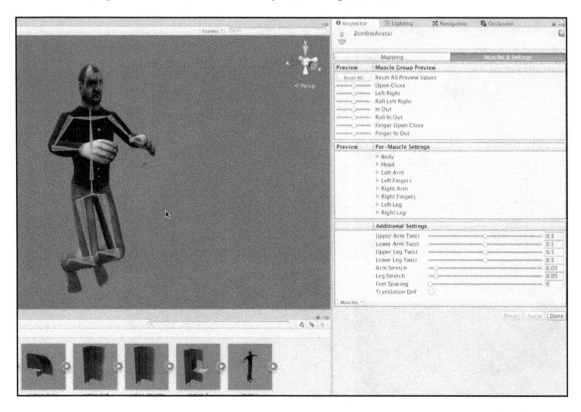

Testing bone mappings

From here, use the character pose sliders in the Inspector object to push the character into extreme poses, previewing its posture in the viewport. The idea is to preview how the character deforms and responds to extremes. The reason such testing is necessary at all is that although bipedal humanoids share a common skeletal structure, they differ widely in body types and heights–some being short and small, and some being large and tall.

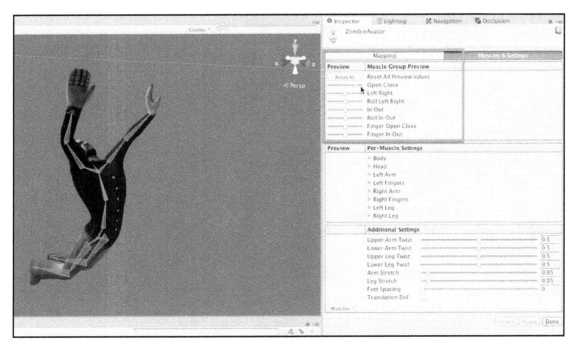

Testing extreme poses

If you feel your character breaks, intersects, or distorts in extreme poses, you can configure the mesh deformation limits, specifying a minimum and maximum range. To do this, first expand the **Per-Muscle Settings** group for the limbs or bones that are problematic, as shown in the following screenshot:

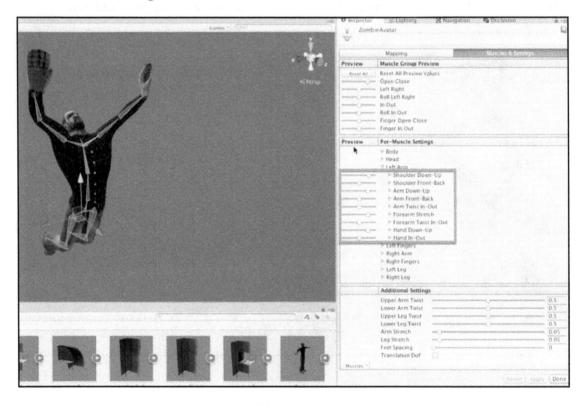

Defining pose extremes

Then, you can drag and resize the minimum and maximum thumb-sliders to define the minimum and maximum deformation extents for that limb, and for all limbs where needed. These settings constrain the movement and rotation of limbs, preventing them from being pushed beyond their intended limits during animation. The best way to use this tool is to begin with your character in an extreme pose that causes a visible break, and then to refine the **Per-Muscle Settings** until the mesh is repaired.

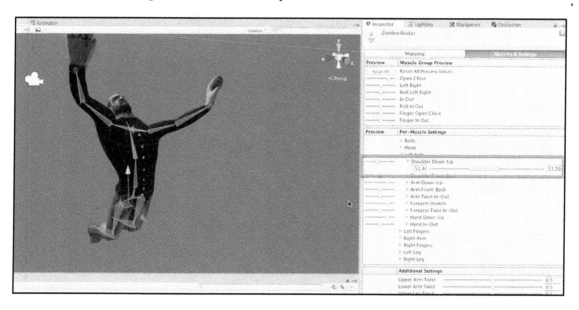

Correcting pose breaks

When you're done making changes to the rig and pose, remember to click on the **Apply** or **Done** button from the **Inspector** object. The **Done** button simply applies the changes and then closes the Rig Configuration Editor.

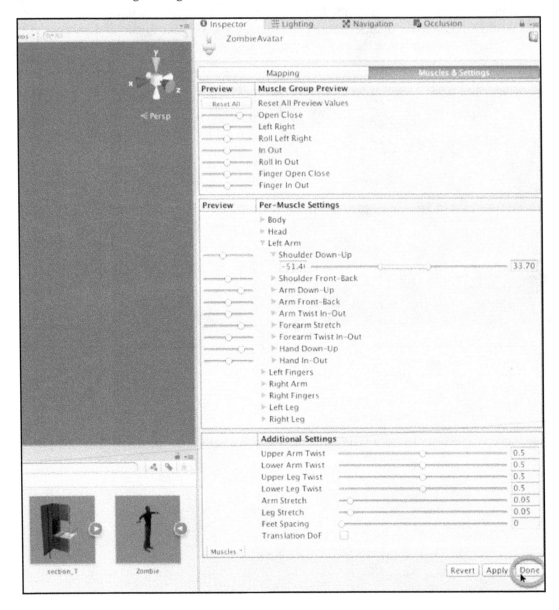

Applying rig changes

Importing animations

The Dead Keys game features character animations for the zombies, namely walk, fight, and idle. These are included as FBX files. They can be imported into the `Animations` folder. The animations themselves are not intended for or targeted toward the zombies, but Mecanim's Humanoid Retargeting lets us reuse almost any character animations on any humanoid model. Let's now configure the animations. Select each animation, and switch to the **Rig** tab. Choose **Humanoid** for the **Animation Type**, and leave the **Avatar Definition** at **Create From This Model**.

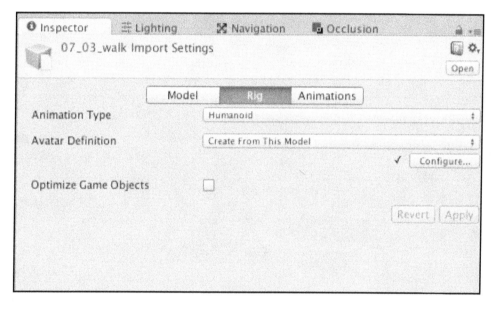

Specifying a Humanoid animation type for animations

Now, move to the Animations tab. Enable the **Loop Time** checkbox, to enable animation looping for the clip. Then, click on **Apply**. We'll have good cause to return to the animation settings in later chapters, for further refinement, as we'll see.

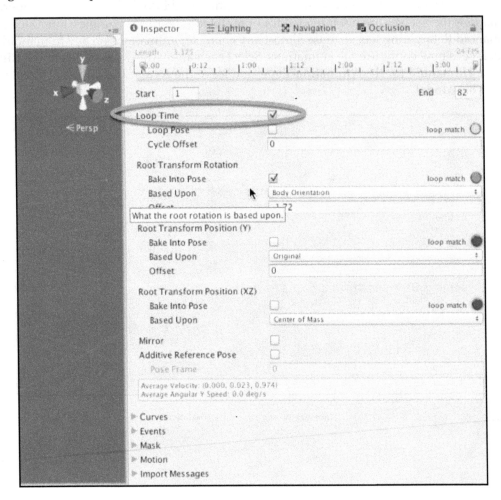

Enabling animation Loop Time for repeating animation clips

Now, let's explore a common problem with loopable walk animations that have root motion encoded. Root motion refers to the highest-level transformation applied to an animated model. Most bone-based animation applies to lower-level bones in the bone hierarchy (such as arms, legs, and head), and this animation is always measured relative to the top-most parent.

However, when the root bone is animated, it affects a character's position and orientation in world space. This is known as root motion. One problem that sometimes happens with imported, loopable walk animations is a small deviation or offset away from the neutral starting point in its root motion. This causes a mesh to drift away from its starting orientation over time, especially when the animation is played on a loop. To see this issue in action, select the walk animation for the zombie character, and from the object **Inspector**, preview the animation carefully. As you do this, align your camera view in the preview window in front of the humanoid character and see how, gradually, his walk deviates slowly from the center line on which he begins. This shows that, over time, the character continually drifts. This problem will not just manifest in the preview window, but in-game too!

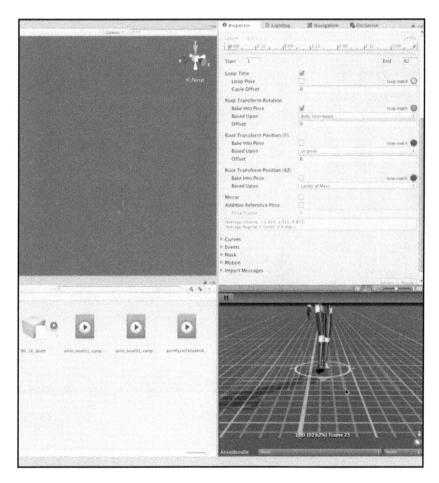

Previewing walk cycle issues

This problem happens as a result of walk-cycle inaccuracies in root motion. By previewing the **Average Velocity** field from the object **Inspector**, you'll see the **X** motion field is a nonzero value, meaning that offset occurs to the mesh in **X**. This explains the accumulative deviation in the walk, as the animation is repeated.

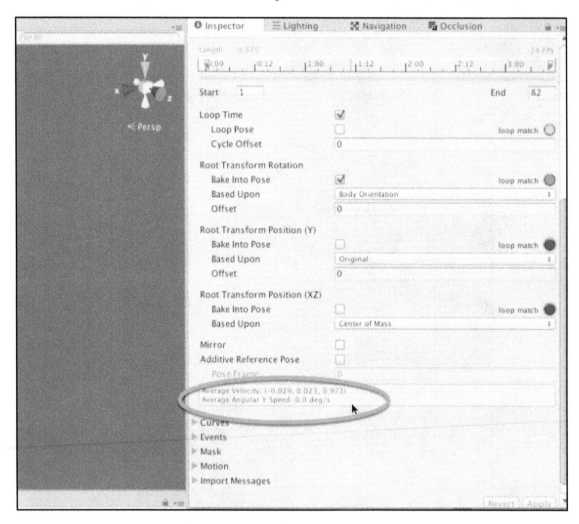

Exploring root motion problems

To fix this problem, enable the **Bake Into Pose** checkbox for the **Root Transform Rotation** section. This lets you override the **Average Velocity** field. Then, adjust the **Offset** field to compensate for the value of **Average Velocity**. The idea is to adjust **Offset** until the value of **Average Velocity** is reset to **0**, indicating no offsetting. Then, click on **Apply**.

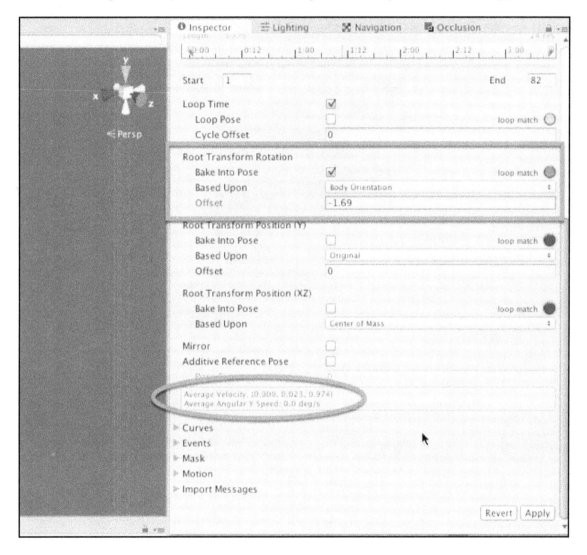

Correcting root motion

Importing audio

Let's import game audio–specifically, the music track. This should be dragged and dropped into the `music` folder (the music track `narrow_corridors_short.ogg` is included in the book's companion files). Music is an important audio asset that greatly impacts loading times, especially on mobile devices and legacy hardware. Music tracks often exceed one minute in duration, and they encode a lot of data. Consequently, additional configuration is usually needed for music tracks, to prevent them from burdening your games.

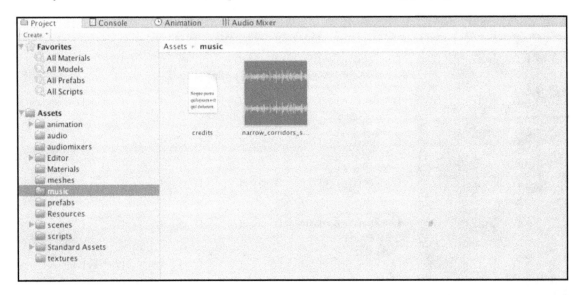

Importing audio files

 Ideally, music should be in a WAV format, to prevent lossy compression when ported to other platforms. If WAV is not possible, then OGG is another valuable alternative. For more information on audio import settings, refer to the online Unity documentation at `http://docs.unity3d.com/Manual/AudioFiles.html`.

Now, select the imported music track in the Project panel. Disable the **Preload Audio Data** checkbox, and then change the **Load Type** to **Steaming**. This optimizes the music loading process. It means the music track will be loaded in segments during playback, as opposed to entirely in memory from the level beginning, and it will continually load, segment by segment. This prevents longer initial loading times.

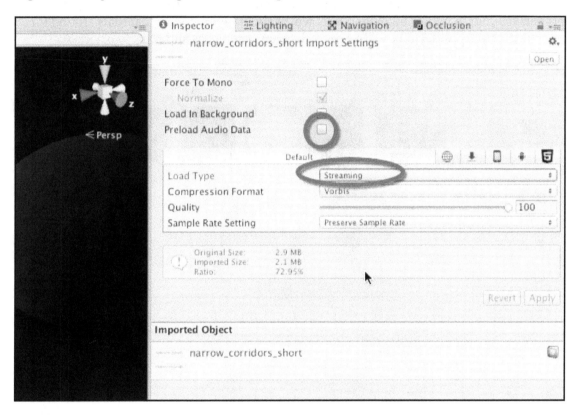

Configuring music for streaming

Configuring materials

As a final step, let's configure mesh materials for the modular environment. By default, these are created and configured automatically by Unity on importing your meshes to the **Project** panel. They'll usually be added to a materials subfolder, alongside your mesh. From here, drag and drop your materials to the higher-level materials folder in the project, organizing your materials together. Don't worry about moving your materials around for organization purposes, Unity will keep track of any references and links to objects.

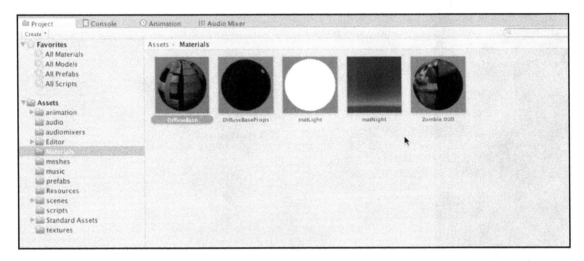

Configuring materials

By default, the **DiffuseBase** material for the modular environment is configured as a standard shader material, with some degree of glossiness. This makes the environment look shinier and smoother than it should be. In addition, the material lacks a Normal Map and Ambient Occlusion map. To configure the material, select the **DiffuseBase** material, and set the **Shader** type to **Standard (Specular setup)**:

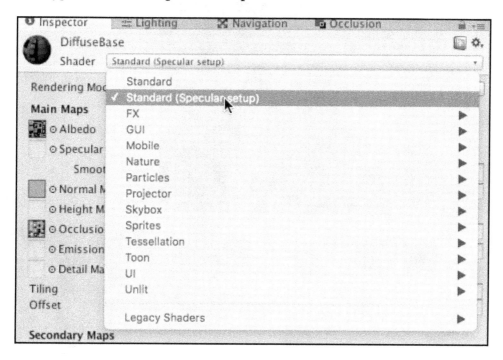

Changing Shader type

Next, assign the **DiffuseBase** texture to the **Albedo** slot (the main diffuse texture), and complete the **Normal Map** and Ambient **Occlusion** fields by assigning the appropriate textures, as found in the textures folder:

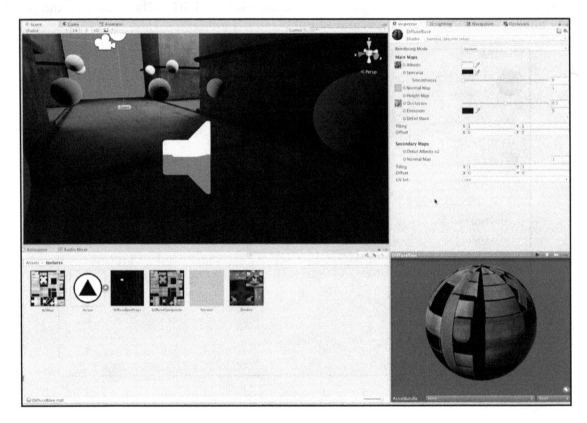

Completing the environment material

Summary

This chapter considered many instrumental concepts for establishing a solid ground work for the *Dead Keys* project. On reaching this point, you now have a Unity project with most assets imported, ready to begin your development work. This will happen in the next chapter. The foundation so far includes imported environment modules, zombie meshes, textures, audio files, and more. In importing these assets, we considered many issues, such as optimal asset construction, import guidelines, and how to solve both common and less obvious problems that sometimes occur along the way. The fully prepared and configured project, ready to begin, can be found in this book's companion files, in the `Chapter02/Start` folder. This saves you from having to import all assets manually. In the next chapter, we'll focus in depth on level design and construction techniques, from skyboxes and lighting to emotion, mood, and atmosphere.

2
Level Design and Structure

This chapter is about designing and building playable levels for Dead Keys. More accurately, Dead Keys consists of multiple levels, and our focus in this chapter will be on the creation of one of those levels in detail. Only one needs be considered because the level-creation process is merely repeated creatively, after creating the first level, to produce all remaining levels at increasing difficulty levels. By *level*, I mean a *scene* in Unity terms–a complete and integrated 3D world where the game evolves according to its internal rules and logic. We'll look in depth at using and reusing modular assets, such as environment meshes, to build interesting levels of any size needed; we'll also see **lightmapping** and lighting overall to enhance realism, as well as **NavMesh** generation for artificial intelligence and Occlusion Culling for rendering optimization, among other issues. By the end of this chapter, we'll have constructed an integrated and atmospheric level, complete with final lighting, that has furnishings and navigation data. However, we'll still be missing agents, that is, the player character and **NPCs** (**Non-Player Characters**). These are considered in later chapters. So, having now imported our assets (covered in the previous chapter), we'll start work on creating the first playable level for Dead Keys (not the menu screen), beginning from an empty scene, created by choosing **File** | **New Scene** (*Ctrl + N*) from the application menu.

If you want to follow along step by step, the starting point for this chapter is found in this book's companion files, in the folder `Chapter02/Start`. This features a starting Unity project.

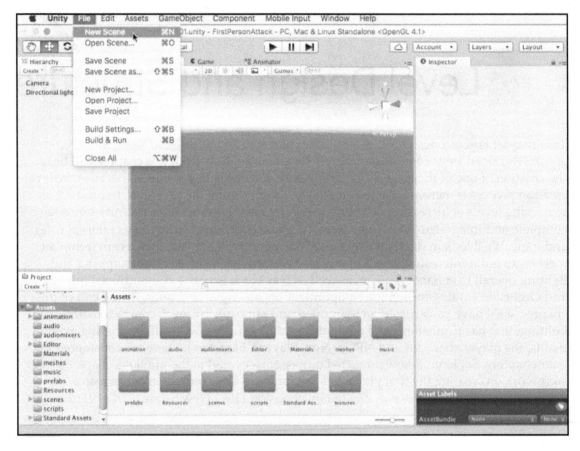

Getting started with a New Scene

Before building any level inside the editor, it's worthwhile getting very clear, conceptually, about the level to create as a whole, in terms of layout and mechanics. For our level (and all levels), we may identify the following key points:

- The objective for the player is to traverse a maze-like network of dark, industrial corridors to reach an end point. On reaching the end point, the next level is accessed; except, of course, for the final level in which the game is completed.

- The player provides input only through keystrokes on the keyboard, typing-in letters that match whatever word appears above the closest attacking zombie. When the entered combination matches the word exactly and in full, the zombie is killed. Otherwise, zombies continue attacking until the player is killed.

- The player does not freely control their movement through the level, as with regular first person controls (*WASD*). Instead, the player experiences a pre-scripted and pre-pathed camera that only moves forward, to the next stopping point, when all attacking zombies are dispatched. This matches the camera and gameplay style of *House of the Dead*, *The Typing of the Dead*, *Lethal Enforcers*, and others.

- The level is made from modular environment pieces, allowing many possible combinations and layouts. It should be dark, eerie, and tense.

- Most objects in the scene (such as walls, floors, and props) will be non-movable. The only movable elements are the player, enemies, and a selection of special effects, such as particle systems and image effects.

This level description is, by no means, comprehensive or complete. But it offers us a good enough platform to get started to build a level that supports our core gameplay. In many cases, artists and designers construct levels from concept art, mood boards, and storyboards; but here we'll improvise using assets made specifically for this book.

Setting the scene with a skybox

Our game environment should be dark, creepy, and suspenseful. But, every new Unity scene is created with a default, procedural skybox representing a cheery daytime, exterior. This needs to be changed. A skybox is ultimately a cube with flipped normals that surround and encompass the environment. Its faces contain an environment texture which, when mapped correctly, appears seamlessly across the model, creating the look of a vast skyline surrounding the scene. The primary purpose of our skybox should be to set a base and ambient lighting. The most appropriate skybox for our usage, then, is a night skybox or, at least, a dark, stormy (and perhaps slightly alien) skybox. There are many ways in Unity to create a skybox. One method is to create a cube-map texture (six separate textures) inside the image-editing software that maps to the faces of a cube. Another method, available in Unity 5, is a procedural skybox. Using this, Unity generates a skybox from some initial creation parameters that we can set through a material.

Let's use the latter, most customizable method. To do this, open the **Materials** folder in the **Project** panel and create a new **Material**. Assign it a meaningful name; I've used matNight.

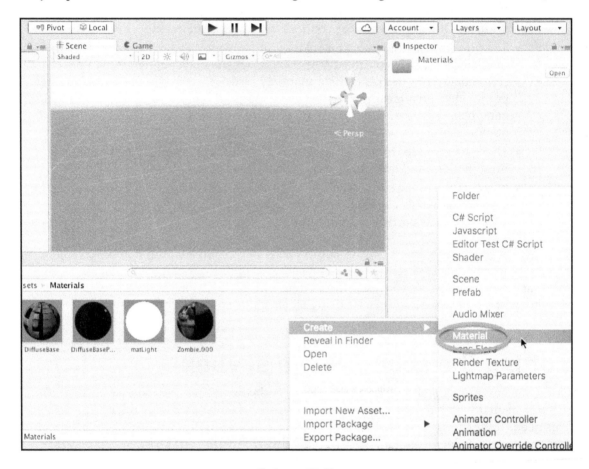

Creating a new Material

 Naming assets and objects appropriately is important for large projects, whether team based or not. It's important to identify an object's type and purpose from its name, and to use a naming convention that'll alphabetically group together related assets in a useful way. For example, I prefixed all material assets with mat_ (mat_Skybox, mat_Marble, and mat_Leather). Using this name, all materials are arranged together in the **Project** panel, and I can determine by the asset name that it's a material and not a texture (_tex), mesh (_mesh), sound effect (_sfx), and so on.

Some may question whether prefixes are needed if folders are used. After all, couldn't you just name your materials anything you wanted, and simply group them together in the same folder, as opposed to using prefixes? In short, use folders to organize and group textures, but name prefixes are still important because assets from different folders can still be viewed together in a consolidate display, when running searches and filters. And in these cases, you'll still want to arrange search results alphabetically.

Newly created materials are configured as a **Standard** shader (PBR material) using the metallic-roughness workflow. This isn't necessary for a skybox, as it doesn't cast light in the same way and isn't affected by shadows and other light sources. Change the material type to **Skybox | Procedural**. Multiple skyboxes are available, but only a procedural skybox gives you out-of-the-box runtime control over the colors and construction of the texture.

Creating a Procedural sky material

Now, let's configure material properties. By default, the skybox is generated as a daytime sky. We'll need to change that. Set the **Sun** field to **None**, as we won't need one. Set the **Sun Size** to 0, **Atmospheric Thicknes** to 0.43, and **Exposure** to 1.3; this adds volume and a horizon glow to the environment. In addition, set the sky and ground colors. These should be dark values, to express a nightscape. I've chosen 021643FF for **Sky Tint** and 1D1A19FF for **Ground**.

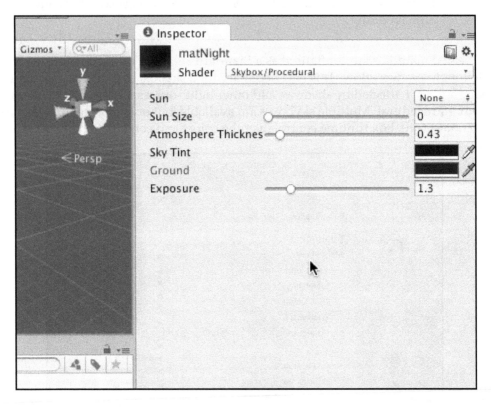

Configuring night time skybox

The skybox can be applied to the scene in several ways. One way is to assign the skybox to a camera as a background. To do this, simply select a camera, and from the **Component** menu, add a **Skybox** component. Navigate to **Component | Rendering | Skybox**. However, for our purposes, we'll avoid this method. We want the background to apply to the scene, and all cameras, as opposed to a single camera:

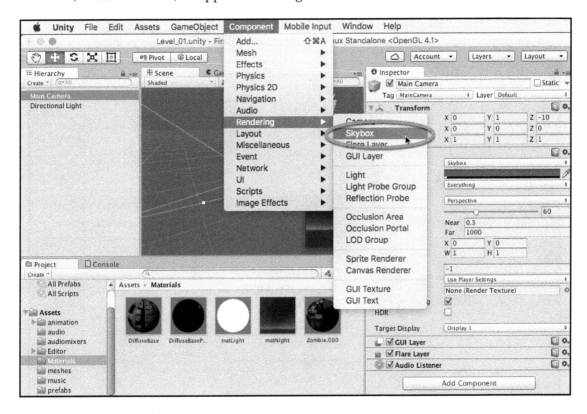

Adding a Skybox component to a camera

Instead of applying a skybox to a camera, we'll apply it to the scene. To do that, open the **Lighting** window by navigating to **Window | Lighting** from the application menu. From the **Lighting** window, drag and drop the newly created skybox material to the **Skybox** field.

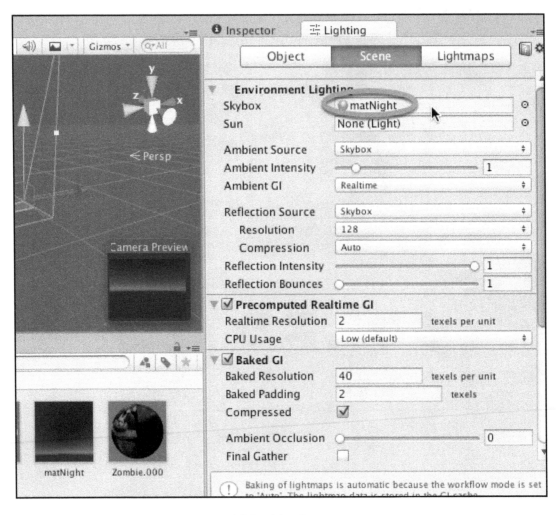

Assigning a skybox to the scene

When the skybox is applied via the **Lighting** window, it should appear from the **Scene** tab, as the world background. If it doesn't appear, be sure to enable Effects Visibility from the **Scene** toolbar.

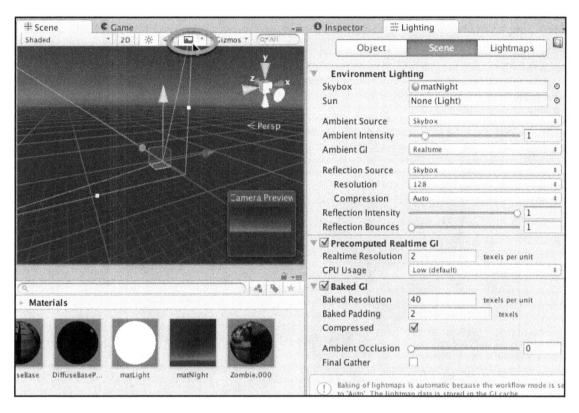

Enabling skybox effect

Level building – modular construction sets

Now the fun begins, though logistically challenging, the process of level building. Our aim is to build a fun and interesting level. But this must be balanced against many factors, including level size, ease of navigation, variety, and more. Creating a level is challenging because misplaced or poorly designed elements stand out for their failings. They break the player's experience. Decisions about architecture and where to include straight sections, turns, jumps, ledges, props, and doors collectively influence the atmosphere and mood of a level. Here, we'll focus on the modular building method, piecing together an expansive level from reusable pieces, exploring reasons, and justifications for our choices along the way. However, let's first see the modular set in its entirety, that is, the complete collection of architectural meshes from which the level must be constructed.

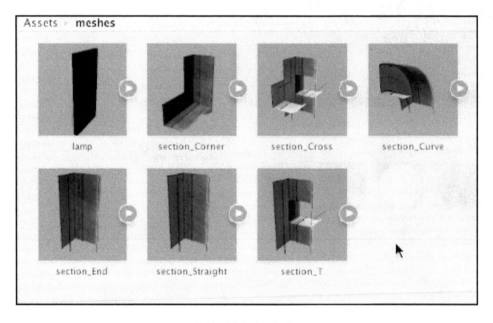

Modular set for level construction

Each mesh is a modular piece (or module). That means each piece is designed to fit seamlessly at the edges with any other piece, in terms of both mesh topology and of texture. This allows all pieces to be combined and recombined, in potentially an infinite number of ways to create any kind of level arrangement. The available modules are as follows:

- **section_Straight**: This is a straight-run mesh for a corridor with open ends. It can be repeated and tiled many times, one after the other at the end vertices, to create a straight corridor of any length.

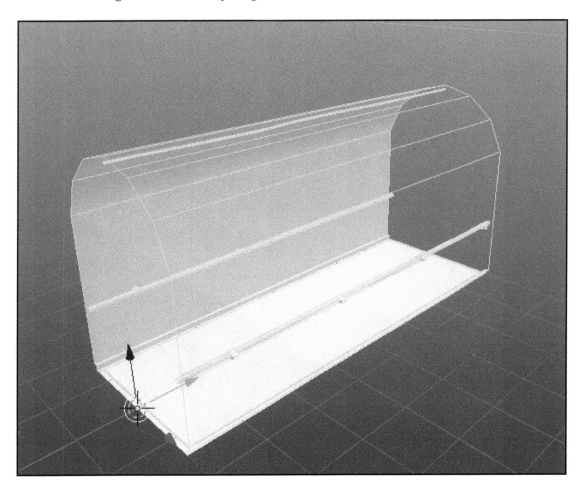

Straight section

- **section_End**: This is a straight section piece with a capped end, representing a wall, preventing the player from passing through. This is useful for creating end-ends. In our case, the piece is a straightforward dead-end, but your own dead-ends need not be so utilitarian. Dead-ends in a modular set come in many forms: broken pipes, fallen debris, toxic gas clouds, wooden boards, plasma barriers, and others.

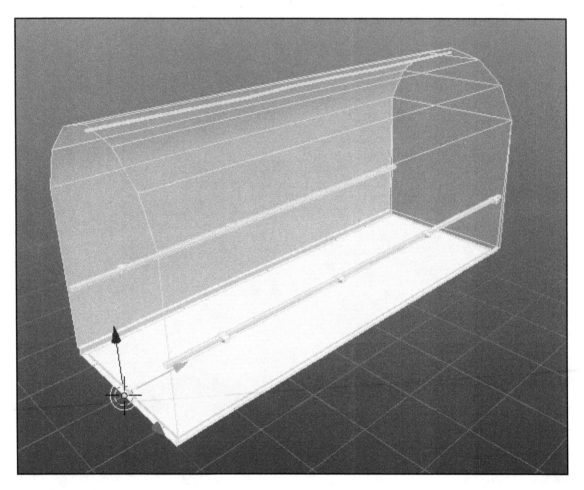

Dead end section

- **section_T**: This piece is formed by the intersection of two straight sections; specifically, by the end of one straight section intersecting with the middle of another. This section presents the player with three possible choices or ways to move.

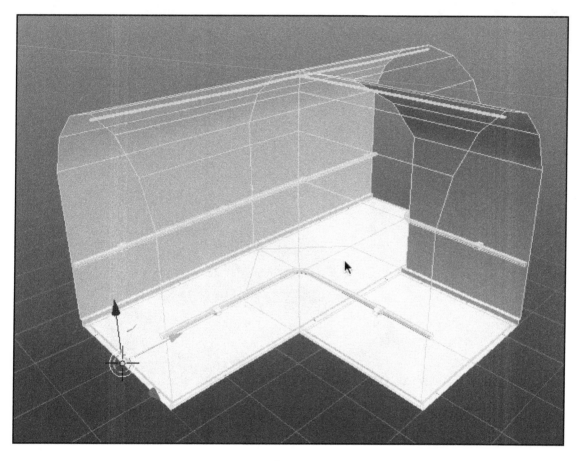

T-section

- **section_Corner**: The corner section is, essentially, an L-formation. It's the intersection of two straight sections meeting at the ends and it allows the player to change direction by 90 degrees.

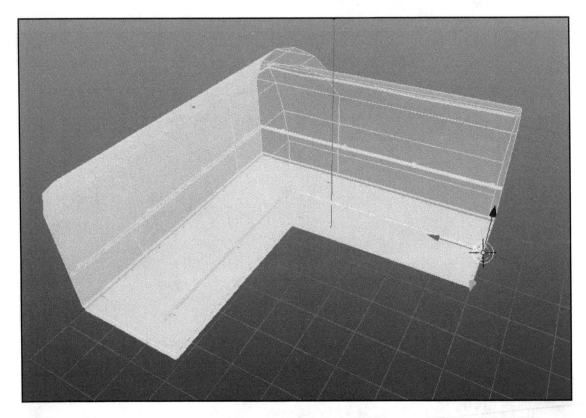

Corner section

- **section_Cross**: The cross section is the intersection of two straights at the middle, allowing potentially four directions of travel. Like all other sections, the cross tiles meet seamlessly with all other modular meshes.

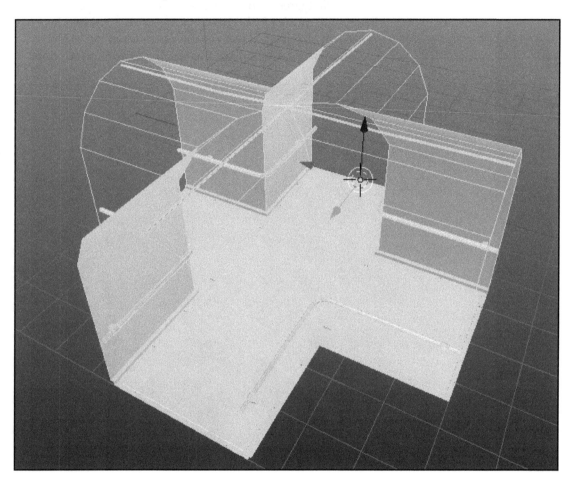

Cross section

- **section_Curve**: The curve section is largely an aesthetic module. So far it achieves exactly the same purpose as the corner section, and thus is functionally unnecessary, but it *looks* and *feels* different. The curve creates a different mood and feeling. With a sharper 90 degree turn, there is an additional suspense and dread, as the player loses sight of *what lurks around the corner*, if anything. In contrast, the curve invites travel, it shapes itself in the direction of travel, and continually allows the same horizon of view for the length of the curve section.

Curved section

Level building – organization and structure

Let's start the level construction process. There are many ways to begin here, but it's a good idea from the outset to develop with a clean workflow in mind. By *clean* I mean an organized, structured, and easy-to-maintain workflow; one that remains maintainable for projects of many scales. First, delete any and all objects in the new scene, and then create a single empty **GameObject** named `root` by navigating to **GameObject | Create Empty** from the application menu. This object will be the top-most object in the hierarchy, from which everything else will be a child directly or indirectly.

Creating a root object for the scene

Next, create a new child object named `env`, which will contain all environment pieces. Make sure that both the `root` and `env` objects are positioned at the world origin at (0,0,0). I typically position the world floor at 0 on the **y** axis, making this the lowest point in the world. It is, of course, possible for objects to fall below this point, but by convention, we can set all negative **Y** values as a kill zone. In this game, where camera paths are predetermined, however, we need not concern ourselves with this, but it's worth considering for free-roaming cameras.

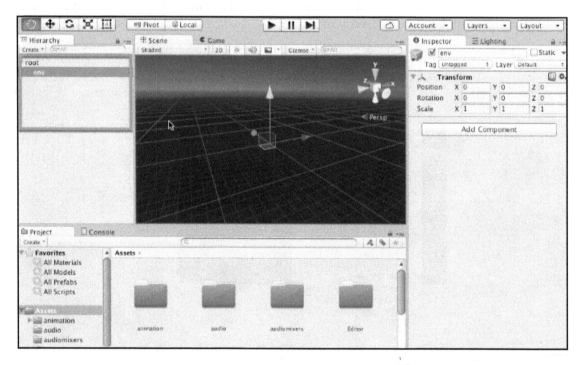

Structuring the scene hierarchy

Now, drag and drop the modular pieces from the **Project** panel into the scene, building a maze-like interior. You can align mesh pieces together exactly at the edge vertices using **Vertex Snapping**. To access Vertex Snapping, switch to the **Translate** tool with *T* on the keyboard, then hold down the *V* key, and then click and drag your mouse from the source mesh to the destination, hovering your cursor over the vertices. When you do this, one mesh snaps to the other automatically. By repeating this process for each mesh module, you can easily align all mesh pieces together.

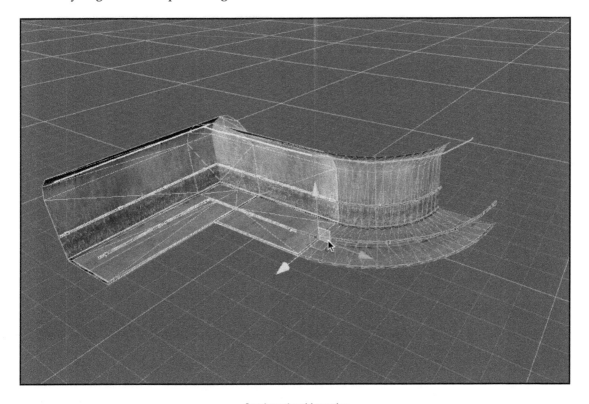

Snapping mesh modules together

When building levels, start by dragging and dropping a single copy of every mesh into the level, to establish a palette of meshes. Then maximize the **Scene** viewport with *Shift* + spacebar, and continue building the level by duplicating the extant pieces as needed in full screen. This saves you from jumping between a maximized and normal view, between the scene and **Project** panel to access your meshes.

After arranging meshes, you'll get an initial level arrangement that should be tested for any obvious problems (such as holes) using a first person controller–or a third person controller, if your game is not first person. Remember to deactivate **Lighting Previews** for the **Scene** tab, for your initial level. This makes it easier to see and position mesh pieces. You can do this using the **Scene** tool bar. Focus first on establishing the overall scene size, general layout and placement of objects, and the starting and end locations. The rest of the scene can be developed functionally and aesthetically alongside these ingredients.

Building an initial level

Level design – tips and tricks

Don't underestimate the design challenges faced when building a level. Arranging mesh modules meaningfully and constructing a layout that encourages exploration and invites interest is challenging. Is a corridor too long or too bendy? Is a walkway too narrow or too wide? Should there be a prop (such as a chair or a desk) in the corner of a room? These types of questions, and others, matter! They're not the kinds of things that should be settled just by flipping a coin. Consider the following design tips and tricks; that is, some guiding principles intended to help you build more interesting levels faster and easier.

Objective and feedback

Always remember the player objective when designing–the goal to be reached by the player during gameplay. This may be reaching a specific location, defeating a specific enemy, achieving a financial target, or something else. Most players like to feel successful, like to feel like they're moving toward that goal. During gameplay, they'll typically look for both *overt signs* of progress (such as mission complete popups and victory sound effects) as well as *convert signs* of progress, such as meeting a friendly unit that offers to help you reach a location, opening a hitherto locked door, finding the murder weapon in a mystery game, or catching sight of the destination from a high-vantage point (such as a watch tower), among others. It's important to reach a balance between these two types of signs or feedback, and to steadily provide them in the level through props, characters, dialog, architecture, special effects, and anything else you can put into a level. If the level features little feedback, the player loses interest, and feels defeated or bored. If the level features too much feedback, the player feels frustrated and overwhelmed.

Narrative

Many games tell a story. Some stories feel like an integral part of the game, while others feel added-on only to facilitate gameplay or a fun mechanic. In any case, the level you build will communicate a story. That is, the engaged player will unconsciously read the environment as they explore (its characters, architecture, and props) for meaningful elements relating to the overarching story. For this reason, ask yourself important questions about the objects that you, as a designer, add to a level, from tables and chairs to doors and windows: Why put an object here? What does that reveal? How does it complement the story, if at all? For example, bloodied footprints found on the floor speak on many levels to the player. They express harm, murder, and intrigue about an event in the past. They encourage exploration right now: where do the footprints lead? And why? Props like these are important for generating interest and excitement. But even a lonely, mundane object such as a chair can take on significance, for example, when positioned alone at the center of a large and creepy room. Who sat there? When and why? It's the curious juxtaposition and relationships between objects that make them interesting and meaningful, and so it's important not to see the objects as *filler*; as simply things thrown in to use up space and reduce emptiness. Emptiness, in that negative sense, arises not so much from a lack of props and objects, but from a lack of significant objects, objects that make a difference and carry meaning. Therefore, add objects and design levels with consideration for purpose and narration; think about how objects relate to the story, which characters would have used them, and what their location now says about recent events.

Believability and convenience

There's an important balance to find between believability and convenience; it's easy to sacrifice one for the other. **Believability** is about creating a world that *makes sense*; one that's consistent with your theme, story, technology, characters, and more. In sci-fi, for example, the player may expect to find starships, aliens, and laser guns–but not elves, dragons, and undead mages. These elements simply don't belong. **Convenience**, on the other hand, is about the creative liberties we, as designers, take with the boundaries of a reality to make things easier, more fun, or more accessible to the gamer. For example, travelling between villages in an RPG may take only minutes in *real time*, but represent weeks in *game time*. We don't make the player wait for weeks; we typically accelerate time for their convenience. When designing levels, we must find a middle point between these two extremes. Sometimes, we'll move closer to one direction than another, depending on the game. For *Dead Keys*, we'll take a *convenience preference* to facilitate the pick-up-and-play arcade feel. This will be reflected by a linear level design allowing only one real route, by the staggered placement of enemies and a fixed-path camera. We'll include some props and objects to express a story now and then, but ultimately the experience needs to be smooth, progressive, and clearly action focused. This damages the believability and narrative, but that's OK! We simply need to recognize that and focus on what's most important for our design and what our aim is–a fast-paced fun experience.

Atmosphere and aesthetic

Believability and *convenience* typically, though not necessarily, exist in tension, both *atmosphere* and *aesthetic* are complementary, though distinct aspects. Atmosphere is part of the aesthetic. Atmosphere is how the whole scene manifests and is experienced by the player; the kind of emotions and feelings it invokes at different times. To decide on the atmosphere, you'll first need to reach decisions about the overarching game aesthetic. This is an artistic decision about how the game looks, feels, sounds, and comes together as a coherent artistic vision–not a specific level, but the game as a whole. Some games are gothic in style, some cyberpunk, some steampunk, and more such styles. These styles define color palettes, sound effects, character types, technology levels, and more. On reaching decisions about the aesthetic, you're thereby given boundaries, visual and audible, for how each level may be styled and structured. Here, concept art, references images, extant music tracks, and even literature can be highly valuable for inspiration that guides level development. In short, don't simply put a scene together without a clear artistic vision guiding the creation of atmosphere. Every level will have an atmosphere, but it should be the result of an intended, planned, and designed atmosphere–as opposed to atmosphere that emerges incidentally from a disjointed mix of meshes.

Simplicity and reuse

Simplicity and reuse work hand-in-hand and are important techniques when level designing. Simplicity is about breaking down the level into reusable blocks or modules, which can be encoded into prefabs. It encourages us too avoid over specificity; that is, to avoid making assets to specific for one purpose. Sometimes this cannot be avoided, but where possible, it should be. For example, when designing a straight-section prefab for a corridor scene, it could be developed with or without a statue mesh. Including the statue mesh alongside the corridor as a single prefab is more specific than omitting the mesh. Therefore, in this scenario, try creating the corridor without the statue, and only add the statue to specific straight-sections where needed. This simplifies the straight-section prefab. From this kind of simplicity comes reusability. That is, the ability to easily reuse the straight section again and again for different purposes, without the repetition being obvious. Such reusability makes it possible to construct complex arrangements, and large levels, from only a limited collection of simple pieces.

Level lighting – preparation

Reaching this far you've now made a complete scene in terms of meshes representing the first level, composed from modular environment pieces (corridor sections). Presently, the level features no lighting, navigation meshes, music or audio, and Occlusion Data; but, we'll add these soon. Let's start with lighting. In Unity, there are three main lighting types or systems, which exist on a spectrum:

- **Baked lighting**
- **Real-time lighting**
- **Precomputed global illumination**

These are discussed in detail further here.

Baked lighting

Baked lighting is the optimal lighting method, but it can only be used under specific circumstances. With Baked lighting, all lighting data (highlights, shadows, and so on) are precalculated and saved to a texture (lightmap). The lightmap is then applied to scene geometry using a second UV channel (Lightmap UVs), on top of their standard materials, using multiplicative blending. This makes geometry appear illuminated by scene lights. This approach is ideal for achieving high levels of realism while maintaining excellent runtime performance, because it saves Unity from having to calculate lighting at runtime. But lightmapping only works properly for static objects (objects that never move), such as walls, floors, ceilings, and architecture.

A lighmap texture for the scene

Dynamic lighting

Dynamic lighting is the opposite of Baked lighting. With Baked lighting, all lighting information is precalculated, that is, calculated ahead of runtime. Dynamic lighting, however, is calculated at runtime. This means Unity accepts all lights affecting an object as input, the object itself, and its surrounding objects, and then produces the best lighting approximation it can. The upside of dynamic lighting is that it changes and updates in real time as objects transform in the scene. The downside is computational expense (it's expensive) and realism, as quality sacrifices are made to produce lighting effects in real time. In short, you never want to use dynamic lighting unless you absolutely have to! Thankfully, Unity offers us some tools (**Light Probes**) for semi-baking lighting data, reducing the impact of dynamic lighting.

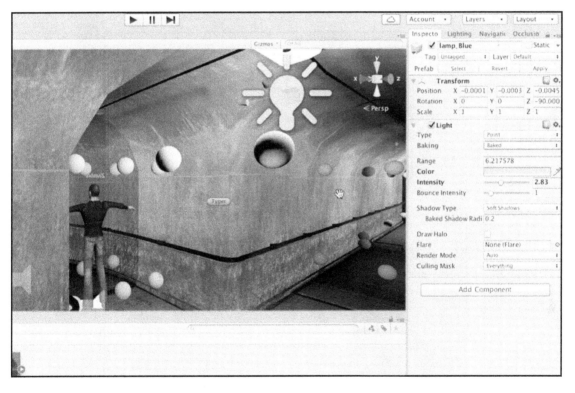

Dynamic lighting

Precomputed global illumination

The problem with Baked lighting is its static and unchanging nature. After a lightmap is baked, it cannot be changed without rebaking. In contrast, the problem with dynamic lighting is its performance intensive nature. Light calculated in real time demands lots of resources and processing time. Since Unity 5, Unity offers a middle-way solution known as precomputed **global illumination** (**GI**). This system lets you recompute (bake) significant lighting data about how light bounces around in the scene, and yet retain the ability to change scene lights at runtime. In short, with precomputed GI you can–move lights, and change their colour and intensity at runtime, and all lighting changes take effect in the scene soon after. However, precomputed GI is restricted only to static objects (non-moving objects). Objects that move must still be illuminated using either dynamic lighting, or a semi-dynamic form, such as Light Probes (as we'll see).

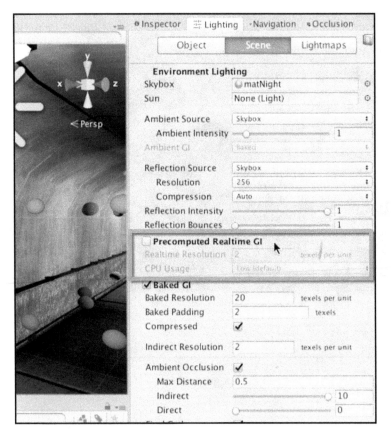

Precomputed global illumination

The three aforementioned lighting systems are not mutually exclusive–they can be used to varying degrees with each other. But for *Dead Keys*, we'll stick with Baked lighting for the environment (since the environment never moves), and semi-dynamic lighting (Light Probes) for animated objects, such as NPCs.

Getting started with lightmapping

To start Baking Scene lighting, we'll first need to activate Lightmap UVs for the environment meshes and then position some lights in the scene where appropriate. To activate Lightmap UVs, select all environment meshes in the **Project** panel and enable **Generate Lightmap UV** from the object **Inspector**. Then click on **Apply**. This method is useful for generating a second UV channel when one doesn't already exist. This defines how lighting is baked to the lightmap texture. Unity applies an auto-unwrap projection using settings from the **Advanced** roll out. If, by contrast, your own meshes already have a custom, second channel, then you can use this channel instead for Lightmap UVs simply by disabling **Generate Lightmap UVs**.

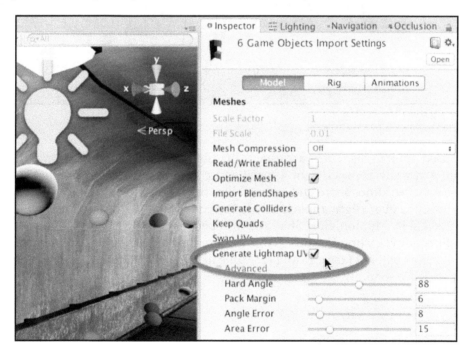

Configuring Lightmap UVs

For meshes with two UV channels, you can enable **Swap UVs** from the object **Inspector** to switch channel order, if needed. This makes the second channel the primary, and the first channel the secondary. The primary channel is used for regular texture mapping and the secondary for Lightmap UVs.

Next, strategically position all lights in the scene, taking care to add as few as possible while maintaining your central artistic vision.

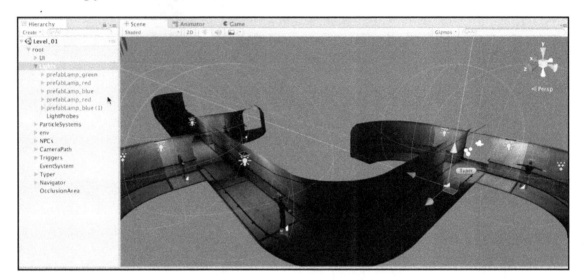

Adding lights

Here, I've used point lights. These are especially useful for simulating interior, artificial lights (ceiling or wall). For each light, I specified a color tint (red, green, or blue) and an intensity to enhance atmosphere and interest. For the **Baking** field, a value of **Baked** is specified, meaning every light applies only to Baked lighting (lightmapping) and not precomputed GI. In addition, **Soft Shadows** are specified for the **Shadow Type**, allowing soft, realistic shadow casting for the environment in the baking process. Remember, being Baked lights, they will not factor in any real-time lighting calculations, except through Light Probes, as we'll see soon.

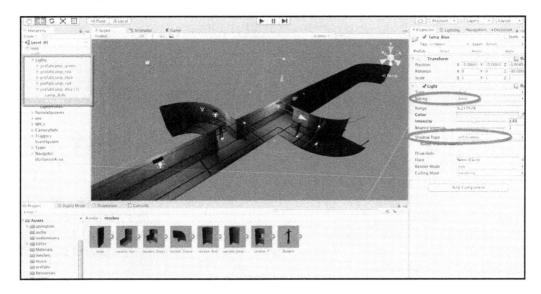

Configuring Baked lights

Finally, enable the **Static** checkbox in the object **Inspector** for all non-moving environment objects. The best approach here is to use the **Hierarchy** panel to append all environment objects as children of a common root node. And then to mark the root node as static. By doing this, the operation cascades downwards automatically to all children. This saves you lots of time from enabling static for each object separately.

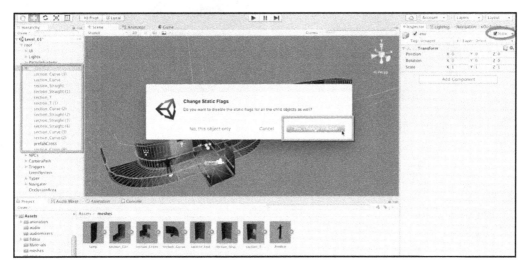

Creating static environments

Don't forget to save your scene before lightmapping! Saving is needed as the scene file encodes some important lightmapping data and connections.

Baking lightmaps – resolution and size

Our scene now features marked static objects, complete with Lightmap UVs, and is ready for lightmapping. The default settings for all Unity scenes and projects is not compatible with a full lightmap setup as we require, and so we must access the lighting settings. To do this, display the **Lighting** window by navigating to **Window | Lighting** from the application menu. Once opened, dock the free-floating window into the object **Inspector** as a separate tab. This is convenient because we can view the lighting settings and inspect the **Scene** viewport side by side.

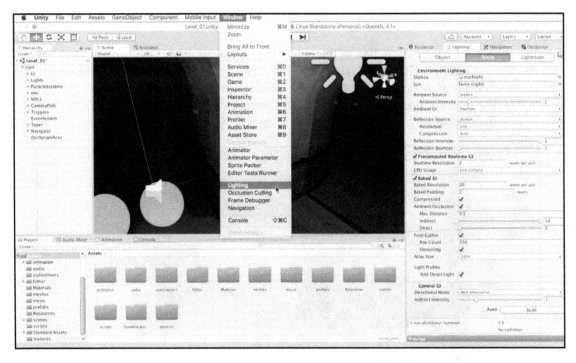

Accessing the Lighting window

First, let's disable all precomputed GI settings, by removing the check mark from the **Precomputed Realtime GI** rollout in the **Lighting** window. This completely deactivates real-time GI for the scene. In addition, specify the night time skybox (created earlier) for the **Skybox** field. This is important for establishing a base, ambient lighting pervading the scene, even in the darkest and most inaccessible areas. Pixels from the surrounding skybox are projected inward into the scene as minor light sources, which are used for defining the lowest lighting level.

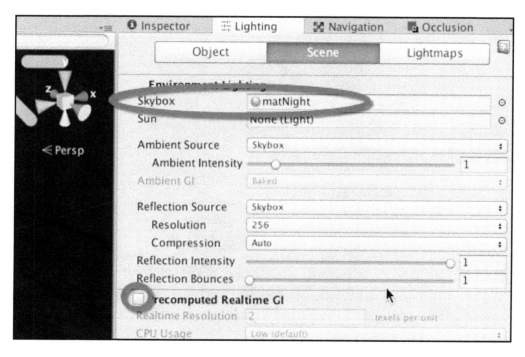

Deactivating Precomputed Realtime GI and establishing an ambient light source

Next, I recommend deactivating the **Auto** checkbox, next to the **Build** button as soon as possible. This step is optional. When enabled, Unity continually rebuilds scene lighting automatically, whenever light-relevant changes are detected in the scene (for example, when static objects are moved, light colors change, and so on). This saves us from initiating a build manually, and for simpler scenes it's both quick and effective. But it can slow down the editor speed while building, invalidates scene lighting temporarily, and is associated with some bugs.

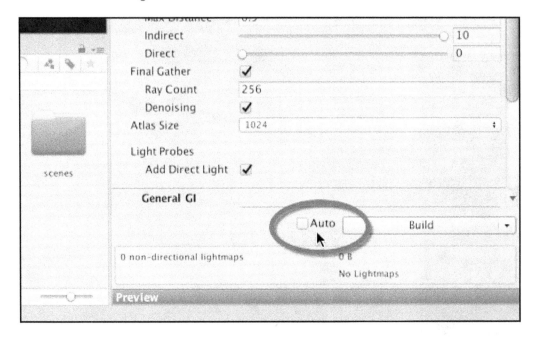

Disabling auto build for lighting

Now, let's establish texel density for the lightmaps to be generated. This is an important process. For lightmapping to be effective, the surface area of the scene must map the lightmap texture, each face of each static mesh mapping to a unique set of pixels for its lighting information. Unity gives you control over how many pixels in the lightmap texture map to a square unit in the scene. The ratio between pixels to world units is defined by the resolution setting for the baked GI rollout. This defines how one pixel in the lightmap relates to a world unit. Lower values produce smaller and fewer lightmap textures, at the expensive of lightmap quality. Higher values improve quality, but at the expense of texture size. We need to arrive at a balance appropriate for our scene. To start, let's visualize the lightmap density. To do this, change the viewport shading mode to **Baked**. This is achieved via the **Shading Mode** dropdown in the **Scene** tab.

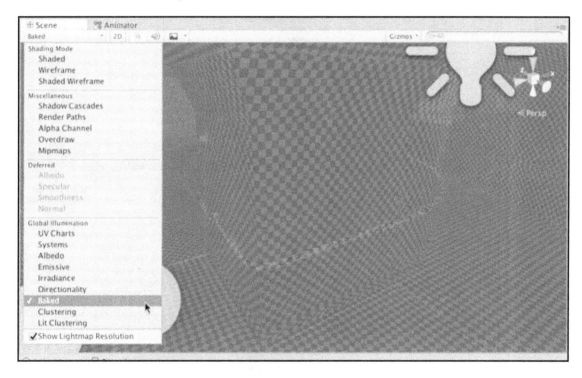

Enabling baked resolution display

When baked shading is activated, the **Scene** viewport flood fills a checker pattern across all meshes in the scene. Each square in the pattern represents one pixel in the lightmap. Thus, the scene view expresses how densely packed texture pixels are from the lightmap to the mesh. You can control texel density using the **Baked Resolution** field. Lower values decrease quality, and thus the size of each square increases as fewer pixels are packed onto the mesh.

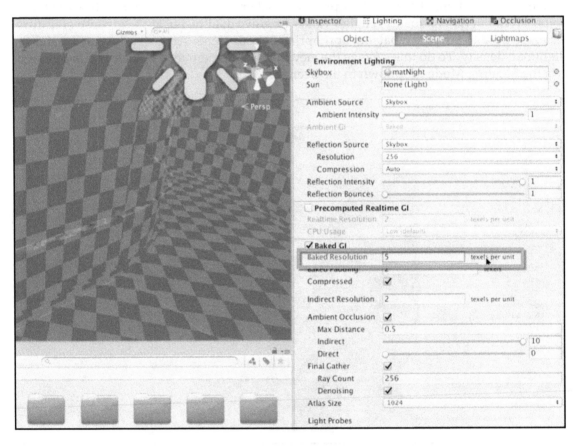

Configuring lightmap resolution

Now, specify an **Atlas Size.** This defines the maximum size in pixels for each square lightmap texture. The number of lightmap textures generated depends on the **Baked Resolution** and **Atlas Size**. If the scene surface area cannot fit into one texture, based on the lightmap resolution, then additional textures are generated. The ideal is to keep lightmap textures as few in number as possible. It's generally better for performance to have one large lightmap than many smaller lightmaps.

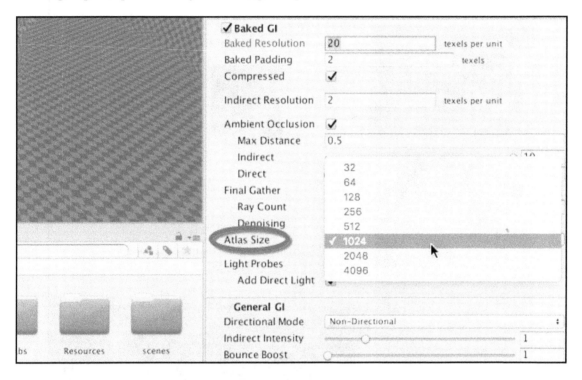

Configuring Atlas Size

Before tweaking further light-mapping details, let's test the existing settings to see how many lightmaps are generated for the scene. Simply click on the **Build** button, and then repeat this process (while refining **Baked Resolution** and **Atlas Size**) until you arrive at textures sized as needed, avoiding pixel wastage. You can view the generated lightmap textures from the **Preview** pane of the **Lightmaps** tab.

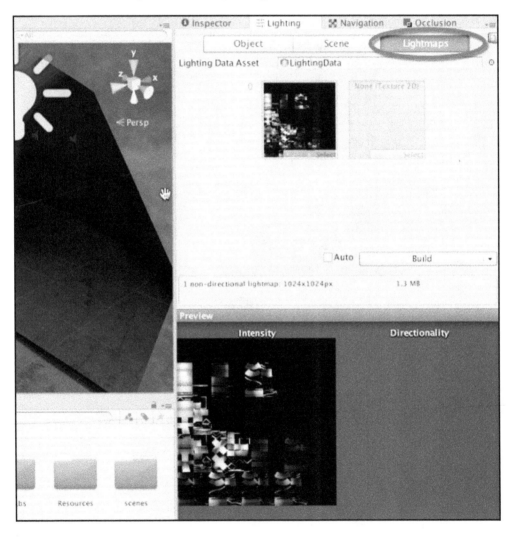

Previewing generated lightmaps

The generated lightmap textures themselves also live in the **Project** panel as a texture asset of the project. These are textures marked with the **Lightmap** type from the object **Inspector**. These are found in a subfolder alongside the saved scene asset.

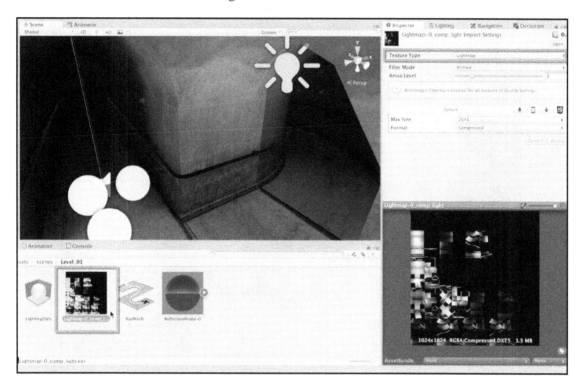

Lightmaps are generated as texture assets

You can often identify pixel wastage in a lightmap texture. This happens when your **Atlas Size** is too high and/or **Baked Resolution** is too low, resulting in textures that cannot be filled or maximized with pixels. This leads to redundant pixels, which are not assigned to any meshes. You'll want to avoid this. Aim to fill lightmaps as much as possible. This gives you the best quality attainable for your settings.

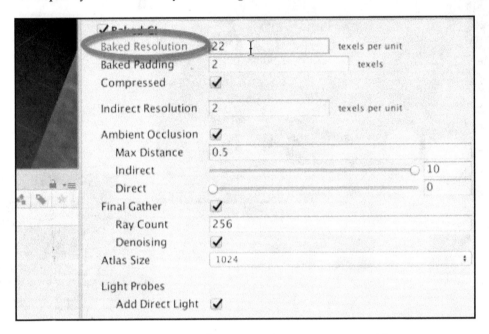

Tweaking lightmap size

Baking lightmaps – details

Having now established a resolution and Atlas Size, we should specify baking details to improve the quality and appearance of our lightmaps. To do this, enable **Ambient Occlusion** and tweak the **Max Distance** field until you get the volumetric effect desired. This requires rebaking. Ambient Occlusion is sometimes called **Contact Shadows** because it generates shadows where two or more solid bodies meet, such as the floor meeting the wall, or crevices and cracks. This creates a volume effect, enhancing the 3D-feel of a scene.

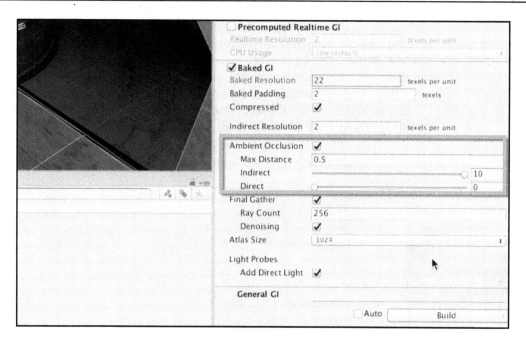

Enabling Ambient Occlusion

In addition, enable **Final Gather**. Set the **Ray Count** to 256. Final Gather reduces noise and improves the quality of lightmapping. Higher values result in smooth, higher quality output, at the expense of the calculation time.

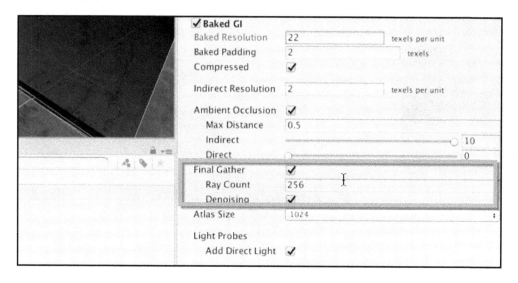

Enabling Final Gather

Finally, you can increase the resolution of specific objects, if needed. We don't need this for DK, but if you have large, eye catching and very important objects in a scene (such as a golden throne or majestic statue), you'll probably want these to receive more lighting detail than obscure areas in darkened regions. Specifically, you'll want to give some objects more lightmap texture space than others. To achieve this, select the object in the scene, to receive more or less detail, and then switch to the **Object** tab of the **Lighting** window. From here, set the object's **Scale in Lightmap** field. By default, all objects have a scale of 1. However, you can raise and lower an object's scale, for each object to increase or reduce its detail, respectively. The value 0.5 is half detailed, 2 is double detail, and so on.

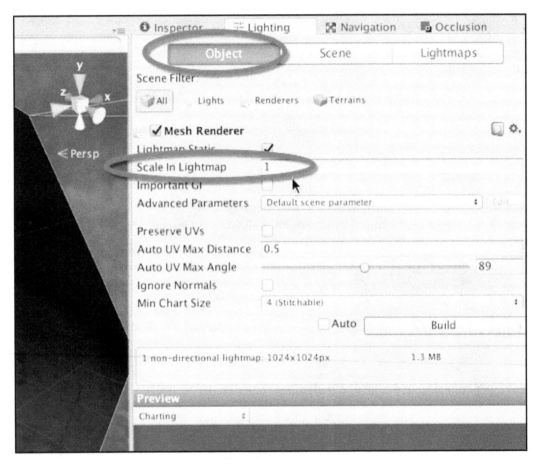

Lightmap scaling

Now you're ready for the final scene bake! Click on the **Build** button, and the final lightmaps are generated. Remember, if you later upgrade to a different version of Unity, you'll probably need to rebake the scene.

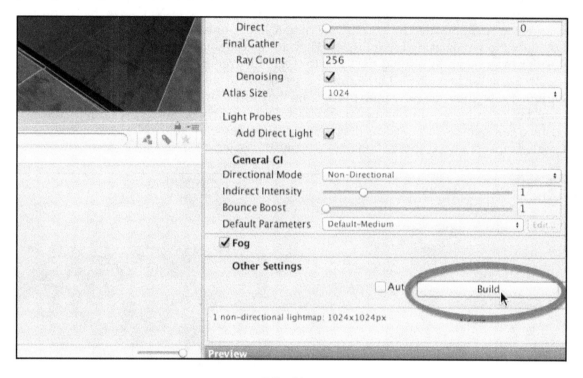

Baking a lightmap

 More information on lightmapping can be found in the Unity documentation online at `http://docs.unity3d.com/Manual/GlobalIllu mination.html`.

Light Probes

The lightmap setup works well for the scene, but applies only to static objects; such as walls, floors, ceilings, and props. Animated and movable objects, such as NPCs, will by contrast continue to be illuminated by expensive dynamic lights, unless additional steps are taken. Let's take those now using Light Probes. They are special sampling objects, which should be positioned strategically around the scene to record an average of light color and intensity at that location. When multiple Light Probes exist, movable objects such as characters are illuminated by interpolated values taken from the nearest probes. Light Probes, therefore, record color and intensity, but they do not cast shadows. To get started with Light Probes, create a new game object to act as the parent of all probes. Navigate to **GameObject** | **Create Empty** from the application menu. Name this object `LightProbes`.

Creating an empty object for Light Probes

Next, add a Light Probe group component to the newly created Empty. This can be added first by selecting the empty, and then by navigating to **Component** | **Render** | **Light Probe Group** from the application menu. Using a Light Probe group, you can add, move, and reposition Light Probes in the scene.

You can also create a Light Probe Group in one operation by navigating to **GameObject** | **Light** | **Light Probe Group** from the application menu.

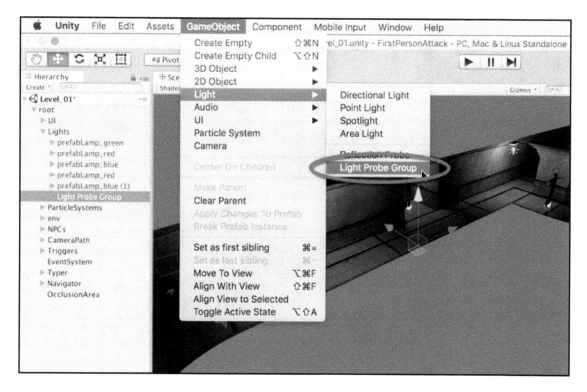

Creating a Light Probe Group

A scene usually has only one Light Probe group, which is responsible for all Light Probes. Each Light Probe samples light color and intensity at a specific location. To add a new probe, select the Light Probe Group object, and from the object **Inspector,** click on the **Edit Light Probes** button, which is part of the **Light Probe Group** component. This unlocks a series of buttons for editing Light Probes.

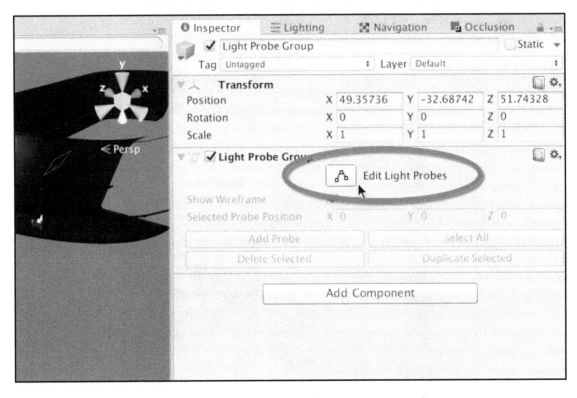

Editing Light Probes from the object Inspector

Now, click on the **Add Probe** button. When you do this for the first time, a collection of probes is added to the scene. The probes may be positioned out of view (press *F* to frame them, if needed). You can use the **Transform** tools to move them into position. The idea is to position them in areas where significant light changes occur, from dark to light, or from one color to the next. Ideally, the probes should record the state of lighting throughout the scene.

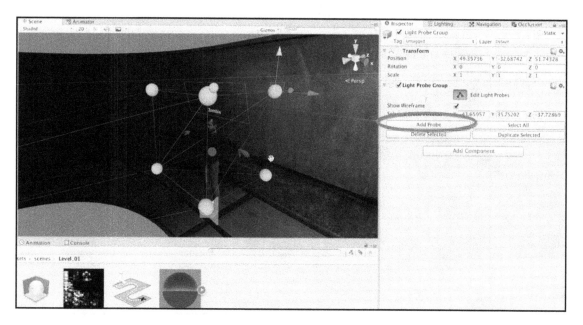

Adding Light Probes

After adding the initial probes, select specific ones and click **Duplicate Selected** to add more. Once duplicated, move the probes into position. Repeat this process to fill the scene with probes in light significant locations.

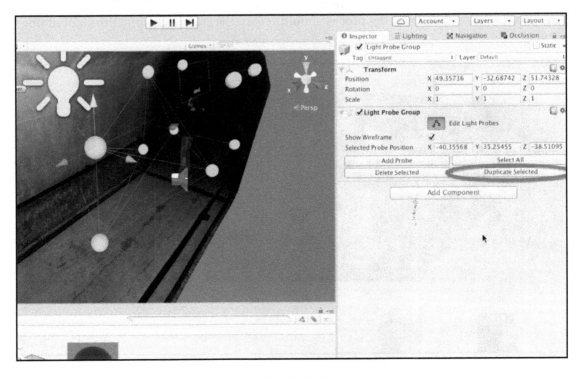

Adding additional probes

A complete network of probes can effectively record scene lighting. In addition, Unity draws connections between probes in the **Scene** viewport, helping you to visualize how lighting will be interpolated.

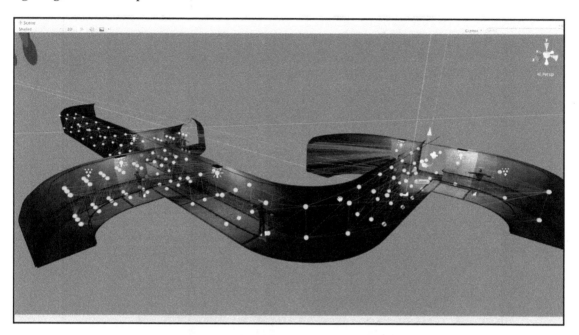

Completing the probe network

If you don't see Light Probes in the **Scene** viewport, ensure you have Light Probe gizmos enabled. To do that, click on the **Gizmos** icon from the **Scene** toolbar and enable **LightProbeGroup**.

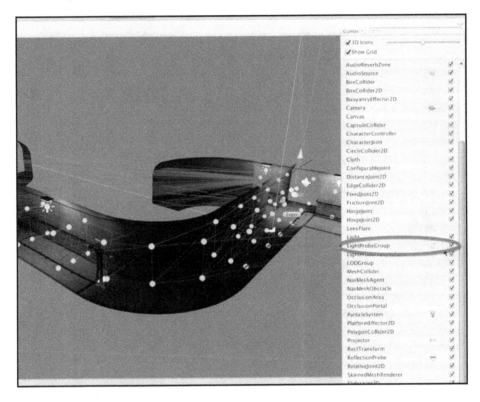

Enabling Light Probe Viewport Visibility

After adding all probes, you'll need to bake them from the **Lighting** window. This process effectively takes the snapshot for the probes, causing each probe to record scene light color and light intensity at the probe location. To achieve this, switch to the **Lighting** window (which can be docked in the object **Inspector**), and click on the **Build** button. That's it! You've now baked Light Probes. Congratulations. Of course, for Light Probes to actually affect dynamic meshes, such as characters, you should select each movable mesh, and examine its properties in the object **Inspector**. For the **Mesh Renderer** (non-character objects) and the **Skinned Mesh Renderer** components (for character meshes), you should specify **Blend Probes** for the **Light Probes** field. This indicates that the selected object receives its lighting from the Light Probes scene, as opposed to dynamically from scene lights.

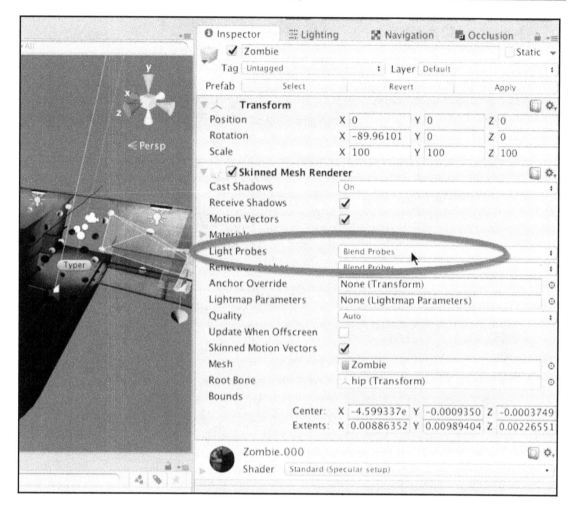

Configuring objects to use Light Probes

 More information on Light Probes can be found at the online Unity
documentation at `https://docs.unity3d.com/Manual/LightProbes.htm`
`l`.

Lighting FAQ

This section takes time out to explore lighting issues and problems that sometimes arise and common methods for resolving them. The issues listed here may not arise for the *Dead Keys* project specifically, but it's likely you'll encounter them somewhere, on some projects. Consequently, it's good to know how the issues are solved or at least avoided. This section takes a Question and Answer format:

- **Scene lighting appears wrong when opening a scene in the editor**: This happens when **Auto** is enabled from the **Lighting** window. As the scene is opened, lighting is rebaked. This may take time or may fail entirely. The result is that scene lighting may not appear correct instantly when a scene is opened. You can resolve this by disabling auto baking from the **Lighting** window and then saving the scene to confirm the change. The next time the scene is opened, the existing baked data will be used instead.

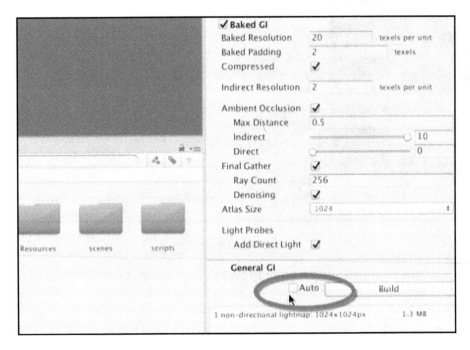

Disabling Auto for baking

- **Scene lighting is baked, but appears messed up in the scene**: If lighting looks wrong on the meshes, such as a jumbled mess with shadows, colors, and highlights appearing in the wrong places, then you can try the following two steps in order. First, make sure all meshes either have a second UV channel for a lightmap or have the **Generate Lightmap UV** option enabled via the object **Inspector**. This is important because lightmaps are baked to a texture through a second UV channel.

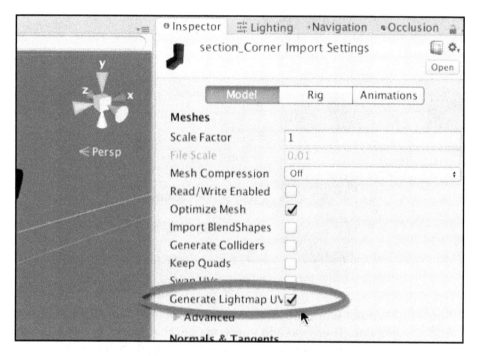

Generating Lightmap UVs

Secondly, you can try enabling the **Swap UVs** option when **Generate Lightmap UV** is disabled, from the object **Inspector**, as the wrong UV channel may have been used for the lightmap. In any case, a complete rebake will be required.

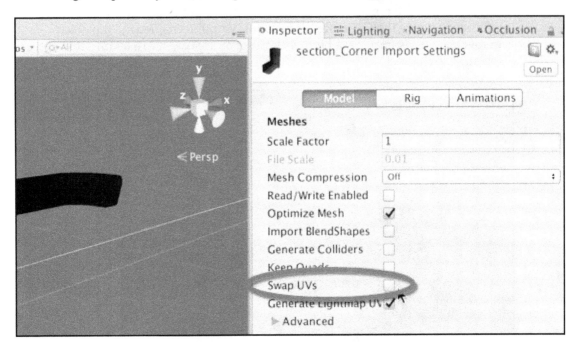

Swapping Lightmap UVs

- **Some lights don't work!**: Here's a common problem. You add a light to the scene and it works fine. Then you add a second, and that works fine too. But then, after adding more, you soon discover that additional lights behave differently in an important way. Some have no affect at all or some illuminate the environment with less or more intensity than expected, despite having the same settings as earlier lights. This problem could be related to the light quality settings and per-pixel Lights. In Unity, there are two main light types: vertex-based and pixel-based. Vertex-based lights are less accurate and typically produce lower quality lighting. But they're cheaper to calculate and work better on legacy hardware. This is because they illuminate meshes by interpolating light across their vertices. Pixel-based lights, in contrast, produce better lighting, but are calculated on pixel basis, as opposed to vertices. This makes them computationally expensive. By default, Unity specifies a maximum of four per-pixel lights in the **QualitySettings**, and it makes a determination at runtime as to whether a light should be pixel-based or vertex-based, in line with the **QualitySettings**.

This means that, after four per-pixel lights are added to the scene and are active, Unity automatically converts additional lights to vertex-based lights, and these illuminate differently. There are two different ways to solve this problem. First, you can increase the number of per-pixel lights permitted at one time in a scene, using the **QualitySettings**. To do this, navigate to **Edit | Project Settings | Quality** from the application menu, to display **QualitySettings** in the object **Inspector**.

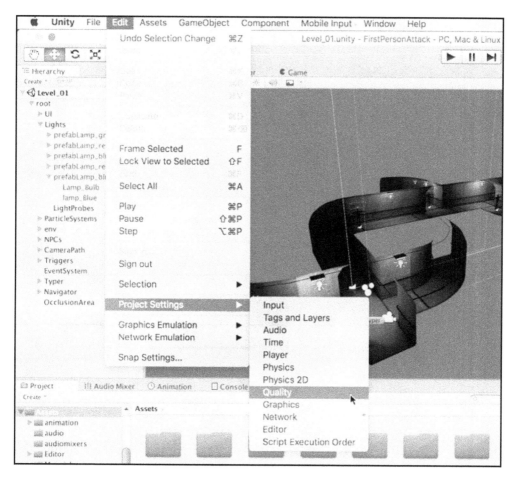

Accessing QualitySettings

From here, specify a new maximum for the **Pixel Light Count** field in the object **Inspector**. This increases the maximum number of pixel lights permitted.

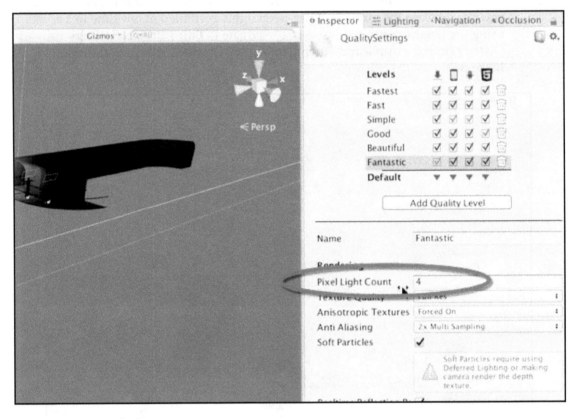

Setting the maximum number of per-pixel lights

You can force Unity to recognize a light as either vertex-based or pixel-based, using the **Render Mode** setting for the light object, in the **Light** component from the object **Inspector**. This overrides the determination Unity makes for each light. Simply change the **Render Mode** from **Auto** (let Unity decide) to either **Important** (pixel-based) or **Not Important** (vertex-based).

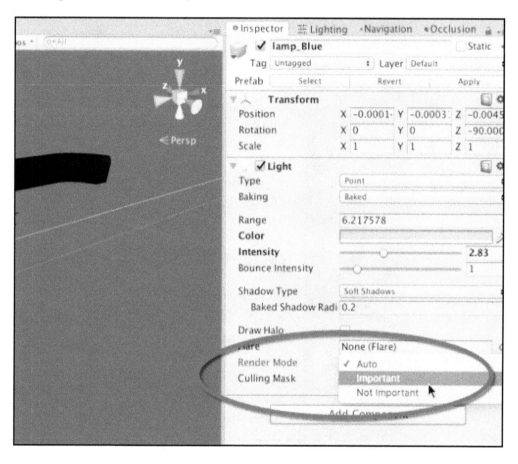

Setting the Light Render Mode

- **Objects don't cast or receive shadows**: If your scene is missing shadows and you don't know why, there are several important stages where problems can occur. First, ensure the selected light is configured for shadow casting. To do this, set the **Shadow Type** field, from the object **Inspector**, to either **Soft Shadows** or **Hard Shadows**.

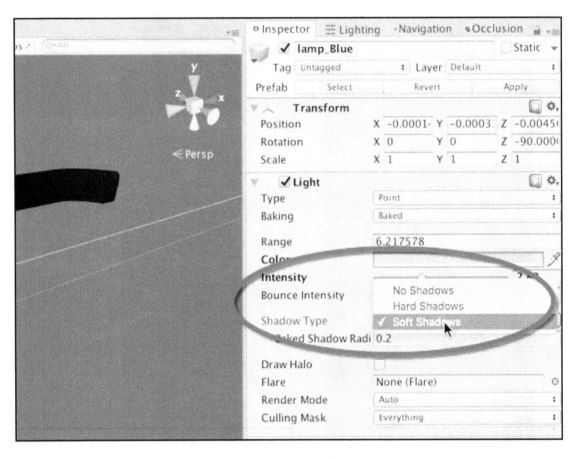

Specifying Shadow Type for a light

Next, make sure other renderable meshes can *cast* and *receive* shadows as needed. Shadow casting is the ability for a mesh to cast a shadow elsewhere; and shadow receiving defines whether the mesh can have shadows cast upon its own surface. To enable these features, select each mesh to cast and/or receive shadows and, from the **Mesh Renderer** component in the object **Inspector**, enable the **Receive Shadows** checkbox. In addition, set **Cast Shadows** to **On**.

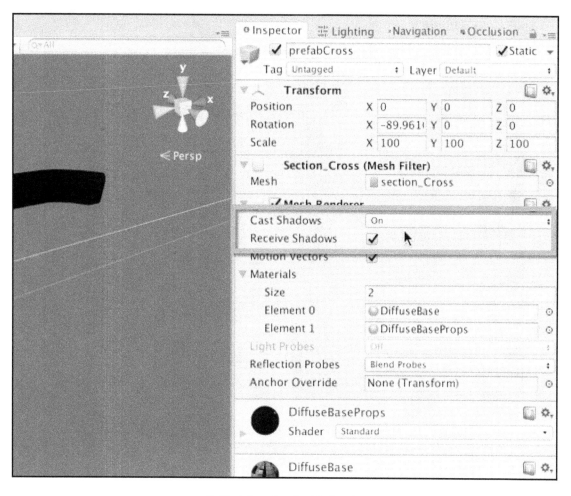

Enabling shadow casting and receiving for meshes

Finally, from the **QualitySettings** window, ensure shadows are enabled overall, and that your viewport and scene camera are within the **Shadow Distance**. The **QualitySettings** window is displayed by navigating to **Edit | Project Settings | Quality**. Both values (**Shadow Casting** and **Shadow Distance**) can be controlled from the **QualitySettings** window. Shadows can be enabled and disabled altogether using the **Shadows** drop-down field. A value of **Hard and Soft Shadows** permits all kinds of shadows, while **None** disables any shadows, regardless of light and mesh settings.

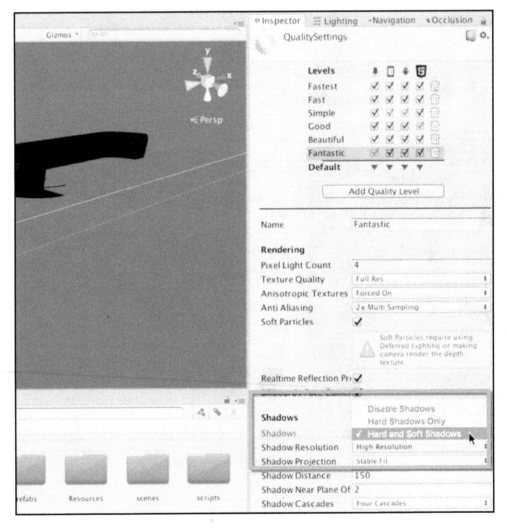

Shadow settings master control

The **Shadow Distance** field specifies a distance in meters from the camera beyond which any shadow casting or receiving is disabled. Shadows beyond the **Shadow Distance** are not rendered, regardless of other shadow settings. Increasing the **Shadow Distance** brings more shadows into view, at the expense of performance.

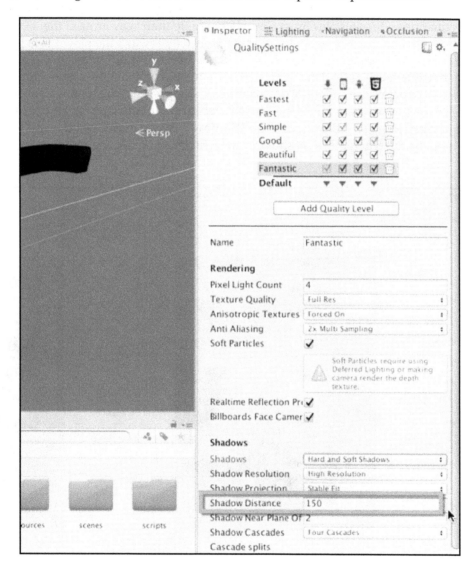

Tweaking Shadow Distance

Navigation mesh

Now it's time to explore NPC intelligence and, specifically, path finding. We'll need our NPC zombies to move around the scene intelligently; that is, to move without bumping into walls, floors, doors, and other obstacles, and without taking the most complex routes to nearby destinations. Our zombies must cleverly navigate their way around the environment, whatever its arrangement, finding their way toward the player to engage in combat, as though they really had brains! To achieve this, a navigation mesh is required. This is a nonvisible mesh asset, generated by Unity, to approximate the scene floor, for both exterior and interior environments. More accurately, it represents the total walkable floor of the scene–the area over which NPCs may maneuver for travelling from point to point. To access the navigation mesh features, click on **Window** | **Navigation** from the application menu. This opens the **Navigation** mesh window, which can be docked into the object **Inspector**.

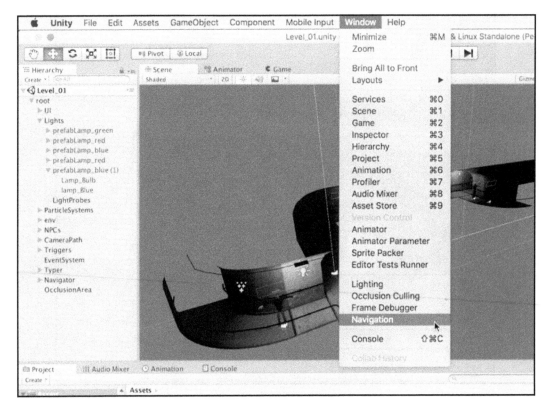

Accessing the navigation mesh features

The **Navigation** mesh window is where you can generate a navigation mesh for the scene. At present, Unity allows you to generate only one navigation mesh per scene, and you cannot import a custom mesh. To get started, use the **Agent Radius** and **Agent Height** fields to specify the radius and height of the smallest possible agent for your game. These values are used by Unity to determine valid areas into which the navigation mesh can be generated. Openings shorter than, or narrower than, the minimum values cause the navigation mesh to break, preventing agents from travelling through. For Dead Keys, the **Agent Radius** should be 0.5, and the **Height** should be 2. For your own projects, these values may differ substantially.

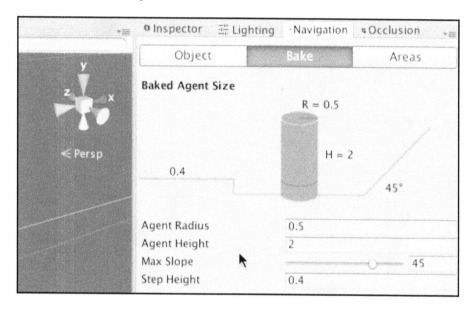

Specifying Agent Radius and Agent Height

Additionally, the **Max Slope** field defines the angle (in degrees) of the maximum incline from ground level allowed. Inclines preceding this angle are classified as non-walkable areas and do not feature in the navigation mesh. The **Step Height** works similarly, except it's based on height (in meters) rather than angle. That is, steps above the threshold are classified as too high for being walkable. For Dead Keys, the default values are acceptable, but for strongly vertical games you may need to tweak these. Having now defined these basic settings, click on the **Bake** button from the **Navigation** mesh window to generate a new navigation mesh.

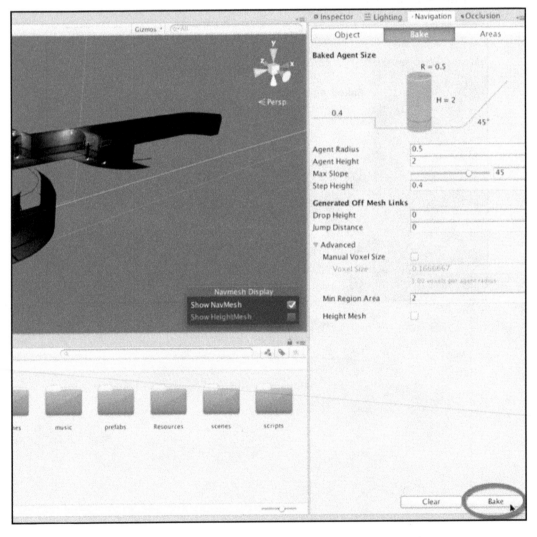

Baking a navigation mesh

Only objects with an active **Mesh Renderer** component, and marked as **Navigation Static**, are included in the navigation mesh bake. All other objects are excluded. To label an object as static, you can enable the **Static** checkbox from the object **Inspector**. You can also click on the static checkbox for a dropdown to be more precise about the applicability of static. This allows you to mark an object as static for navigation, but not for lightmapping, if necessary.

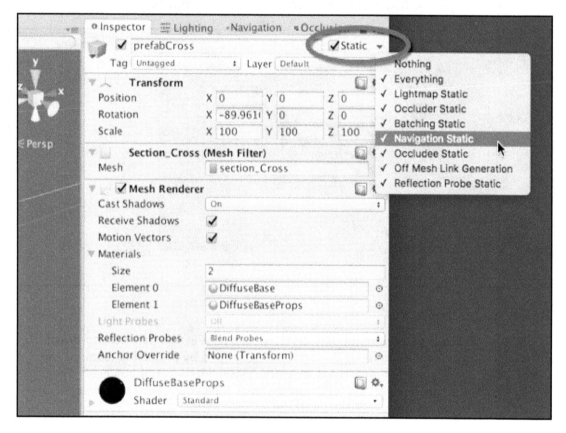

Enabling Navigation Static

After the navigation mesh is generated, it appears inside the **Scene** viewport as a blue mesh-based floor. This appears *only if* the **Navigation** window is open and the **Show NavMesh** checkbox is enabled from the **Navmesh Display** dialog. Remember, the navigation mesh is not visible to the player; it simply represents the walkable area of the scene for intelligent NPCs. A player controlled character is not restricted to the navigation mesh, and nor is an NPC that moves through its transform component.

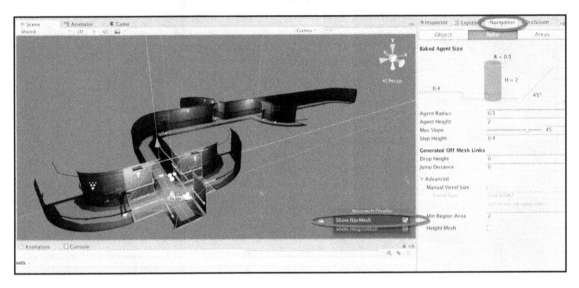

Previewing a navigation mesh

 An important limitation of navigation meshes is that they are top-down based. That is, a navigation mesh is generated by projecting from the top downwards. In most cases, this works well. However, if you need characters to walk on walls and ceilings, then you'll need to develop a custom solution.

For Dead Keys, the floor is divided into only walkable and non-walkable areas, and all walkable areas are the same. This makes things simpler for us. But for some games, this simplicity is not applicable. In real-time strategy games, for example, there are many types of walkable areas, including sand, swamp, grass, rock, concrete, wood, and others. These terrain materials influence how easily a unit may walk on the terrain. In some cases, specific terrain types should be avoided, if preferable, even if it means taking a longer route. Lava is walkable, but dangerous compared to grass, for example. You can encode this preference behavior into a navigation mesh using Areas. By switching to the **Areas** tab, you can define different terrain types, using a custom name, and assign a cost of travel to each type that is used to influence how a path is generated. Higher costs represents less desirable areas.

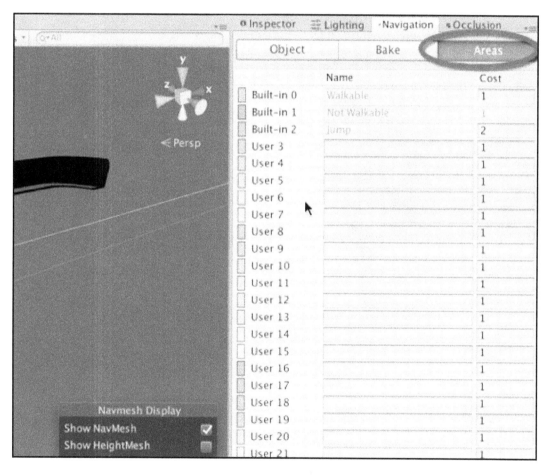

Defining navigation mesh Areas

Having defined terrain types from the **Areas** tab, you can assign specific types to meshes in the scene through the **Object** tab. This tab lets you adjust navigation properties for the selected object in the scene. The **Navigation Area** dropdown is where you assign a type to an object.

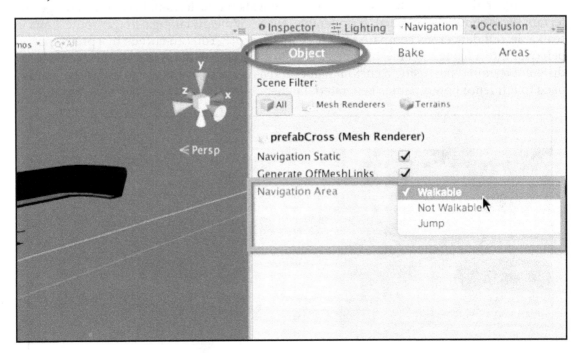

Assign terrain types to objects

Great! We now have a navigation mesh in the scene. This exists as an independent asset of the project too, which can be found in the **Project** panel in the same folder as the saved scene. The navigation mesh does nothing in itself, that is, the existence of a navigation mesh has no tangible effect immediately on any game objects in the scene. Rather, it's an asset whose importance becomes apparent only as we add intelligent NPCs, such as zombies, to the level, which is covered in later chapters.

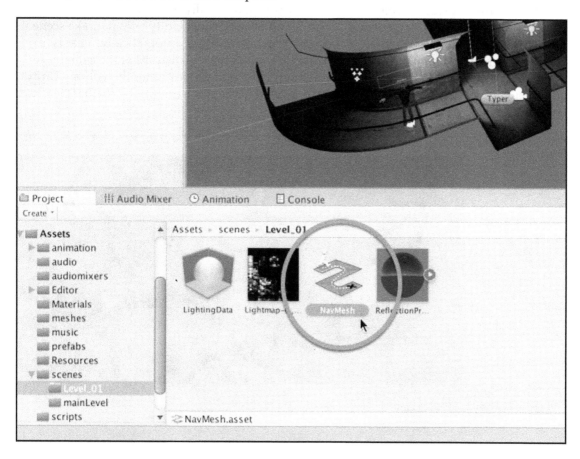

Navmesh objects are saved as an asset

Occlusion Culling

Unity imposes no official limits on the size of your scene, and there's no established convention or industry-standard making recommendations about scene size. This is a decision largely in your hands. But there will certainly be a limit in a practical sense. The complexity of meshes, materials, and special effects combine together with the number of meshes and their spread to determine just how computationally expensive a scene is when presented to a camera with a specific frustum and field of view. Unity tries to make scene rendering easier on the computer by applying **Frustum Culling** automatically. That is, it silently deactivates (culls) objects outside the viewing volume (frustum) of the camera. As objects leave the frustum, Unity ceases to render them, and as they enter the volume Unity starts rendering them. This optimization works well in many cases, for objects that clearly enter and leave the Frustum.

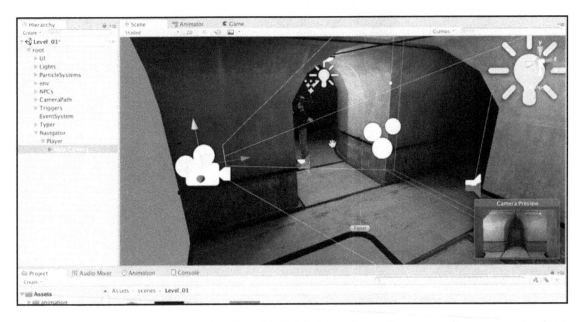

Camera frustum defines the limits of what can be seen

Using Frustum Culling, it becomes possible to create large scenes with many meshes, without worrying about whether the camera will be burdened by unmanageable render workloads. However, despite this, it's important to emphasize that the camera frustum is a volume, which follows the camera, and defines the region inside which all objects could potentially be visible. That is, only objects within the frustum can possibly be seen. But, not all objects in the frustum are necessarily seen.

For example, if a camera moves close to a wall, the objects beyond it may technically come into the frustum, but they will not, in fact, be seen by the camera, because they will be occluded by the wall. Even so, Unity continues to process and render all frustum objects, even though it actually wastes time doing so, because it doesn't check their visibility after entering the frustum. This can be problematic because even objects within the frustum can still hinder render performance, if they're high-poly and detailed. However, in identifying the problem we see a new window of opportunity for optimization, which Unity supports. Specifically, we can use Occlusion Culling. This lets Unity make further culling decisions about whether objects within the Frustum should be rendered, based on their visibility. To get started with Occlusion Culling, create a new empty object by navigating to **GameObject | Create Empty** from the application menu.

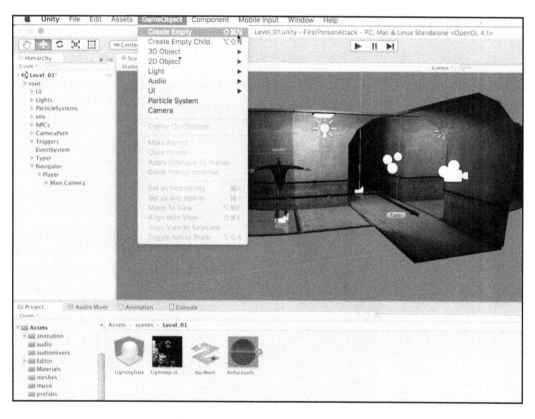

Creating a new empty in preparation for Occlusion Culling

After creating a new, empty object, rename it to `OcclusionArea`, and then position it to the world origin (0,0,0). This step is not essential, but it makes for a cleaner workflow.

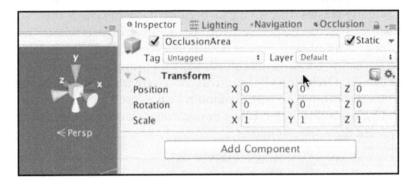

Resetting the Occlusion Area to the world origin

Next, select the empty and navigate to **Component | Rendering | Occlusion Area** from the application menu. This adds an **OcclusionArea** component, which will contain all Occlusion Data for the scene. It defines how objects relate to each other, making it quicker for cameras to determine whether any object in the frustum is visible.

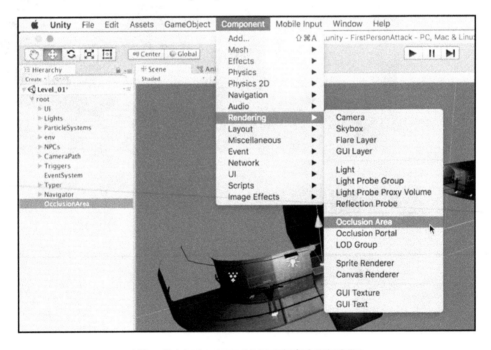

Adding an Occlusion Area component in preparation for Occlusion Culling

By adding an **Occlusion Area** component to the empty, you can use the **Size X, Y,** and **Z** fields to resize a boundary volume around the scene. The idea is to resize the volume to fully encompass either the entire scene or the area in which Occlusion Culling applies if it's not the entire scene. Ideally, the volume should be sized tightly around the scene, leaving little empty space at the fringes. You may also need to adjust the **Center** field to better size the volume. You can resize the volume through typeins, via the object **Inspector,** or you can interactively resize with the mouse from the viewport by clicking on and dragging the gizmo handles.

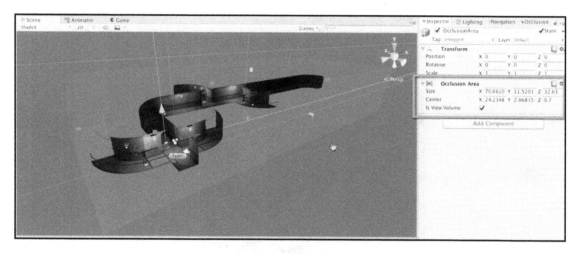

Sizing the Occlusion Culling volume

After creating an `OcclusionArea`, defining an area with densely populated meshes, open the **Occlusion Culling** window by navigating to **Window** | **Occlusion Culling** from the application menu. This displays a free-floating window, which can be docked into the object **Inspector**. This window is used for baking Occlusion Data based on all active Occlusion Areas in the scene.

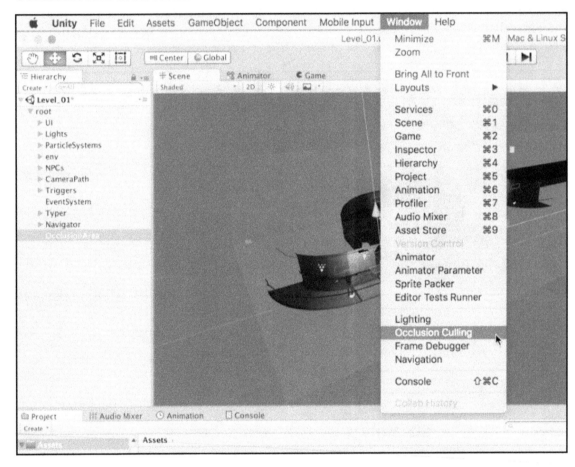

Accessing the Occlusion Culling Bake Features

From the **Occlusion** Culling window, the default settings can often be left as is for scenes using real-world scales. Simply click on the **Bake** button, and Occlusion Data is generated. The bake time varies, depending on the scene and its contents, but it is usually less than a minute. Once completed, the scene is surrounded by gizmo boxes representing spatial divisions that are integral to the culling algorithm.

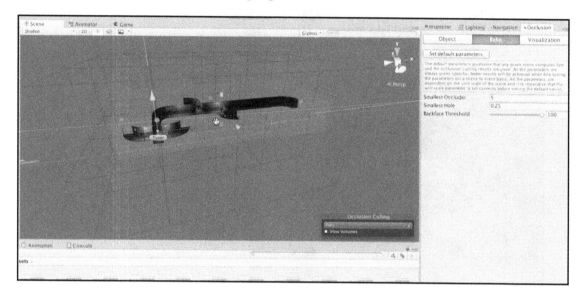

Baking Occlusion Data

You can preview the effects of Occlusion Culling, and its implications for specific cameras, by switching to the **Visualization** tab in the **Occlusion** Culling window, and then selecting a perspective camera in the scene. When you do this, the viewport rendering changes, showing only the meshes visible to the camera given its position, field of view, and frustum. The preview updates in real time as the camera moves. This is helpful for showing how Occlusion Culling works from any camera and perspective, and the extent to which it's optimized for your scene and cameras.

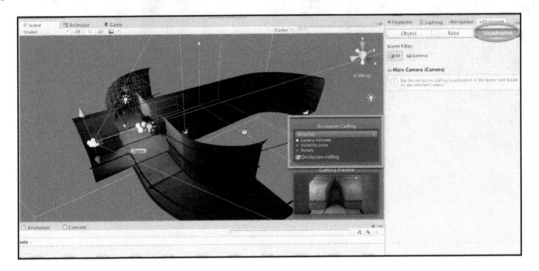

Previewing Occlusion Data

Excellent! Occlusion Culling is now successfully configured for the scene. Next, we just need to add a camera to the scene for the player character.

Creating a player camera

The camera object is, in many ways, the most important in any scene because without the presence of at least one camera, the scene can't be rendered at all. Dead Keys will eventually feature multiple cameras, each with a dedicated purpose. But now, let's focus on the main camera; that is, the player perspective in the scene. For first person games, you could create a camera easily by dragging and dropping a **First Person Controller** from the **Project** panel into the scene, from the **Characters** asset package. However, for Dead Keys, we don't need that; our camera path is fixed as it moves through the level and the user doesn't need free-look controls with the mouse or *WASD* keys. Consequently, we'll create a custom camera from the ground upwards.

Let's start by creating a camera object, by navigating to **GameObject** | **Camera** from the application menu. This adds a fresh, new camera to the scene.

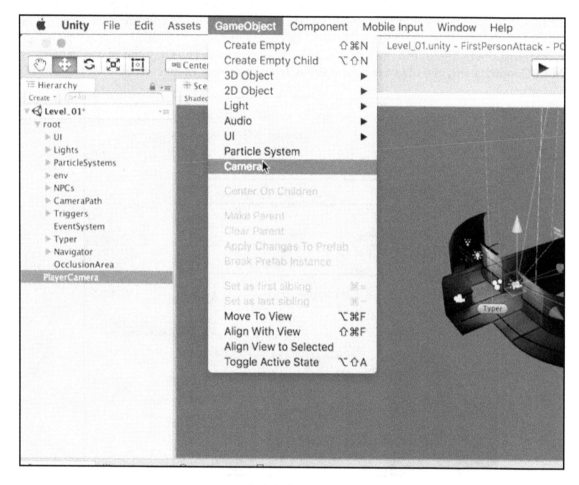

Previewing Occlusion Data

Each object in the scene may be tagged, using either a predefined tag or a custom tag. The purpose of a tag is to help Unity quickly and easily identify specific objects or types of objects quickly, especially in code. Each scene should have one and only one **MainCamera**. That is, one camera object tagged as **MainCamera**. For Dead Keys, and for most games, this should be the main player camera. This will be highly important for our code, as it relies on the **MainCamera** tag to find the one and only player camera. Thus, tag the player camera as **MainCamera**, using the object tag dropdown, from the object **Inspector**.

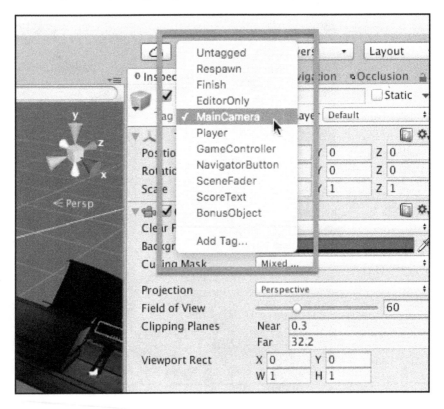

Tagging cameras as the MainCamera

Set the camera **Projection** method to **Perspective**, which renders the scene in *true 3D*, applying foreshortening effects to objects, making them smaller in the distance. In addition, set the **Field of View** to 60, to more closely imitate the human field of vision, and adjust the **Clipping Planes** to 0.3 for **Near**, and 32.2 for **Far**. You may need to use trial and error for adjusting the latter settings. The ideal value for **Near** is the highest value that allows the camera to move closest to a mesh without clipping, and the ideal for **Far** is the lowest value that allows the furthest object to be seen.

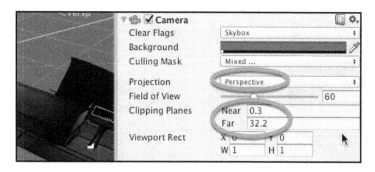

Configuring projection, Field of View and Clipping Planes

Now, ensure **Occlusion Culling** is enabled for the player camera from the **Camera** component. Furthermore, any and all cameras that can display scene meshes should have **Occlusion Culling** enabled.

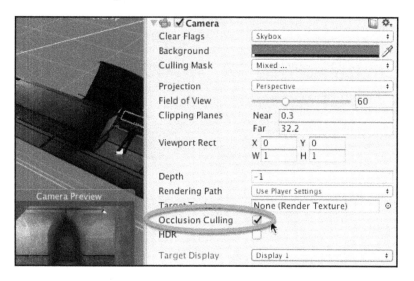

Enabling Occlusion Culling

Finally, let's apply a **Culling Mask** to the camera. This specifies which scene layers (and their associated game objects) should be included or excluded from the camera. For the player camera, exclude the UI layer, to prevent double rendering of the UI. A separate camera will be dedicated to UI rendering, as we'll see later. To exclude the UI from renders, click on the **Culling Mask** dropdown and disable the **UI** layer.

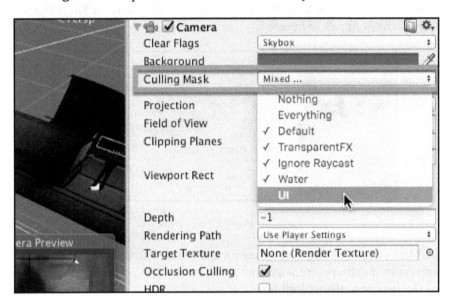

Specifying a camera culling mask

Good work! You've now configured a camera, at least initially, for Dead Keys; a prescripted first-person game. We'll have reason later to tweak some camera settings, but for now, these will work fine.

Particle systems

Particle systems are great for creating effects such as rain, snow, steam, sparkles, hordes of birds, foot prints, armies of ants, and more. Unity ships with preconfigured particle systems ready to use, and it lets you create your own from scratch. Here, we'll use some premade systems that can be added easily to the scene, for drama and tension. To access the premade systems, import the **ParticleSystem** package into the project. Choose **Assets** | **Import Package** | **ParticleSystems** from the application menu, if you've not imported the package already. From the **Import** dialog that appears, accept the default settings and click on the **Import** button.

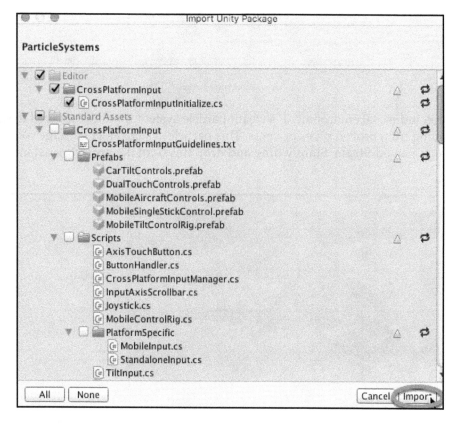

Importing Unity particle systems

Once imported, you can access all premade particle systems via the **Project** panel; through the **Standard Assets** | **ParticleSystems** | **Prefabs** folder.

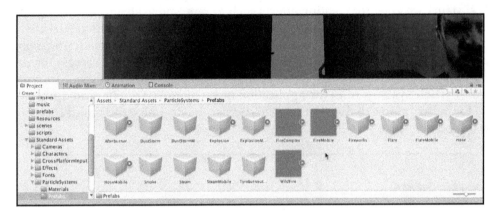

Access ParticleSystem packages

For our eerie, industrial environment, a steam particle system should work well to simulate steam escaping from broken pipes or vents. This particle system asset package contains a steam system, named **Steam**. Simply drag and drop this from the **Project** panel into the scene.

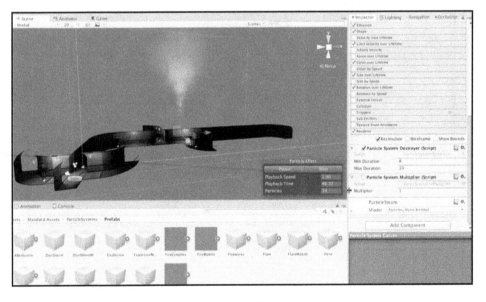

Creating a steam particle system

By default, the steam particle system prefab features a **Particle System Destroyer** component, which deletes the particle system after a specified duration elapses. We don't need this behavior, so let's remove the component. Click on the cog icon on the component and select **Remove Component** from the context menu. Then choose **GameObject | Apply Changes to Prefab** to propagate the change upwards to the original prefab asset.

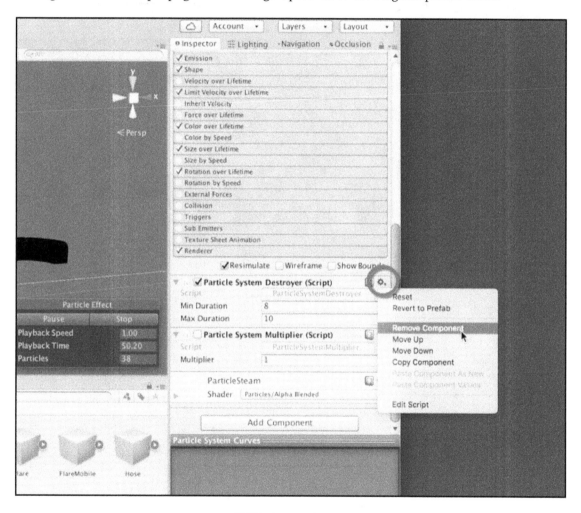

Modifying the steam particle system

Now, position the steam system and duplicates strategically around the level to enhance the mood. Again, appropriate placement of the systems will depend on level layout and where the camera stops. For this reason, placement will likely be an ongoing trial-and-error process.

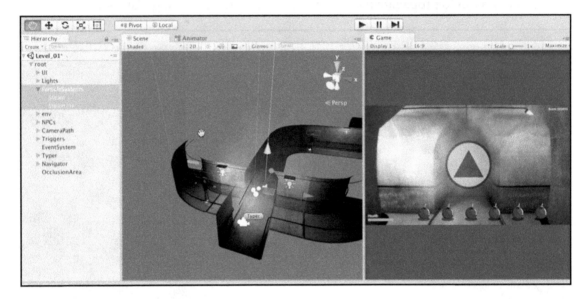

Placing steam particle system

Music and audio

To complete basic level configuration and structure, let's add music. Specifically, the main background music, which should play continuously throughout the level. In the previous chapter, we imported audio assets, both music and sound effects, and configured these optimally. As discussed previously, it is most important that music is configured for **Streaming** as the **Load Type**, and the **Compression Format** should be set to **Vorbis**. This ensures that Unity doesn't load the complete track into memory, which would be performance prohibitive, especially for mobile devices and legacy hardware.

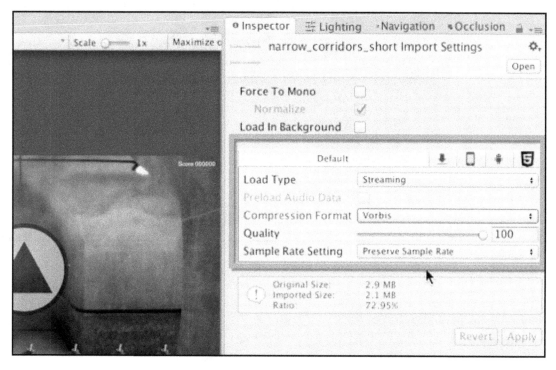

Configuring music audio

In addition to importing music assets, let's create an Audio Mixer asset. This is optional in theory, as Unity can play audio without a mixer. But mixers give you more control over different audio types and their independent volumes and balance (SFX, music, voice, and more). To create an Audio Mixer asset, right-click inside the **Project** panel and navigate to **Create | AudioMixer** from the context menu. As with all assets, this should be contained in an appropriately named folder.

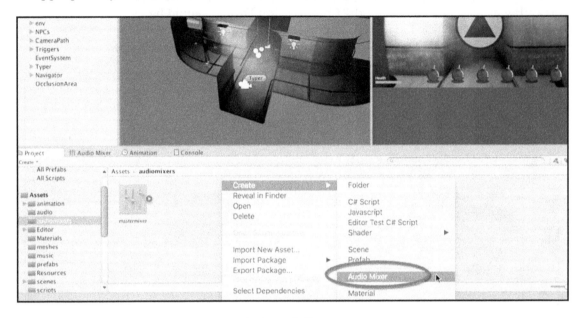

Creating an Audio Mixer asset

By double-clicking on the **Audio Mixer** asset from the **Project** panel, it'll open automatically in the **Audio Mixer** window, which can also be shown by navigating to **Window** | **Audio Mixer** from the application menu. By default, the Audio Mixer is created with a **Master** group, which controls the volume for all audio (hence, the name **Master**). This is displayed in the Audio Mixer as both a visual controller, and a named listed in the **Groups** hierarchy.

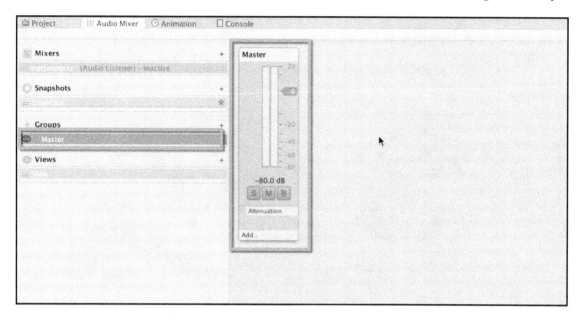

A new Audio Mixer

In addition to the **Master** volume group, we want independent control over the volume for music, sound effects, and voice, as appropriate. This lets us balance volume levels to arrive at a harmonious soundtrack. To achieve this, right-click on the **Master** group from the hierarchy and choose **Add child group**. Repeat this process to create three child groups, and then rename them **Music**, **SFX**, and **Voice**.

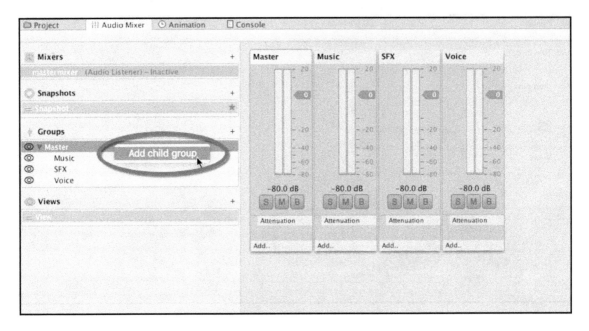

Adding child groups; Music, SFX and Voice

Because the **Music**, **SFX**, and **Voice** groups are children of the **Master** group, their volume is dependent. That is, volume changes in SFX, music, or voice does not change the master volume, but the master volume cascades downwards to child groups. Having now configured the Audio Mixer in this way, we can now route scene audio through a specific group to have high-level control over its volume. Select the root object in the scene (topmost object), and drag and drop the music asset on to it from the **Project** panel. This creates an Audio Source component automatically on the root object, wired to the music track. Alternatively, you can select the root object and navigate to **Component | Audio | Audio Source** from the application menu to add an Audio Source Component. Once added, you should drag and drop the music track from the **Project** panel into the **AudioClip** slot to assign the track to the component.

Assigning a music track to the Audio Source component

The **Audio Source** component features an **Output** field, defining the mixer group to which the audio should be routed. For the music track, this should route to the **Music** child group of the **Master** group. To choose this, simply click on the **Group Selection** button in the object **Inspector**, and then choose the appropriate group.

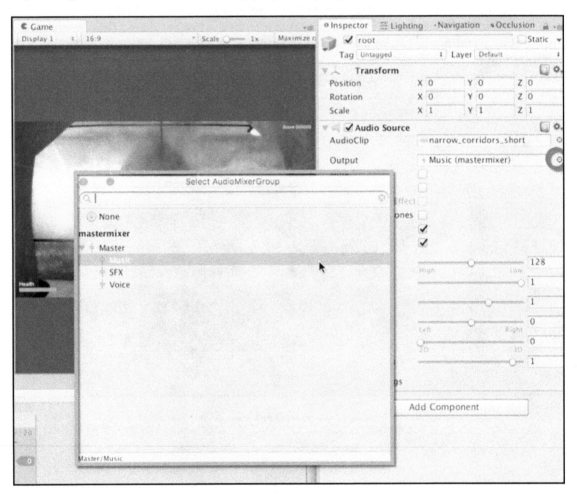

Selecting an Output group

The **Audio Source** component for the music track is almost configured. The music should play as the scene begins and it should play endlessly on a loop. This behavior can be created in code, but we can simply enable the **Play on Awake** and **Loop** checkboxes, from the **Audio Source** component.

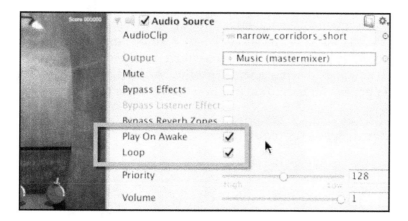

Enabling Play on Awake and Loop

In addition, the music track should be a 2D type of audio; that is, its volume and speaker-pan is unrelated to player position: the music should play at a consistent volume regardless of player movement. To achieve this, ensure the **Spatial Blend** of the **Audio Source** component is set to **2D**.

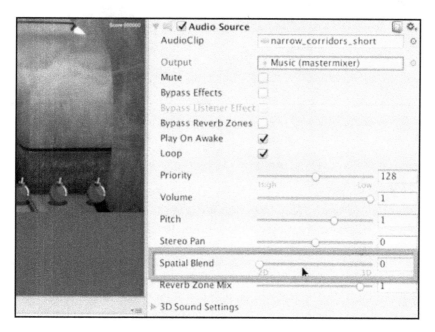

Setting Spatial Blend to 2D

The **Audio Source** component for the music track is now configured. To hear audio, however, the scene should have one and only one **Audio Listener** component. This is typically attached to the player camera, representing the player ears. Select the player camera, and then navigate to **Component | Audio | Audio Listener** to attach a listener to the camera, if not present already. That's it! You can now test out the level, complete with music.

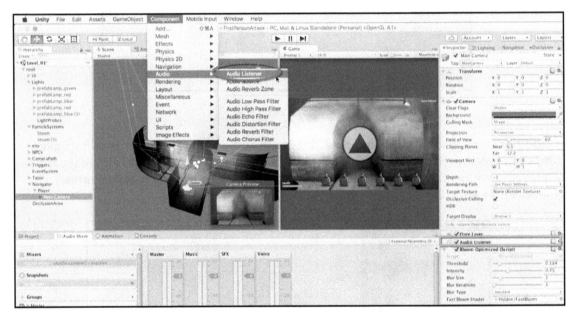

Adding an Audio Listener to the Scene

Summary

Congratulations! You've now created the first level of Dead Keys. Of course, more will be added, but let's first focus on creating one functional level, whose behaviors may be easily recycled to produce more levels, as needed. This chapter focused on many level design issues, both practical and theoretical. Specifically, we explored level design tips and tricks–methods for producing levels more simply and conveniently. In addition, we examined the modular building technique, alongside more advanced tools, such as lightmapping, navigation meshes, and Occlusion Culling. In the next chapter, we'll examine how to take the first person camera and build player functionality, using animation and scripting.

3
Player Controls - Movement

This chapter focuses in depth on building cross-platform player controls. This process involves making animations using the animation editor, developing animation graphs with **Mecanim**, creating user interface elements with Unity UI, and scripting core functionality in C#. Let's start by clarifying how the player controls work for the majority of gameplay. The player has two main input types:

- They have limited control over how the camera moves and when it moves
- They can press alphanumeric keys on the keyboard to spell words during combat with zombies

These two input types are now considered in more depth.

Player movement

Dead Keys is played inthe first-person perspective, meaning that the camera is positioned at the eye point of the player character. However, the player doesn't get free-roaming control as with many first-person games using the *WASD* keys. Here, camera movement through the level is pre-scripted. Specifically, the camera moves from point to point along a carefully defined path when the player progresses by killing zombies. Nevertheless, the player still has some control over character movement, albeit minor. After defeating a wave of zombies by typing words, the game essentially pauses until the player confirms they're ready to move forward by clicking/tapping a forwards icon. This gives the player opportunity to prepare and creates dramatic tension about the possible dangers lurking ahead.

Moving forward at player prompting

Zombie combat

The player primarily engages in combat with zombies. This is the central mechanic and main challenge. Each zombie is associated with a word or short phrase chosen randomly from a dictionary for each zombie at level start-up. The player must speed-type letters on the keyboard during combat to match the word or phrase for the nearest attacking zombie. If the player makes a mistake by entering the wrong letter, then the current word match is reset; that is, the player must retype the complete word or phrase from the beginning. Only a completely correct entry, letter for letter, qualifies as a match, after which the associated zombie is destroyed. This mechanic means we must accept keyboard input from the player, such as a standard keyboard for PC and Mac, and on-screen keyboard input from mobile devices, like iPhones. Traditional keyboard input for typing, however, is only meaningful during combat sections.

Type letters to match words

If you want to follow along step by step, the starting point for this chapter is found in the book companion files, in the folder `Chapter03/Start`.

Creating player waypoints

The remainder of this chapter focuses on creating the first input type; namely, player movement. The second type is explored in the next chapter. In building movement functionality, we'll bring together many Unity features operating harmoniously – including animation, Mecanim, scripting, and others. We'll start by creating empty objects (empties) in the scene, representing important locations for the camera to stop at on its journey from the beginning of the level to the end. These are locations of *attack* and *ambush*; where zombies approach for combat. When a combat sequence is completed (by killing all zombies), the camera is free to move forward at the player's prompting. To create waypoints, create an empty object for each stopping point, then parent all of those to a single object for organization. I have created five stopping points for the first level: *A*, *B*, *C*, *D*, and *E*. These empties are primarily for reference and not for scripting purposes; they help us easily remember where the camera should stop, in terms of *X*, *Y*, and *Z* location (3D coordinates).

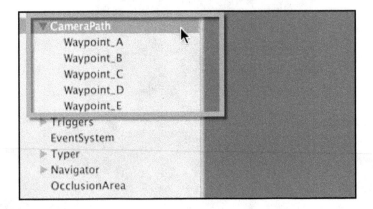

Creating waypoint objects

By default, empties are created without any visual representation in the view port, except for a gizmo axis that appears when selected. You can, however, assign the objects a custom icon or graphic via the object **Inspector** to make them permanently visible and easily selectable. Select each empty by clicking on it in the view port, or from the **Hierarchy** panel, and then, from the object **Inspector**, click the avatar icon.

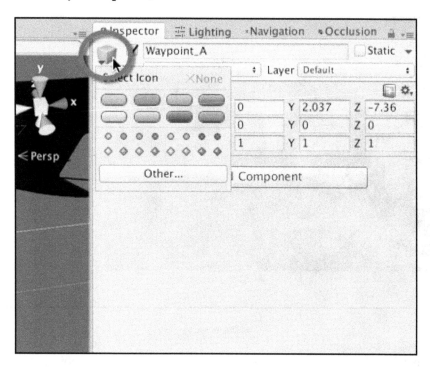

Customizing game object icons

From here, you can select various icons for display. The topmost, horizontal icons (named icons) show the object name in the view port, in addition to a solid background color and the squarer icons beneath display only icons. You can also click the **Other...** button to browse the **Project** panel for a texture to display instead. For *Dead Keys*, I'll simply choose the named icons.

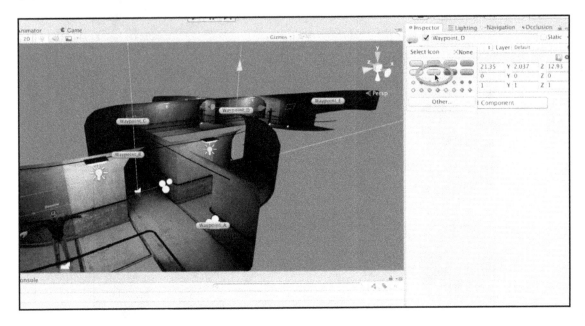

Selecting a named icon

Now we've established waypoint objects for the camera track. These objects are for our reference only when animating the camera through the level. We'll turn to that subject next.

Animating the camera

Dead Keys needs a first-person camera that's effectively on rails. The camera must slowly follow a pre determined path through the scene; its staggered movement from one location to the next is a sign of player progress. So far, a set of specific waypoints have been created (in the previous section), defining locations the camera stops at on its journey to engage with oncoming zombies.

To create this motion for the camera, multiple animations must be created; one for each journey between waypoints (one for A to B, then another for B to C, and then another for D to E, and so on). Before creating the animations, however, it's important to first structure your object hierarchy for the camera, as needed. Changes to your object hierarchy after creating an animation can invalidate how the animation works. I've used several empty objects nested in parent-child relationships, with camera objects as children, to create an organized and structured hierarchy. It takes the form of **Navigator** | **Player** | **Main Camera**. The **Navigator** and **Player** objects are both empties and the **Navigator** is the top-level player object that'll be animated through the level.

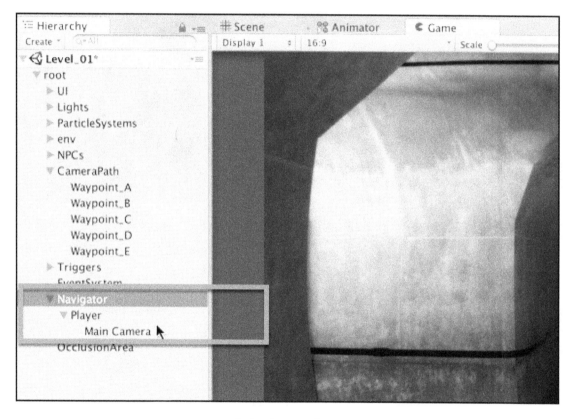

Creating a player camera hierarchy

Now select the top most navigator object and display the **Animation** window (not Animator) by choosing **Window | Animation**. The **Animation** window is a horizontal interface (viewed from left to right) and is best docked at the bottom of the editor.

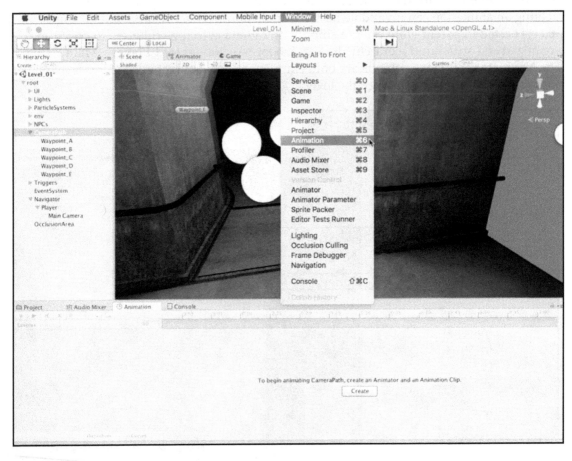

Showing the Animation window

Using the **Animation** window, you can create, and then attach, multiple animations to the selected object. Click the **Create** button from the **Animation** window to make the first animation. Before clicking this, ensure the top-level navigator object is selected from the **Hierarchy** panel. Unity prompts you to name the animation, which will be saved in the project as an animation clip asset. I've used the name anim_Level01_camath_01, as this specifies the asset type (anim), the scene applicability (Level01), and the order it should be played in (camath_01). I recommend saving all animation clips to a dedicated **Animation** folder in the **Project** panel.

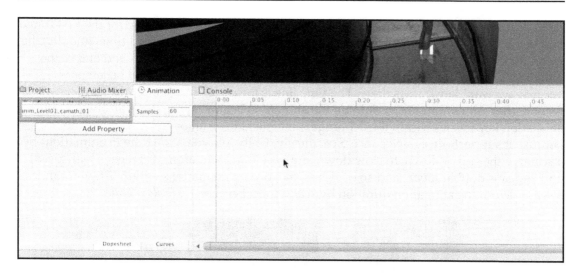

Creating a new animation

Let's focus on the workflow for building our first travel animation, moving from Waypoint A to Waypoint B. To achieve this, use the **Animation** window to create two new entries, listing the properties to be animated. In our case, the **Position** and **Rotation** of the player will be changed. Click the **Add Property** button from the **Animation** window, and then select **Transform | Position** and **Transform | Rotation**.

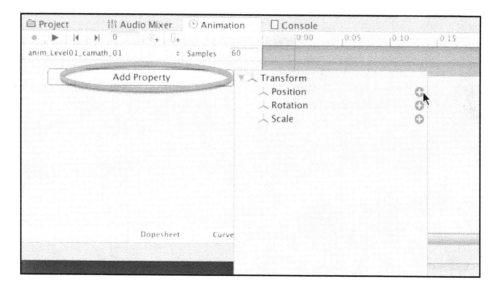

Adding properties for camera position and rotation

After adding both properties, key frames are auto generated for each, one for the first frame and one for the last. Key frames define the state of an object at a specified time. Initially, the generated frames hold the position and rotation for the player at the start and end of the animation. These key frames span the 0-1 range and their position should be left as is because we want key frames there. The time line is measured in seconds, thus 1 means 1 second after animation start, assuming the animation begins at 0. In general, always define animation key frames within the 0-1 range, unless you have an overriding reason not to, because it supports design elegance. Specifically, Unity lets you scale time in animations by a scalar, either up or down, to slow down and speed up animations. 0.5 means half speed, and 2 means double speed, and so on. Thus, by keeping animations within 0-1, you can always determine animation duration by scale alone; because *1 x Scale = Scale*.

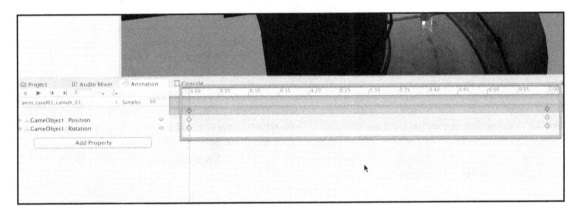

Keep key frames in 0-1 time

 Defining key frames outside 0-1 is acceptable and sometimes justifiable. You'll need times greater than 1 if your animation has lots of key frames, or if events have exact times.

Start by defining the position and rotation of the camera for the first key frame, using the established waypoints. Select **Waypoint_A** in the level and, from its **Transform** component in the object **Inspector**, click the cog icon and choose **Copy Component**. This copies the position, rotation, and scale values to the clipboard.

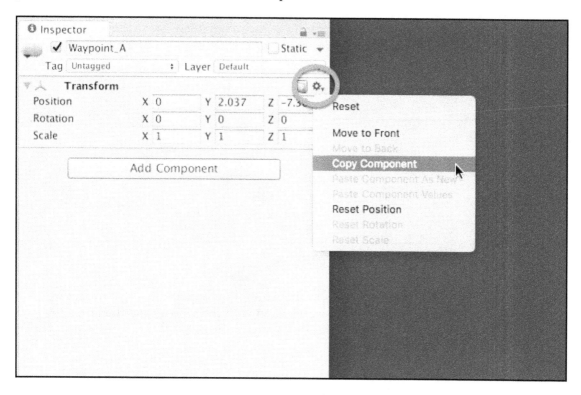

Keep key frames in 0-1 time

Now paste the values to the destination: select the navigator object again and click and drag the time slider in the **Animation** window, moving to the first frame. Finally, select the cog icon in the navigator **Transform** component and choose **Paste Component** Values to paste the copied values to the navigator object. You may want to tweak the **Y** value for the navigator to position it where it should be at that time. On doing this, the position and rotation for the navigator is set at the first frame. Once completed, move the time slider to the last frame and set the navigator to **Waypoint_B**. This defines where the navigator begins and ends for the animation.

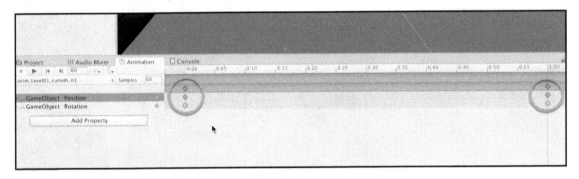

Defining start and end key frames

 Remember, you can auto size the **Animation** window to fit all frames by selecting them all (using box selection with the mouse) and then pressing *F* on the keyboard. This centers all frames into view.

Unity generates all frames between the key frames and these are known as **tweens** (*in-between*). The process by which tweens are generated is known as **interpolation**. Interpolation uses a look-up line graph, with a curve to determine which values (along the horizontal axis) should be used for the position and rotation tweens as the animation plays back (reading from the vertical axis). By default, linear interpolation is used. This means the navigator will travel in a straight line, at a consistent speed, from **Waypoint_A** to **Waypoint_B**, even if that leads it to travel through walls and solids. This is clearly not the behavior we want, because the camera should take an intelligent and believable route through the scene, making turns where needed.

To achieve this, we'll need to insert additional key frames between the start and end keys to fix the position and rotation of the navigator at intermediary moments. This will necessarily change how Unity interpolates the tweens. Hence, move the time slider across the timeline in the **Animation** window, previewing the camera route in the **Scene** and **Game** view port. Then, move the time slider to frames where the camera begins deviating from its intended course, repairing that course by repositioning and rotating the camera as appropriate. This auto generates key-frames for the camera at the selected times. Repeat this process until the route from **Waypoint_A** to **Waypoint_B** is correct over the complete time line.

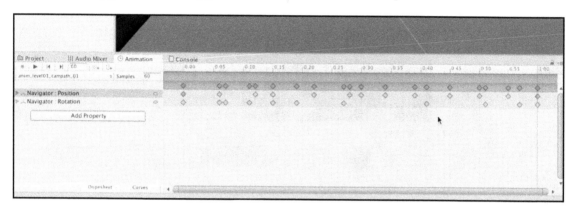

Creating camera path key-frames

 You can copy and paste key frames with *Ctrl* + *C* and *Ctrl* + *V* respectively. And you can drag key frames over the time line to reposition them.

Preview the animation carefully by scrubbing the time slider back and forth in the timeline, ensuring the camera route is appropriate. In addition to creating the route as we've done, you'll probably want to change the interpolation curves for the start and end key frames, creating an *ease-in* and *ease-out* effect. Right now, the camera jumps into motion at in the first frame and comes to a sudden and complete stop at the end. While this is acceptable, it doesn't *feel* smooth. Instead, we can use *ease-in* to slowly bring the camera into motion at in the first frame, and *ease-out* to gradually bring the camera to a stop at the end. To achieve this, start by opening the **Curves** editor from the **Animation** window; just click the **Curves** button.

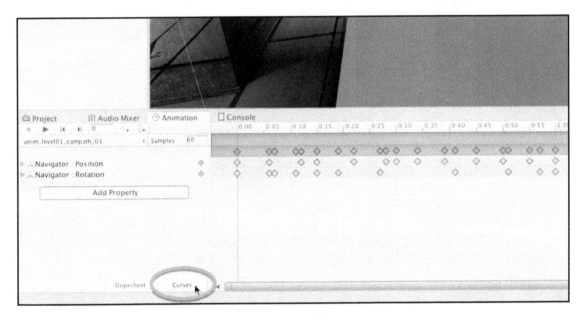

Displaying the animation curve editor

The curve editor may initially display a mess of curves, or an otherwise indecipherable graph. This may be because the view is not appropriately zoomed in or out. You can click and drag a box selection around all points and curves, then press the *F* key on the keyboard to frame all curves into the **Animation** window.

 Remember, you can press *Shift* + Space bar on the keyboard to maximize the **Animation** window, making its contents full screen.

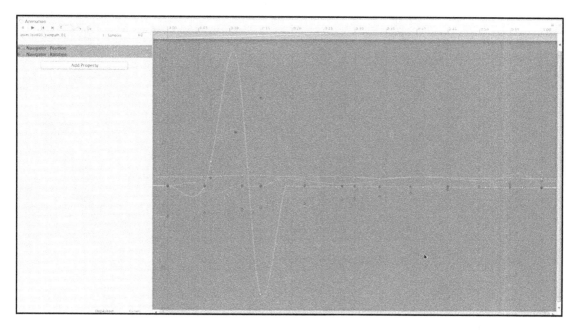

Maximizing the curve editor

Select the **Position** field from the property list to filter the graph, viewing only the **X**, **Y** and **Z** position curves. Notice the straight lines that run from the first frame and terminate at the final frame, with no curve or damping to soften the motion. This represents sudden changes, from motionlessness to motion and from motion to motionlessness.

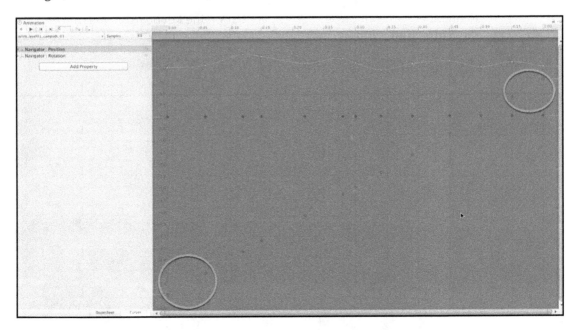

Identifying sudden and inappropriate changes in motion

Right-click the first and last keys for the **X**, **Y**, and **Z** fields. From the context menu, choose the **Flat** option to flatten the bezier handle for the key frame. This creates a soft transition in the curve, creating an *ease-in* and *ease-out* at the animation start and end respectively. The result is smoother, more believable camera motion.

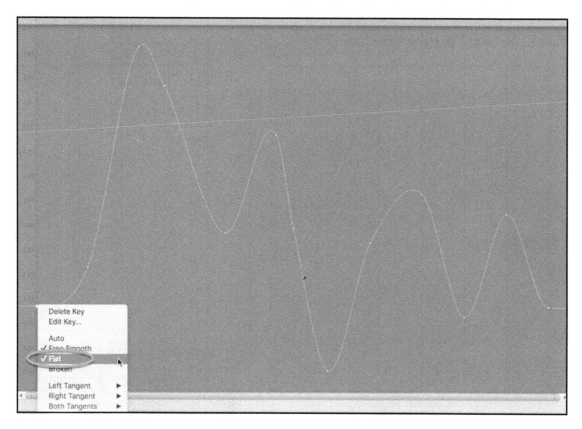

Creating ease-in and ease-out for camera movement

Now your first animation is complete, moving from **Waypoint_A** to **Waypoint_B**! You can test this from the **Scene** view port, even in **Game** mode. By default, Unity creates and applies an animator asset and component to the navigator object, which plays the created animation at level start up (we'll change that behavior later). You'll probably want to disable animation looping, as well as reducing the playback speed. The speed can be adjusted later. To disable looping, select the animation clip asset in the **Project** panel and disable the **Loop Time** check box.

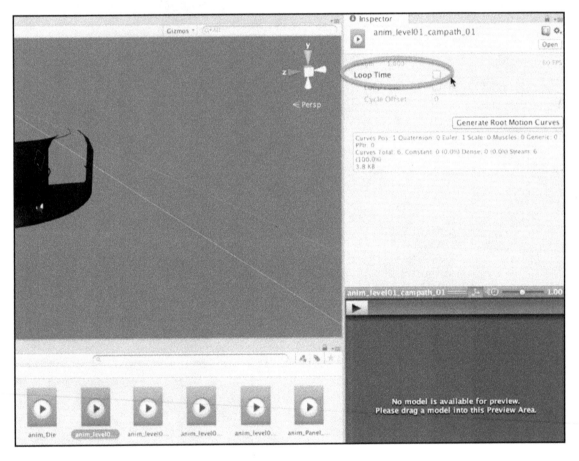

Creating play-once animation clips

Having created one travel animation, let's create the remaining ones. More animations can be easily added to the selected object via the **Animation** window by clicking the **Animation** name drop-down menu. This reveals a drop-down menu, including the option to **Create New Clip...**. Select this option and Unity prompts you again to name and save the clip as an asset of the project.

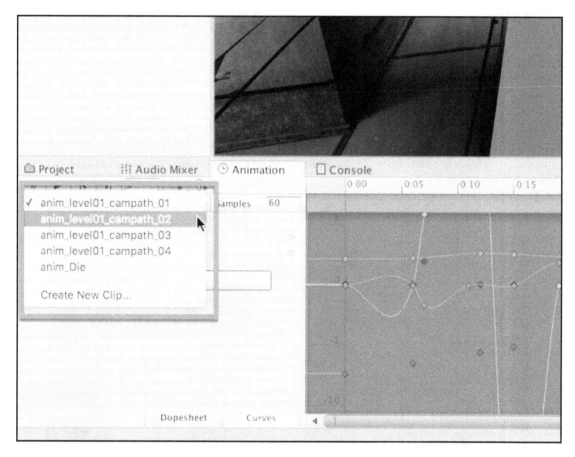

Adding animation clips

Great work! You've now created all camera animations. The next step consists of configuring a Mecanim graph to play them at appropriate times.

Configuring an animator graph

The animation clip defines an animation, in terms of key frames, graphs, and states. This includes all camera animations created so far. Specifically, an animation clip defines the content of an animation. However, the animation clip doesn't define when it should play during gameplay. To control playback, an **Animator** component and animator controller is needed for the navigator object. Unity creates these assets automatically when you create your first animation clip. Additionally, Unity configures the assets and attaches them to the selected object so that it always plays the first animation when the level begins. However, this is not the behavior we actually want. We could easily tweak the generated assets to behave differently, to play when instructed, for example. But, let's start this process from scratch, deleting all the auto generated assets (the **Animator** component and animator controller). This is not essential, but doing this demonstrates how an animator is configured manually. To remove all auto generated assets for animation, select the navigator object and remove the **Animator** component from the object **Inspector**. Click the cog icon and choose **Remove Component**.

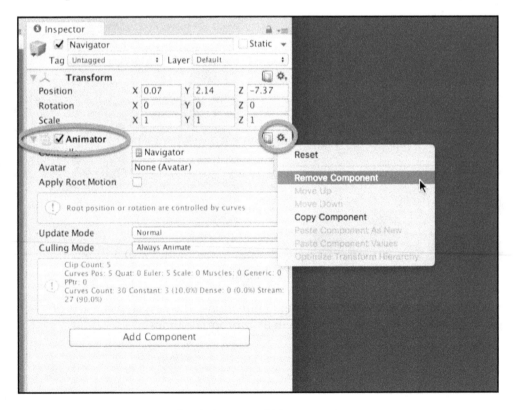

Removing the auto-generated Animator component

Next, find the generated animator controller asset in the **Project** panel and delete it. This removes all auto generated assets for animation, allowing us to begin again from a clean slate.

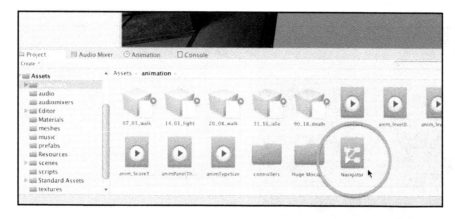

Removing animator controllers

To start again, create a new animator controller named `animControl_Navigator`, by right-clicking the **Project** panel and choosing **Create** | **Animator Controller** from the context menu.

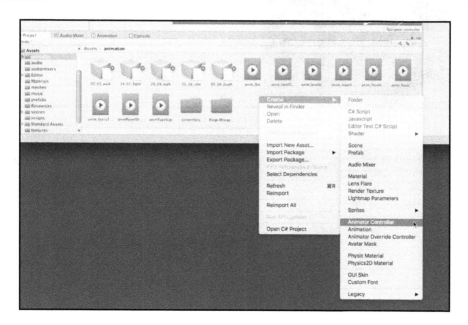

Creating an Animator Controller

You now need to add an **Animator** component to the camera (or rather, to the **Navigator**, which is a top-level object), and then drag and drop the newly created Animator Controller asset into the **Controller** field of the **Animator** component. This assigns an **Animator Controller** to the **Animator** component.

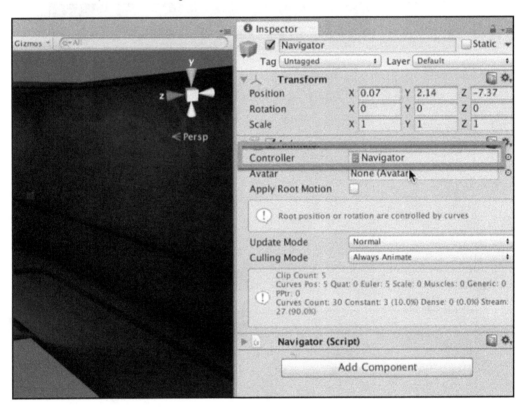

Assigning an Animator Controller

Ensure **Apply Root Motion** is not enabled and that **Update Mode** is **Normal** and **Culling Mode** is **Always Animate**. The **Culling Mode** field, when set to **Cull Completely**, effectively links animation playback to the visibility of the object's mesh renderer. This can enhance performance, as animations only play when the mesh is actually visible. But this, of course, doesn't apply to the camera object, which has no mesh renderer component. To configure the animator controller for animation playback, double-click it inside the **Project** panel. This opens the controller by default in the animator window. This offers visual scripting control over high-level animation playback. By default, the node graph features two auto-created nodes; specifically, **AnyState** and **Entry**.

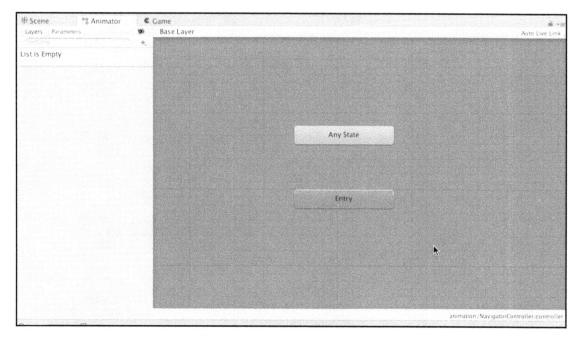

Accessing the animator graph

The **Entry** node is fired once; for the first time the animator component becomes enabled on an active object. Unless an object is deactivated in the editor, through script, or the animator component is disabled, then the **Entry** node will fire normally on level start up. The **Entry** node is therefore useful for connecting to any other nodes, or states, that must execute as the level begins. For the camera object, however, we don't need an animation played; but we do need the camera to simply remain as it is until further notice. To achieve this, we'll create an empty node, which simply leaves the camera unchanged and remains this way in a loop (idle state). That is, it holds graph execution at that node and it remains there until a condition causes the state to change. Right-click inside the graph and choose **Create State | Empty** from the context menu. This adds a new, empty node to the graph.

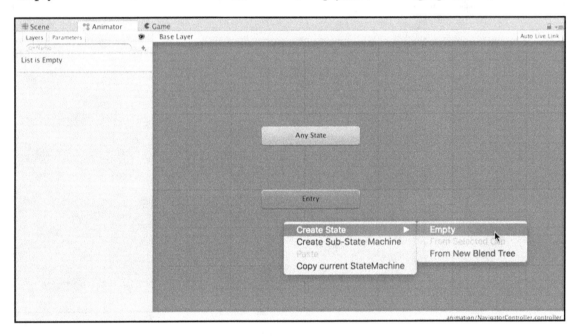

Creating a new animator state for the camera

By default, the first added node becomes the default node and is highlighted in orange. The default node is always connected to the **Entry** node. Select the newly created node by clicking on it and rename it `Idle`. The **Motion** field should specify **None (Motion)**. This represents the animation clip that should play when the node is activated. When this field is set to **None (Motion)**, no animation clips play and the camera object will be left as is; that is, unchanged from its starting state. Remove the check mark from the **Write Defaults** check box too (which resets the object's state back to its default settings when the animation clip completes playback).

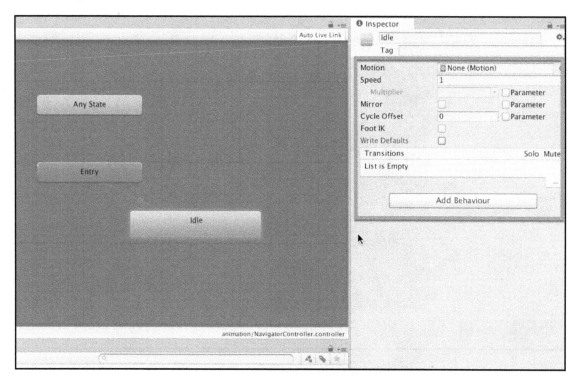

Setting properties for the Idle state

The **Idle** node represents the camera when it's neither animated nor moving through a path in the scene. It should always be active whenever the camera is motionless. This will usually be because the player is fighting zombies by matching words. Thus, the **Idle** node is the first and neutral state in a **Finite State Machine** (**FSM**). More on FSMs later in this chapter, and later in this book. This means that all other nodes will, in some way, be connected to the **Idle** node, as the camera changes from being in motion to being motionless. To start building the graph, drag and drop all camera animation clips from the **Project** panel into the animator graph, where they will be added automatically as new nodes.

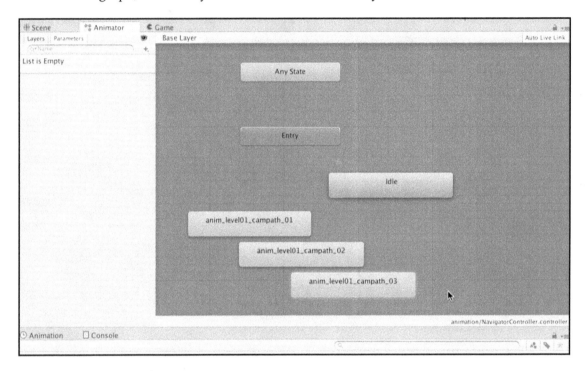

Adding animation nodes to the animator graph

Once added, rename each clip appropriately and connect them in a sequence (or chain) to the *Idle* state. Because the movement of the camera in *Dead Keys* is linear (moving from point to point), the graph nodes can be connected one after another in an unbroken sequence. Specifically, the camera stops, the player attacks, and then the camera moves to the next destination, and so on. Although the potential exists for branching paths, the first level has only one possible route that may be taken. To create connections between nodes, simply right-click from the first node and choose **Make Transition** from the context menu. Then, select the destination node to establish the connection.

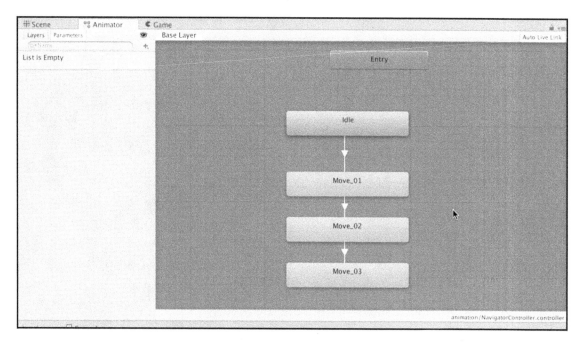

Mapping the camera path as a linear sequence of nodes

The linear sequence is made between the nodes, but the transitions themselves need configuring. A transition determines when one state should change to another. By default, all transitions are unconditional, they simply allow the first state to move to the second when playback is completed. Let's now configure some conditions for each transition. Start by creating an Int parameter, called `NavState`. The values of this variable will reflect the states of the camera (0 = starting state, 1 = travel to next location, 2 = travel to next location, and so on). To create the parameter, click the + icon from the **Parameters** list, and choose **Int**.

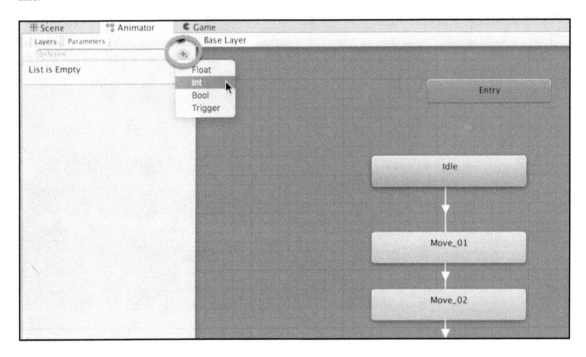

Creating an Int parameter in the animator graph

The **Int** parameter should have the default value of 0. If not, it can be specified in the **Parameters** list. Now select each transition in turn (the arrow connecting the nodes), and set the condition from the object **Inspector** using the equals operation. Specifically, to transition from **Idle** to **Move_01**, the `NavState` parameter should be equal to 1. A value of 2 transitions between **Move_01** and **Move_02**, and so on. By using an **Int** parameter in this way, we have the ability to transition between any number of nodes.

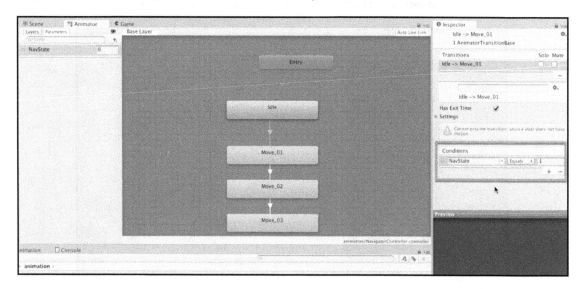

Specifying transition conditions

Each transition features a **Has Exit Time** Boolean field. When enabled, as it is by default, the full length of the animation always plays when the node is activated, and the state can only change after the animation completes. Or, more accurately, the settings roll-out specifies an exit time field, defining animation duration in normalized time (between 0-1). When **Has Exit Time** is enabled, the state can only exit or change after the specified exit time elapses. In our case, **Has Exit Time** should be disabled, as there are some conditions (such as *death*) which can potentially interrupt an animation at any time and must be allowed to do so.

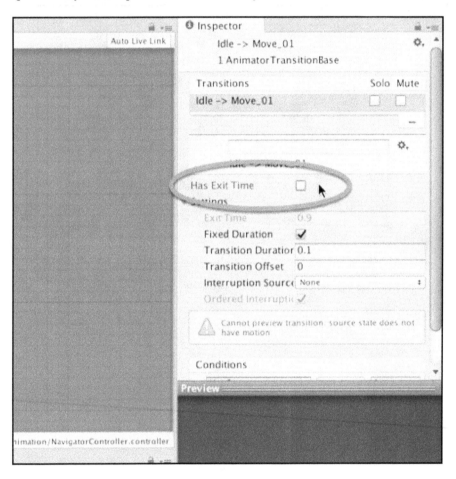

Disabling exit time

Finally, you'll probably want to tweak the **Speed** value for each node. This determines how fast or slow the animation plays back. This value is expressed, again, in normalized time. Thus, a value of 1 means default (since *time x 1 = time*), 2 means double speed (since *time x 2 = 2 time*), and 0.5 means half speed (since *time x 0.5 = time/2*), and so on. For my animations, I've specified a value of *0.15*. I arrived at this value by trial and error; that is, by repeatedly playing back the animation at different speeds to observe the result.

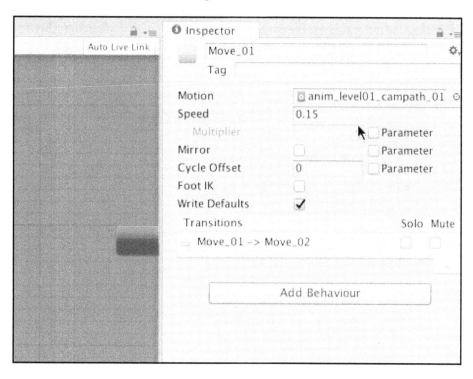

Configuring animation speed by trial and error

Excellent! The animator graph is now fully configured for camera navigation. The nodes should be set up in a linear sequence, allowing the camera to move forward on its path as the `NavState` Int parameter is updated. Right now, nothing actually changes this parameter; this explains why the camera won't move or change as the level begins. We'll need to access the `NavState` and its value from script to gain control over camera movement.

Working with animation – creating the navigator

The animator is now created for the camera object, and the camera object itself is configured in a hierarchy that'll make our work organized and clean going forward. The object structure is Navigator > Player > Main Camera, as shown earlier in the screenshot in the section *Animating the camera*. Now it's time for us to define the core functionality for the main camera by scripting. Specifically, we'll create a new class, called `Navigator`. This will be responsible for moving the camera across its network of paths. To create a new script, right-click in the **Project** panel and choose **Create | C# Script**. Name this `Navigator`. Then, double-click the file, open it inside **MonoDevelop** or another associated code editor, such as Visual Studio or Microsoft Code. The auto-generated class template will appear as follows:

```
using UnityEngine;
using System.Collections;

public class Navigator : MonoBehaviour
{
    // Use this for initialization
    void Start () {
    }
    // Update is called once per frame
    void Update () {
    }
}
```

Customizing and changing MonoDevelop

Going forwards, I'll assume you're using MonoDevelop for coding and editing text files from within Unity. MonoDevelop is a third-party, cross-platform application for editing text files and compiling code in many languages. Unity is configured by default to work with MonoDevelop as the standard editor. This means that MonoDevelop will open automatically when you double-click a valid script file from the **Project** panel. However, if you want to change the default editor, you can do this by choosing **Edit** | **Preferences** from the application menu, then choosing the **External Tools** tab.

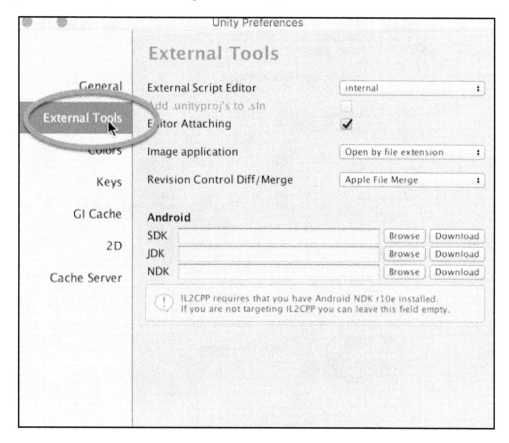

Accessing the Unity Preferences dialog to change the default code editor

From the **External Tools** tab, click the **External Script Editor** field and select your preferred code editor. MonoDevelop is an available option and you can browse your computer for other applications, like Visual Studio or Microsoft Code.

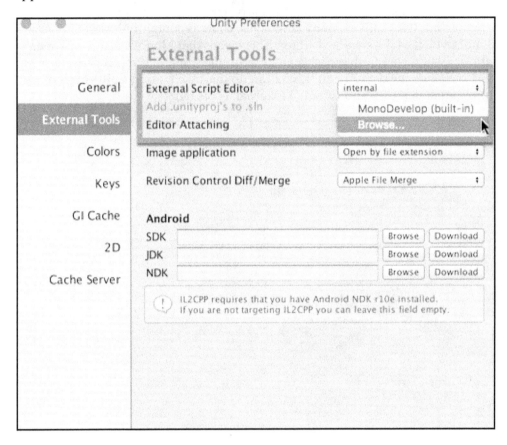

Customizing the Unity code editor

On launching MonoDevelop for the first time, your code editor will probably appear as shown in this screenshot, the very light color scheme can be hard on the eyes:

MonoDevelop default color scheme

Some people find a darker color scheme easier to view for long periods. You can easily change this, first by choosing **Edit** | **Preferences** from the MonoDevelop application menu. This displays the user **Preferences** window.

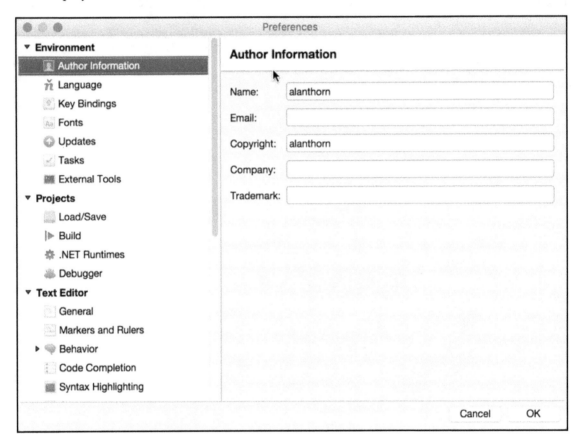

User Preferences window

From here, choose **Syntax Highlighting** and select the **Oblivion** color scheme.

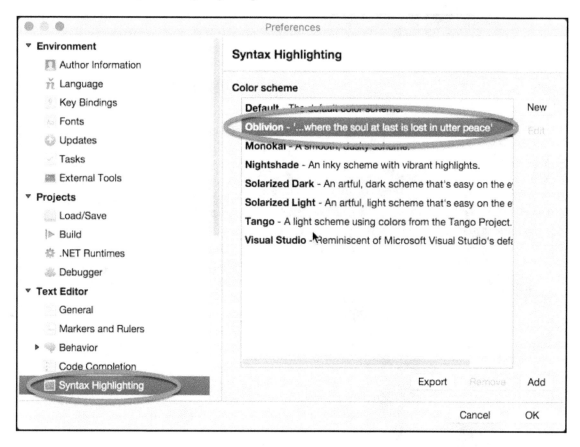

Choosing Oblivion

This Oblivion scheme darkens the editor background, making the code easier to read.

```
     MonoDevelop-Unity   File   Edit   View   Search   Project   Build   Run   Version Control   Tools   Window   Help

           ▶       ☐ Debug ▸ ▮ Unity Editor

     ◂  ▸    Navigator  ×   GameMan:  ×   KeyPressE  ×   UIScore.cs  ×   UIFader.cs  ×   UIHealth.c  ×   Typer.cs  ×   UIBonus.c  ×   AIEnemy.c  ×   NewBehav  ◇   ▾

     Navigator  ▸    ThisInstance
    1  //
    2  using UnityEngine;
    3  using System.Collections;
    4  using UnityEngine.UI;
    5  using UnityEngine.EventSystems;
    6  using UnityEngine.Events;
    7  //
    8  public class Navigator : MonoBehaviour
    9  {
   10      //
   11      public int CurrentNode = 0;
   12      private Animator ThisAnimator = null;
   13      private int AnimStateHash = Animator.StringToHash("NavState");
   14
   15      //Reference to NPC die event
   16      public UnityEvent EnemyDie;
   17
   18      //Reference to navigator button
   19      private Button NavigatorButton = null;
   20
   21      //Reference to singleton instance
   22      public static Navigator ThisInstance
   23      {
   24          get
   25          {
   26              //Get or create singleton instance
   27              if (mThisInstance == null)
   28              {
   29                  GameObject GO = new GameObject ("Navigator");
   30                  mThisInstance = GO.AddComponent<Navigator> ();
   31              }
   32
   33              return mThisInstance;
   34          }
   35
   36          set
   37          {
   38              //If not null then we already have instance
   39              if (mThisInstance != null)
   40              {
   41                  //If different, then remove duplicate immediately
   42                  if(mThisInstance.GetInstanceID() != value.GetInstanceID())
   43                      DestroyImmediate (value.gameObject);

                                                                                    ⚠ Errors      Tasks
```

The Oblivion color scheme in action!

Splendid. You've now customized MonoDevelop in preparation for coding, which we will use in many ways over the coming chapters, including this chapter.

Singletons

The Navigator class is associated with the player and represents player controls. There can be one, and only one, player in the scene at any one time. For this reason, the Navigator class should be coded as a Singleton object. A Singleton object is a class that is specifically designed so that it cannot be instantiated more than once. Note, the Singleton design is not a convention by which we agree, with ourselves and other developers, not to instantiate the class more than once. Rather, the Singleton class is so designed as to make multiple instantiations impossible. Let's start implementing Singleton behavior. The class is re-coded as follows and comments follow:

```
using UnityEngine;
using System.Collections;

public class Navigator : MonoBehaviour
{
    //Reference to singleton instance
    public static Navigator ThisInstance
    {
        get
        {
            //Get or create singleton instance
            if (mThisInstance == null)
            {
                GameObject GO = new GameObject ("Navigator");
                mThisInstance = GO.AddComponent<Navigator> ();
            }

            return mThisInstance;
        }

        set
        {
            //If not null then we already have instance
            if (mThisInstance != null)
            {
            //If different, then remove duplicate immediately
        (mThisInstance.GetInstanceID() != value.GetInstanceID())
                    DestroyImmediate (value.gameObject);

                return;
            }

            //If new, then create new singleton instance
            mThisInstance = value;
        }
```

```
    }

    private static Navigator mThisInstance = null;

    void Awake()
    {
        ThisInstance = this;
    }

}
```

 Remember, static variables are very different from non-static. Variables prefixed with static belong to the class itself and not to a specific instance of the class. Thus, they are shared across all instances of that class. If the value of a static variable changes, then it changes for all instances. More information on statics and Unity can be found online here: `https://unity 3d.com/learn/tutorials/topics/scripting/statics`.

Comments

- The navigator Singleton features two new variables: the private static variable `mThisInstance`; and the public static property `ThisInstance`.
- The `mThisInstance` variable should always maintain a reference to the one and only currently activated instance of the navigator. All other instances are to be regarded as invalid and should be removed.
- The only way to access and read the `mThisInstance` variable is through the `ThisInstance` property. The `set` method controls which values are written to `mThisInstance` and the `get` method controls which values are returned.
- The `Awake` event, which is called when an instance is created, uses the *set* method for the `ThisInstance` property. This property validates the passed value (the current instance) and determines whether an instance has been created before by checking the `mThisInstance` variable. Since the `mThisInstance` variable is static, its value will hold across all instances. Hence, we can always know if `mThisInstance` has been previously assigned.
- If an instance has already been assigned to `mThisInstance`, then any differing instances must be later instances and may be removed. Here, all addition instances are destroyed with `DestroyImmediate`.

- The function `GetInstanceID` determines whether two object references refer to one and the same object. This makes sense as each object in the scene is guaranteed a unique instance ID. This is needed to prevent the Singleton from deleting itself; that is, the one and only instance.

Great work! We've now applied the **Singleton Design Pattern** to the navigator object and this class should be dragged and dropped to the top-level navigator object in the scene. The `Navigator` class will then be instantiated on the navigator object as a component.

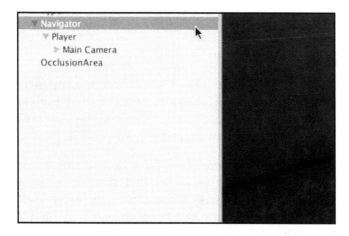

Assigning the Navigator script to the navigator object

Connecting to the navigator component

The navigator must connect with the animator component to change the Int parameter `NavState`. Specifically, our code needs to identify when the camera should move and then make that happen via the animator. Additionally, the navigator should also identify when the camera finishes travelling to its next waypoint. We know the camera is ready to move when all currently attacking zombies are defeated; the next wave of zombies begins again only after the camera has arrived at its next destination. Based on these requirements, there are some limitations to what we can achieve here presently, because we still have lots of dependent functionality to define, like the zombies and attacking behaviors. Consequently, we'll return to the navigator in later chapters to implement the final functionality. However, we know enough here to get started on the navigator and to block in basic functionality. This is absolutely fine; jumping back and forth between connecting and dependent classes, refining their functionality. To get started, we'll retrieve a reference to the navigator component inside the `Awake` function.

Remember, the `Awake` function on an object is always called before start. `Awake` is useful for retrieving object references, such as a reference to the navigator, on which later functions (including start) may depend.

```
void Awake()
    {
        ThisInstance = this;
        ThisAnimator = GetComponent<Animator> ();
    }
```

Comments

It's always a good idea to retrieve a reference to the animator component inside `Awake`, and then store its value in a private class variable, which can be used anywhere throughout the class. An alternative is to call the `GetComponent` function wherever you need a reference, but this is comparatively expensive computationally, so avoid it.

The animator component offers us a method for directly accessing Int parameter; namely `SetInt`. This function accepts two arguments: the first identifies which Int parameter must be set (we could have multiple parameters); the second is the value itself, which should be assigned to the parameter. Now, there are two versions of this method, and each differs by how the Int parameter is named. We can name the parameter literally by string (specifying the name of the parameter as it appears in the **Animator** window; for example, `NavState`), or by an integer ID. The latter method is preferred, as it doesn't rely on any string processing, which can be computationally expensive. To achieve this, we'll need to generate a hash from the parameter name. Specifically, Unity can generate a hash from a string; a unique number from a string. This is valuable because the generated number is guaranteed to be unique for the specified string, and no other string produces the same number. To achieve this, we can declare a new integer variable for the class as follows:

```
private int AnimStateHash = Animator.StringToHash("NavState");
```

Comments:

- The `AnimStateHash` variable is an integer that stores a numerical representation of the `NavState` string
- This variable should be used as an argument to the `Animator.SetInt` function, to specify the named parameter to change

Thus, we can now access the `NavState` parameter anywhere in code, as follows:

```
ThisAnimator.SetInteger (AnimStateHash, MyVal);
```

So, we now know how to access the Int parameter in the graph, but when should we do this? For testing purposes, we could implement a call to `SetInteger` in the `Update` function when a key is pressed. This, at least, means we can easily test the functionality by pressing keys on the keyboard to move the camera on its path. But, in its final implementation, the player must kill all zombies and, when killed, a prompting arrow should appear on screen, which the player can click to move the camera forward. The details of zombie attacks and typing are covered in later chapters. But, for now, we'll focus on the UI which appears when zombies are killed. To implement this behavior, we'll need to work with the Unity UI.

Navigator GUI

Let's now start work on the UI for *Dead Keys*, which covers a broad range of important subjects. As mentioned, the main interesting area of the UI here is the forward pointing UI arrow (navigator button), which should appear after all zombies are killed and allows the player to continue on their journey through the environment, moving to the next ambush point. As we create this, we'll explore many interesting UI tips and tricks.

Navigator button

First, let's create a new empty object to contain all UI elements, including the navigator button to be added in this section, and the remaining elements for later. In addition, add this object to the UI layer in the scene using the object **Inspector**. In general, strive to keep all UI elements on the UI layer, or another dedicated layer that's separate from the non-UI objects. Doing this gives the power and flexibility to easily show and hide UI elements, as well as delegate their rendering to specific cameras.

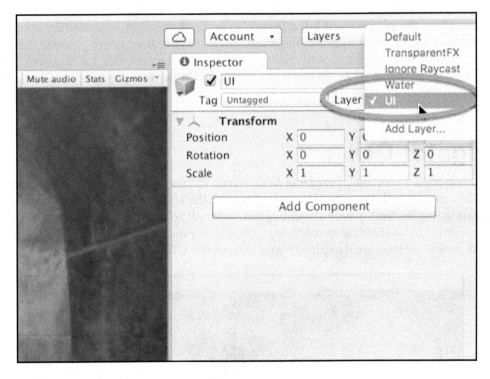

Assigning an object to the UI layer

Next, create an UI canvas object. The canvas is a special UI object which acts as a surface or layer onto which UI elements may be rendered to cameras. As you create the canvas in the scene, assuming this is your first UI object, Unity automatically creates an **EventSystem** in the hierarchy. This object is essential for linking the UI to input, allowing UI objects to detect keyboard, click and tap input events. If your scene doesn't have an **EventSystem**, you can always create one manually, by choosing **GameObject | UI | Event System** from the application menu.

Assigning an object to the UI layer

The **EventSystem** features two notable components: an **Event System** component, and an input module. The **EventSystem** is the nerve center for events and its main duty is to match up abstracted player input (from the input module) to specific objects and events in the scene, like button clicks on UI buttons. The input module is responsible for mapping hardware specific input into a generalized abstracted input that the **EventSystem** uses for firing events. There are several kinds of input module components and each varies to accommodate specific hardware types. These are **Standalone Input Module** (for handling keyboard and mouse input from desktop systems), and touch input modules, for mobile devices like phones and tablets.

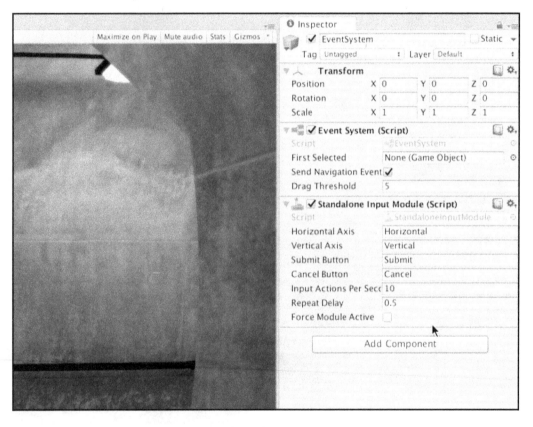

EventSystems with input modules

Input axes

The input module features several named Axes. An input axis is a named, linear space that maps to an input device and typically generates normalized values when input events are received. For example, the horizontal axis, by default, maps to the left and right keys on the keyboard. Left corresponds to -1, right corresponds to 1, and pressing nothing corresponds to the neutral 0. This convention is especially convenient for creating movement scripts with vectors. Other input Axes are officially buttons, which have an on and off (Boolean) status instead. The named input Axes can be accessed, edited, and configured from within the Unity editor, by choosing Edit | **Project Settings** | Input from the application menu.

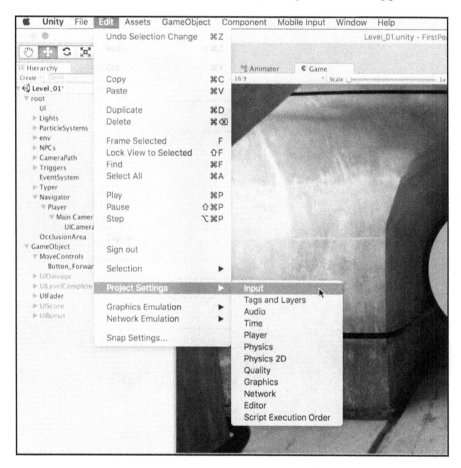

Accessing input Axes

Using the Axes menu from the object **Inspector**, you can customize input mappings. That is, you change how keyboard, mouse, touch, and gamepad controls relate to the input axis and generated values. You can add additional input Axes with any name and configure them to specific controls (like mouse presses and keyboard events), and you can even add multiple Axes with the same name, mapping them to different controls. This is useful when you need two key assignments to perform the same action in-game; for example, *WASD* and keyboard arrows both mapping to horizontal and vertical Axes controlling character movement.

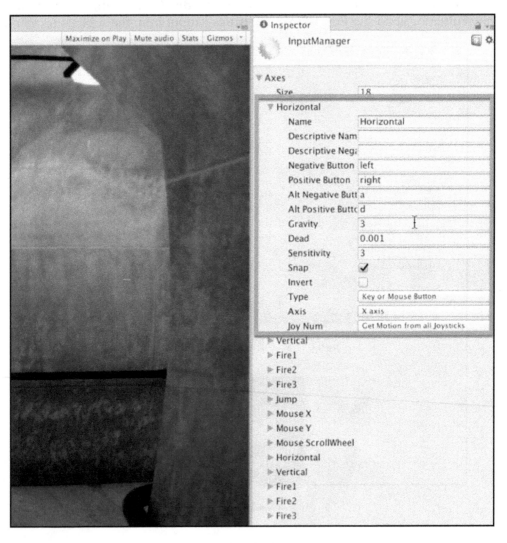

Configuring input Axes

For *Dead Keys*, the default controls may be left as is; they work as intended. Be careful not to delete the default Axes, as this can invalidate many standard asset packages that ship with Unity, causing problems with your game.

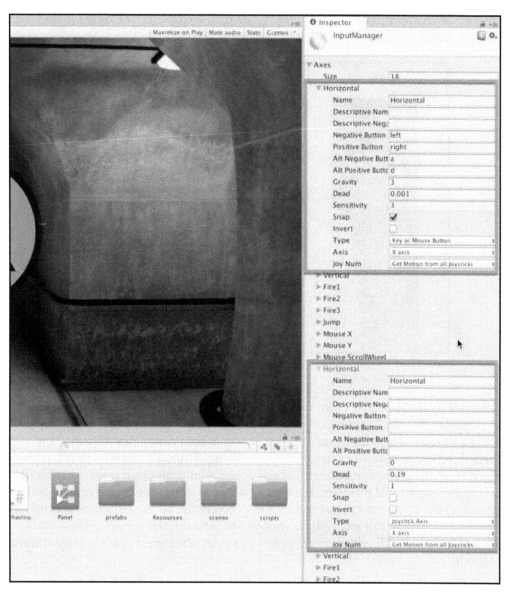

Duplicating input Axes

The canvas

On creating a canvas object, you can now build a user interface. First, let's fix the resolution of our game to 16:9 from the **Game** tab. This will be important for previewing the UI in screen space at an appropriate aspect ratio. To do this, switch to the **Game** tab and choose **16:9** as the screen aspect ratio.

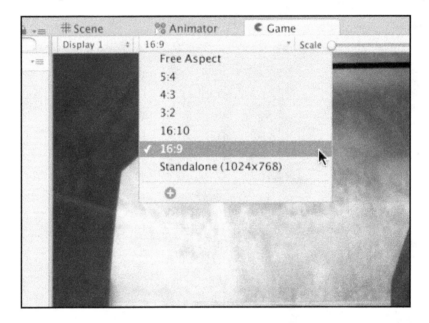

Setting aspect ratio

Now, select the canvas object. From the object **Inspector**, set the **Render Mode** to **Screen Space – Overlay**, via the **Canvas** component, if this mode is not already selected. In this mode, the UI on the selected canvas appears on top of everything, literally. It is the highest rendered object and needs no camera for its rendering. Thus, all cameras could, in theory, be deleted from the scene and still our canvas object would render if it were visible. This can be both beneficial and problematic. Beneficial because we don't need any additional scene cameras to render the UI; but sometimes problematic because we lack control over depth sorting of objects. For example, if we want to fade-out the screen using a black overlay, or obscure the UI with other objects or stencils, then we'd need to use a different render mode.

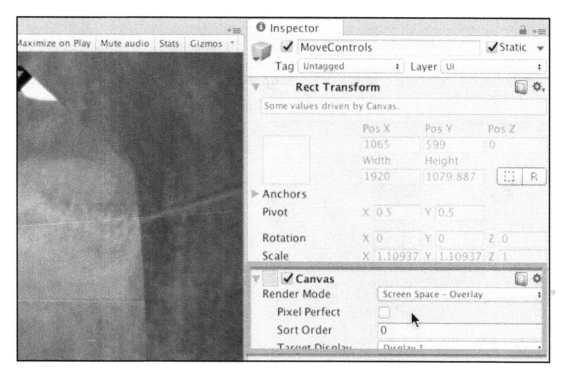

Changing canvas Render Mode

Next, let's focus on the **Canvas Scaler** component, which can be especially important for resizing your UI to fit different resolutions and devices. Change the **UI Scale Mode** to **Scale with Screen Size**. This property can be one of three modes, discussed here:

- **Constant Pixel Size**: This ensures that UI textures all display on screen at their pixel-accurate sizes, in both width and height. Thus, a texture of *100×100* pixels will consume that many pixels in each dimension, regardless of screen size. This means that higher resolutions (with more pixels) can make your textures look smaller, as they remain at their original size.
- **Scale With Screen Size**: This proportionally stretches or shrinks the width and height of UI textures according to the screen resolution. If the resolution increases, the textures increase in size proportionally, and so on. This mode can be useful for resizing UI elements for different resolutions, but it can cause stretching or pixelation when stretched to a differing aspect ratio or to a much higher or lower resolution than the original.
- **Constant Physical Size**: In this mode, the UI textures retain their sizes based on measurements other than pixels. Valid forms of measure include: points, centimeters, millimeters, inches, and picas.

[205]

After choosing **Scale With Screen Size**, set the **Reference Resolution** to *1920×1080*. This specifies the default resolution – or more accurately, the resolution at which the UI was designed. It may be displayed at runtime at potentially many resolutions, both higher and lower, but it will have been designed at a specific, native resolution. This is the **Reference Resolution**.

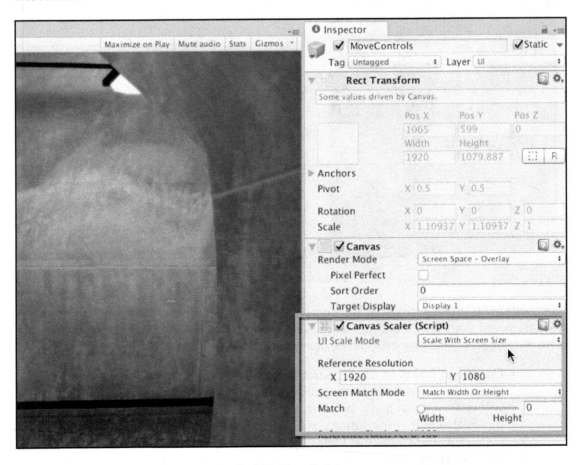

Changing the Reference Resolution

Make sure the canvas object has a **Graphic Raycaster** component. This ensures that touch and keyboard input, from the input module, is dispatched to graphical elements in the UI as events, which are sent to the appropriate objects. In short, without this module, all input (clicks, tabs, and key presses) will be ignored for UI objects on this canvas.

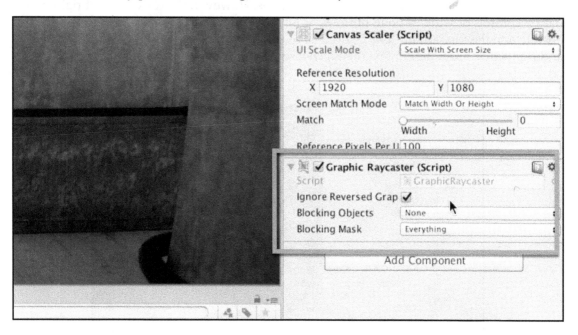

Enabling the Graphics Raycaster

 Remember, the canvas object should be attached to the UI layer.

The button

The canvas object is now properly configured for a multi-resolution setup. Due to the **Canvas Scaler** component, it can be resized automatically to fit many resolutions and devices, from desktop computers to mobile devices. However, the canvas object right now has no controls or widgets on it; buttons, or images, or text edits, and so on. Specifically, we need to add the forward button. To do this, select the canvas object in the hierarchy panel, and right-click. From the context menu, choose **UI** | **Button**.

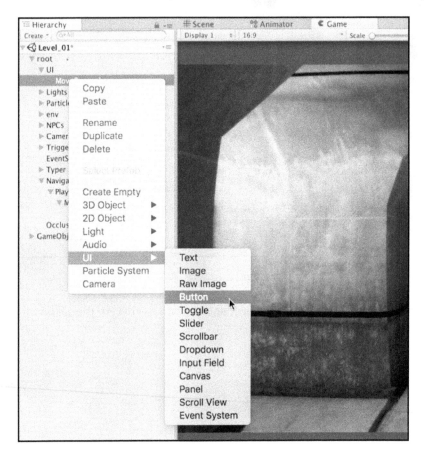

Adding the UI button

All newly added buttons appear as a default, white button, which should be clickable. When adding your first interactive object, however, it's a good idea to test-play your game, moving your mouse cursor over the button to confirm that it responds by changing appearance – detecting input. If it doesn't, then you should check your EventSystem setup and the **Graphic Raycaster** component on the canvas object.

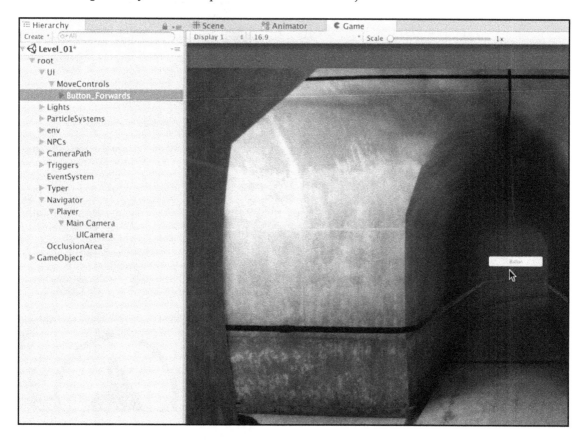

Adding a forwards button

Assuming the default button works as intended (that is, responds to user input), we're ready to customize its appearance. To do that, select the button and, from the object **Inspector**, drag and drop your button texture into the **Source Image** field of the **Image** component.

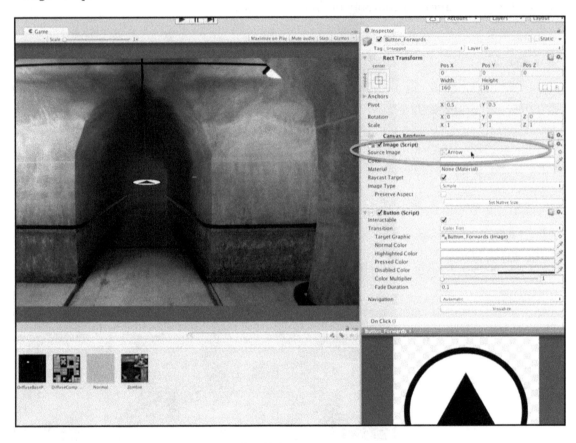

Customizing button appearance

Normally, the reconfigured **Source Image** field leaves the button distorted and wrongly sized. You can correct this easily by clicking the **Set Native Size** button from the object **Inspector**. This returns the button to its native size, combined with the settings of the **Canvas Scaler** component.

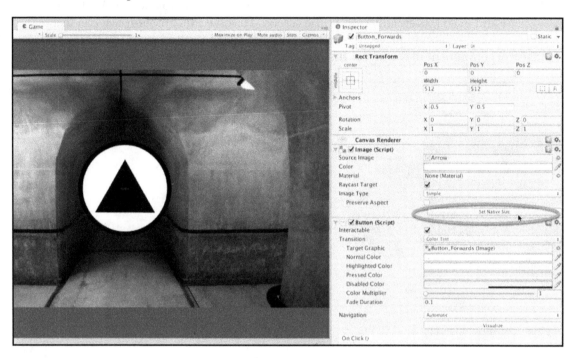

Setting a button to native size

In addition to configuring button size, its position should also be carefully defined. Although the newly created button happens (in this case) to be at the screen center, in the appropriate place, your buttons may not always be aligned like that. You can use the transformation tools (move, rotate, and scale) to move the objects into place on screen, but if the screen resolution and aspect ratio change at runtime, it's possible for the button to *slip out of place* and even (potentially) out of the screen. To solve this problem, we can use anchors to fix the object in place. To do this, click the anchor button from the **Rect Transform** component in the object **Inspector** to view a selection of anchor presets.

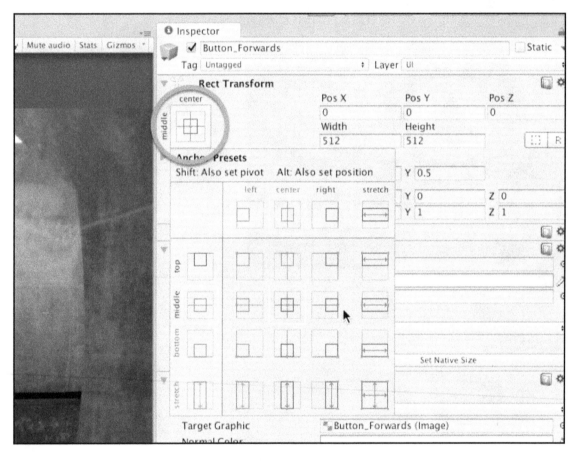

Choosing an anchor point

 Rect Transform is the 2D, UI equivalent of the transform component. More information on **Rect Transform** can be found in the online Unity documentation here: `https://docs.unity3d.com/Manual/class-RectTransform.html`.

Each UI object has four anchor points, one at each corner. These points can be locked (anchored) to known screen locations, which all screens have (namely, top-left, top-right, bottom-right, bottom-left, center, middle-left, middle-right, middle-top, and middle-bottom). The anchors therefore align the edges of a UI element in line with specific screen edges so that, if the screen is resized, the element may move or change (if needed) except for the edges where it is anchored. Thus, by centering the button at the screen-center, we lock the button position and it will always be at the center for every resolution and every aspect ratio.

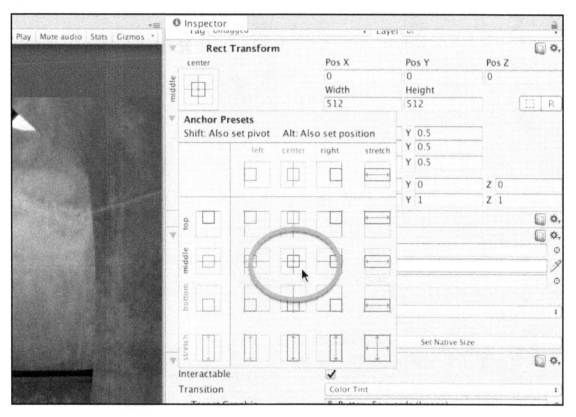

Centering the anchor

In addition to the anchor, each UI element has a pivot point, as specified in normalized coordinates. The pivot point represents the coordinate center of an object (its center of rotation); the position within a UI rectangle that actually moves to the specified X, Y, and Z position in world space when an object is translated. The **Pivot** for the forwards button should be its center. In normalized coordinates, this is *0.5 x 0.5*.

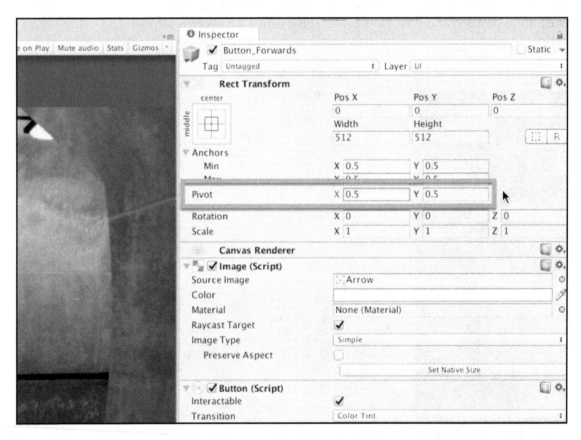

Centering the pivot point

Finally, let's tag the button appropriately, as we'll use this soon from script. Select the button object on the canvas and assign it a **NavigatorButton** tag via the object **Inspector**.

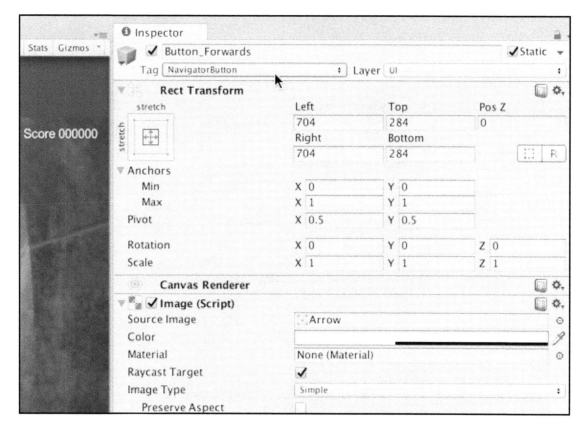

Assigning a tag to the navigator button

Coding button behavior

Now, we'll link button clicks to the `Navigator` class for moving the camera forward. First, let's refine the `Navigator` class, which we started earlier, to support camera movement from the animator graph. The latest code for this class appears as follows:

```
//------------------------------------
using UnityEngine;
using System.Collections;
using UnityEngine.UI;
using UnityEngine.EventSystems;
using UnityEngine.Events;
//------------------------------------
public class Navigator : MonoBehaviour
{
```

```
        //-----------------------------------
//Reference to current camera position
    public int CurrentNode = 0;
    private Animator ThisAnimator = null;
    private int AnimStateHash = Animator.StringToHash("NavState");

    //Reference to navigator button
    private Button NavigatorButton = null;

    //Reference to singleton instance
    public static Navigator ThisInstance
    {
        get
        {
            //Get or create singleton instance
            if (mThisInstance == null)
            {
                GameObject GO = new GameObject ("Navigator");
                mThisInstance = GO.AddComponent<Navigator> ();
            }

            return mThisInstance;
        }

        set
        {
            //If not null then we already have instance
            if (mThisInstance != null)
            {
                //If different, then remove duplicate immediately
                if(mThisInstance.GetInstanceID() != value.GetInstanceID())
                    DestroyImmediate (value.gameObject);

                return;
            }

            //If new, then create new singleton instance
            mThisInstance = value;
        }
    }

    private static Navigator mThisInstance = null;
    //-----------------------------------
    void Awake()
    {
        ThisInstance = this;
        ThisAnimator = GetComponent<Animator> ();
        NavigatorButton = GameObject.FindGameObjectWithTag
```

```
("NavigatorButton").GetComponent<Button>();
    }
    //------------------------------------
    public void Next()
    {
        ++CurrentNode;
        ThisAnimator.SetInteger (AnimStateHash, CurrentNode);
    }
    //------------------------------------
    public void Prev()
    {
        --CurrentNode;
        ThisAnimator.SetInteger (AnimStateHash, CurrentNode);
    }
    //------------------------------------
    //Show button if there are no remaining enemies
    public void ShowMoveButton()
    {
        //To be defined

        NavigatorButton.gameObject.SetActive (true);
    }
    //------------------------------------
}
//------------------------------------
```

Comments

- The CurrentNode variable is an integer representing the progress of the camera through the animator graph and through the scene. It corresponds directly to the NavState parameter.
- This NavigatorButton variable maintains a reference to the UI button on the canvas. This reference is retrieved in the Awake function using the FindGameObjectWithTag method. Thus, the UI navigator button is required to have an appropriate tag.
- The Next and Prev methods are responsible for incrementing and decrementing the CurrentNode variable and then for updating the NavState parameter in the graph. Once updated, Mecanim automatically fires any relevant nodes in the graph.

Select the canvas button object in the scene and, from the object **Inspector**, scroll to the **OnClick()** section of the **Button** component. Here, you can **visually script** what should occur when the button is pressed. Click the + icon to add a new entry for the event.

Adding a new action to the OnClick event

Next, click and drag the navigator object from the **Hierarchy** panel into the target slot, identifying the object with a component whose function we should run when the button is clicked. Select the **Navigator** component and choose the **Next** function. This means that **Next()** will execute as the button is pressed, driving the camera forward to the next location on each increment.

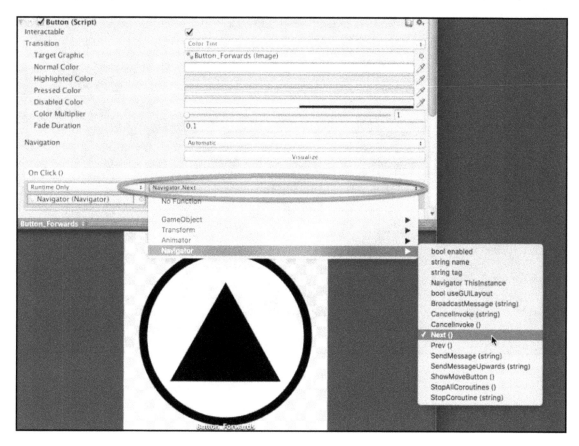

Choosing the Next function as the button's action

The navigator button is now configured to run the `Next` function on the navigator object when clicked. This moves the camera forward. Right now, the button remains visible even when the camera is travelling, but for test purposes this is acceptable. In the next chapter, we'll be refining the controls even further.

Using the navigator button

Creating player death

In addition to building a player camera that moves from point to point, let's also establish a death animation which will feature in the Mecanim graph. With the death animation, the camera simply falls to the floor and rolls over, and this can interrupt gameplay at any time. The death animation will, of course, occur when the player is killed by a danger in the scene, such as a zombie attack. To get started on creating this, select the navigator object, then add a new animation from the **Animation** window by clicking **Create New Clip**. Create a new animation clip called `anim_Die`.

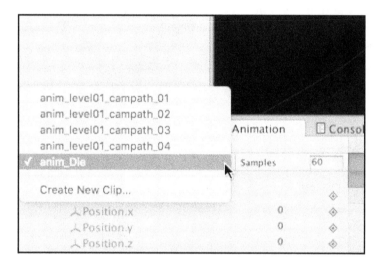

Creating a new animation clip (anim_Die)

Creating this clip involves a challenge concerning object transformation. Specifically, the death animation may potentially occur anywhere in the scene, at the beginning, middle, end, or elsewhere. That is, the world position (X, Y, Z) at which death can occur is undefined; it could be anywhere. Consequently, we cannot animate for death at the root level of the navigator object because its position values are baked into the animation in world space. If we created a death sequence on the navigator object, as death occurs, the camera will always snap to a single, specified position, as this is coded into the animation. To fix this, we'll use a relative transformation. That is, we'll animate a child object of the navigator – namely the **Player** object. To do this, click the **Add Property** button from the **Animation** window and, instead of selecting the **Transform** component (which applies to the navigator object), choose the **Player** child object, then select its **Transform** component, both position and rotation.

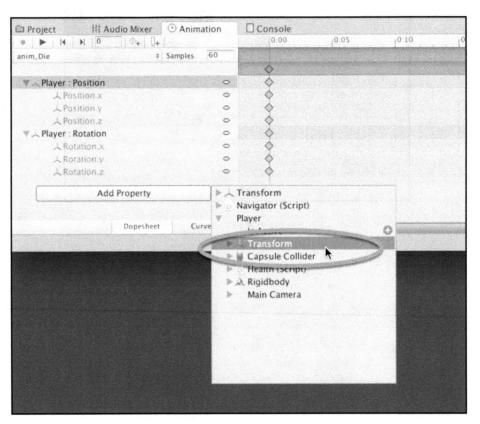

Selecting the Player Transform component

This adds an animation track for both the position and rotation keys for the player object, which is a child of the navigator. This ensures that, wherever the navigator moves, the death animation (when played) will be run as a relative offset from the player position, allowing the player to *die anywhere*. Now animate the camera to a falling position over time, using the **Animation** window to create the death animation.

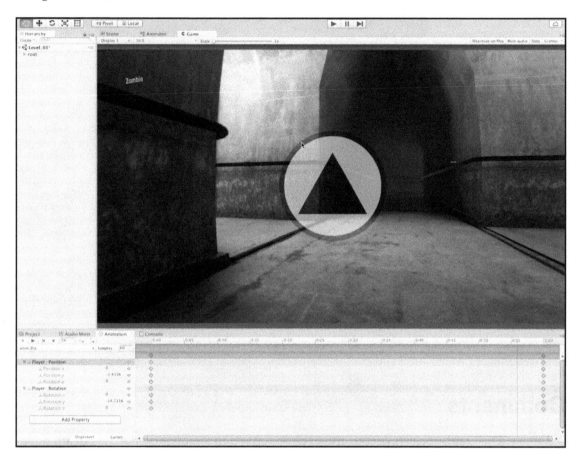

Creating a death animation

Great! The death animation is now created. Let's connect that to the animator graph to mix with the existing nodes. The final node graph looks as follows, featuring all major states and stopping points in the scene:

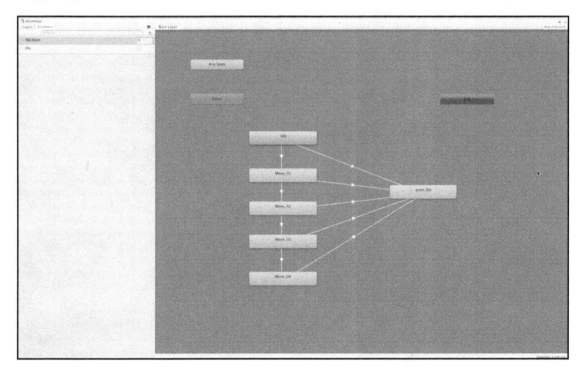

The camera node graph

Comments

- The graph consists of four travel nodes linked in a sequence, and one death node.
- Transitions between travel nodes is controlled via the integer `NavState` parameter.
- The death animation is trigged by the die trigger parameter.
- All travel nodes have the potential to lead to the death animation node. The death animation node has no outward connections, since death is a one-way trip.

Summary

Good work. In reaching this far, we've developed the first half of the player controls – namely, first person camera navigation, complete with camera animations, Mecanim graph, and a UI button. Using these features, we can navigate the player around the scene using fixed animations. However, the first-person functionality is still incomplete; we lack the ability to type and attack zombies, we lack dictionary functionality, enemies, and lots more. These topics are addressed in the next chapter.

Summary

4
Player Controls - Typing and Health

The previous chapter began development of player controls by coding a camera waypoint and navigation system. This chapter completes player controls development by creating a typing-combat system. Specifically, zombies approach the player to attack, sometimes alone and sometimes in waves. When this happens, a word or phrase is randomly selected from a dictionary and assigned to each attacking zombie; the player must frantically type the matching phrase to destroy the zombies one by one, thereby making progress in the level. This functionality involves many different features within Unity. We'll need a dictionary database, a random select feature, an input system for typing instructions, and UI elements to provide graphical feedback for the input. So, let's jump in and get started.

Word combat

Let's consider the work ahead in more detail. Combat in *Dead Keys* is ultimately an exercise in speed typing. A complete word or phrase in English is randomly selected from a large dictionary, then presented in UI form above the head of an attacking zombie. One or more zombies may attack the player at any one time, each associated with a unique word or phrase. The player must use the keyboard to type the matching phrase as quickly as possible, mitigating the attack and destroying the zombie. Hence, they must type under time pressure. When a word or phrase is entered in full correctly, letter for letter, the zombie is destroyed. Mistakes in typing reset progress, forcing the player to retype the phrase from the first letter.

Zombies and Words!

If you want to follow along step by step, the starting point for this chapter is found in the book's companion files, in the folder `chapter_04/start`.

Creating a word list

One of the most important ingredients for *Dead Keys* is an extensive word list, allowing for a wide selection of words and phrases. The word list should be encoded as a text file, with a new word on each line. This file could be built manually if you know enough words and have enough time, but you'll probably want to download and use an existing list. A word list can be downloaded from

`http://dreamsteep.com/projects/the-english-open-word-list.html`. This is the **English Open Word List**, which can be used for many purposes. Additionally, this book's companion files feature the `WordList.txt` file (in the `chapter_04` folder), which can be imported into Unity as a text resource.

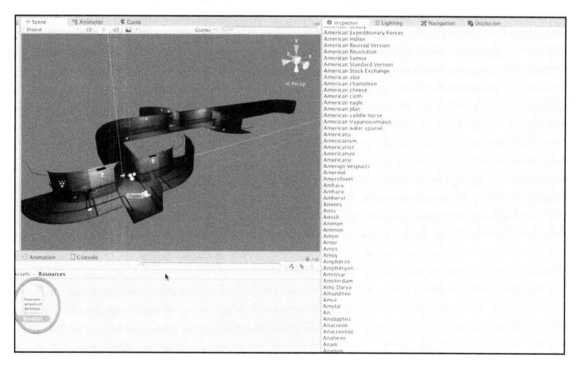

Importing a word list text file

For *Dead Keys*, I've added the `WordList.txt` to a `Resources` folder. Any folder named `Resources` is considered special by Unity. Unity allows resource assets to be loaded and unloaded dynamically at runtime by pathname, rather than by object reference. This means you can delete and replace, and re-import, the word list file in the **Project** panel without Unity and its scripts losing a reference to the asset. This is because they access and read the asset at runtime by pathname, which is always valid so long as the asset remains in the same folder and retains the same file name. More information on resource folders can be found in the Unity documentation at: `https://docs.unity3d.com/ScriptReference/Resou rces.html`.

You may want to edit or remove specific words from the dictionary, or remove specific characters (such as £, %, & , and so on). These are not so easy to speed-type on a regular keyboard or mobile device, as the user must press key combinations, like the *Shift* key. Ideally, every typed character should be a one-button-press operation (for quick-fire), as opposed to two or more. This enhances the intense, action-packed nature of gameplay. Of course, you could argue the opposite (why not try it and find out?). You can speed-edit text files using a powerful text-editor application, such as Notepad++, Sublime Text or Visual Studio Code. These offer find and replace features, as well as other text replacement tools, focused on being lightweight and fast text editors. Notepad++ can be downloaded from `https://notepad-plus-plus.org/download/v6.9.2.html`, Sublime Text from `https://www.sublimetext.com`, and Microsoft Visual Studio Code from `https://code.visualstudio.com`.

Using Visual Studio Code

Let's edit the dictionary text file using a text-editor. For *Dead Keys*, I've chosen Microsoft Visual Studio Code because it is free, cross-platform, lightweight and supports many different extensions to enhance its functionality.

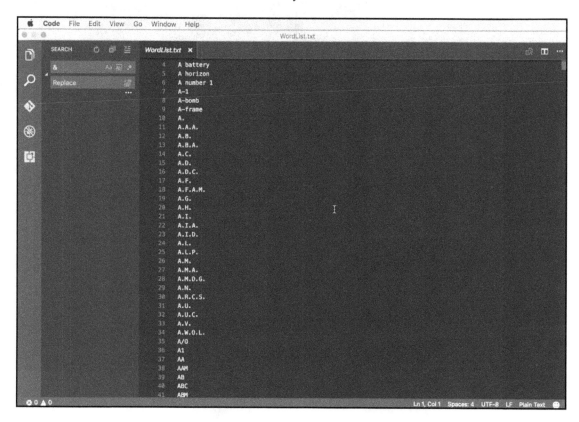

Replacing difficult character using a text editor application (Visual Studio Code)

First, I want to change all text into lowercase, to prevent a mix of upper and lowercase featuring in the word selection. To do this, I'll install the change-case extension. Click **View | Extensions** from the application menu, or press the **Extensions** button from the tool box.

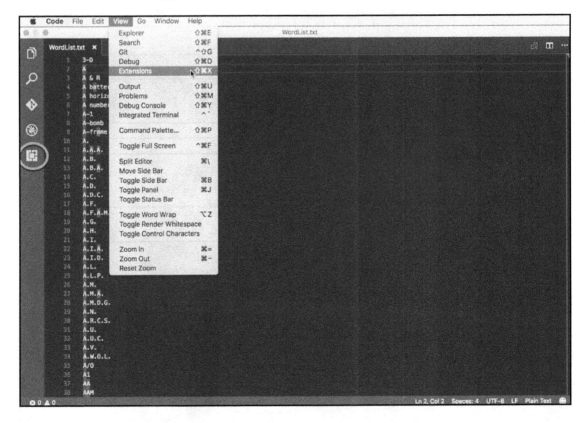

Accessing the Extensions menu

From the **Extensions** palette, search for **change-case**. Then click the **Install** button for the **change-case** extension, afterwards clicking **Enable** to activate it. Once activated, we can change the case of the selected text.

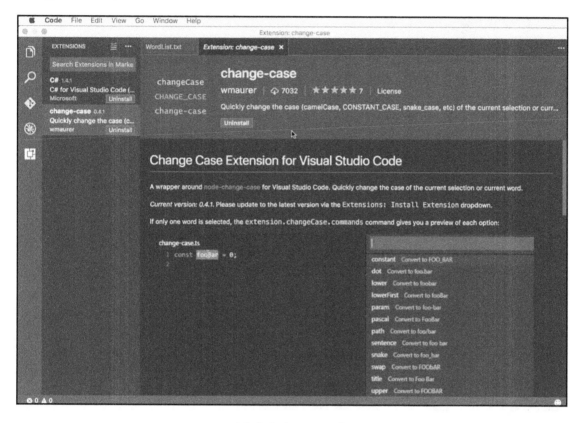

Activating the change-case extension

Now select all text in the file and choose**View | Command Palette** from the application menu, or press *Ctrl + Shift + P* on the keyboard. This displays the Command Palette, from which many text-based operations can be performed, to batch edit the selected text.

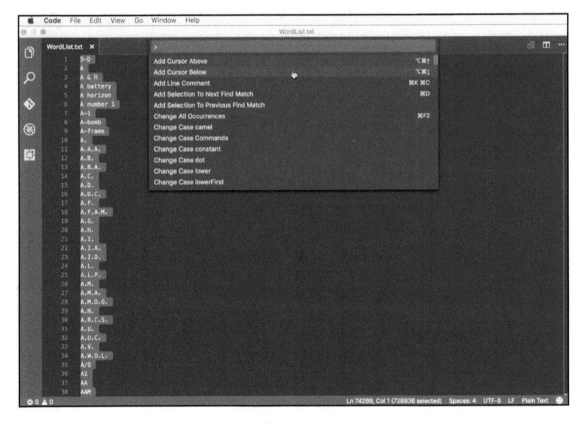

Accessing the Command Palette

From the Command Palette, choose **Change Case Lower**. This may take some time to process for large quantities of text, but eventually all text in the file will be converted to lowercase.

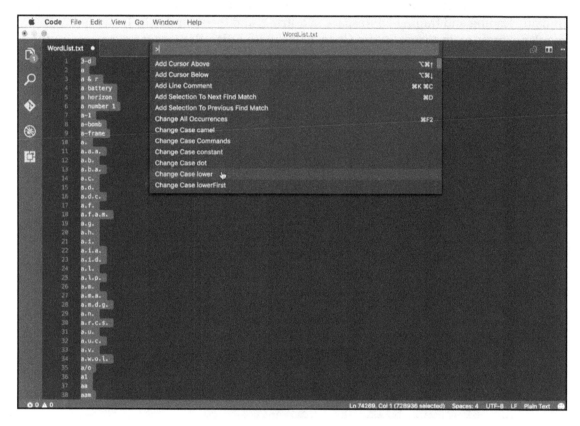

Change text case to lower

Visual Studio Code also supports regular expressions. These are special string statements defining patterns and structures within text that can be searched for. More information on regular expressions can be found online at: `https://msdn.microsoft.com/en-us/library/az24scfc(v=vs.110).aspx`. Let's use the following regular expression (^[\t]+|[\t]+$) to find any leading and trailing whitespace in a string, and then remove it. To apply this regular expression in Visual Studio Code, first choose **Edit** | **Replace** from the application menu.

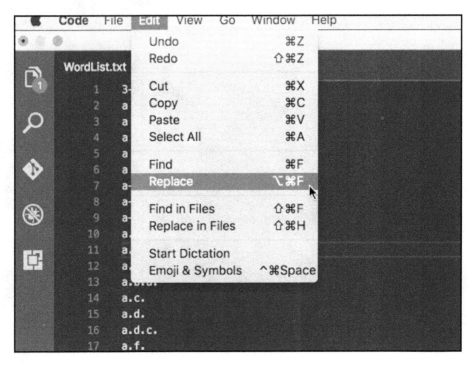

Accessing the text replacement feature

Enable regular expressions by clicking the regular expression button from
the **Replace** dialog.

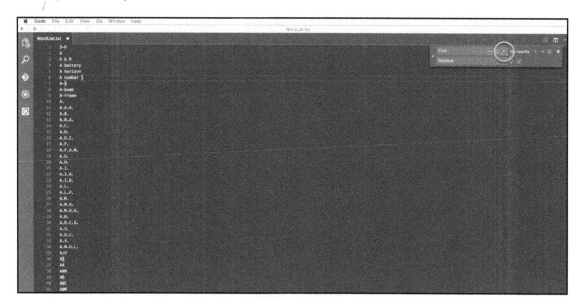

Enabling regular expressions

Next, enter the expression ^[\t]+|[\t]+$ into the **Find** field and leave the **Replace**
field empty to remove all whitespace. Press *Enter* on the keyboard to confirm. The operation
may take from several seconds to a minute to complete, depending on text length and
computing hardware.

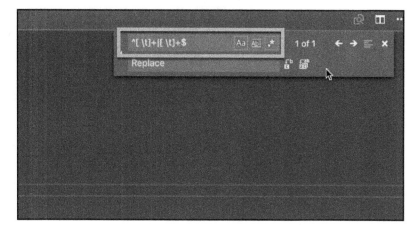

Searching with regular expressions

Now let's remove complete lines that contain specific characters that make them inappropriate for *Dead Keys*. For example, lines that contain space characters indicate multiple words and these should be removed (if we don't want to allow multiple words). Also, lines containing other characters, such as *, / (), are more difficult to type and make little sense. We can construct a regular expression to achieve this, as follows: ^.*\b(.| |-|/)\b.*$.

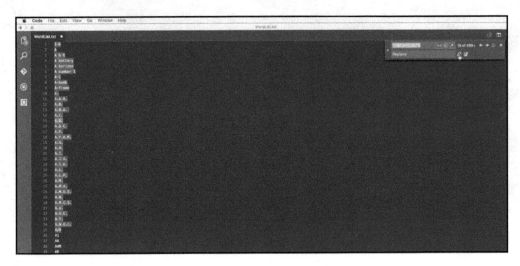

Removing invalid lines

By clearing problematic lines by character, we may end up with completely empty lines. These can also be removed with a regular expression, (\r?\n){2,}.

Trimming empty lines

Finally, you'll end up with a text file dictionary that has many unnecessary lines removed, including complex phrases, special characters, and multiple words. You can now save the file, updating it inside the Unity project folder, and the changes are automatically reflected in Unity.

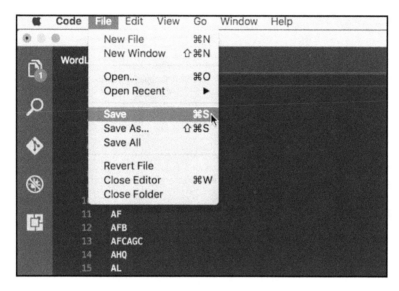

Saving the updated dictionary

Creating a WordList class

Now we must build a class to process the word list asset. This involves a class that can open and read the word list itself, select a word at random from the list, and compare two words for a match. The latter is needed to compare the typed word with the selected word from the dictionary. To start with, a new Singleton class `WordList.cs` should be created. The basic skeleton follows:

For more information on Singleton objects, see chapter 3, *Player Controls – Movement*. In addition, you can view the Unity online Wiki here: `http://w iki.unity3d.com/index.php/Singleton`.

```
using UnityEngine;
using System.Collections;
using System.Collections.Generic;
//----------------------------------
public class WordList : MonoBehaviour
```

```
{
    //----------------------------------------
    //Members for Singleton
    public static WordList ThisInstance
    {
        get
        {
            //Get or create singleton instance
            if (m_WL == null)
            {
                GameObject GO = new GameObject ("WordList");
                ThisInstance = GO.AddComponent<WordList> ();
            }
            return m_WL;
        }
        set
        {
            //If not null then we already have instance
            if (m_WL != null)
            {
                //If different, then remove duplicate immediately
                if(m_WL.GetInstanceID() != value.GetInstanceID())
                    DestroyImmediate (value.gameObject);
                return;
            }
            //If new, then create new singleton instance
            m_WL = value;
            DontDestroyOnLoad (m_WL.gameObject);
        }
    }
    private static WordList m_WL = null;
}
//----------------------------------------
```

Comments

- The `WordList` class features `Get` and `Set` properties to control class instantiation, making it a Singleton.
- In addition to being a Singleton, `WordList` also calls the `DontDestroyOnLoad` function. This prevents the object from being destroyed when the scene ends, allowing it to carry over to the next scene.
- Take care when using `DontDestroyOnLoad`, as all child objects and associated texture and mesh resources on the object will also survive and continue to the next scene.

The first programmatic step in working with the WordList is to tokenize the text file. This means we need to generate a complete array of all words in the file; separating the words as distinct units, as opposed to being part of a long string spanning the length of the file. For our word list, each word is separated by a new line. Or rather, there is one word or phrase per line. Each line should therefore become its own entry in the word array. We can achieve the tokenization process simply in the Awake function.

```
//-----------------------------------
// Use this for initialization
void Awake ()
{
    //Set singleton instance
    ThisInstance = this;

    //Now load word list, if available
    if (FileWordList == null)
        FileWordList = (TextAsset) Resources.Load("WordList");
    Words = FileWordList.text.Split (new[] { "\r\n" },
System.StringSplitOptions.None);
}
//-----------------------------------
```

Comments

- Two variables should be added to the class to support the Awake function: firstly, FileWordList (declared as TextAsset FileWordList), which references the Word List text asset, as loaded from the Resources folder; and, secondly, Words, which is an array of strings (string[] Words). This represents the tokenized file (the words from the file separated into unique elements).
- The function Resources.Load is called to load the text asset resource at runtime from the file, loading the resultant string into FileWordList.
- After FileWordList has been created and populated with string data from the word list file, the Split function is called with the string argument "\r\n", indicating that words should be separated by new lines. This returns an array in which each element is a separate word.

Next, a random word can be selected from the `Words` array by using the `Random.Range` function. This function generates a random number between a minimum and a maximum, and this can be passed as an index for the `Words` array. Here is a new method for the `WordList` class, which selects a random word:

```
//Returns a random word from the word list
public string GetRandomWord()
{
    return Words[Random.Range(0, Words.Length)].ToLower();
}
//----------------------------------
```

 All returned words are converted to lower case, if needed, preventing case sensitivity issues disrupting gameplay. You can use a text editor to convert case, but it's useful to safeguard against this in code too. For *Dead Keys*, the player should not have to worry about whether upper or lowercase is used, so either case is acceptable.

Matching words

Determining whether two words match is an important function for *Dead Keys*. When a player enters a word during combat, we must ascertain several features of that word compared to the chosen one from the word list:

- **Complete word matches**: A complete word match occurs when the player fully and correctly types the selected word, letter for letter. This results in a zombie being killed and is a measure of progress in the scene. Detecting complete word matches is therefore important for progressing gameplay.
- **Failed matches**: A failed word match occurs when the player's most recent keypress fails to match any selected words (there could be multiple zombies) and therefore invalidates any partial matches there may have been up to that point. When a failed match occurs, the player's input is reset and they must retype the word from the first letter.

- **Partial word matches**: A partial match occurs when the player is on their way to entering and completing a word but has yet to type every letter. Some letters will have been entered correctly, but there are additional letters outstanding to make a complete match. Detecting partial matches is important for two main reasons: it helps us identify which zombie the player is targeting, as each zombie represents a different word; and it lets us update the UI with appropriate feedback, indicating how much of the selected word has been matched so far, through color coded text or interface elements.

The following function `CompareWords` should be added to the `WordList` class. Its return value indicates which of the three matches above is true.

```
//-----------------------------------
//Compares two strings and returns the extent of a match
//EG: s1="hello" and s2="helicopter" the result = "hel"
public static string CompareWords(string s1, string s2)
{
    //Build resulting string
    string Result = string.Empty;

    //Get shortest length
    int ShortestLength = Mathf.Min(s1.Length, s2.Length);

    //Check for string match
    for (int i = 0; i < ShortestLength; i++)
    {
        if (s1 [i] != s2 [i])
            return Result;

        Result += s1[i];
    }

    //Output result
    return Result;
}
//-----------------------------------
```

Comments

1. The `CompareWords` function accepts two string arguments for comparison.
2. The comparison proceeds by comparing letters for the length of the shortest string.
3. The return value is a string whose contents reflect the extent of a match. An empty string results i *no match,* and either partial or complete strings are returned for partial or complete matches. Thus, the strings `hel` and `hello` return `hel`, and the strings `door` and `don't` return `do`. Thus, the function returns a new string defining a letter by letter match from the first letter onwards.

That's it! We've created a `WordList` class. Let's see the full source code for that:

```
//-----------------------------------
using UnityEngine;
using System.Collections;
using System.Collections.Generic;
//-----------------------------------
public class WordList : MonoBehaviour
{
    //-------------------------------------
    //Text asset featuring word list
    public TextAsset FileWordList = null;
    public string[] Words;

    //Members for Singleton
    public static WordList ThisInstance
    {
        get
        {
            //Get or create singleton instance
            if (m_WL == null)
            {
                GameObject GO = new GameObject ("WordList");
                ThisInstance = GO.AddComponent<WordList> ();
            }

            return m_WL;
        }
        set
        {
            //If not null then we already have instance
            if (m_WL != null)
            {
                //If different, then remove duplicate immediately
```

```
            if(m_WL.GetInstanceID() != value.GetInstanceID())
                DestroyImmediate (value.gameObject);

            return;
        }

        //If new, then create new singleton instance
        m_WL = value;
        DontDestroyOnLoad (m_WL.gameObject);
    }
}
private static WordList m_WL = null;
//---------------------------------
// Use this for initialization
void Awake ()
{
    //Set singleton instance
    ThisInstance = this;

    //Now load word list, if available
    if (FileWordList == null)
        FileWordList = (TextAsset) Resources.Load("WordList");
    Words = FileWordList.text.Split (new[] { "\r\n" },
System.StringSplitOptions.None);
}
//----------------------------------
//Returns a random word from the word list
public string GetRandomWord()
{
    return Words[Random.Range(0, Words.Length)].ToLower();
}
//----------------------------------
//Compares two strings and returns the extent of a match
//EG: s1="hello" and s2="helicopter" the result = "hel"
public static string CompareWords(string s1, string s2)
{
    //Build resulting string
    string Result = string.Empty;

    //Get shortest length
    int ShortestLength = Mathf.Min(s1.Length, s2.Length);

    //Check for string match
    for (int i = 0; i < ShortestLength; i++)
    {
        if (s1 [i] != s2 [i])
            return Result;
```

```
            Result += s1[i];
        }

        //Output result
        return Result;
    }
    //--------------------------------------
}
//--------------------------------------
```

Most classes in Unity must be added to game objects as components. This often requires us to create empty objects in the scene and then drag and drop our scripts onto them from the **Project** panel. However, we don't need to do this for `WordList` because its Singleton functionality automatically instantiates a new instance, if one is not already instantiated, whenever it's referenced anywhere in the script through the `ThisInstance` C# property.

The Typer object

The `WordList` class supports the import and tokenization of a dictionary, generating an array of words on a line by line basis. The `GetRandomWord` function returns a randomly selected word from the dictionary and the `CompareWord` function determines whether a typed word matches the chosen one entirely, partially, or not at all. Having now created this class, we begin work here on the `Typer` class, which actually accepts typed input from the keyboard, processes that input and displays UI complements for player feedback. Let's start by creating an object hierarchy. Create a new, empty object at the scene origin to act as the topmost node for the **Typer**. Name the object `Typer` and then create a `Canvas` object as a child. The canvas contains all objects for the associated UI.

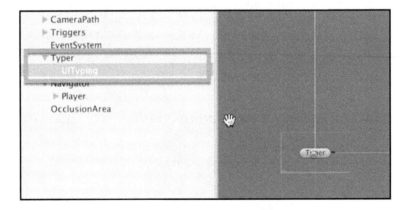

Creating a Typer object

As with previous canvas components, we'll configure it to support multiple resolutions with a scaling technique. Set the **UI Scale Mode** to **Scale With Screen Size** and specify a **Reference Resolution** of 1920 X 1080. The rationale for this is covered in depth in Chapter 3, *Player Controls – Movement*.

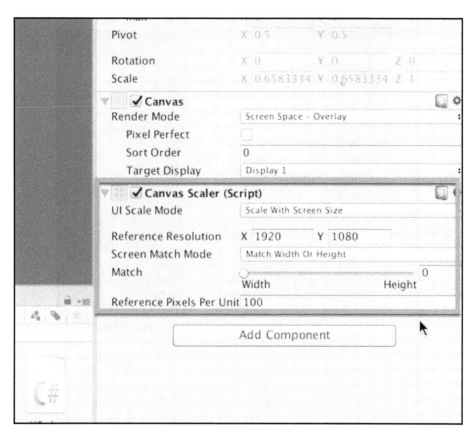

Configuring the Canvas Scaler for multiple resolutions

The canvas is necessary for showing UI elements as the player types on the keyboard during zombie combat. Specifically, as a new letter is typed, it should appear in the center of the screen as UI text and then zoom inwards into the scene (away from the camera), as though it were a projectile being thrown at an oncoming zombie. To achieve this, start by creating a new `Text` object as a child of the `Canvas` object.

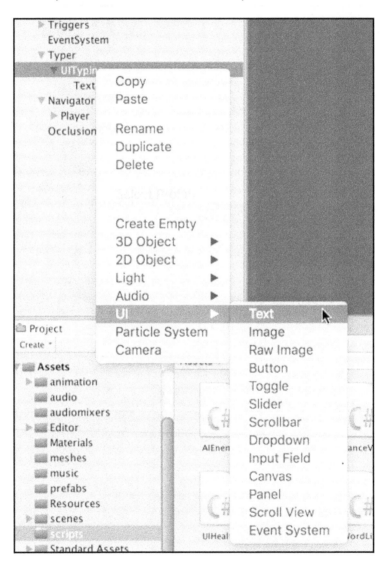

Creating a Text object as a child of the Typer's Canvas Scaler

Position the text to the screen center, previewing your results in the game tab, then use **stretch** anchoring to align the left, right, top and bottom text borders to the screen edges. In addition, from the **Text** component in the object **Inspector**, set the text horizontal alignment to screen center and text vertical alignment to screen center. This ensures the text is always positioned at the center of the screen.

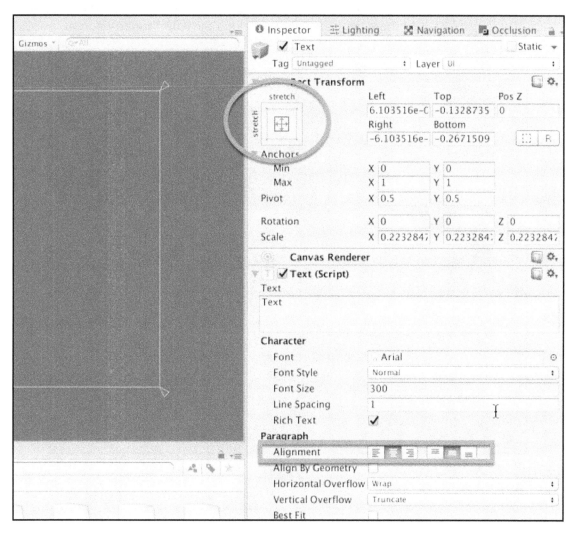

Aligning text to the screen center

The text will be an animated UI element to express motion, impact and attack whenever the gamer presses keys on the keyboard. Specifically, the text will zoom inwards, growing smaller as it moves towards the screen center, replicating the effect of being thrown into the world toward attacking zombies. To start creating the animation, select the text object, and open the **Animation** window by choosing **Window** | **Animation** from the application menu. Two channels should be animated, namely **Scale** (for changing text size) and **Color** (for fading the alpha). Add these two channels by clicking the **Add Property** button.

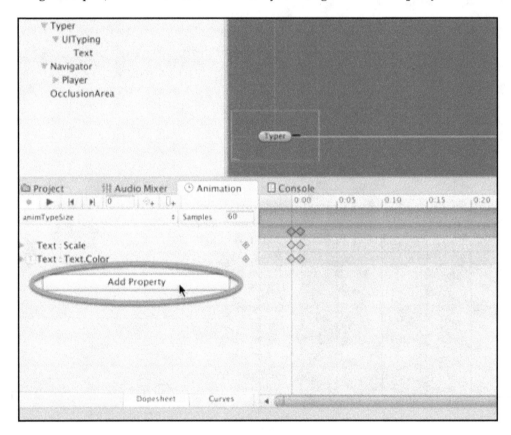

Creating animation channels for Scale and Color

Use the first key frame (*Frame 0*) to reset all text properties back to their defaults each time it plays. Specifically, set the **Text : Scale** to 2 (a scale that fills the screen) and set the **Text : Color** to an alpha of 0, making the text invisible. Using the first key frame to reset object properties can be an effective strategy, especially for animations that play repeatedly or regularly but not on a loop.

Keep the animation timeline between zero to one second for the text attack animation. This means we can rescale the duration up or down as needed, while retaining control over total duration. Hence, *1 x t = t, 2 x t = 2t*, and so on.

Setting text Scale and Color for the starting frame

For the second key frame (that is, *Frame 1*), change the **Text Color** to Alpha 1, making the text visible. It doesn't matter what the text object actually says in the view port at design time, because the text will change programmatically based on keyboard input.

Showing the text for an attack animation

Before inserting intervening frames, add the last frame to the timeline. It's good practice to *block in* an animation, first by creating core key frames at the beginning, middle, and end. These define the main structure of motion. Then, later, refine those frames by adding intervening ones describing the changes between them. In our case, the last frame should shrink the text to a **Scale** of 0.2, and reset the color Alpha back to 0. This creates the effect of text being thrown into the scene, before disappearing, or fading, as it moves further from us.

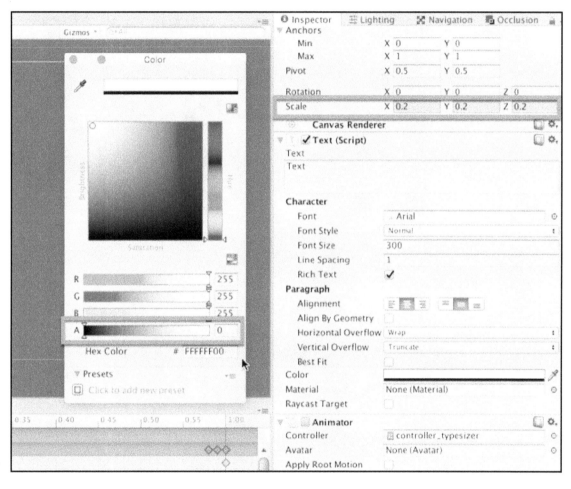

Defining the last key frame

Right now, with only the start and end frames defined, text transparency fades to Alpha 0 from start to end. To keep the text visible and clearer for longer, we'll need an extra frame, between the start and end to retain text visibility. Move to **0.33** in the timeline, and insert a color frame, keeping the Alpha at 255 (or 1 in normalized values). This holds text color between times **0–0.33**.

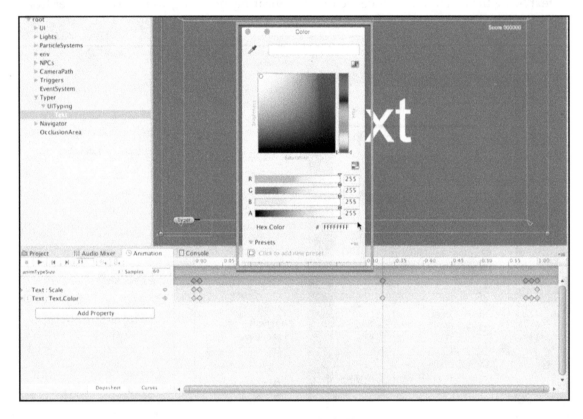

Holding text color between time 0-0.33

Remember to disable animation looping for the clip. The animation will probably play frequently, but not on a loop. Select the clip from the **Project** panel and disable the **Loop Time** check box.

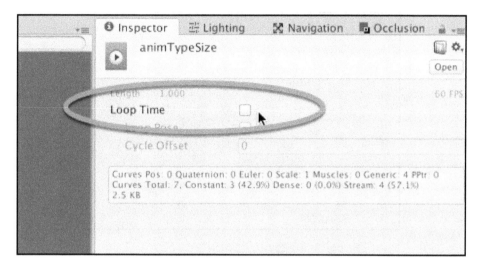

Disable animation looping

This completes the text animation itself. It's pretty simple but, despite this simplicity, its importance in-game cannot be understated for usability reasons. It will serve several important design functions. Firstly, it offers feedback (confirming that a key was pressed); secondly, it educates by asserting the primary game mechanic (text typing as an aggressive and combative act); and, thirdly, it expresses the *direction of action* (text moving away from the viewer) as an action that damages enemies in front of us. Thus, wrapped up in a simple UI animation, without reliance on text instructions, we educate the player on how to play and on the importance of their actions.

Now let's configure the associated animator graph which, by default, always plays the first animation clip at level startup. Open the graph editor and create a new trigger parameter called **ThrowText**. This parameter will be invoked whenever text is typed in combat.

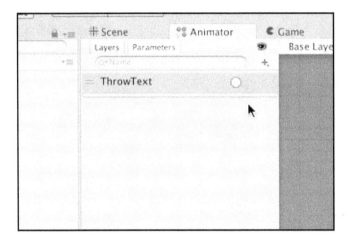

Creating a ThrowText trigger parameter

Next, create an empty node as the starting, default node for the graph by simply right-clicking and selecting **Create State** | **Empty** from the context menu. Then, right-click the node and select **Set as Layer Default State**. Connect the empty node to the **ThrowTextAnim** animation, and use the **ThrowText** trigger as a condition.

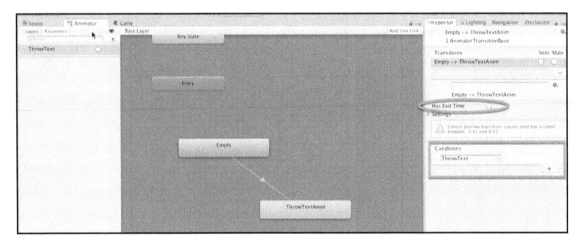

Connecting the starting node to Throw Text by a trigger condition

Don't forget to add a backwards transition from the animation node to the idle node. Simply create a transition without a condition and enable **Has Exit Time**. This ensures animation flow returns to the idle node after the text animation completes. You may also need to select the animation node and change its **Speed** to match your needs. I've set my speed to five.

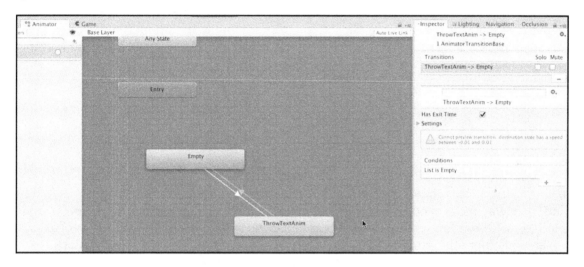

Creating a two-way node connection

Voila! We've now created a text-throw animation and configured this alongside an animator graph with a trigger. The next step is to link the animation to code that accepts user input.

Progressing with the Typer class

The Typer object (the root object) will be associated with a new class, defining its functionality. This class (the `Typer` class) will accept keyboard input and link that to a combat mechanic. We haven't yet developed any enemies to fight (like zombies), but this will be dealt with in forthcoming chapters. Consequently, we'll have reason to return to the Typer class later. As it stands, we can still link player input to important functionality already in place, such as UI animations and sound effects too. Let's begin with a new, empty class, as follows:

```
using System.Collections;

public class Typer: MonoBehaviour
{
}
```

The first step in developing the `Typer` class is to build an extensible event framework. `Events` are critically important for the `Typer` because it must listen for a keypress (`Events`) and then relay those to other processes, which should respond as needed. There are multiple solutions for developing an integrated event system. One method, which I've covered in other titles, such as *Mastering Unity Scripting, Packt,* is to use a notifications manager. You can download and use a free notifications class, if preferred, from here: `http ://wiki.unity3d.com/index.php?title=CSharpNotificationCenter`.

However, for *Dead Keys*, we'll use a different approach. Specifically, we'll use a dedicated `UnityEvent` class, which enables us to customize what happens on specific events through visual scripting, directly in the object **Inspector**, so that there is no need to recompile code. To get started with this, include both the `UnityEngine.EventSystems` and `UnityEngine.Events` namespaces into the source file, as follows:

 In C#, a namespace refers to a collection of related classes. By using namespaces, you can avoid naming conflicts that commonly arise when working on complex projects with many source files. Namespaces let you group classes into a larger unit, which can be selectively included and excluded like libraries from other source files. More information on namespaces in Unity can be found online here: `https://docs.unity3d.co m/Manual/Namespaces.html`.

```
using UnityEngine;
using System.Collections;
using UnityEngine.EventSystems;
using UnityEngine.Events;

public class Typer : MonoBehaviour
```

```
    {
    }
```

Next, we'll add a `UnityEvent` to the class, called `OnTypingChanged`. This is a special object type that we'll invoke when a typing event happens (a keypress), to run specific behaviors and functions that we specify from the object **Inspector**. See the following code:

```
using UnityEngine;
using System.Collections;
using UnityEngine.EventSystems;
using UnityEngine.Events;
public class Typer : MonoBehaviour
{
    //Typing changed event
    public UnityEvent OnTypingChanged;
}
```

When this variable is added as public to the `Typer` class, it appears in the object **Inspector** as a customizable field.

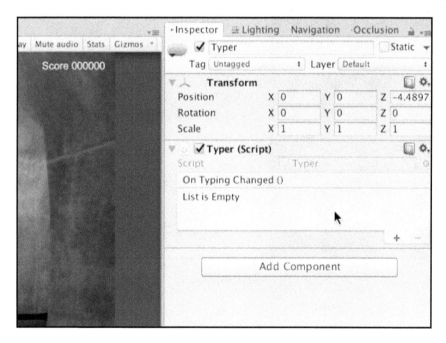

Adding a Unity event to the class

Unity events can be customized easily from the object **Inspector**. You simply click the +
button to add an action to the event and there's no limit to the number of actions that may
be added or combined. In our case, when a typing event occurs, we'll play the text
animation on the UI panel to express an attack. To achieve this, drag and drop the text
object in the UI from the **Hierarchy** panel into the **Object** field for the event inside the object
Inspector. This indicates the target or subject of action. In this case, the text animation
should play on the text object (this object has the animator component); thus, it should be
added to the **Object** field.

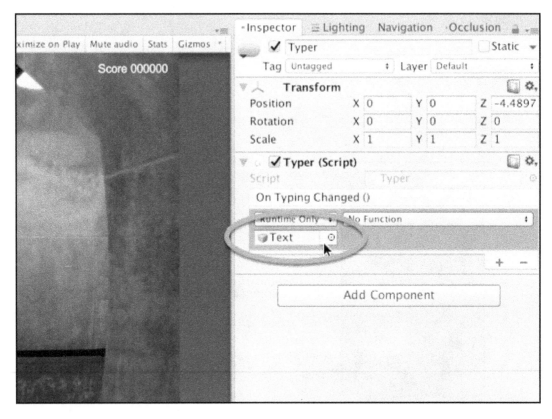

Specifying the action target

With the target object specified, indicate the function to run from the Function drop-down list. In our case, we should call the **Animator | SetTrigger** (string) function. For the string argument field, we need to specify the name of the trigger to invoke for a typing event. This should be **ThrowText**, matching the name of the trigger parameter in the animator graph.

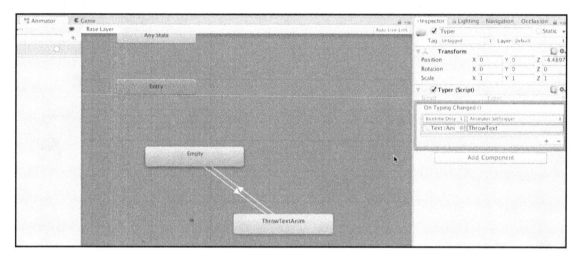

Running the SetTrigger function from the object Inspector

By configuring the `OnTypingChanged` event with visual scripting from the **Inspector**, we always activate the `ThrowText` trigger, playing the text animation. We didn't even need to type a line of code, which is convenient. Plus, we don't need to rely on expensive and slow functions, like `SendMessage` or `BroadcastMessage` for dispatching event notifications. In addition to activating the `ThrowText` trigger, we also want to play a punch sound.

Again, this is to emphasize the attack and the impact on our enemies. The *Dead Keys* project contains punch sound effects, as well as an *AudioMixer* asset configured to play sounds across three main groups (channels): **Music**, **SFX** and **Voice**. This was configured in Chapter 2, *Level Design and Structure*.

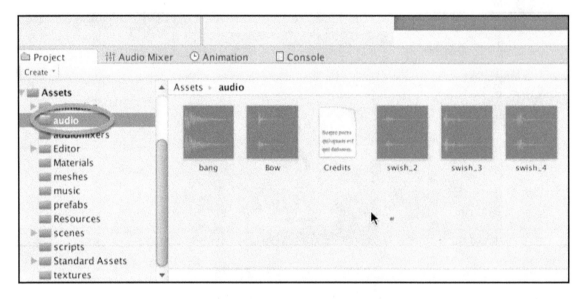

Accessing punch sound effects

Now, we could configure the Typer as it stands to play the same punch sound on every type event, but ideally we want some randomization to enhance credibility and to avoid annoying the player with too much repetition. Specifically, for each keypress event, we should select and play a random punch sound from a larger collection of punch sounds. We can do this easily using only two lines of code. First, we need an array of sounds to choose from. For this, add an array of audio clips to the class as a public variable with the following code:

```
//Collection of combat sounds
public AudioClip[] CombatSounds;
```

Next, a clip can be randomly selected using the `Random.Range` function, as follows. This code should feature wherever sounds are selected at random (see the sample project in the course companion files).

```
SelectedClip = CombatSounds [Random.Range (0, CombatSounds.Length)];
```

Working from this, we can now assign all punch audio clips from the project panel to the array variable, dragging and dropping them into the array slots.

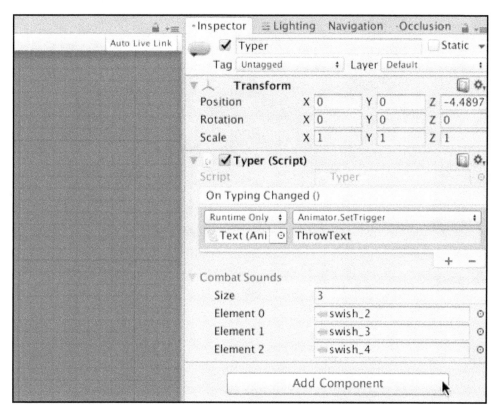

Building an array of combat sounds

In addition to the combat sound array, the Typer object will also need an **Audio Source** component to play the selected sound. To add this, select the Typer object and choose **Component | Audio | Audio Source**. Once added, route the **Audio Source** component through the configured **AudioMixer | SFX** channel for the project by using the **AudioMixer** field from the object **Inspector**.

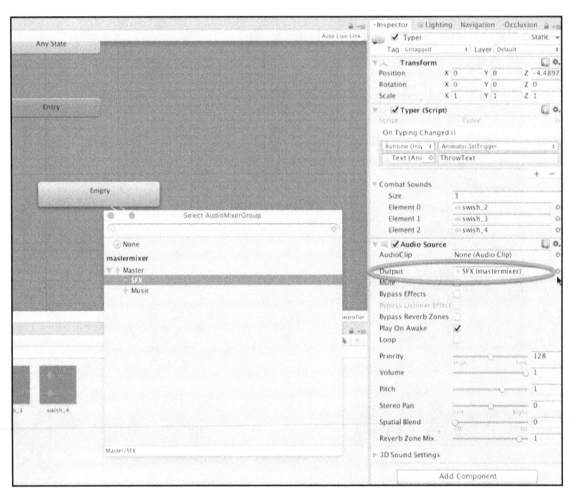

Setting the Audio Mixer output for the Typer Audio Source

Now the Typer object is configured in terms of components and setup, let's complete the code for the `Typer` class overall with the following code. A more detailed exploration of the class and its functionality follows this:

```
//-----------------------------------
using UnityEngine;
using UnityEngine.UI;
using UnityStandardAssets.CrossPlatformInput;
using System.Collections;
using UnityEngine.EventSystems;
using UnityEngine.Events;
//-----------------------------------
public class Typer : MonoBehaviour
{
    //Reference to typed word
    public static string TypedWord = string.Empty;

    //Text object for showing type
    private Text TyperText = null;

    //Reference to audio source component
    private AudioSource ThisAS = null;

    //Typing changed event
    public UnityEvent OnTypingChanged;

    //Time elapsed since last reset
    public static float ElapsedTime = 0.0f;

    //Record words per second
    public static float RecordLettersPerSecond = 2f;
    //-----------------------------------
    //Collection of combat sounds
    public AudioClip[] CombatSounds;
    // Use this for initialization
    void Awake ()
    {

        //Get audio source
        ThisAS = GetComponent<AudioSource>();
        ThisAS.clip = CombatSounds[0];

        TyperText = GetComponentInChildren<Text>();
    }
    //-----------------------------------
    // Update is called once per frame
    void Update ()
    {
```

```
        //Update types string
        if (Input.inputString.Length > 0)
        {
            TypedWord += Input.inputString.ToLower();
            UpdateTyping ();
        }
    }
    //-----------------------------------
    //Update enemy type event
    private void UpdateTyping()
    {
        //Update GUI Typer
        OnTypingChanged.Invoke();

        Reset ();
    }
    //-----------------------------------
    public void Reset()
    {
        //Reset typing
        TypedWord = string.Empty;

        //Reset time
        ElapsedTime = 0.0f;
    }
    //-----------------------------------
    // Update is called once per frame
    public void UpdateTyperText()
    {
        TyperText.text = Input.inputString;
        ThisAS.clip = CombatSounds [Random.Range (0, CombatSounds.Length)];
    }
    //-----------------------------------
}
//-----------------------------------
```

Comments

- The `TypedWord` static variable will reference the complete word being typed as a string; that is, an accumulation of the letters typed, letter by letter, until a word match is found with a zombie or a mistake is made which resets the typing.
- The `TyperText` variable references the `Text` UI object for displaying the text animation. This variable is automatically assigned in the `Awake` event. There, the `GetComponentInChildren` function is called, which searches downwards in the hierarchy for the first matching component. In this way, the text component on the child object can be found. More information on `GetComponentinChildren` can be found in the Unity online documentation at: `https://docs.unity3d.com /ScriptReference/Component.GetComponentInChildren.html`.
- The variable `ThisAS` references the `AudioSource` component on the object. This is needed for playing sounds when keys are pressed.
- The `ElapsedTime` and `RecordLettersPerSecond` variables are currently place-holders for functionality to be implemented later. They'll determine the fastest typed words and phrases for bonus points and rewards.
- The `Update` function (called once per frame) references the `Input.InputString` variable to determine which keys, if any, have been pressed since the last update cycle.
- All input strings are converted to lowercase to make string matching simpler. This also means *Dead Keys* is not case-sensitive.
- The `UpdateTyping` event is called when new keys are pressed. This calls the `OnTypingChanged.Invoke` method, which activates all visually scripted behavior for the typing event inside the object **Inspector**.
- The `UpdateTyperText` method is responsible for selecting and playing a random attack sound.

The `Typer` script should be attached to the root Typer object, and that's it! We now have a class that can type text, throwing it inwards into the scene, ready to whack a zombie!

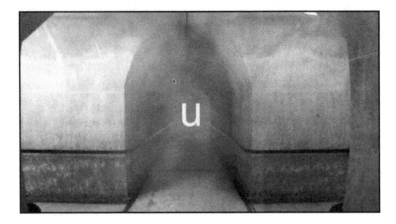

Testing the Typer class

Health and damage

Next up, we consider health and damage. Health is an interesting property, especially because it is abstract. That is, many characters have health: the player character and enemies, including the zombies. Though zombies are neither alive nor dead, but are *undead*, they still normally have an equivalent metric corresponding to health. When that property or resource is exhausted for any character, they expire, die, or are removed from the game. Because of the generic quality of health, it's a good idea to code it once such that it can be applied limitlessly as a component to any entity that has that property. For this reason, we'll create a `Health` class. Consider the following full source code and the comments that follow it:

```
//------------------------------------
using UnityEngine;
using System.Collections;
using UnityEngine.EventSystems;
using UnityEngine.Events;
//------------------------------------
public class Health : MonoBehaviour
{
    //------------------------------------
    public float Value
    {
        get{return fValue;}
```

```
        set
        {
            fValue = value;
            OnHealthChanged.Invoke();
            if (fValue <= 0f)
                OnHealthExpired.Invoke();
        }
    }

    [SerializeField]
    [Range(0f,100f)]
    private float fValue = 100f;
    //-----------------------------------
    //Events called on health change
    public UnityEvent OnHealthExpired;
    public UnityEvent OnHealthChanged;
    //-----------------------------------
}
```

Comments

- The `fValue` private float variable stores the health value itself. It's declared with two C# attributes, `SerializedField` (to show the value in the Inspector) and `Range`, to display as a slider.
- The `fValue` variable is accessed through the `Get` and `Set` methods for a C# property. The `Get` method simply returns `fValue`. The `set` method updates the value and validates it.
- The `Set` method invokes the `HealthChanged` event, since the health has changed. And, if the health equals or falls below zero, the `HealthExpired` event is invoked, allowing any visually scripted events in the object **Inspector** to run.

With the `Health` script coded, you can now attach it to any object that should have a health property, including the player and all his/her enemies. This demonstrates an effective coding practice when working in Unity, namely **Component Based Design**. The basic idea is to encapsulate abstract and general properties (like health, or spell books, or character sheets), which can potentially apply to many different characters, into a single class. This class can then be attached to an object as a component, perhaps alongside other components, to collectively define that object, so that the object becomes the sum of its component parts.

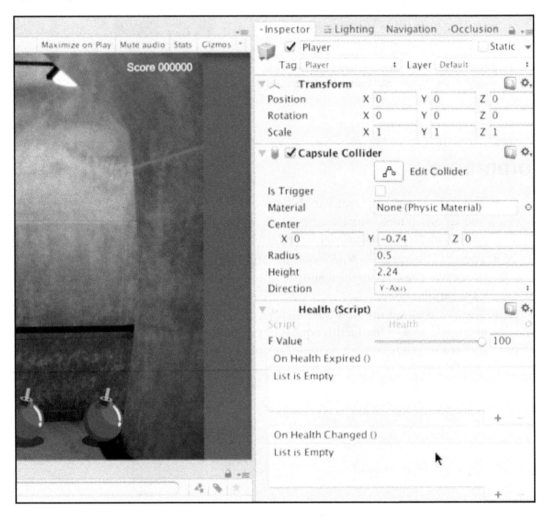

Attaching the Health script to the Player object

Excellent! We now have a `Health` class. This alone doesn't do much, besides encode a health value for an object. But in collaboration with other classes and components, it'll make a big difference. To see this, let's create a health bar UI element for the player which will update as the health changes to reflect the current health of the player. To achieve this, create a new canvas object, by choosing **GameObject** | **UI** | **Canvas** from the application menu. This adds a new canvas object to the scene, which will be dedicated to a health bar. Name this object `UIDamage`.

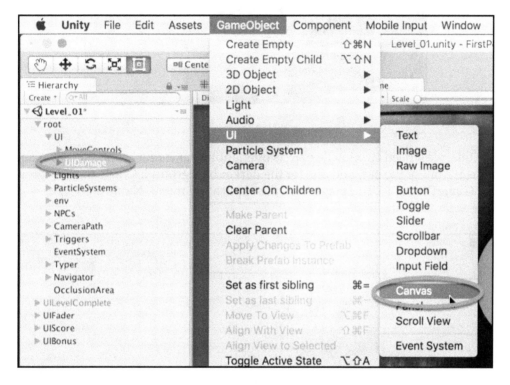

Creating a UI health canvas object

The health bar should act much like a traditional health bar in video games. It's presented as a horizontal bar or gauge. When full, the bar appears completely green, from left to right. When damage occurs, the green section of the bar moves further to the left, revealing a darker background behind it. When health has been exhausted, the bar fully retracts to the left, appearing empty.

Creating a health bar

To create this, we'll need two image objects overlapping each other in the screen space; one for the green front of the bar, and one for the darker background. Create the background by choosing **GameObject** | **UI** | **Image** from the application menu. Name this object `Image_Health_Background`.

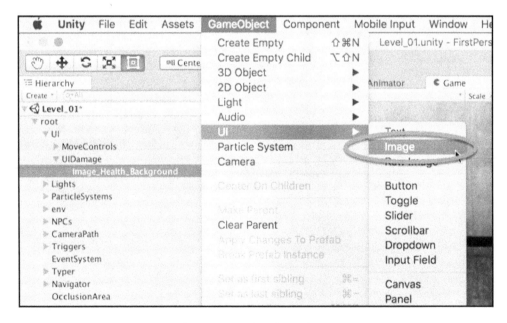

Creating a background image for the health bar

The health bar should be positioned at the bottom-left corner of the screen and the bar itself should be explicitly left-aligned so that, when damage occurs, the right-hand edge of the bar retracts leftwards, while the left-hand side remains in place. The width of the bar is therefore equivalent to the health value, so set it to 100. To configure the bar this way, change its **Pivot** in the **Rect Transform** component to 0,0 from the object inspector (positioning the pivot at the bottom-left corner). In addition, set the bar anchor to the bottom-left screen corner, fixing the bar in place.

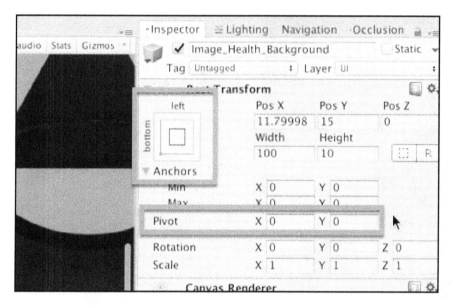

Setting the pivot and anchor for the health bar background

Good work! We've created the bar background, so let's now create the foreground. To do that, simply duplicate the background and then rename it to `Image_Health`. From the **Image** component in the object **Inspector**, select a green color for the **Color** field, and leave the source image field empty to fill the image with a bold color.

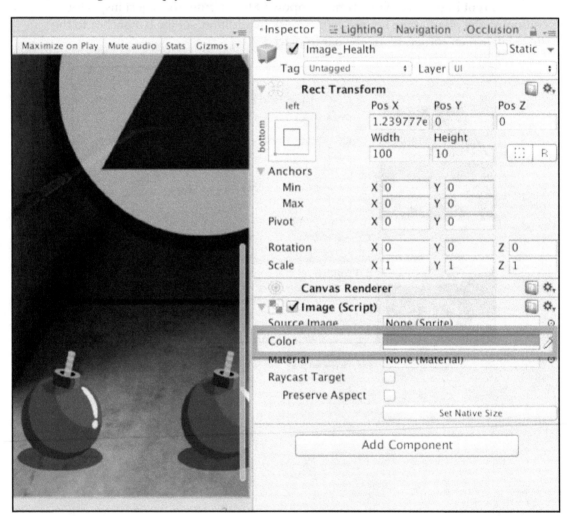

Setting the image color for the foreground

You can already test the health bar by simply reducing the width of the `Image_Health` object; reducing it from `100` to a lower value above `0`. When you do this, the health bar should retract from the right to left, revealing a solid bar background behind.

Testing the health bar

We also need to connect the health bar to the health value for the player. To do this, we'll create a new script for the health bar UI and call it `UIHealth`. The following full source code includes comments afterwards. This script should be attached to the health bar foreground image:

```
//------------------------------------
using UnityEngine;
using System.Collections;
//------------------------------------
public class UIHealth : MonoBehaviour
{
    private Health PlayerHealth = null;
    private RectTransform ThisTransform = null;
```

```
    // Use this for initialization
    void Awake ()
    {
        GameObject GO = GameObject.FindGameObjectWithTag ("Player");
        PlayerHealth = GO.GetComponent<Health> ();
        ThisTransform = GetComponent<RectTransform> ();
    }
    // Update is called once per frame
    public void UpdateHealth ()
    {
        //Update player health
        ThisTransform.sizeDelta = new Vector2(PlayerHealth.Value,
ThisTransform.sizeDelta.y);
    }
}
//------------------------------------
```

Comments

- The `PlayerHealth` variable references the health component on the player object. This variable is assigned during the `Awake` function by searching the scene for an object tagged as `Player`. Once found, the health component is retrieved. You could display health for other characters (like zombies), however, by exposing the `PlayerHealth` field as public and manually assigning a reference to a different object.

- The `UpdateHealth` function updates the `Width` of the health bar based on the health of the player. The variable `RectTransform.sizeDelta` controls the width of the health bar.

The `UpdateHealth` function could be called on every frame (such as in *Update*) to update the GUI health status. However, continually using update in this way is performance prohibitive. Functionality like this, when distributed across classes, soon accumulates over all updates, which substantially impacts performance. For this reason, we should opt for an event-based approach. This means identifying all possible occasions when the health can change and then invoking an appropriate event. When the event occurs, the health must update. Using this technique means the health UI code only updates when health changes are possible, as opposed to indiscriminately on every frame.

Make sure the health component is attached to the *foreground* health image and not the *background*.

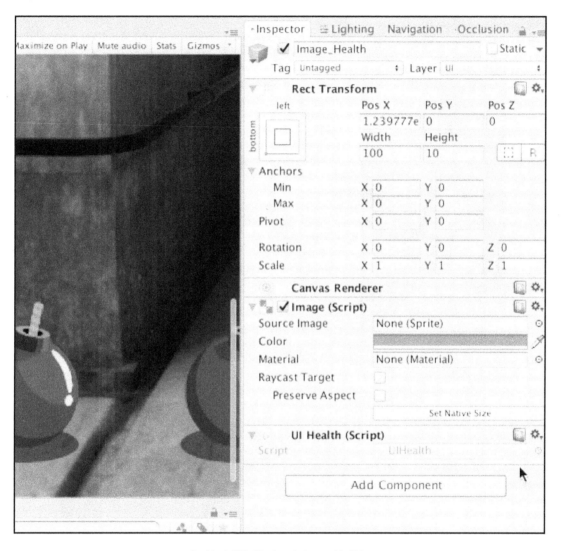

Attaching the UI health script to the foreground health bar

Now we need to generate a health change event; we already have the mechanism in place to do this from the Health class. Select the **Player** object and, from the **Health** component, add an action for the **OnHealthChanged** event in the object **Inspector**.

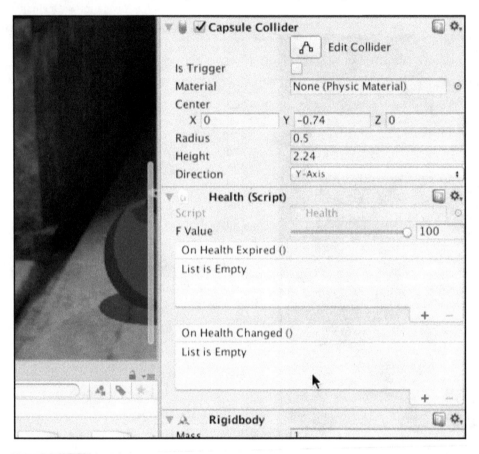

The health script features two events, coded with Unity events

Next, add the HealthUI object to the target field, and run the `UpdateHealth` function from the **UIHealth** component.

The Health script features two events, coded with Unity Events

That's it! The health changed event is now successfully linked to UI health updates. Right now, there is nothing dangerous in the scene to damage our health, but this will change in the next chapter! You can, of course, test out the damage functionality by using key presses inside an `Update` function.

In addition to responding to damage, we should also link the health expired event to the camera death animation that we created in the previous chapter. In that chapter, we developed an animation for the camera falling to the ground up on death. Having developed this, we can now link that to the health expired event from the object **Inspector**, just as we did for the **OnHealthChanged** event.

Simply create a new action for **OnHealthExpired** (on the player's health component) and call the **Animator.SetTrigger** (string) function to activate the **Die** parameter in the graph.

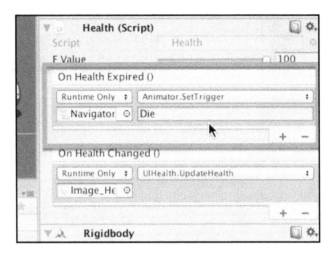

The health script features two events, coded with Unity events.

The **Die** parameter is simply a trigger in the animator graph that activates the death sequence. This was created in the previous chapter.

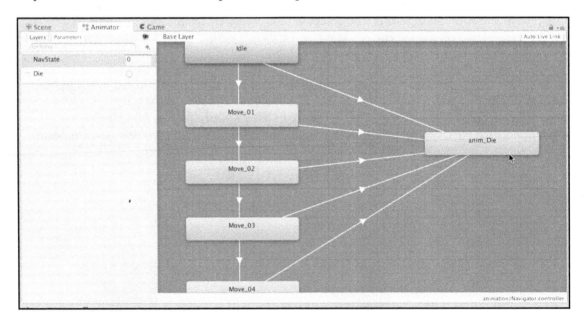

Invoking the death sequence on health expired events

Damage and feedback

The **Health** component allows objects to have health and therefore to take damage during attacks; but, we also want more UI feedback for the player during a battle. Specifically, when the player is attacked and hit by a zombie, the screen should throb or flash red, indicating that damage has been sustained. We can achieve this by using a colored sprite overlay whose opacity is animated from transparent to visible and then back again. To achieve this, create the colored overlay by choosing **GameObject | UI | Image** to create a new image object. Name this `Panel_Damage_Throbber`. Add this as a child object of the `Health UI Canvas` created previously. Select red for the **Color** field to express danger, damage and pain, or you can use a custom texture.

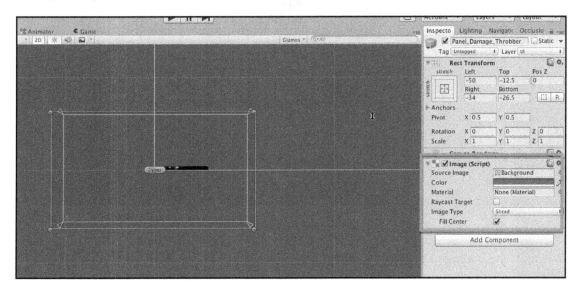

Creating a red, damage UI object

Use the **Rect** Transform tool (*T*), as shown in the following screenshot, to resize the image plane to fill the canvas, and thereby the screen. Then use anchoring to attach each corner anchor to the respective edges of the screen (stretch anchoring). This ensures the damage panel fully occupies screen space.

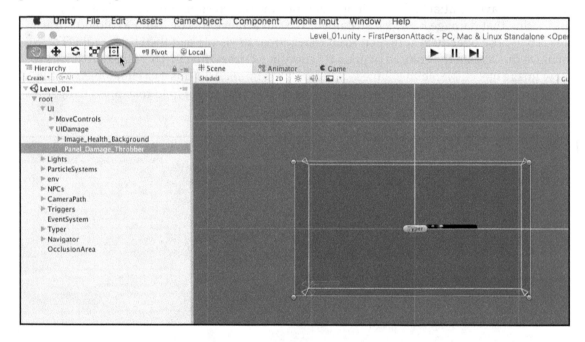

Resize the damage panel overlay

To create the damage animation, simply open the **Animation** window, add a new animation, and insert three key frames: one at the start of the animation, one in the middle, and one at the end. Each key frame animates the sprite color (alpha component). Start with an Alpha of 0, move to 1, and then back to 0 by the final frame. This creates a ping-pong, back and forth, for the alpha. Again, work within the 0–1 space for the animation duration, as the **Speed** can always be tweaked from the mecanim graph.

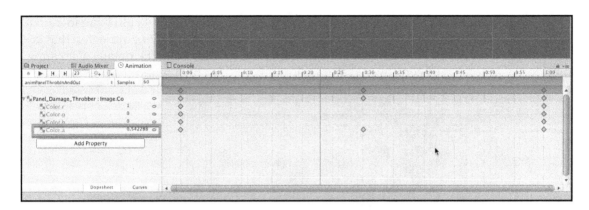

Creating a Throb animation

Flatten the key frame handles for the start and end frames, using the **Curves** view in the animation editor to smooth out the fade, creating a more natural transition. You can also click and drag the handles in the editor to further refine the curve.

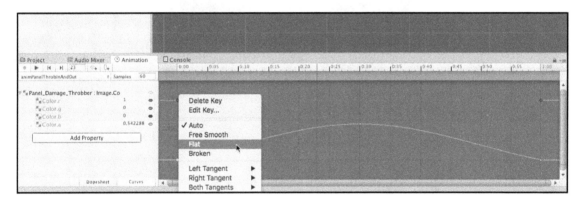

Flattening keyframe handles to create smoother motion

Finally, add an animation controller to the damage object. This should begin in an idle node (empty state) and transition to the damage animation based on a trigger parameter: that is, by enabling a trigger parameter, the damage animation should play. The details of creating this kind of graph have been covered amply throughout this chapter and the previous chapter. The final graph should look like this:

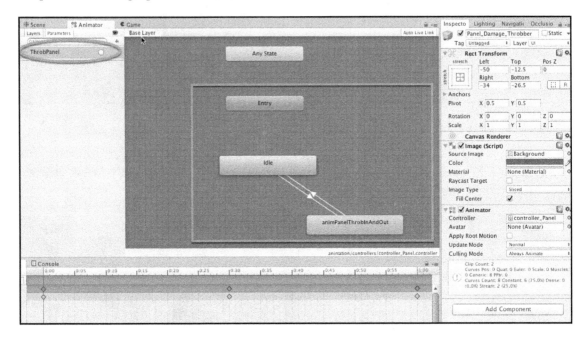

Creating an animation graph for the damage fader

To connect player health to the damage fader, select the **Player** object and, from its health component, we can set the animation trigger for damage from the **OnHealthChanged** event directly from the object **Inspector**. Again, no additional code needed!

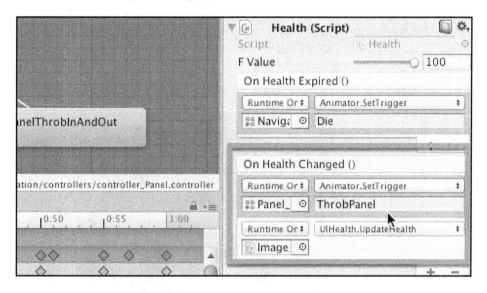

Link the OnHealthChanged event to the damage object

Great! Now health is linked to the damage effect. We can test this, if needed, by simply changing the player health at runtime.

Player score

In many games, the player has a score to express their achievement and progress. *Dead Keys* will be no different and we'll use a traditional scoring system. Specifically, the player will earn points for each zombie killed; we'll create the potential for assigning different scores (points) to different zombies, depending on difficulty and strength. To implement this, we'll work with UI elements and script, as before.

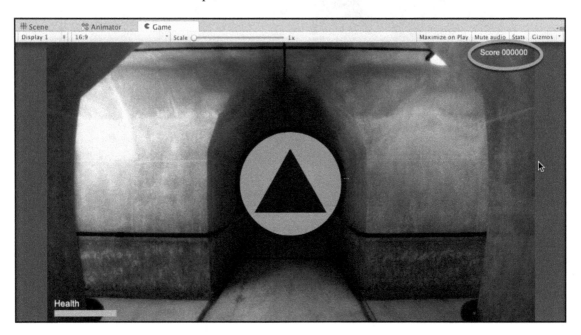

Creating a score display

The score feature will essentially be a text object displaying a numerical score, representing the kill count for zombies. Most games complement a score with some animation and effects. Our score will feature two behaviors: firstly, it'll expand and contract in scale as the score changes; and secondly, the score will catch up and Lerp. That is, the numbers in the score text will animate upwards as the score changes to represent the latest value, as opposed to changing instantly. Creating the throb animation works much like the damage panel. We'll create a three-key-frame animation, with the start and end frames identical on a smaller scale, and the middle frame on a larger scale.

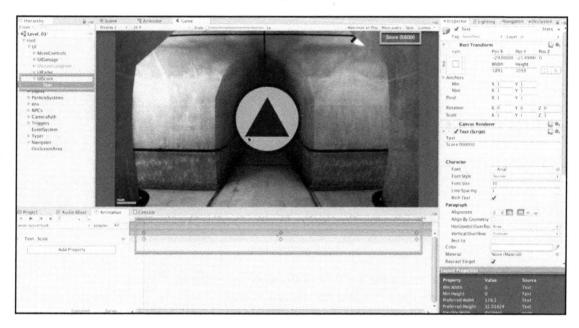

Creating a score display

As with the **Damage Throb** object, the score has an associated animator graph, featuring a trigger parameter to initiate the throb animation when the score changes.

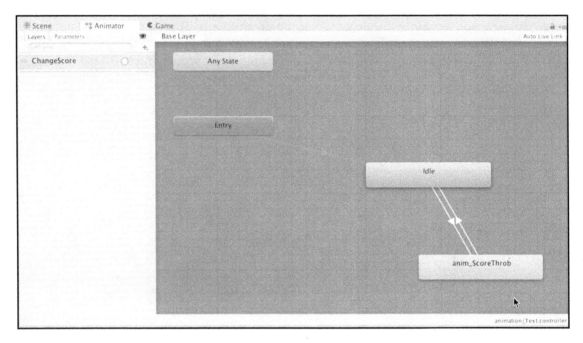

Configuring the score animator

In addition to the score animator, we'll need to create a dedicated score UI class (UIScore.cs) to update the score and initiate any score animations. The following script is lightweight but contains important code worth considering, and is followed by comments:

```
//------------------------------------
using UnityEngine;
using System.Collections;
using UnityEngine.UI;
using UnityEngine.EventSystems;
using UnityEngine.Events;
//------------------------------------
public class UIScore : MonoBehaviour
{
    public float DisplayScore = 0;
    private Text ThisText = null;
    public float CatchUpSpeed = 1f;

    public UnityEvent OnScoreChange;
```

```
// Use this for initialization
void Awake ()
{
    ThisText = GetComponent<Text> ();
}
// Update is called once per frame
void Update ()
{
    DisplayScore = Mathf.Lerp (DisplayScore,
GameManager.ThisInstance.Score, CatchUpSpeed * Time.deltaTime);
    ThisText.text = "Score " + Mathf.CeilToInt (DisplayScore).ToString
("D6");
}
}
//------------------------------------
```

Comments

- The CatchUpSpeed variable defines the speed at which the score text animates from its current value towards its destination value as the score changes.
- The DisplayScore variable represents the score actually shown for the GUI text element.
- The Mathf.Lerp function is used to **Linearly Interpolate** (**Lerp**) smoothly between two values, a and b. This function accepts a time value for controlling how quickly a changes to b.

Excellent! We now have a score object added to the scene too. Of course, right now, we can't score any points as there are still no enemy zombies to kill. Nevertheless, the potential for scoring points exists. In the next chapter, we'll focus on creating zombie enemies that can both attack and be destroyed.

Bonus items

Now let's focus on a distinct and extensible feature, namely bonuses or rewards. Rewards systems and positive feedback are important properties for games wherever the player repeatedly encounters time-critical challenges. When provided judiciously and appropriately, rewards reinforce the player's successes, making them feel good, and encouraging them to play on. It's important not to over or under-reward. By under-rewarding, you make the game seem too difficult or boring, and by over-rewarding, you remove the challenge and desensitize the player to rewards completely.

Rewards take many forms, from steam achievements, certificates, and badges, to power-ups and extra items. For more information on player motivation and in-game achievements, see the book *Gamification with Unity 5.x, Packt* (`https://www.packtpub.com/game-development/gamification-unity-5x`). In *Dead Keys*, we'll reward the player with collectible badges. These are issued based on typing time: that is, when the player types and completes a word successfully, while also beating a minimum *letters per minute record*, they'll be rewarded with an achievement badge. These will appear horizontally at the bottom of the screen and accumulate through the level as the player collects rewards. The reward asset is included in the book companion files and should be imported into the project (if you've not already imported it) as a 2D sprite texture.

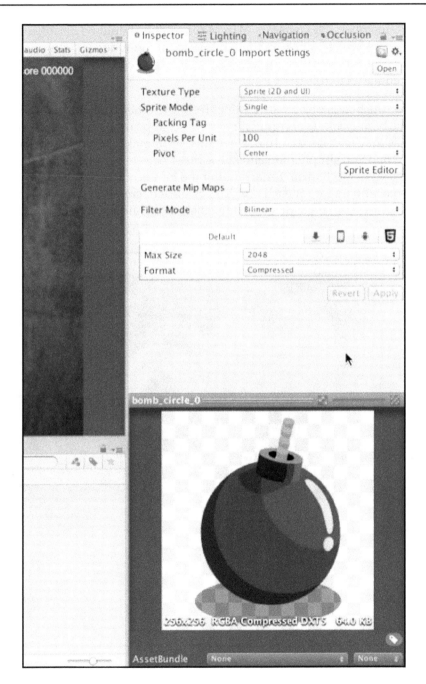

Importing a rewards badge icon

Remember, the **Generate Mip Maps** option should be disabled for 2D sprites which appear in the UI. Mip mapping reduces texture quality as it moves further from the camera. We neither need nor want such quality reduction in this case.

The UI needs for the bonus objects are distinct from the other UI elements we've been working on. The bonus objects accumulate over time, appearing one by one, in a row at the screen-bottom as they're collected. To achieve this, we'll make some bonus objects in the editor and the game will simply hide and show these objects as needed. However, we still want a clean and easy mechanism for arranging the bonus objects in a row, as opposed to relying on manual alignment for each one. To get started, create a canvas object, configured to *Stretch with Screen Size*. Then add an image object as a child, configured to display the bonus sprite.

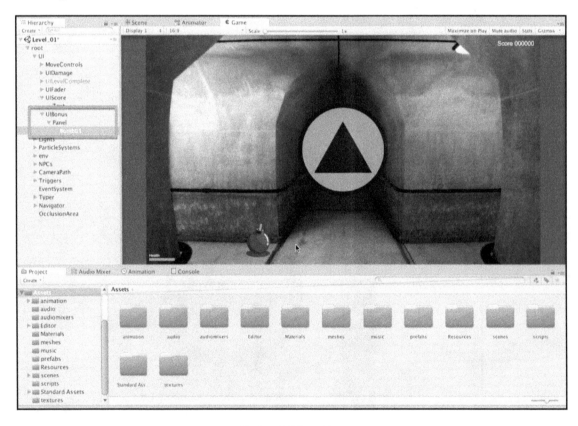

Creating an initial bonus object

Now, we could create more bonus objects by duplicating the existing ones and repositioning them wherever they're needed. However, this grows tedious quickly, especially when creating many objects. Instead, we can use a Horizontal Layout Group, which forces Unity to automatically align and position horizontal elements. Let's see how this works. Select the parent canvas object, then choose **Component | Layout | Horizontal Layout Group** to add a **Horizontal Layout Group** component to the object. Doing this may change the appearance, size or layout of the bonus graphic.

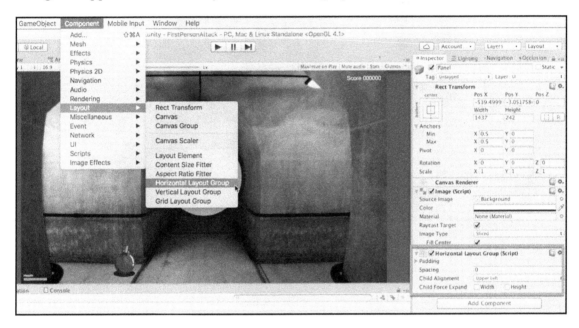

Adding a Horizontal Layout Group

After adding a **Horizontal Layout** Group to the canvas object, you can duplicate the bonus objects to add more. When you do this, all new instances are automatically aligned side by side, in a row because of the **Horizontal Layout Group**.

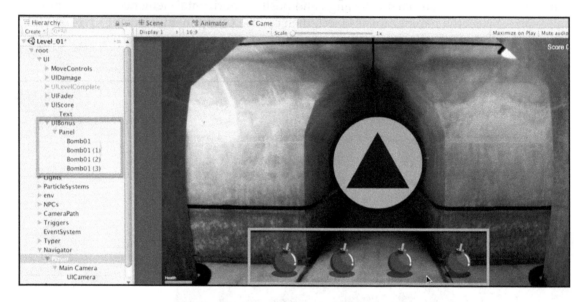

Duplicating bonus objects, aligning them in a row via the Horizontal Layout Group

The relative spacing between elements can be controlled from the **Horizontal Layout Group**. Simply increase or decrease the spacing field from the object **Inspector**. In my case, the bonus icons appear with too much pixel spacing between them. We can reduce the spacing by setting the spacing field to a negative value.

Changing the pixel spacing between UI elements

By default, the **Horizontal Layout Group** overrides the width and height settings for each element, working to accommodate the total number of elements in a row. This can often be problematic when you want specific sizes, or different sizes, for each element. You can control this, however, by adding a Layout Element component to each element in the row. To do this, select each bonus object and choose **Component | Layout | Layout Element** from the application menu. This adds a **Layout Element** component to each object.

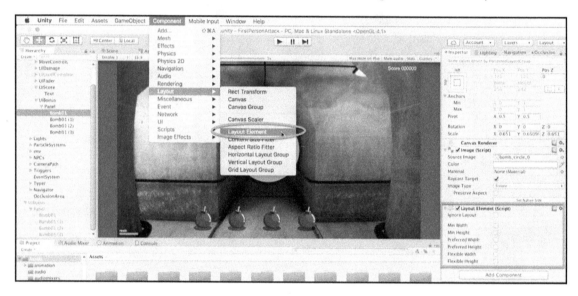

Adding a Layout Element to a bonus object, controlling the size of each element.

Next, use the minimum and preferred size fields to control the size of the bonus object. For *Dead Keys*, the bonus object is *256×265* pixels. The minimum field specifies the smallest size an element can possibly be in any circumstances and Unity will never shrink an element smaller than that size, even if more elements are added to the row and cannot fit on screen. The preferred field instead specifies the ideal size for an element whenever that size is possible, otherwise the element may be resized to smaller dimensions if it's necessary to make room for more elements.

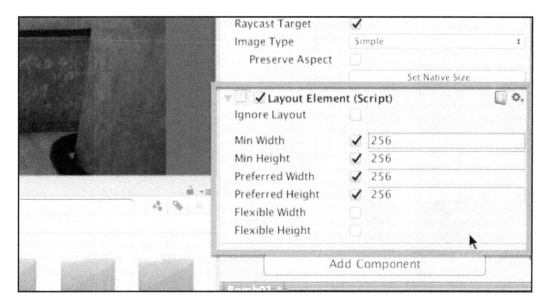

Configuring a Layout Element within a group

Now label all the bonus objects with a **BonusObject** tag (create this tag, if necessary). This is important for helping Unity quickly identify bonus objects in code at scene startup, as these should be hidden until a bonus is achieved.

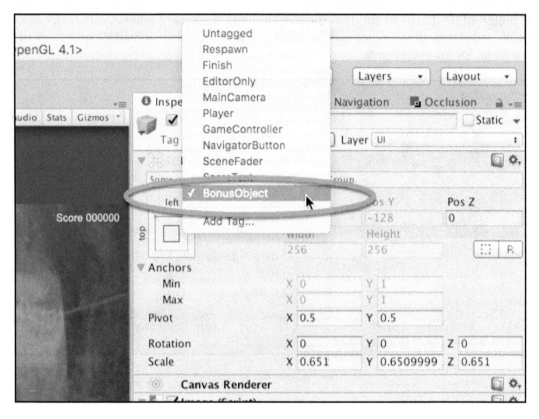

Tagging bonus objects

Next, create a UIBonus.cs script file and assign this to the canvas parent object. This script hides all bonus objects at level startup and determines whether a bonus object should be hidden. Comments are included after the following code sample:

```
using UnityEngine;
using System.Collections;

public class UIBonus : MonoBehaviour
{
    public GameObject[] BonusObjects;

    // Use this for initialization
    void Awake ()
```

```
    {
        BonusObjects = GameObject.FindGameObjectsWithTag ("BonusObject");
    }
    // Update is called once per frame
    void Update ()
    {
        ///Set bonus level
        //Hide/Show all bonus objects
        for (int i = 0; i < BonusObjects.Length; i++)
        {
            if (i < GameManager.ThisInstance.BonusLevel)
                BonusObjects [i].SetActive (true);
            else
                BonusObjects [i].SetActive (false);
        }
    }
}
```

Comments

- The `BonusObjects` array references all scene objects tagged as `BonusObject`. This will refer to one or more objects.
- The `GameManager` class, which is an overarching class that persists across scenes, maintains the variable `BonusLevel`. This is an integer determining how many bonus objects have been collected, if any.
- The `Update` function cycles through all bonus objects, and enables them depending on the size of the `BonusLevel`. This makes sense because, as additional bonus levels are reached, more bonus objects should become visible.
- The order of bonus objects in the array is irrelevant as the **Horizontal Layout Group** automatically resizes and reorders only active objects. Thus, as bonus objects become active, they'll be added and resized as needed within the Layout group.

Excellent work! We've now coded a bonus system from which specific bonus objects may be unlocked by using an integer variable `BonusLevel`. This is good, but still we don't have the functionality to actually collect a bonus in-game, even though the framework is now in place. To achieve this, we'll need a zombie to destroy.

Summary

In this chapter, we completed the player input system by creating a Typer object and implemented a range of related classes and UI elements that accompany that feature; specifically: health, damage effects, a score, and a bonus system. None of this functionality, however, links together or coheres as one yet, due mainly to the lack of enemy objects to destroy. For this reason, the next chapter focuses on zombie enemies, their intelligence, and their role as a functional part of the whole application.

5
Enemies and Artificial Intelligence

This chapter brings the *Dead Keys* project to an important developmental stage, adding a certain roundness and completeness by adding enemy characters (zombies). In creating an enemy, we'll bring together many features that we've already created, from health and damage, to combat mechanics and UI elements. Specifically, we'll build a zombie enemy that can wander the level in search of the player, then chase the player when found, and finally attack them when close enough. In addition, the player will be able to engage and attack the zombie in word-combat. To create this functionality, we'll work with **Prefabs**, **Navigation Meshes**, **Artificial Intelligence**, and **Finite State Machines**. So let's get started.

Configuring the zombie character

To start building the zombie character, all related assets (meshes, textures, and animations) should be imported and configured correctly. Import details for meshes and textures were covered in-depth in Chapter 1, *Preparation and Asset-Configuring*, but it's worth recapping the important assets here:

- **Zombie mesh**: The **zombie mesh** is a fully rigged, biped zombie, compliant with *Unity Mecanim*. This file is included in the book companion files and can be imported into the project by simply dragging and dropping into the **Project** panel. The mesh should be configured as a **Humanoid** rig type:

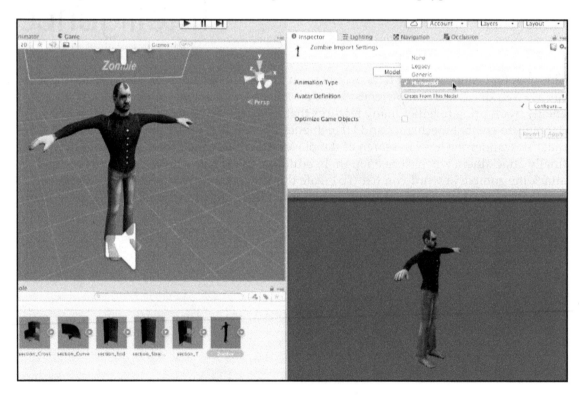

Importing and configuring a zombie mesh

- **Zombie texture**: The zombie mesh comes with an accompanying texture (`Zombie.png`). This maps to the zombie via *UV Channel 2*. This texture should be assigned to the **Albedo** slot for the zombie material:

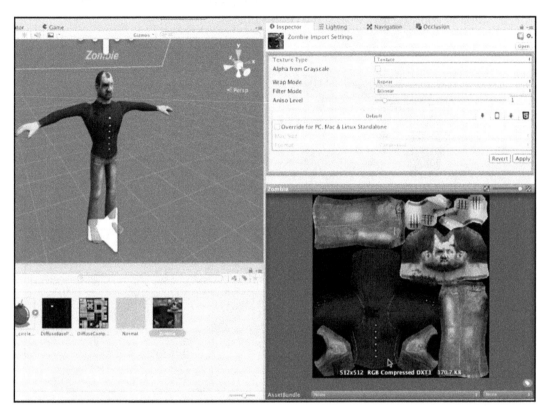

Importing a zombie texture

- **General animations**: Lastly, the zombie depends on several key character animations. These are: **Idle**, **Walk,** and **Attack**. Each of these animation files should be configured as a **Humanoid** rig, using the **Rig** tab in the object **Inspector**. Additionally, root motion may need to be corrected, preventing the zombie walking away from the center line:

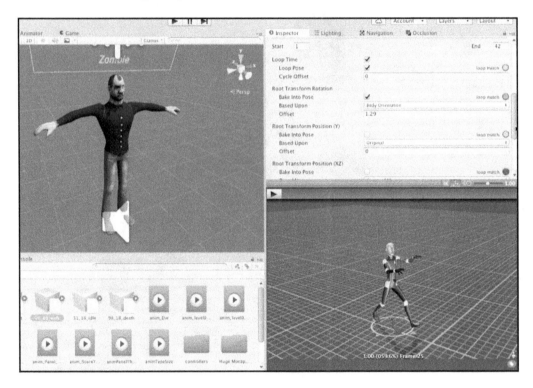

Importing character animations

 If you want to follow along step by step, the starting point for this chapter is found in the book companion files, in the folder Chapter05/Start.

Getting started with the zombie Prefab

The zombie character will appear many times throughout a level, and other levels. For this reason, we'll build one zombie in the **Viewport** and, from that, create a **Prefab**. This may be reused as many times as needed. To start, drag and drop the zombie from the **Project Panel** into the **Scene**, and set its **Scale** to 1.3 for all axes:

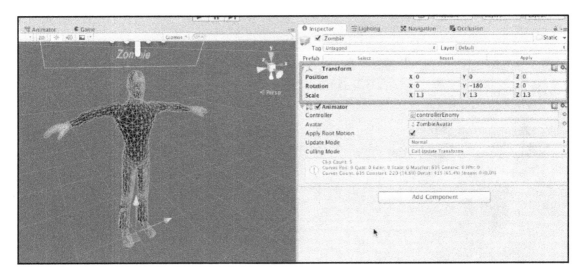

Adding a zombie character to the Scene and setting object Scale

Next, add a **Nav Mesh Agent** to the zombie, configuring it for a navigation mesh. Set the **Radius** to 0.26, fitting the **Cylinder** collider tightly to the character.

 This volume approximates the character on the navigation mesh. If it's too large, the character won't fit through tight but passable spaces; and if too small, the character will pass through impossibly narrow spaces.

Additionally, set the **Speed** to 0.6, and the **Stopping Distance** to 3. The **Stopping Distance** variable specifies how close to its destination an agent should reach before stopping:

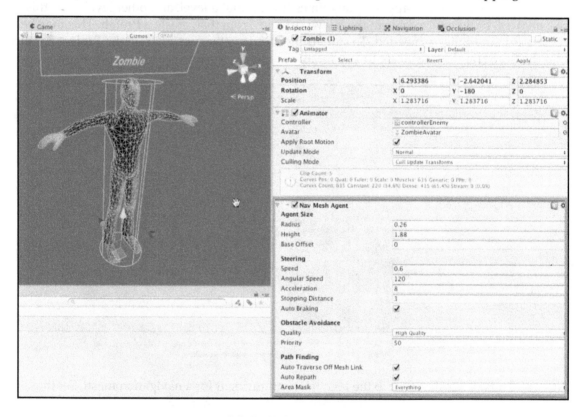

Configuring a Nav Mesh Agent component

Finally, add a **Capsule Collider** component to the zombie, making it a part of the physics system. And then add a **Health** component, coded in the previous chapter, to give the zombie a health value. This will be important for combat sequences:

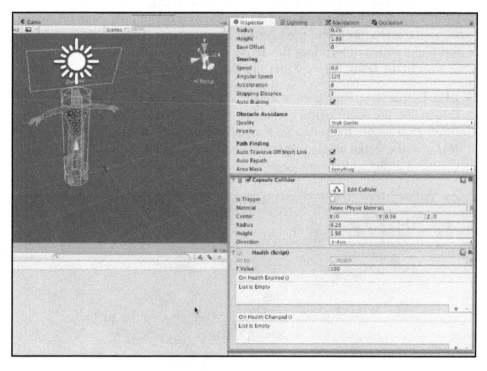

Adding a Capsule collider and Health component

Planning the zombie Artificial Intelligence

The zombie character needs intelligence, that is, the ability to take appropriate actions and responses in front of the player. Specifically, the zombie should balance actions between idling, chasing, and attacking at appropriate times. To achieve this, we'll need **Artificial Intelligence (AI)**. This essentially involves coding functionality to help the computer make good decisions under specific conditions where multiple outcomes are possible. AI (for video games) is not, however, about coding an inward consciousness or phenomenology; and it's not about replicating the workings of the human mind. Rather, it's about deciding how NPCs behave, creating the illusion or appearance of intelligence, to enhance the experience and realism for the player. For the zombie, we'll code AI by using **Finite State Machines (FSMs)**.

The FSM is essentially a decision-making structure. The simplest example of an FSM is a traffic light. This exists in only one of three possible states at any one time: red, amber, or green. The active color indicates what nearby traffic may legitimately do (for example, red means stop, and green means go). The FSM, conceptually, begins from the assumption that anything, from a traffic light to a zombie, has a finite number of behaviors or modes, and that only one of these may apply to the agent at any one time. The decision-making structure and logic, which determines the active state, is the FSM. When we think about a zombie character in the level, we may identify three possible states. These are as follows:

- **Idle:** In this state, the agent is standing still, playing an Idle animation on loop. In this mode, the agent neither wanders nor attacks, but they have the potential to move into action; the potential to "come alive". Idle is a constant state of standby. It is also the initial or default state for all NPCs in *Dead Keys*. The default state could be different for your game

Idle state

- **Chase**: If, and when, an agent sees the player character, and when the player is also beyond the attack range, the agent enters Chase mode. In this mode, the agent continually moves towards the player using the navmesh, intending to get closer for an attack:

Walk state

- **Attack**: After chasing the player, an agent may enter the attack range. That is, a measured distance or radius from the player character inside which an enemy agent can successfully attack and inflict damage. On entering the attack range, the enemy will repeatedly launch attacks. If the enemy leaves the attack range (for example, if the player runs away), the enemy will revert back to chase mode:

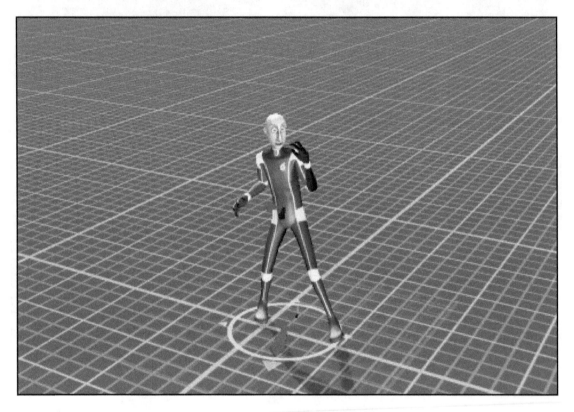

Attack state

- **Death**: If the agent health falls to zero or below, it will die. In this state, the agent does nothing but play a death animation, fall to the floor and become inactive. The Death state is, in many respects, a dead-end state: once entered it has no route to any other state:

Death state

Based on these three states, we can start coding an enemy class (`AIEnemy.cs`) and FSM, as follows:

```
//----------------------------------
using UnityEngine;
using System.Collections;
using UnityEngine.EventSystems;
using UnityEngine.Events;
using UnityEngine.UI;
//----------------------------------
```

```
public class AIEnemy : MonoBehaviour
{
    //-----------------------------------
    public enum AISTATE {IDLE = 0, CHASE = 1, ATTACK = 2, DEAD=3};

    [SerializeField]
    private AISTATE mActiveState = AISTATE.IDLE;
}
```

Comments

- The `AIEnemy` class encapsulates all enemy behaviors, controlled by an FSM
- To start coding an FSM, all possible states are encoded into an enumeration: Idle, Chase, Attack, and Dead
- The `mActiveState` variable represents the currently active state right now, within the FSM

Developing state structure

The zombie character has four main states, and therefore the zombie FSM must decide which state should be activated at any time, and which logic should govern the relationship between states. To start implementing the FSM, we'll write the following code, to create a state change function which sets the FSM to a specified state from any of the four available states. Comments follow the code:

```
//-----------------------------------
using UnityEngine;
using System.Collections;
using UnityEngine.EventSystems;
using UnityEngine.Events;
using UnityEngine.UI;
//-----------------------------------
public class AIEnemy : MonoBehaviour
{
    //-----------------------------------
    public enum AISTATE {IDLE = 0, CHASE = 1, ATTACK = 2, DEAD = 3};

    [SerializeField]
    private AISTATE mActiveState = AISTATE.IDLE;

    public AISTATE ActiveState
    {
```

```
    get{ return mActiveState; }
    set
    {
        //Stops any running coroutines, if there are any
        StopAllCoroutines ();
        mActiveState = value;

        //Run coroutine associated with active state
        switch(mActiveState)
        {
        case AISTATE.IDLE:
            StartCoroutine (StateIdle());
            break;

        case AISTATE.CHASE:
            StartCoroutine (StateChase());
            break;

        case AISTATE.ATTACK:
            StartCoroutine (StateAttack());
            break;

        case AISTATE.DEAD:
            StartCoroutine (StateDead());
            break;
        }

        //Invoke state change event
        OnStateChanged.Invoke ();
    }
}

//Events called on FSM changes
public UnityEvent OnStateChanged;
//-----------------------------------
public IEnumerator StateIdle()
{
    //ADD BODY HERE
    yield break;
}
//-----------------------------------
public IEnumerator StateChase()
{
    //ADD BODY HERE
    yield break;
}
//-----------------------------------
public IEnumerator StateAttack()
```

```
    {
        //ADD BODY HERE
        yield break;
    }
    //-----------------------------------
    public IEnumerator StateDead()
    {
        //ADD BODY HERE
        yield break;
    }
    //-----------------------------------
}
```

Comments

- The C# `ActiveState` property sets and gets the private variable `mActiveState`. This expresses the current state of the FSM.
- Each of the four states (Idle, Chase, Attack, and Dead) correspond to a unique and associated `Coroutine` in the class. Right now, the `coroutine` is a placeholder. But when implemented, each `Coroutine` runs on its own cycle or update loop for as long as a state is active.
- The event `OnStateChanged` is invoked whenever a state is changed.
- The `set` function for the `ActiveState` property updates the current state, stops any existing state by stopping all `Coroutines`, and invokes the `OnStateChanged` event, allowing Object Inspector level control for state change events, if needed.

Developing an NPC Animator Controller

The FSM must be complemented by a Mecanim animator graph, as each state involves a unique animation and each one should play at the appropriate time. You create a new animator asset simply by right-clicking inside the Project Panel and choosing **Create |Animator Controller** from the context menu. Name this `controllerEnemy`.

Be sure to add this as an animator component to the zombie in the scene by dragging and dropping the asset from the Project Panel to the mesh in the Scene Viewport:

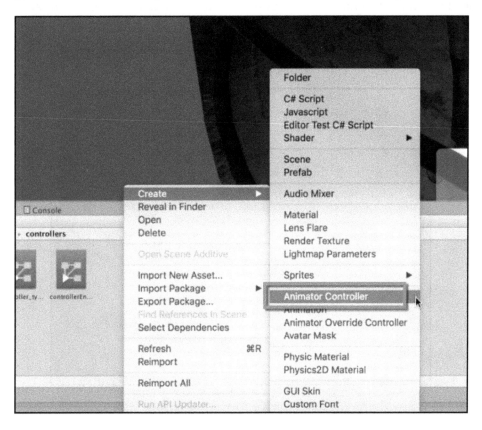

Creating a new Animator Controller for the zombie NPC

First, create a new animator integer parameter, and name this `AnimState`. This parameter represents the currently active state of the zombie in the graph. Its values will match exactly the value of the `AIState` enum, coded for the `AIEnemy` class: 0 = `Idle`, 1 = `Chase`, 2 = `Attack`, and 3 = `Dead`:

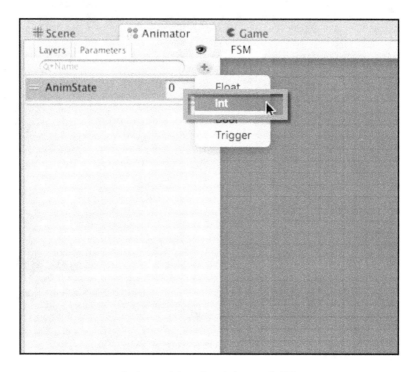

Creating a new Animator Controller for the zombie NPC

Now for the starting state, create a new Empty state by right-clicking in the graph and navigating to **Create** |**Empty** from the context menu. Name the state **Start**, and make it the default state (if it's not already) by right-clicking the state and choosing **Set as Layer Default State** from the context menu. This ensures the zombie *does nothing* when the level begins, until we explicitly force it into a state:

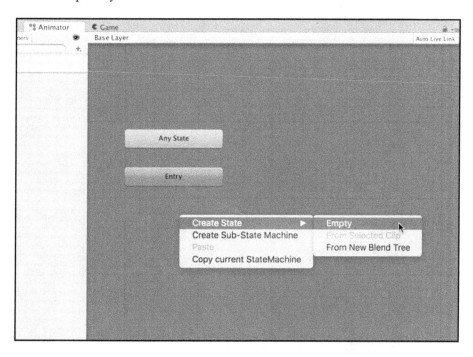

Creating the zombie Start state

Now drag and drop each state-animation clip from the Project Panel into the animator graph, to create a new animation node for each state; one each for idle, chase, attack and death. These animations are included in the book's companion files:

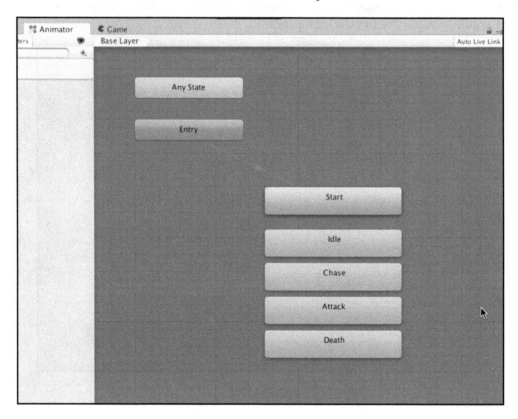

Adding zombie Animation-States to the graph

Remember, the animator graph features three default nodes: **Entry, Any State**, and **Exit**. These nodes are auto-created with the animator graph. The **Entry** node is invoked when the animator graph (state machine) begins, and any connected nodes are initiated too. The **Any State** node effectively links to all other nodes and initiates those whenever the transition conditions (connections) are satisfied. The **Exit** node is initiated on leaving any sub-state machine (this node is useful for creating nested animator graphs). For more information on these states and transitions, see the online Unity documentation at:
`https://docs.unity3d.com/Manual/StateMachineTransitions.html`

Once the states have been added to the graph they must be wired together logically and consistently using the state machine code. Specifically, the zombie may transition from **Idle** to **Chase**, from **Chase** to **Attack**, back from **Attack** to **Chase**, and from **Chase** to **Idle**. The **Death** state may, potentially, be invoked from anywhere. First, let's wire the connection from **Start** to **Idle** which happens when the **AnimState** parameter is equal to 0:

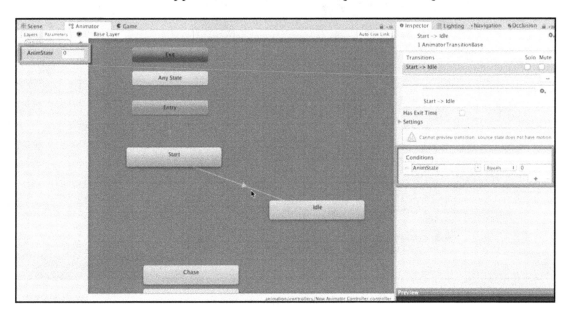

Setting the Idle state from the Start node

The **Idle** state simply plays a standing animation. However, it doesn't last long enough in itself and doesn't loop as well as I want. We can easily fix this type of looping problem directly from the **Animator**, without changing any frames in the animation. We can do this simply by playing the animation forwards once and then playing it again backwards, looping back and forth with a ping-pong effect. Select the **Idle** node in the graph and then duplicate it, and set the **Speed** to −1 to play backwards.

Now the two duplicates can be wired together to play continuously:

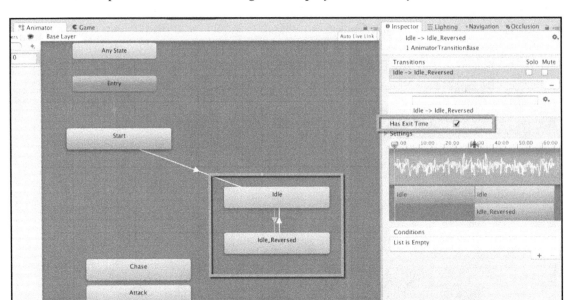

Looping an Idle through a ping-pong sequence

The Idle state (whether it's playing forwards or backwards) may transition to the Chase state (usually when the player's character appears). Conversely, the Chase state may transition back to the **Idle** state. This can be configured in the graph with transitions that depend on the **AnimState** field being equal to 1 (for **Chase**) and 0 (for **Idle**).

Be sure to uncheck the **Has Exit Time** checkbox for each transition, as these force the state to change immediately from one to another, as opposed to waiting for the animation to complete before changing:

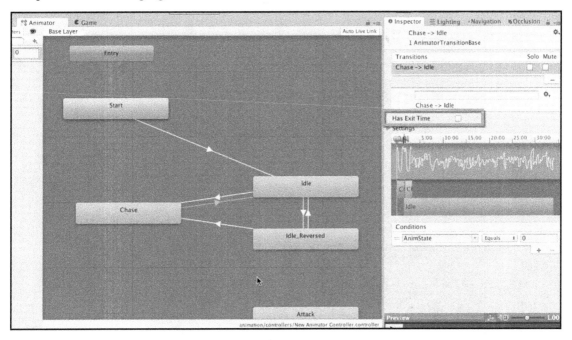

Creating connections between Idle and Chase

The **Chase** state can also change to the Attack state, and the **Attack** state can change to the **Chase** state. Again, the change depends on the **AnimState** parameter:

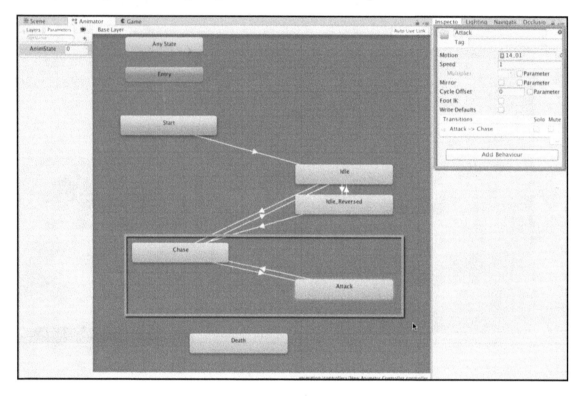

Creating a transition between Chase and Attack

Any State should have a connection to **Death**. This makes sense because the enemy AI could be in Idle, Chase, or Attack and, effectively, be killed. Create a transition from **Any State** to **Death**, based on the `AnimState` parameter being equal to 3:

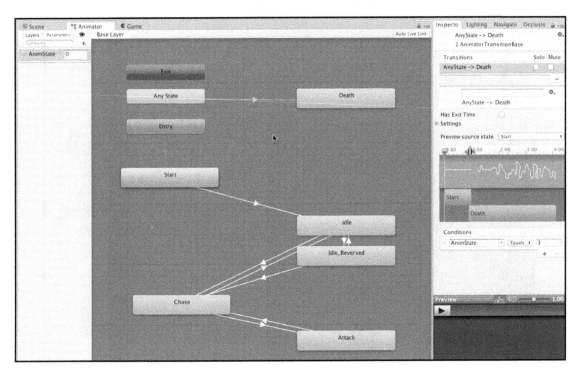

Building the Death state in the animator graph

The animator graph is now fully configured to support the FSM for the zombie character. **Save** the animator asset and associate it to an **Animator** component for the zombie, if you've not already done so. The next step is to return to the AIEnemy script to code the remaining AI for the zombie:

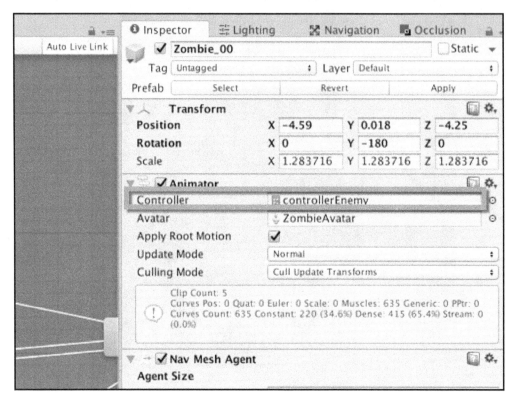

Configuring the zombie animator

Developing the Idle state

The Idle state is ultimately the starting state for a zombie, and a passive state. Normally, an NPC in Idle will stand around and just look about. It's a state from which action may begin. For *Dead Keys*, the zombies remain in Idle until instructed to change, based on camera movement and the position of the player:

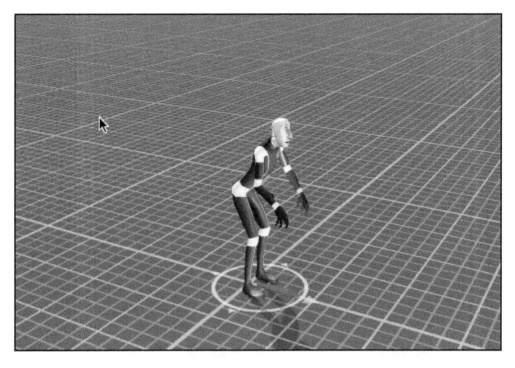

Idle state

As the player enters the Chase range of an NPC, the NPC comes to life. In many games, a deciding factor will be line of sight. The enemy chases, or pursues the player as they enter their line of sight. However, for *Dead Keys*, this is unnecessary because camera movement, as the player progresses from one point to the next, determines whether an NPC moves into view. For this reason, the StateIdle coroutine will remain almost empty. However, the SetInteger function will be called to the set the animator integer parameter:

```
public IEnumerator StateIdle()
{
    //Run idle animation
    ThisAnimator.SetInteger("AnimState", (int) ActiveState);

    //While in idle state
    while(ActiveState == AISTATE.IDLE)
    {
        yield return null;
    }
}
```

Although the `StateIdle` coroutine represents everything needed for an NPC in *Dead Keys*, let's take a small detour and consider an NPC for other uses and games. What about cases where NPC states rest on whether the player can be seen (line of sight)? An example is when a NPC chases the player because the player has been seen. Consider the following sample code for an enemy object, with a **Nav Mesh Agent** attached. This code finds a player object in the level and determines whether it can be seen. Comments follow:

```
using UnityEngine;
using System.Collections;
//----------------------------------------------------
public class Enemy_Script : MonoBehaviour
{
    private Transform Player = null;

    //----------------------------------------------------
    // Use this for initialization
    void Start () {
        Player = GameObject.FindGameObjectWithTag ("Player").transform;
    }
    //----------------------------------------------------
    // Update is called once per frame
    void Update () {
        CanSeeAgent (transform, Player, 10f, 30f);
    }
    //----------------------------------------------------
    //Function to determine if enemy can see player
    //Agent = The enemy character
    //Target = The player who may be seen
    //NearDistance = How close player must be within field of view
    //FieldofView = Viewing angle enemy must have to be classified as
facing player
    public static bool CanSeeAgent (Transform Agent, Transform Target, float
NearDistance, float FieldofView)
    {
        //Determine if player is within field of view
        Vector3 VecDiff = Target.position - Agent.position;

        //Get angle between look at direction and player direction from
enemy
        float Dot = Vector3.Dot (Agent.forward.normalized,
VecDiff.normalized);

        //If player is behind enemy, then exit
            if(Dot < 0) return false;

        //If player is not within viewing angle then exit
                if(FieldofView < (90f - Dot * 90f)) return false;
```

```
        //Enemy is facing player. Is player within range and is there a
direct line?
        NavMeshHit Hit;
        if(!NavMesh.Raycast(Agent.position, Target.position, out Hit,-1))
        {
            //Has direct line, is within range?
            if((Agent.position - Target.position).sqrMagnitude >
NearDistance) return false;
            //Can be seen (the enemy (Agent) can see the player (Target)
                    return true;
        }

        return false;
    }
    //-------------------------------------------------
    //Draw forward vector of enemy for line of sight
    void OnDrawGizmos()
    {
        Gizmos.color = Color.red;
        Vector3 direction = transform.TransformDirection(Vector3.forward) *
5;
        Gizmos.DrawRay(transform.position, direction);
    }
    //-------------------------------------------------
}
//-------------------------------------------------
```

Comments

- The `CanSeeAgent` function returns true or false indicating whether a specific NPC (represented by the `Transform` component) can see the player (an object tagged as player). True means the player can be seen. False means the player cannot be seen.
- There are several steps in determining player visibility. The first is to establish a field of view for the NPC. That is, an angle threshold either side of the forward vector, representing the angular limits of view.
- To determine whether the player is within the angular limits, the `Vector3.Dot` function is used. This function takes two vectors as input and returns information about the angle between the vectors, assuming they were laid out from a common starting point.

- If `Vector3.Dot` returns −1 then the two vectors are pointing in exactly the opposite direction. The closer a value moves towards −1, the further apart the vectors are in orientation.
- If `Vector3.Dot` returns 1, then both vectors are pointing in the same direction. The closer a value moves towards 1, the closer together the vectors are in orientation.
- If `Vector3.Dot` returns 0, then the two input vectors are perpendicular. That is, intersecting at 90 degrees to each other.
- `Vector3.Dot` is therefore used to determine whether the angle between two vectors is within the field of view. If so, the player can potentially be seen. But, there are additional considerations to explore before we can finally conclude that the player is seen by the NPC.
- In addition to the player being in the NPC's field of view, he or she must be within a specified radius from the NPC. This is because the NPC has a specific horizon or distance beyond which they cannot see. Even when the player is within the field of view, they must also be close enough to be seen. Additionally, there cannot be intervening obstacles (like walls) between the player and NPC. To solve this, the `Raycast` function of the `NavMeshAgent` is used. This determines whether an unbroken line can be traced between two points, without its leaving the navmesh. If so, a line of sight exists between the NPC and player. Soon we'll code the functionality to change between states!

 A sample line of sight project is included in the course companion files, in the folder `Chapter05/LineofSight`.

Developing the Chase state

The Chase state occurs when the NPC is following and moving towards the player. In *Dead Keys*, this happens whenever the scene camera moves into a trigger volume or area where zombies are waiting:

Chase state

The following is the Chase coroutine (for the Chase state). It contains some interesting features, considered further in the comments section:

```
//-------------------------------------
public IEnumerator StateChase()
{

    //Run chase animation
    ThisAnimator.SetInteger("AnimState", (int) ActiveState);

    //Set destination
    ThisAgent.SetDestination (PlayerTransform.position);

    //Wait until path is calculated
    while (!ThisAgent.hasPath)
        yield return null;

    //While in chase state
    while(ActiveState == AISTATE.CHASE)
    {
```

```
        if (ThisAgent.remainingDistance <= ThisAgent.stoppingDistance)
        {
            ThisAgent.Stop ();
            yield return null;
            ActiveState = AISTATE.ATTACK;
            yield break;
        }

        yield return null;
    }
}
//-------------------------------------
```

Comments

- The `StateChase` corotuine begins by setting the `AnimState` integer parameter in Mecanim, for playing the walk/chase animation. This is configured to play on a loop.
- Next, the **Nav Mesh Agent** component is used to set the destination for the zombie. This will be the player location. This causes the zombie to move, walking towards the player, using the navigation mesh.
- After setting the navmesh destination, the coroutine waits for the `NavMeshAgent` to fully calculate the zombie's path. The calculation often happens quickly, but it runs asynchronously and can take more than one frame. That is, the path is not necessarily fully calculated immediately after calling `SetDestination`.
- Next, the couroutine loops continuously, frame by frame, until the `remainingDistance` (the distance left to travel) is less than the `stoppingDistance` (the distance for stopping). In other words, the zombie should continue travelling in Chase mode until it reaches the destination.
- On reaching the player, the state changes to Attack.

Developing the Attack state and more

The Attack state is entered when the zombie arrives within the attack distance to the player. During this state, the zombie repeatedly attacks the player until either the player dies or the player leaves the attack distance:

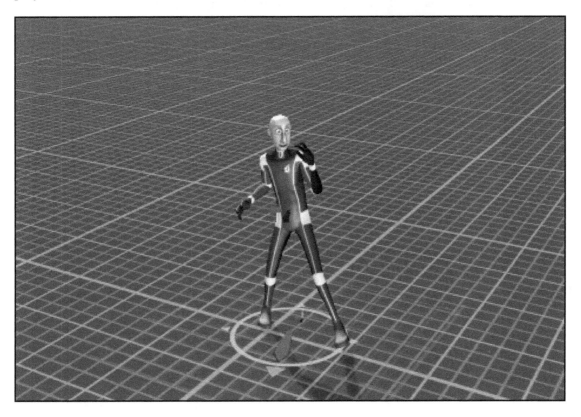

Attack state

Consider the following code:

```
//-----------------------------------
public IEnumerator StateAttack()
{
    //Run attack animation
    ThisAnimator.SetInteger("AnimState", (int) ActiveState);

    //While in idle state
    while(ActiveState == AISTATE.ATTACK)
    {
        //Look at player
        Vector3 PlanarPosition = new
Vector3(PlayerTransform.position.x, ThisTransform.position.y,
PlayerTransform.position.z);
        ThisTransform.LookAt(PlanarPosition, ThisTransform.up);

        //Get distance between enemy and player
        float Distance = Vector3.Distance(PlayerTransform.position,
ThisTransform.position);

        if (Distance > ThisAgent.stoppingDistance*2f)
        {
            ThisAgent.Stop ();
            yield return null;
            ActiveState = AISTATE.CHASE;
            yield break;
        }

        yield return null;
    }
}
//-----------------------------------
```

Comments

- The `StateAttack` coroutine begins and remains throughout the Attack state.
- The function `Transform.LookAt` is called during the coroutine loop, on each frame, to reorient the enemy to always face the player character.
- If the enemy falls outside the Attack distance, he reverts to the Chase state to catch up with the player. The distance between player and enemy is determined by the `Vector3.Distance` function.
- If the zombie reaches the `StoppingDistance` from the player, they stop moving and continue to attack.

The Attack state, as it stands, is not sufficient to actually inflict damage on the player. The `StateAttack` coroutine, for example, contains no code to interact with the player character and therefore causes no damage for each punch or attack. To achieve this, we'll use **Animation Events**. That is, we'll invoke player attack functions from the animation keyframes themselves. To get started, let's add some new class variables and a function, `DealDamage`. This function inflicts damage on the player, by an `AttackDamage` amount, representing the amount of damage inflicted by the enemy. The class variables to add are as follows:

```
//Reference to player transform
private Transform PlayerTransform = null;
//Player health component
private Health PlayerHealth = null;
//Amount of damage to deal on attack
public int AttackDamage = 10;
```

The `DealDamage` function is a short, public function written as follows:

```
//------------------------------------
//Deal damage to the player
public void DealDamage()
{
    PlayerHealth.Value -= AttackDamage;
    HitSound.Play ();
}
//------------------------------------
```

Now we've added the necessary functionality to the `AIEnemy` class, let's configure the animation clip asset for Attack state. Specifically, we need to configure the attack animation for synchronizing enemy punches (actions) with punch sounds. Select the **Attack** animation in the Project Panel, and switch to the **Animator** tab in the object Inspector:

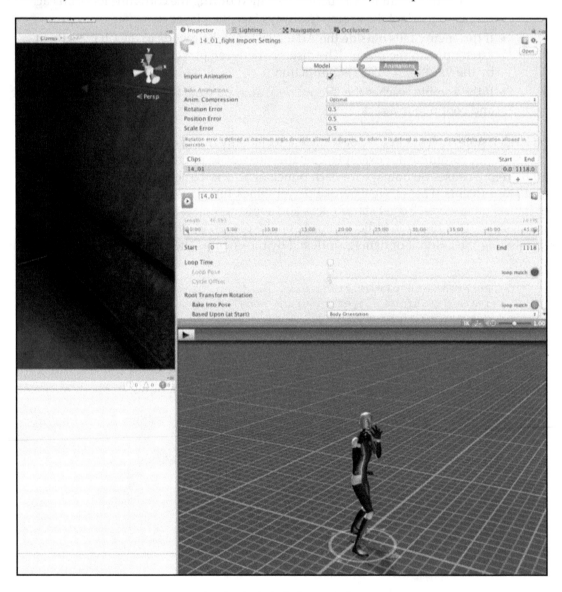

Accessing animation data for the attack animation

Next, expand the Events section, to reveal the attack animation timeline, representing the complete attack animation. From here, we should click and drag the red time slider from the **Animation** preview window to preview key frames:

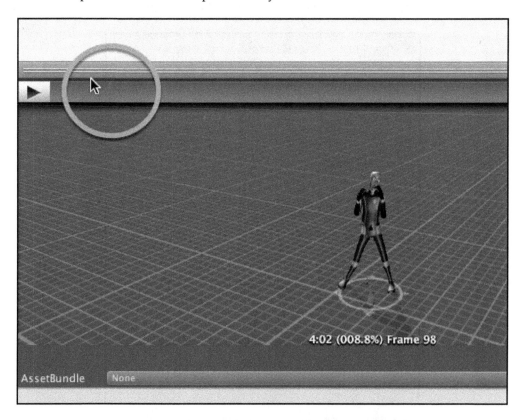

Previewing attack key frames

Expand the **Events** section to add animation events. Use the time-slider from the preview window to find each key frame where a zombie punch lands (strikes) the player. This is where a punch sound should play. To achieve this, an event should be added for each punch frame. To add an animation event, click the **Add Event** button from the Inspector:

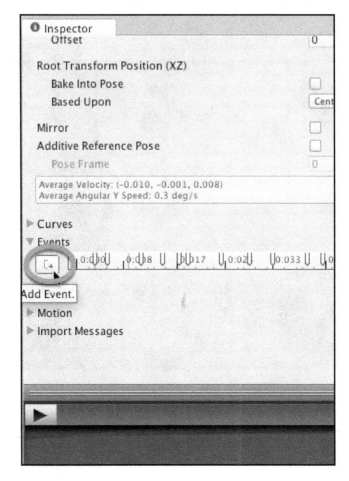

Creating animation events

For each event, run the **DealDamage** function. The name is case-sensitive and should match the function name as specified in the `AIEnemy` class:

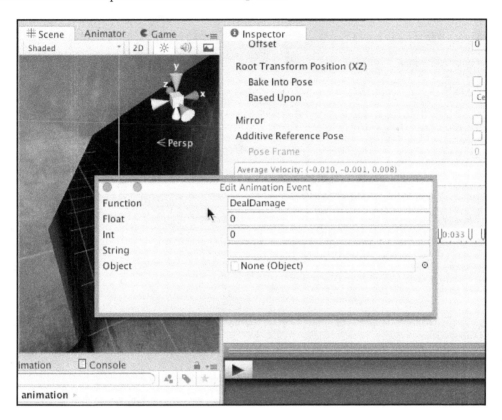

Detailing animation events

Repeat this process for each punch event in the timeline, adding a single and unique event calling the **DealDamage** keyframe:

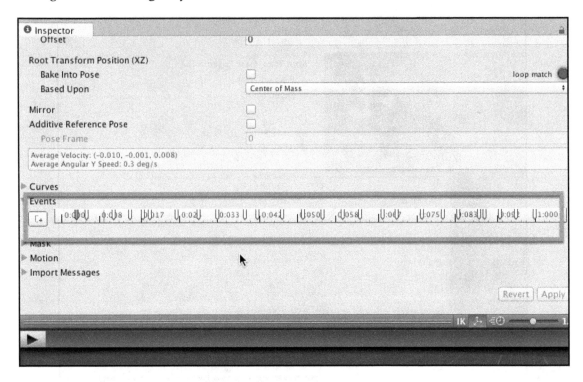

Creating an animation event for each punch key frame

For the **DealDamage** function to execute successfully, the zombie also needs a fully configured **Audio Source** component associated with the punch or damage sound. Add the **Audio Source** component by navigating to **Component | Audio | AudioSource** from the application menu:

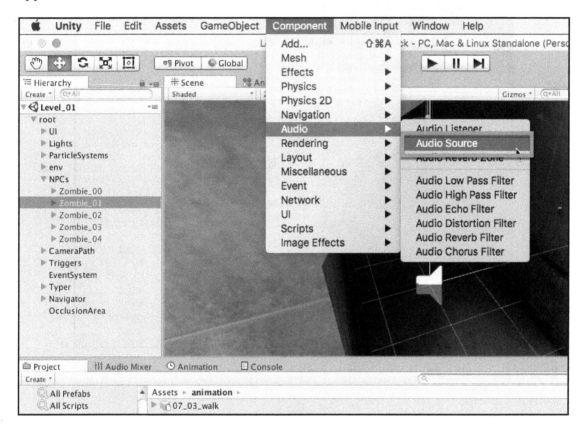

Adding an Audio Source component

Then drag and drop the punch sound into the **AudioClip** slot, making sure to deactivate both the **PlayOnAwake** and **Loop** checkboxes. The **AudioClip** should only play when the zombie deals damage:

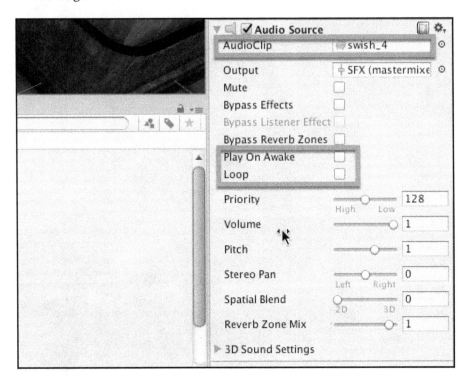

Configuring the zombie Audio Source component

Now let's create a zombie Prefab. This is a great idea because, as mentioned, a Prefab is a special asset type allowing us to easily package and reuse objects from our scene anywhere else. Zombies should feature many times in a single level, as well as across multiple levels. To create a zombie Prefab, simply drag and drop the zombie from the **Hierarchy Panel** into the Project Panel (into a `prefab` folder):

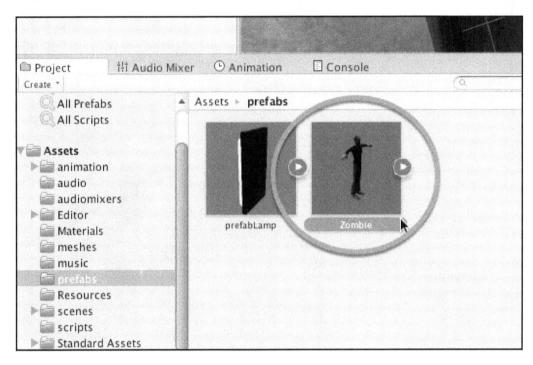

Creating a zombie Prefab

If you later change a single instance of the zombie in a scene and then want to apply the change to all other instances, you can do this by updating the prefab. To achieve this, select the zombie you have changed, then navigate to **GameObject|Apply Changes to Prefab** in the application menu:

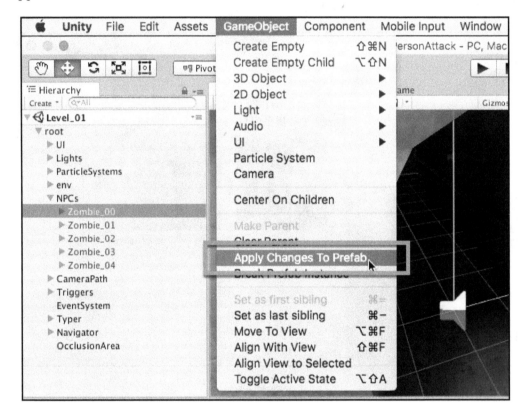

Applying changes to the Prefab

Developing the Dead state

After the zombie enters the Death state within the animator graph, it remains there and cannot revert to any other state. The animator graph simply suspends, without linking to any new state:

Death state

The code is therefore pretty simple:

```
//------------------------------------
public IEnumerator StateDead()
{
    //Run dead animation
    ThisAnimator.SetInteger("AnimState", (int) ActiveState);

    //While in idle state
    while(ActiveState == AISTATE.DEAD)
    {
        yield return null;
    }
}
//------------------------------------
```

Zombies and text input

In addition to the FSM for zombie behaviors, like Idle, Chase, Attack, and Death, zombies respond to player input. Specifically, the player may attack by typing letters on the keyboard, matching the complete word above the zombie's head:

Attacking zombie with typed text input

To achieve this, we must firstly display a word above the zombie's head, then keep track of the word being typed, and finally determine whether a match has been made. We already have some code to achieve much of this, but we should now link it specifically to the zombie character. Let's start by creating a text object that hovers above the zombie's head. Select the zombie NPC and expand its hierarchy in the **Hierarchy** panel. Select the **Armature** object and locate the **head** bone. This represents an empty game object used to move the character head during animation. Any object attached to the head bone therefore moves with the character head:

Selecting the character head bone

Now right-click the selected head bone, and from the context menu navigate to **UI** | **Canvas**. This creates a new UI canvas object that is a child of the **head** bone. Alternatively, you can navigate to **GameObject** | **UI** | **Canvas** from the application menu, and then drag-and-drop the newly created **Canvas** to the **head** bone:

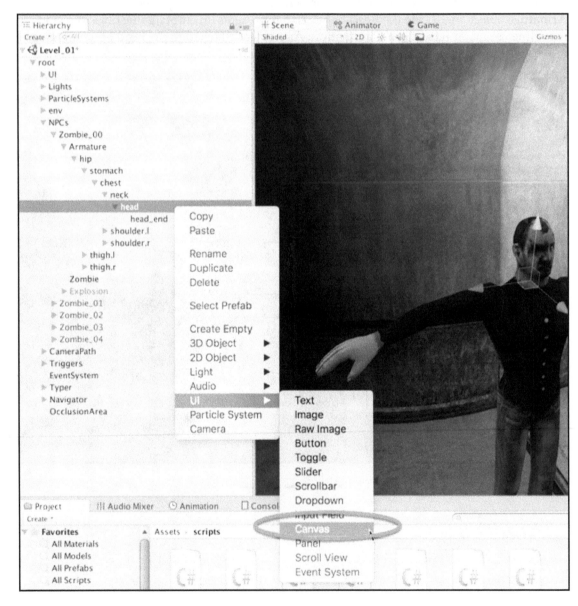

Creating a Canvas object as a child of the head bone

By default, a UI Canvas object is configured with a render mode of **Screen Space – Overlay**. This means the interface will always appear on top of everything else in 2D screen space. For the head text, however, we'll need a **World Space** UI element. That is, a UI object existing as a 2D object in a 3D world (with its own position, rotation, and scale), as opposed to a flat object aligned in screen space. After selecting a **World Space Render Mode**, you'll need to select a camera for rendering the element. For our scene, choose the **Main Camera**:

Creating a Canvas object as a child of the head bone

Next, create a **Text** object as a child of the **World Space** canvas, simply by right-clicking the **Canvas** object in the **Hierarchy** panel and navigating to **UI** | **Text** from the context menu. Assign the text a yellow color to attract attention, and set the **Font Size** to **20**. Ensure **Rich Text** is enabled, to allow for font color changes and other formatting effects, to allow for text effects while the user is typing. In addition, change the text-alignment to both vertical and horizontal center:

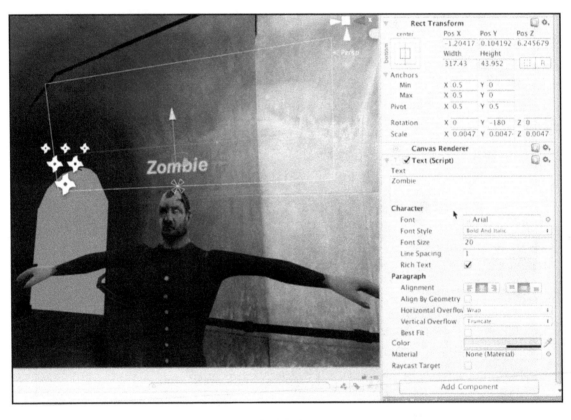

Creating head text

The text object, though existing in world space above the zombie head, should always face the camera wherever it is located. This is to prevent the text from being shown at grazing angles, or from behind, where it becomes difficult to read. The player must always be able to see the text to enter the right combination of letters. To achieve this, we'll need to create a short but important script (CameraFacing), which should be attached to the text (and any other object) that must always face the camera. The following is the featured code:

```
//-------------------------------------
using UnityEngine;
using System.Collections;
//-------------------------------------
public class CameraFacing : MonoBehaviour
{
    //-------------------------------------
    //Reference to local transform
    private Transform ThisTransform = null;
    //-------------------------------------
    // Use this for initialization
    void Awake ()
    {
        ThisTransform = GetComponent<Transform> ();
    }
    //-------------------------------------
    // Update is called once per frame
    void LateUpdate ()
    {
        ThisTransform.LookAt (Camera.main.transform);
    }
    //-------------------------------------
}
```

The `CameraFacing` script should be attached specifically to the Canvas object:

Attaching the CameraFacing script to the zombie character

Now we must refine the `EnemyAI` script further to select a word from the word list, at random, for the zombie character when the level begins. In addition, once the word is selected from the list, we'll update the zombie text to show the selected word. This is achieved by the `UpdateText` function. Consider the following code, for both the `Start` function and the `UpdateText` function, included in the `EnemyAI` script:

```
//---------------------------------------
void Start()
{
    //Set active state
    ActiveState = mActiveState;

    //Get random word
    AssocWord = WordList.ThisInstance.GetRandomWord();

    UpdateText();
```

```
    }
    //-----------------------------------
    public void UpdateText ()
    {
        //Build UI String
        NameTextComp.text = "<color=red>" + MatchedWord + "</color>" +
AssocWord.Substring(MatchedWord.Length,AssocWord.Length-
MatchedWord.Length);
    }
    //-----------------------------------
```

Comments

- The `Start` function uses the `WordList` class to select a word at random from the word list. This list is loaded from a text file. The selected word is stored in the string variable `AssocWord` (meaning Associated Word).

- Next, the `UpdateText` function simply displays the selected word, from the `WordList`, in the text object attached to the zombie head. This function should be called whenever the zombie text changes. The `MatchedWord` variable, as we'll see, determines how much of the associated word has been successfully typed by the player:

Stylizing the enemy text

The `UpdateText` function uses the **Rich Text** functionality in Unity to stylize the displayed text. Specifically, all typed letters in the associated word are shown in red, while all untyped letters remain in yellow. This is achieved by inserting HTML style tags within the string itself. When **Rich Text** is enabled for the text field, all HTML style tags are removed and replaced with corresponding stylizations. Unity supports the following tag types: <b> for bold, <i> for italic, <size> for font size, and <color> for font color. More information on **Rich Text** can be found online at the Unity documentation at https://docs.unity3d.com/Manual/StyledText.html.

Zombies and the Typer class

We've now configured the zombie to display the selected word, and also to add text stylizations based on player input. However, we still haven't linked player input through the `Typer` class (coded in the previous chapter) with the zombie NPC. Let's do this now by adding a new function to the `EnemyAI` class, namely `UpdateTypedWord`. This function compares the typed word with the associated word to determine the extent of a match. The purpose is twofold, firstly, to generate the `MatchedWord` string, for highlighting the typed portion of the `Associated Word`; and secondly, to fire a word matched event (`OnTypingMatched`), which causes the zombie to die. Consider the following code:

```
//-----------------------------------
public void UpdateTypedWord()
{
    //If not chasing or attacking, then ignore
    if(ActiveState != AISTATE.CHASE && ActiveState != AISTATE.ATTACK)
        return;

    MatchedWord = WordList.CompareWords (Typer.TypedWord, AssocWord);

    //Check for typing match
    if (MatchedWord.Length != AssocWord.Length)
        return;

    if (MatchedWord.Equals (AssocWord))
        OnTypingMatched.Invoke (); //Match found. Invoke matched event
}
//-----------------------------------
```

Comments

- The `UpdateTypedWord` function starts by determining the zombie state, as player typing and combat only applies when the zombie is chasing or attacking.
- Next, the `CompareWords` function determines the extent of the match, if any, between the typed word and the associated word. This function is part of the `WordList` class, coded in the previous chapter. It returns a string representing the amount of match between the typed string and the associated word. If there is no match, the string length will be 0. If there is a partial match, the string length will be > 0 but less than the associated word length. There is a complete match when the associated word length and the typed-string length are identical.
- When a match is detected, the `OnTypingMatched` event is invoked. This is a Unity Event on the zombie character, and this should initiate the zombie death sequence.

To initiate the death sequence from the object Inspector (in the `OnTypingMatched` event), we'll need a public `Die` function. This is important because only public functions can be launched as actions, inside Unity Events, from the object Inspector. Let's look at the code for this, as follows:

```
//-------------------------------------
public void Die()
{
    //Update Game Score
    GameManager.ThisInstance.Score += ScorePoints;
    ScoreText.OnScoreChange.Invoke ();

    //Calculate Bonus, if achieved
    float LettersPerSecond = AssocWord.Length / Typer.ElapsedTime;

    //If we beat best times, then get bonus
    if (LettersPerSecond < Typer.RecordLettersPerSecond)
    {
        //Bonus achieved
        ++GameManager.ThisInstance.BonusLevel;
    }

    ActiveState = AISTATE.DEAD;
    --ActiveEnemies;

    //Reset matched word
    MatchedWord = string.Empty;

    //Update Navigator
```

```
        Navigator.ThisInstance.EnemyDie.Invoke();
    }
    //------------------------------------
```

Comments

- The `Die` function starts by incrementing the player score by the `ScorePoints` variable. This is an integer property and represents the number of points achieved for killing the enemy.
- The game then determines if a bonus should be unlocked, because a new record has been set by typing the full word (total number of letters) in the fastest time.
- In addition, the `ActiveEnemies` field is a static integer property. Being static it is, in effect, shared across all instances. It represents the total number of active enemies in the level. That is, the total number of enemies who are either searching, chasing, or attacking the player right now and, thus, who can be dispatched through typing combat.
- As the enemy is destroyed, the `ActiveEnemies` field is decremented. If this value falls to 0, the in-game camera can move forwards to a new destination.
- The camera `Navigator` class is notified of each enemy death through the `EnemyDie` event.

Now we can configure the zombie for a death event through the object Inspector event interface. Select the zombie, and from the `OnTypingMatched` field, call the `Die` function and enable an explosion particle:

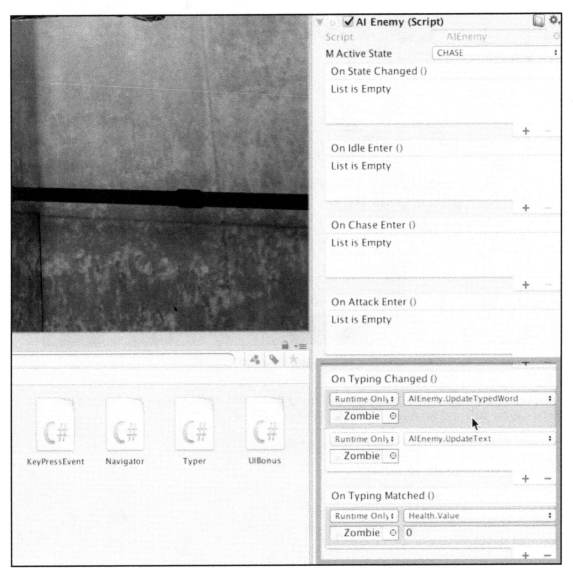

Configuring the zombie typing matched event

The explosion system is included in the standard particle system package. Remember, this can be imported from **Assets** | **Import Package** | **Particle Systems**, from the **Assets** menu:

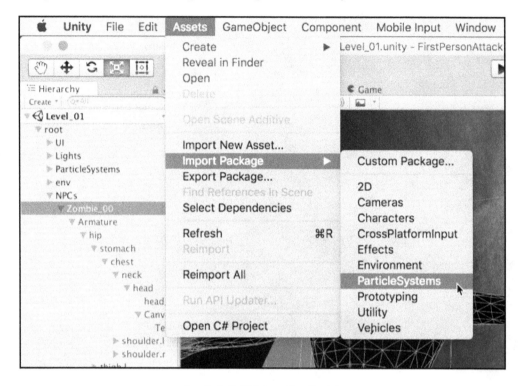

Importing the ParticleSystems package, if needed

At this point we have completed the AIEnemy class, and we're almost ready for a test run. Let's see the full and final enemy class code, as follows:

```
//------------------------------------
using UnityEngine;
using System.Collections;
using UnityEngine.EventSystems;
using UnityEngine.Events;
using UnityEngine.UI;
//------------------------------------
public class AIEnemy : MonoBehaviour
{
    //------------------------------------
    public enum AISTATE {IDLE = 0, CHASE = 1, ATTACK = 2, DEAD=3};
    public AISTATE ActiveState
    {
        get{ return mActiveState; }
```

```
        set
        {
            StopAllCoroutines ();
            mActiveState = value;

            switch(mActiveState)
            {
            case AISTATE.IDLE:
                    StartCoroutine (StateIdle());
                break;

                case AISTATE.CHASE:
                    StartCoroutine (StateChase());
                break;

                case AISTATE.ATTACK:
                    StartCoroutine (StateAttack());
                break;

                case AISTATE.DEAD:
                    StartCoroutine (StateDead());
                break;
            }
            OnStateChanged.Invoke ();
        }
}
[SerializeField]
private AISTATE mActiveState = AISTATE.IDLE;
//------------------------------------
//Events called on FSM changes
public UnityEvent OnStateChanged;
public UnityEvent OnIdleEnter;
public UnityEvent OnChaseEnter;
public UnityEvent OnAttackEnter;
public UnityEvent OnTypingChanged;
public UnityEvent OnTypingMatched;
//------------------------------------
//Component references
private Animator ThisAnimator = null;
private NavMeshAgent ThisAgent = null;
private Transform ThisTransform = null;

//Reference to player transform
private Transform PlayerTransform = null;

//Points for enemy
public int ScorePoints = 10;
```

```
    //Reference to Score Text
    private UIScore ScoreText = null;

    //Player health component
    private Health PlayerHealth = null;

    //Word associated
    public string AssocWord = string.Empty;

    //Extent of word match with associated word
    public string MatchedWord = string.Empty;

    //Amount of damage to deal on attack
    public int AttackDamage = 10;

    //Text component
    private Text NameTextComp = null;

    //Active enemy count (how many enemies wandering at one time?)
    public static int ActiveEnemies = 0;

    //Sound to play on hit
    public AudioSource HitSound = null;
    //-----------------------------------
    void Awake()
    {
        ThisAnimator = GetComponent<Animator> ();
        ThisAgent = GetComponent<NavMeshAgent> ();
        PlayerTransform = GameObject.FindGameObjectWithTag
("Player").GetComponent<Transform> ();
        PlayerHealth = PlayerTransform.GetComponent<Health>();
        //Find and get associated UI Text
        NameTextComp = GetComponentInChildren<Text> ();
        ThisTransform = GetComponent<Transform> ();
        HitSound = GetComponent<AudioSource> ();
        ScoreText = GameObject.FindGameObjectWithTag
("ScoreText").GetComponent<UIScore> ();

        //Hide text
        NameTextComp.gameObject.SetActive(false);
    }
    //-----------------------------------
    void Start()
    {
        //Set active state
        ActiveState = mActiveState;

        //Get random word
```

```
        AssocWord = WordList.ThisInstance.GetRandomWord();

        UpdateText();
    }
//-----------------------------------
public IEnumerator StateIdle()
{
    //Run idle animation
    ThisAnimator.SetInteger("AnimState", (int) ActiveState);

    //While in idle state
    while(ActiveState == AISTATE.IDLE)
    {
        yield return null;
    }
}
//-----------------------------------
public IEnumerator StateChase()
{
    ++ActiveEnemies;

    //Run chase animation
    ThisAnimator.SetInteger("AnimState", (int) ActiveState);

    //Set destination
    ThisAgent.SetDestination (PlayerTransform.position);

    //Wait until path is calculated
    while (!ThisAgent.hasPath)
        yield return null;

    //While in idle state
    while(ActiveState == AISTATE.CHASE)
    {
        if (ThisAgent.remainingDistance <= ThisAgent.stoppingDistance)
        {
            ThisAgent.Stop ();
            yield return null;
            ActiveState = AISTATE.ATTACK;
            yield break;
        }

        yield return null;
    }
}
//-----------------------------------
public IEnumerator StateAttack()
{
```

```
            //Run attack animation
            ThisAnimator.SetInteger("AnimState", (int) ActiveState);

            //While in idle state
            while(ActiveState == AISTATE.ATTACK)
            {
                //Look at player
                Vector3 PlanarPosition = new
Vector3(PlayerTransform.position.x, ThisTransform.position.y,
PlayerTransform.position.z);
                ThisTransform.LookAt(PlanarPosition, ThisTransform.up);

                //Get distance between enemy and player
                float Distance = Vector3.Distance(PlayerTransform.position,
ThisTransform.position);

                if (Distance > ThisAgent.stoppingDistance*2f)
                {
                    ThisAgent.Stop ();
                    yield return null;
                    ActiveState = AISTATE.CHASE;
                    yield break;
                }

                yield return null;
            }
    }
    //------------------------------------
    public IEnumerator StateDead()
    {
        //Run dead animation
        ThisAnimator.SetInteger("AnimState", (int) ActiveState);

        //While in idle state
        while(ActiveState == AISTATE.DEAD)
        {

            yield return null;
        }
    }
    //------------------------------------
    public void UpdateTypedWord()
    {
        //If not chasing or attacking, then ignore
        if(ActiveState != AISTATE.CHASE && ActiveState != AISTATE.ATTACK)
    return;

        MatchedWord = WordList.CompareWords (Typer.TypedWord, AssocWord);
```

```
        //Check for typing match
        if (MatchedWord.Length != AssocWord.Length)
            return;

        if (MatchedWord.Equals (AssocWord))
            OnTypingMatched.Invoke (); //Match found. Invoke matched event
    }
    //-----------------------------------
    //Deal damage to the player
    public void DealDamage()
    {
        PlayerHealth.Value -= AttackDamage;
        HitSound.Play ();
    }
    //-----------------------------------
    // Update is called once per frame
    public void UpdateText ()
    {
        //Build UI String
        NameTextComp.text = "<color=red>" + MatchedWord + "</color>" +
AssocWord.Substring(MatchedWord.Length,AssocWord.Length-
MatchedWord.Length);
    }
    //-----------------------------------
    public void Die()
    {
        //Update Game Score
        GameManager.ThisInstance.Score += ScorePoints;
        ScoreText.OnScoreChange.Invoke ();

        //Calcluate Bonus, if achieved
        float LettersPerSecond = AssocWord.Length / Typer.ElapsedTime;

        //If we beat best times, then get bonus
        if (LettersPerSecond < Typer.RecordLettersPerSecond)
        {
            //Bonus achieved
            ++GameManager.ThisInstance.BonusLevel;
        }

        ActiveState = AISTATE.DEAD;
        --ActiveEnemies;

        //Reset matched word
        MatchedWord = string.Empty;

        //Update Navigator
        Navigator.ThisInstance.EnemyDie.Invoke();
```

```
    }
    //----------------------------------
    public void WakeUp()
    {
        ActiveState = AISTATE.CHASE;
    }
    //----------------------------------
}
//----------------------------------
```

Activating enemies and camera paths

We've now achieved a lot for the *Dead keys* game. We've created health, enemy AI, and the ability for enemies to change between different states. However, if we add enemies to the level right now, they'll begin in a sleeping or deactivated state and, as yet, nothing changes that state. To move forwards, we'll need to link the camera position in the level with enemies so that, as the camera moves near to an enemy, the enemy wakes up and becomes an active participant in the game. This allows us to pace our game with the camera. To achieve this, we'll use strategically positioned **Trigger Volumes**, with a GameTrigger script. The script is as follows:

```
//----------------------------------
using UnityEngine;
using System.Collections;
using UnityEngine.EventSystems;
using UnityEngine.Events;
//----------------------------------
public class GameTrigger : MonoBehaviour
{
    public UnityEvent OnTriggerEntered;
    //----------------------------------
    // Update is called once per frame
    void OnTriggerEnter (Collider Other)
    {
        //If not player then exit
        if(!Other.CompareTag("Player")) return;

        OnTriggerEntered.Invoke ();
    }
    //----------------------------------
}
//----------------------------------
```

As the game camera enters each trigger, one or more zombie NPCs will be activated, approaching the game to attack. To create a trigger, simply navigate to **GameObject** | **Empty** from the application menu, and then add a **Box Collider** with **Component** | **Physics** | **Box Collider** from the application menu. Ensure the **Collider** is marked with **Is Trigger**, from the object Inspector:

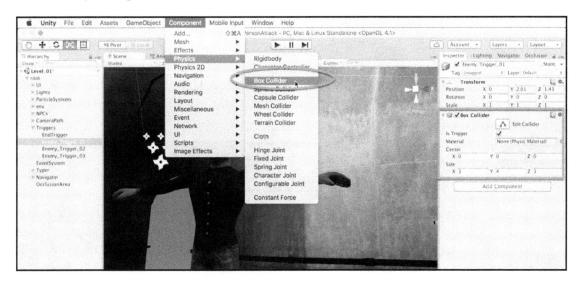

Creating a trigger object

Now add the **Game** Trigger script to the object, and configure the **TriggerEnter** event, from the Inspector, to activate nearby sleeping zombies to bring them into the game. This is achieved by calling the `WakeUp` function for all zombies that should awaken when the player enters the trigger area:

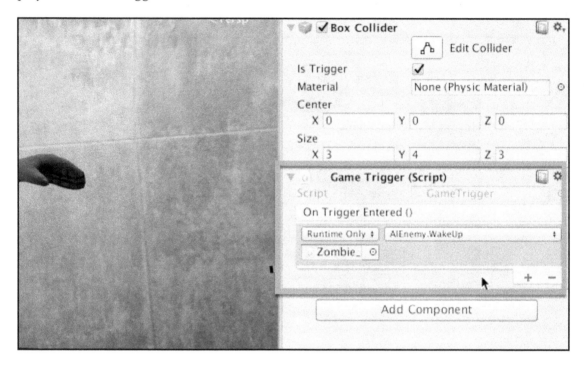

Calling the AIEnemy.Wakeup function

Now add more triggers to the level by duplicating the original, repeating this process for important way-points. This paces the level, activating zombies as the camera progresses from point to point:

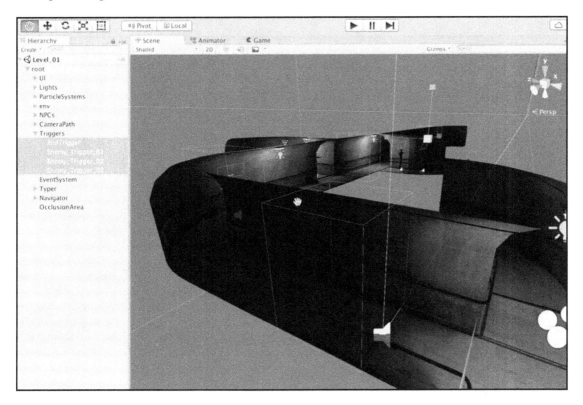

Positioning trigger volumes to activate enemies

Don't forget to duplicate zombies around the level, placing them to add difficulty. Position zombies around corners and at important intersections where the camera stops. Zombies should not appear while the camera is moving. For the gameplay mechanic to work and feel right, zombies should appear as the camera stops:

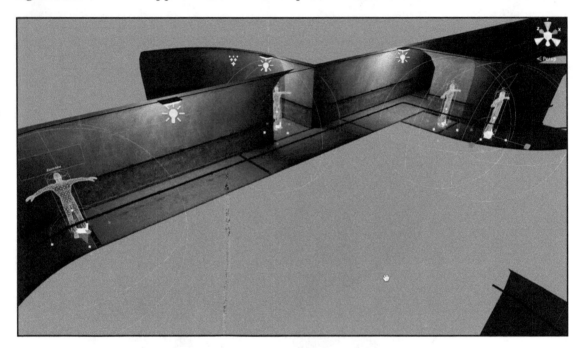

Duplicating and positioning enemies

If you test the level right now, you'll notice that the text above the zombie head will display for sleeping zombies and even for zombies a long distance away. This may conflict with game difficulty and feel, damaging the gameplay because players can potentially dispatch enemies long before they get close, by quickly typing their associated word. To solve this, we should configure the head text to display only when the zombie is closer to the player. To achieve this, add a **Sphere Collider** to the zombie, marked as a **Trigger** (Just navigate to **Component** | **Physics** | **Sphere Collider**). This will approximate the distance or range of the zombie for showing the head text:

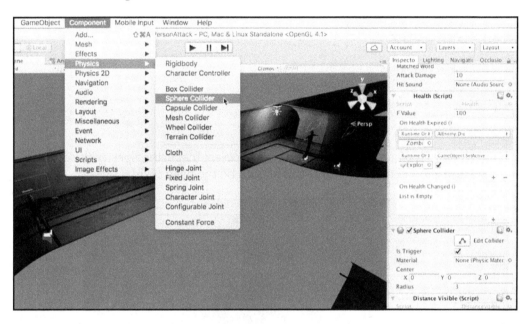

Adding a radius Sphere Collider to the zombie

Next, create a new script file (`DistanceVisible`), which hides and shows the head text based on distance to the player, as the following shows:

```
using UnityEngine;
using System.Collections;

public class DistanceVisible : MonoBehaviour
{
    //Reference to local sphere, marking distance
    private SphereCollider ThisSphere = null;

    //Object to show hide
    public GameObject ShowHideObject = null;
```

```
    void OnTriggerEnter(Collider Col)
    {
        if (!Col.CompareTag ("Player"))
            return;

        if (ShowHideObject != null)
            ShowHideObject.SetActive (true);
    }

    void OnTriggerExit(Collider Col)
    {
        if (!Col.CompareTag ("Player"))
            return;

        if (ShowHideObject != null)
            ShowHideObject.SetActive (false);
    }
}
```

Attach the script to the zombie and then, from the object Inspector, specify the object which should hide and show. For the zombie, this should be the head text UI object:

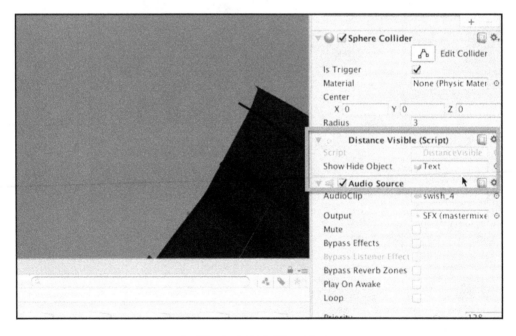

Specifying a target object for hiding and showing

Excellent work! Now you're ready to test the level. Simply click the **Play** button, and away you go! Enemies should approach as you enter the trigger, and should take damage as you type the appropriate letters on the keyboard:

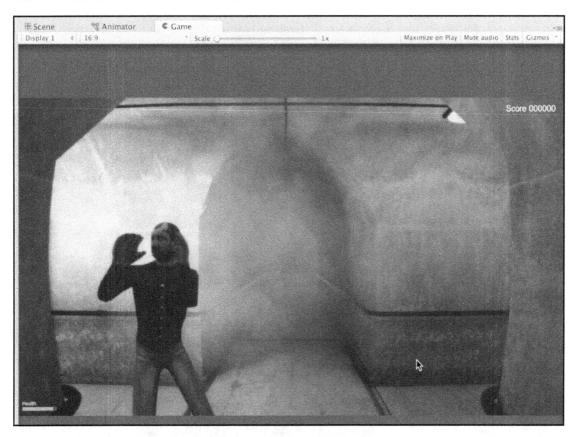

Playtesting with zombies added!

 One of the great benefits of implementing zombies as a self-contained Prefab is that you can easily add and remove zombies from a level without affecting any other functionality of behavior.

Working with Play mode

It's important to start play-testing the game at this point, checking the zombie NPCs, making sure animations play and states change. You should specifically test that the player can approach a zombie, that a zombie can chase and attack the player, and that the player can attack and defeat enemies:

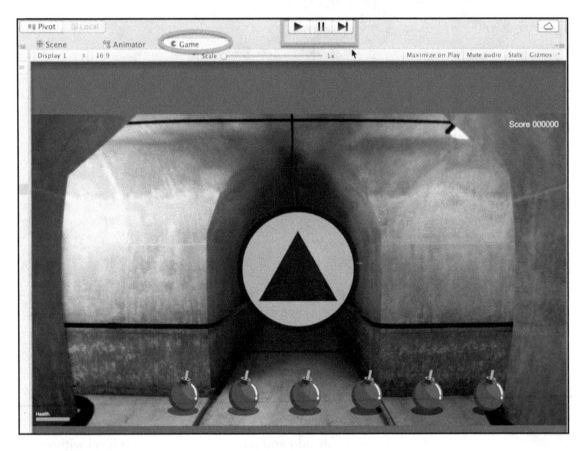

Working in Play mode

During testing you may decide to make changes, tweaking speeds, stopping distances, health points, and more. Remember, any changes made in **Play** mode are automatically reverted when playback is stopped. However, you can copy values on components from Play Mode to edit Mode. This makes it easier to adjust values from the Inspector and to take them back to edit Mode. To do this, click the **Cog** icon from the component being changed, during Play mode, and select **Copy Component** from the menu:

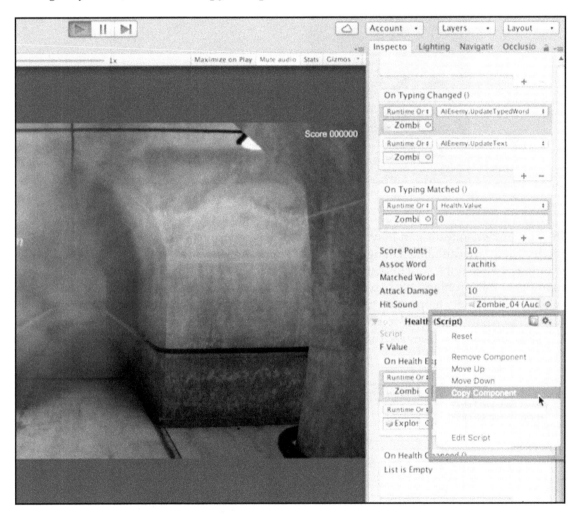

Copying component values

Then, back in edit mode, select the same component and click the **Cog i**con. From the context menu, choose **Paste Component Values**. This copies the values between the modes, allowing you to retain your changes from Play mode:

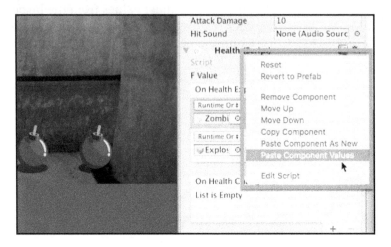

Pasting component values

In addition, when testing in Play mode, it can be easy to forget that we're actually in Play mode. There, we can make changes, and then later realize we made them in Play mode and should not have done so. This can be frustrating. However, Unity does offer us something to mitigate this problem. We can use a feature (**Play Mode Tint**) to colorize the interface while in Play mode, helping us to remember the currently active mode. To access this feature, navigate to **Edit** | **Preferences** (on a PC) or **Unity** | **Preferences...** (on a Mac). This displays the **User Preferences** dialog:

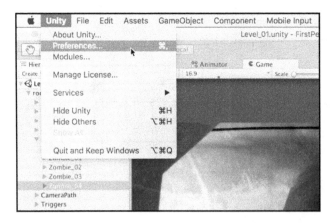

Accessing User Preferences

From the User **Preferences** dialog, select the **Colors** tab. Click inside the **Playmode tint** swatch and select a color for the interface:

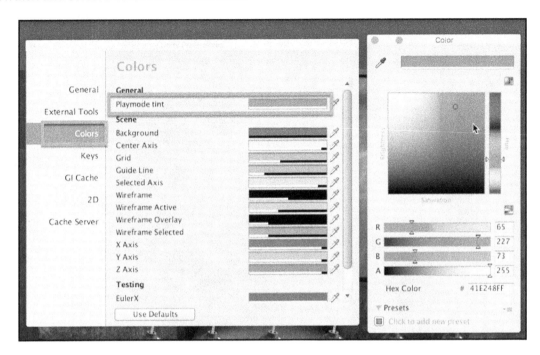

Selecting Playmode tint

Now press Play from the application tool bar to launch Play mode, and the interface is immediately colorized with the tint color:

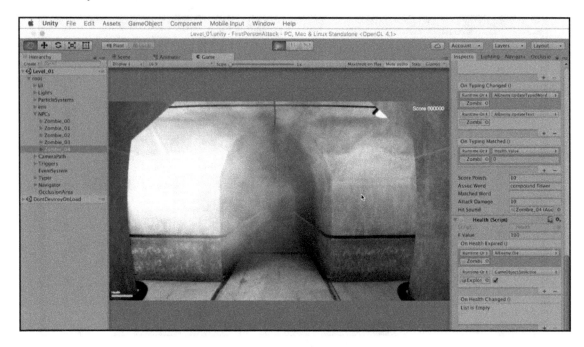

Working with Playmode tint

Summary

Good work! In this chapter, we completed a critical part of *Dead Keys*. Specifically, we've created an intelligent zombie NPC that wanders the level, attacks the player and can themselves be attacked by typing combat. This is a significant milestone in the project because now, we have united many classes and features to create a working core mechanic. In the next chapter we'll move forwards to enhance our workflow even further.

6
Project Management and Version Control

In this chapter, we'll take a detour away from the *Dead Keys* project specifically, and into related development fields, such as **Project Management** and **Version Control**. These are critically important for organizing your work, ensuring development is focused and completed as per the schedule and with the intended quality. You might think these practices are unnecessary for people working alone or in very small teams, but this is not true. Teams of all sizes, from one person to hundreds, need some degree of Project Management skill, and version control is a technology (alongside others) that can really help. Speaking generally, Project Management is about understanding the project design, aspirations and required workload, and then creating a schedule to support that workload, distributing tasks to qualified people, at the right times, for completion by an appropriate deadline. Version Control, as we'll see, is a technology we can use to save ourselves time. It effectively lets us take periodic snapshots of our work throughout development, whether in Unity or other software, allowing us to revert the status of our work back to an earlier stage, if needed. This is useful for undoing wrong-turns and mistakes in development. So let's get started.

Project Management

Project Management is really important. We all have to do it to some extent in our everyday lives, but especially when developing games. We must think carefully about the work needed, and then figure out the most practicable way to pursue it. Project Management is, essentially, about planning your time, workload and resources to achieve success optimally. The idea is to identify all the work needed, and then to divide it into a sequence of manageable chunks. The following terms and phrases emerge with the Project Management process.

Research, design, and work assessment

Project Management begins by careful analysis of the design. This involves examining the **game design document** (a clear statement of the game) and determining how, when properly conceived, it can be implemented optimally. Previous chapters outlined the design for *Dead Keys*, and from this, we can extrapolate various levels of work. Try thinking about these, and then write them down using a tree structure. At the highest level, you should include art, sound, and development work. Within the development, for example, we have many systems to develop, from player controls and enemy AI to level logic and camera systems, plus lots more. The degree to which you can dig down into lower levels of work is, potentially, endless. For this reason, you'll need to make informed decisions about when to stop digging, by arriving at small, achievable **tasks** (or **tickets**) that can be fully assigned to specific team members within a reasonable **deadline**.

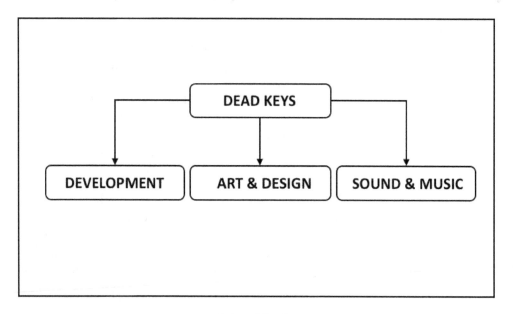

Project work hierarchy

Workload plan

The **workload plan** begins when you have atomized the full workload into discrete, manageable tasks that can be assigned to specific team members, like: *create player controls, animate a walk cycle for a character model, create brick texture,* and so on. Each task will have an *assignee* (a person responsible for its completion), and a *deadline* (the time and date the task should be completed). In addition, the Project Manager should arrange tasks sequentially in a timeline or *calendar*, representing the order in which they should be completed: after all, there's no point texturing a character model before the model has actually been made!

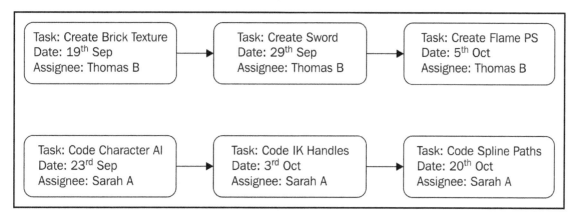

Task progression

Task status

Each task has a **status** within the development timeline, representing how far (or not) work has progressed. The exact name and nature of a status varies from project to project, but there are some general states that a task can be. First, a task can be in a **To-Do** state. This means a task exists in the plan, has been assigned, but has not yet been started by the assignee. Thus, it's on their list of things *to do*. Next, a task can be **In Progress** or **Open**; which means the task is currently being addressed by the assignee. And finally, a Task can be **Completed** or **Closed**. This means the task has, in the judgment of both the assignee and the team, been completed according to the plan, and the assignee is now working on something else. Sometimes, however, a task can be **Blocked** or **Suspended**.

This happens when a task was started but cannot now be completed. This can be caused by an oversight from the Project Manager (perhaps not all necessary tasks were planned), or an unfortunate disruption to the workload (a team member fell ill). Most often, it is caused when *tasks* depend on each other, and an assignee for another related task has fallen behind schedule so that you are now waiting for them to complete it. The **Blocked** status is not usually a persistent state; it typically changes back to **In Progress** when the blocking condition is removed.

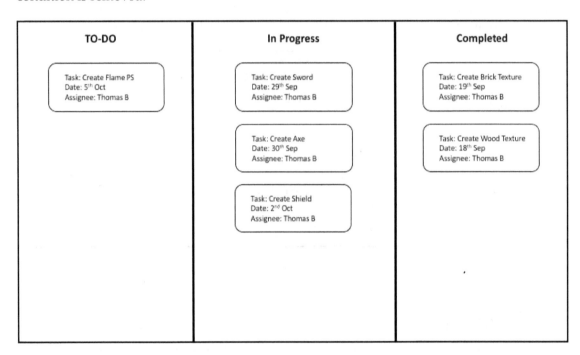

TO-DO	In Progress	Completed
Task: Create Flame PS Date: 5th Oct Assignee: Thomas B	Task: Create Sword Date: 29th Sep Assignee: Thomas B	Task: Create Brick Texture Date: 19th Sep Assignee: Thomas B
	Task: Create Axe Date: 30th Sep Assignee: Thomas B	Task: Create Wood Texture Date: 18th Sep Assignee: Thomas B
	Task: Create Shield Date: 2nd Oct Assignee: Thomas B	

Task status

Risk Analysis

Each task has associated *risks*, which should be stated, and these risks can vary in kind. Sometimes, the risk will be financial: How much time and money will task-completion cost, and is it worth it? Sometimes, the risk will be technical: What software, hardware, and skills are needed to complete the task to the required standard? Sometimes the risk will be logistical or economic: Will task completion satisfy a market demand? There can be other risks too, but each risk outlines a potential problem that is foreseen, with a reasonable probability, and it should further recommend a solution to the problem or, at least, a workaround. **Solutions** define how to solve and tackle problems, and **workarounds** define ways of working so that difficult problems are not encountered at all.

Resources and skills needed

Each task has requisites, and not just in terms of other tasks. These are all the things needed to complete the task on-time and to the specified standard. Each task requires software (like Unity, Blender, MonoDevelop and so on), hardware, skills, finances and time. *Time* itself is a *wasting resource* meaning that it cannot be refunded once it's spent. This makes time a particularly expensive resource.

Testing plan

It's easy to underestimate the testing work for any project. After the game is developed, people must spend time testing it, searching for bugs and issues. It's important to allocate time for testing in advance by creating a testing plan as part of the development schedule. The plan should include tasks specifically for testing. You'll need to test specific components and features, as well as general testing. In addition, you should allocate time for debugging and fixing any problems found. This can be difficult when estimating time and deadlines because you're allocating time for unknown bugs with unknown solutions. As a result, allocate the maximum time your schedule allows for testing.

Applied Project Management using Trello

Let's now look at a practical tool for managing our workload for *Dead Keys*. There are many tools available, ranging in features, complexity and cost. Here, we'll focus on **Trello**, a free web-based work management program. You can access Trello from its official homepage at http://www.trello.com. Trello lets you design your workload using a vertical, column-based **Kanban** board, as we'll see. More information on a Kanban Board can be found online at: https://en.wikipedia.org/wiki/Kanban_board.

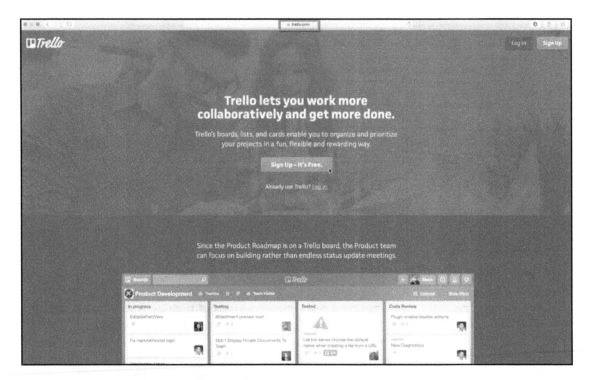

Accessing Trello

After signing up to Trello you should create a new team. A *team* represents a collection of Trello users who can share site content together for collaboration. It's a good idea to add all members of your team, so everybody can view and track project progress. To do this, click the **Create a new team...** button from the main interface.

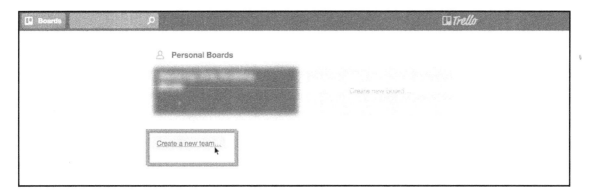

Creating a new project

Assign your team a meaningful name and description, clearly outlining the project to be created in a way that's accessible to everybody on the team. Take your time writing an appropriate title and description. These small details are important and make a big difference to how people see and value your project.

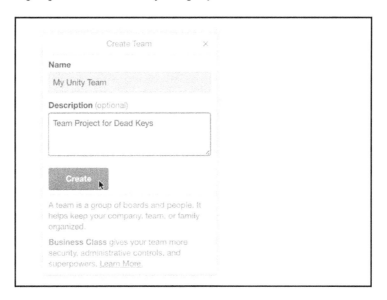

Describing a new project

Now you've created a team and the contents can be shared by one or more Trello users. Let's start by adding members to the team, where needed. To do this, switch to the **Add Members** tab, and click the **Add by Name or Email** to add a single and specific user, or else choose **Bulk Add Members** to paste in a list of e-mail addresses and add members in the block.

Adding team members

After adding all your team members, you're ready to create a new board. A good approach is to create a single board for each team member and their work. Sometimes you'll need more if the workload is heavy. Each board works like a billboard or notice board where notes, pictures, tasks and information can be viewed and changed by the team. To create a board, just click the **Create new board...** option from the website menu; or use the **Boards** tab from the team page.

Creating a new board

Every new board begins empty; clear of all tasks and information. At this point, we should first structure the board, to arrange our tasks and deadlines within an established framework. One approach is to use the **Kaban** method. This refers to a vertical column format in which four columns are created: To-Do, In Progress, Completed, and Blocked. Tasks are then moved individually, like sticky notes, between the columns as they are started and completed. This helps us easily visualize the status of particular tasks in the workload. To get started using the Kanban method, click **Add a list...** from the **Boards** page.

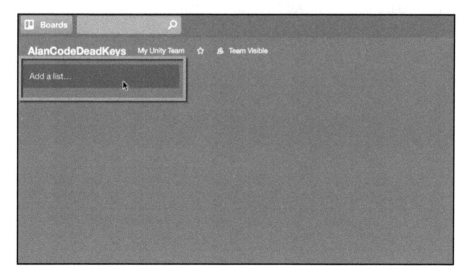

Creating a new list

Each created list needs a name. Name them: **To-Do**, **In-Progress**, **Completed**, and **Blocked**. Arrange the lists from left to right chronologically. You can drop and drop the lists to reorder them if needed.

Creating a Kanban board

Having created a Kanban board, it's time to add tasks to the list. Trello names them **Cards**. Select the **To-Do** list, and click the **Add a card...** button on the list.

All newly created tasks should begin in the **To-Do** list.

Give the card an appropriate name for the task. I'll start by creating some coding/development tasks. Once named, click the **Add** button. We can adjust its properties afterwards.

Creating a new development card

Now the first task has been created, let's adjust its properties: Add an assignee and a Deadline, as well as notes and any attached information. To do that, click the Pen icon to edit the task's properties.

Accessing a task's properties

Let's first assign the task a deadline (due date). Click the **Change Due Date** button, and then select a date from the **Calendar** field. Be sure to assign all tasks a deadline because a real, concrete date applied to a task helps you focus on getting the task completed. *Deadlines protect you from procrastination and putting off tasks to an unspecified time.*

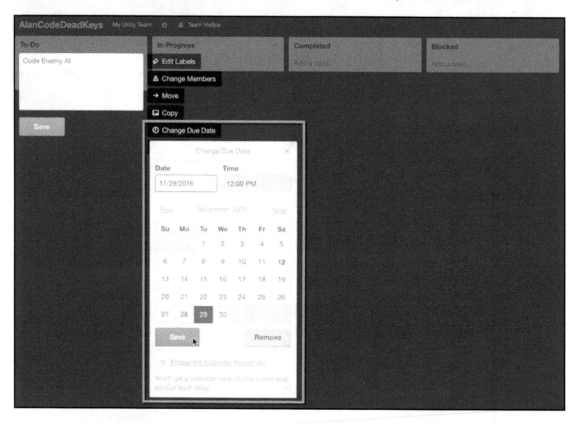

Setting a task deadline

Now let's assign the task a team member, and apply a label to it. **Labels** let you color code tasks to *visualize importance* or *priority*. The color red should indicate high-priority. Click **Team Members** to assign members to the task, and then click **Labels** to choose a color.

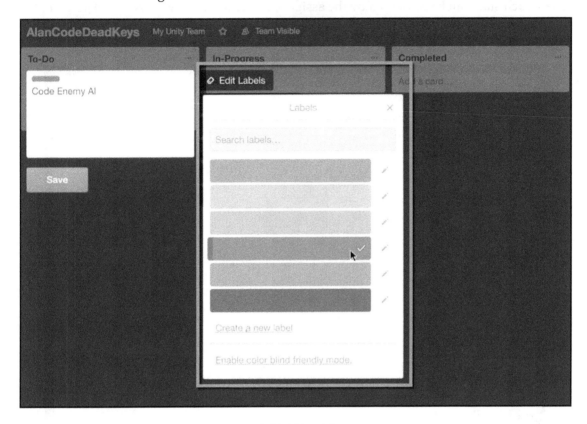

Applying labels to a task

Completing some tasks may involve multiple steps or discrete stages: for example, *Enemy AI* can be broken into the implementation of several states (Patrol, Chase, Attack, and Death) as we've seen in earlier chapters. We add these details to a task through **checklists**, where each state can be *checked-off* by the assignee as the relevant work is completed. To do this, click on the task name from the list, and then choose the **Checklist** button from the **Properties** dialog:

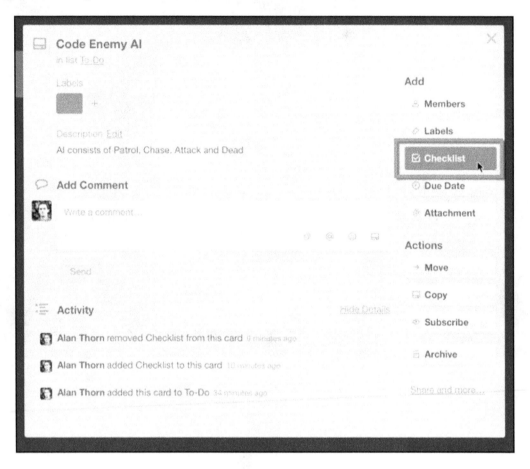

Creating a checklist

Assign the checklist a unique and meaningful name. Then, from the Checklist creator, add checklist fields for each of the **AI States**. Name these items: `Patrol`, `Chase`, `Attack`, and `Dead`. Be sure to click the **Add** button after naming each state, adding the state to the checklist.

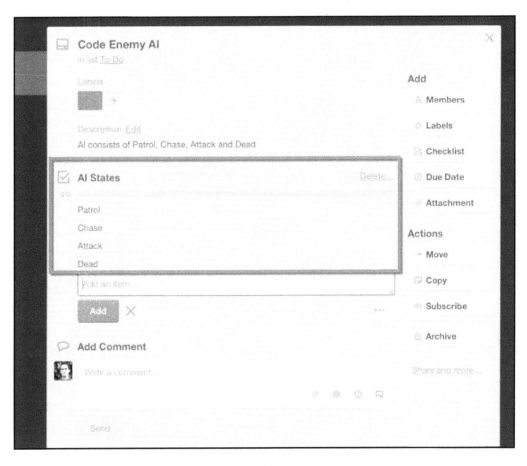

Adding checklist Items...

Now, by activating the checkboxes in the list, you increment the progress status of the task. This appears both in the progress bar view from the properties dialog, and in the summary view from the tasks list. This is a handy way to keep track of progress for specific tasks.

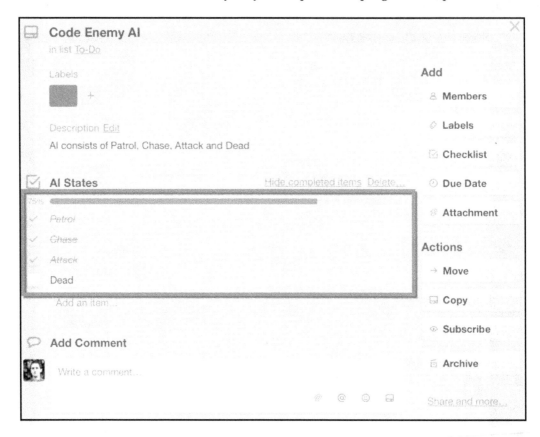

Making progress with checklists

You can also use the **Subscribe** option on another member's task to be automatically notified by e-mail whenever progress or changes are made to the task status. This is useful if you have many people to keep track of and don't want to repeatedly log in to Trello to review their status.

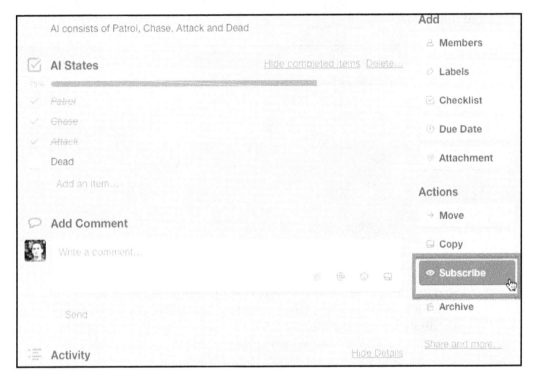

Subscribing to a task

Now repeat the process to create more *tasks*, building up a workload schedule for the complete Dead Keys project. As you add more tasks and populate the Trello board, you'll be able to move tasks between columns to reflect their completion status. Great work! Being able to project manage your work collaboratively in this visual way will help you work faster and empower your team, especially when different members are located in different countries and time-zones.

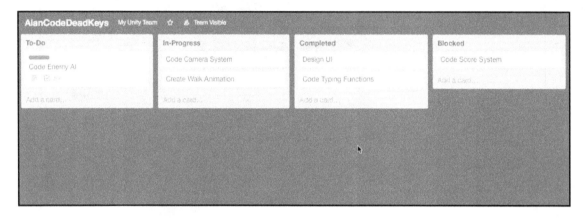

Building a Kanban board for Dead Keys

So we've seen how *Trello* helps us manage our work effectively and easily both for small teams and large, whether they are locally based or distributed across the globe. However, Trello is not the only option. There are valuable alternatives, which achieve the same or similar purposes, some free and some commercial. Here are some others to check out:

- Basecamp (https://basecamp.com)
- Freedcamp (https://freedcamp.com)
- Bittrix24 (https://www.bitrix24.com)
- Unfuddle (https://unfuddle.com)
- Visual Studio Team Services
  (https://www.visualstudio.com/vsts-test/)

Collaboration with cloud storage

Being able to effectively manage people, tasks and resources is an important skill in games development. Working at a high organizational level, Trello helps us break down tasks, costs and time. But, for developers going about their work every day, more is needed. Artists, animators and other creatives frequently need to share files with each other, like textures, meshes, movies, animations, and more. To do this, you can use e-mail attachments and memory sticks, but this soon grows tedious: e-mail attachments are very limited in size, and memory sticks require people to be located close to each other if they're to be effective. Ideally, artists need a central, internet-accessible storage space for their files, which can be accessed by all team members. This is where cloud storage and synchronization clients can be very useful. Cloud storage refers to a *remote server* where users can upload and download their files. It's simply a storage place somewhere on the net. All users can access it, provided they have the appropriate login credentials. There are many cloud storage options available, some free and some commercial. The free options normally have important limitations: such as limited space (*like 10 GB of total storage*), or limited bandwidth (*like a 10 GB transfer limit per month*), and sometimes limited file types (*like PNGs, or ZIPs*), or file sizes (*like 4 GB for a single file*). Some common cloud storage solutions include (in no special order):

- Google Drive (https://www.google.com/drive/)
- OneDrive (https://onedrive.live.com)
- DropBox (https://www.dropbox.com)
- Amazon Cloud Drive (https://www.amazon.co.uk/clouddrive/)
- BackBlaze (https://www.backblaze.com)
- HiDrive (https://www.free-hidrive.com)

 Remember to check out the terms and conditions of any cloud storage provider before signing up for an account. Each provider has different policies on acceptable file sizes, usage, and content.

Signing up to one or more of these providers gives you access to storage space for sharing your files between team members. One problem that arises for most solutions is easy file synchronization between systems and users. Specifically, how can saving your files on one computer automatically update other computers, keeping all machines updated with the latest changes for everybody? Some storage solutions (like Google Drive, DropBox, and OneDrive) offer desktop client applications that can auto-sync files. However, these are usually solution specific – for example, the *OneDrive* client synchronizes files across all OneDrive linked computers only. This solution is workable and easy if you're using only one storage solution. But if you decide to use multiple, you'll probably want a solution that synchronizes files automatically across all the storage systems, treating them as a single consolidated cloud drive. You can achieve this using the freely available **ODrive** system. This is available at: `https://www.odrive.com`.

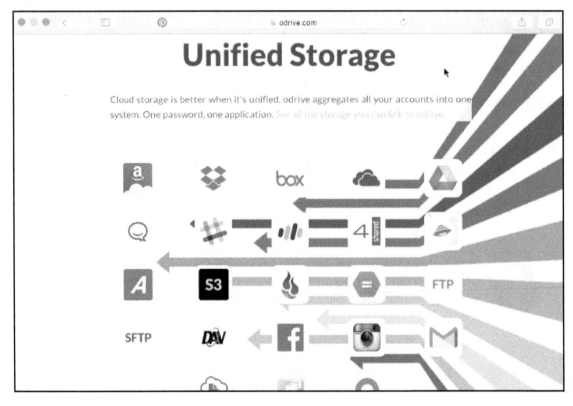

ODrive aggregates cloud storage systems into a Unified Interface…

Version control using Git

Cloud storage is an effective solution for artists sharing files, such as textures and meshes, across computers. However, for programmers and developers, the situation is different. Programmers work collaboratively with code and script files, and this creates some important needs that are substantially different or acute:

- First, coders frequently work together on the same source code. This may involve collaborating on different functions or areas of the same project, but also collaborating on the code in the same file. Consequently, they need an easy way to identify lines that have changed between edits, who made the changes and when and why.
- Second, coding often requires developers to explore and experiment with different solutions and techniques. The aim is to reach decisions about which solution is best. This means coders need an easy way to reverse small or large scale changes, restoring a project back to an earlier state before the changes were made.
- Third, coders normally like to reuse code from other sources, like libraries and source files, where it's relevant and saves us work. The basic idea is that code created for earlier projects may be relevant to the latest ones too, so why not merge that code into the existing project, instead of reinventing the wheel. Thus, the ability to merge code between projects is really useful!

To conclude, then, coders benefit from a file-system that identifies and tracks file changes, allows those changes to be reversed, and supports merging behaviors that allow us to reuse and integrate code from external sources. These features and more are supported by *version control* with *Git*. **Version control** as a concept lets us track, reverse and merge changes, and **Git** is simply one program that supports version control features.

Git is a free of cost, open source program that can be downloaded, installed, and then used to apply version control to your files. When used and configured appropriately, it can be an incredible asset to your workflow. One way to obtain Git is by visiting the Git homepage at `https://git-scm.com`.

The Git homepage

The Git homepage provides you access to the standard, command-line Git tool. However, by default, this tool has no GUI interface. You use it by typing commands and instructions into a console which is syntax sensitive. That means spelling, grammatical and structural errors will not execute at all, or at least not as intended. This can be awkward for newcomers, who must learn a new syntax, and unintuitive for experienced users, who may be seeking a graphical, point-and-click simplicity. For this reason, we'll consider a specific **Git client** (a program that builds on the fundamental Git framework to extend its features and make it easier to use). Specifically, we'll use **GitKraken**, which is a graphical, free and cross-platform Git client. It works on Windows, Mac, and Linux. This program is a completely stand-alone download and installation, so you don't need to download or install any pre-requisite files and packages. To access GitKraken, visit the homepage `https://www.gitkraken.com`, and click the **Download** GitKraken button.

Downloading GitKraken

The **GitKraken** homepage should auto-detect your operating system, allowing you to download the best version for you when selecting the **Download** button. However, if the wrong version is selected, you can manually choose a download by selecting the **See All Platforms** option below the download button.

After downloading the GitKraken package, run the installer program to the install the software to your computer. Great work!

Getting started with Git and GitKraken

So let's start using the Git client, GitKraken, to manage the *DeadKeys* project using version control with Git. By doing this, we'll be able to keep track of every change made to *DeadKeys* from here onwards, and we'll also be able to reverse and forward development history, as needed. Before getting started with Git, let's clarify a few technical terms. These are presented in point form in a carefully selected order, as below:

- Git is software for tracking changes to a group of files and folders. The total collection of tracked files, including Git meta-data for storing information about the changes, is known as a **Repository** (or **Repo**). This is essentially a folder containing many files.
- A Repo can be remote (stored on a web server) or local (stored on a local hard drive). Often both types are involved. As a user downloads the remote version onto their local machine, they are creating a clone.
- Creating a new Repo from scratch is called **Initializing** a Repo (or **Init** for short).

When you first start GitKraken you'll be faced with three main options: **Open**, **Clone**, and **Init**.

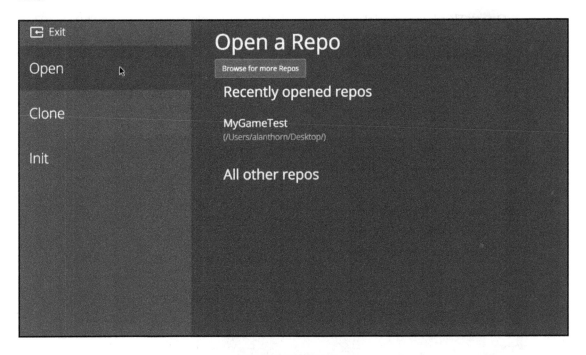

Gettingstarted with GitKraken…

These three main options (**Open**, **Clone**, and **Init**) have a technical meaning in the world of Git.

- **Open**: This lets you pick a folder on the computer that contains a local Repo. This contains all your Unity project files (as well as additional Git files for version control).
- **Clone**: This lets you specify a Remote Repo to download.
- **Init**: This lets you create a new and empty Repo. Let's a create new Repo. To do this, click the **Init** button.

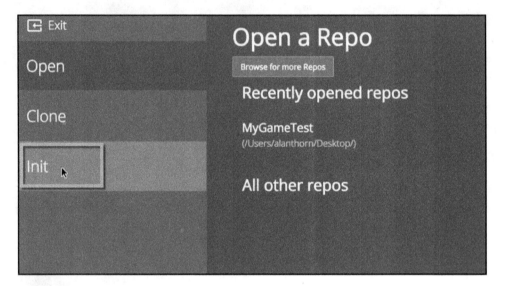

Creating a new Repo

After selecting **Init**, you can choose where the Repo is created. You can create a local Repo on the computer, or a repo on **Github** or **BitBucket**. These are free, web-based servers for hosting Git repos. Later, we'll use BitBucket. For now, let's create a local Repo. To do this, select the **Local** tab, and enter a **New repository path** (this references a folder on the computer where the Repo should be created). The folder should be empty.

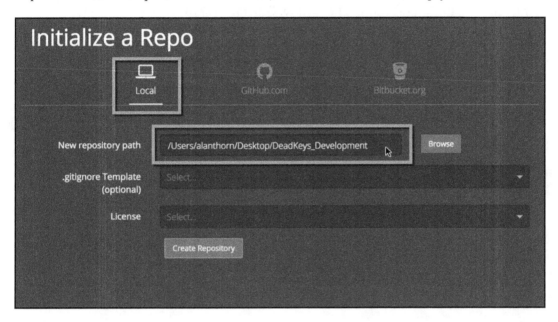

Naming and locating the Repo

Next, we should choose a **GitIgnore Template**. This is a special text file included in the Git Repo, listing all file and folder types that Git should ignore when tracking. This is important because some files, like user preference data and UI customizations, should remain local to a specific user. These should not be shared because each user has their own UI preferences and customizations. The only files we should track are the development-relevant files, and any files needed to support those. Thankfully, GitKraken ships with pre-configured GitIgnore files for specific programs that we can use immediately. Click the **GitIgnore** field, and then choose **Unity** from the dropdown. This configures the Repo to ignore user-preference data for Unity.

Selecting a GitIgnore file

The GitIgnore file conforms to a specific Git syntax, and it uses wildcard symbols (*) to specify the different file types and naming conventions to be ignored. The GitIgnore file for Unity is as follows:

```
/[Ll]ibrary/
/[Tt]emp/
/[Oo]bj/
/[Bb]uild/
# Autogenerated VS/MD solution and project files
*.csproj
*.unityproj
```

```
*.sln
*.suo
*.tmp
*.user
*.userprefs
*.pidb
*.booproj
# Unity3D generated meta files
*.pidb.meta
# Unity3D Generated File On Crash Reports
sysinfo.txt
```

Now click the **Create Repository** button, to generate a new Repo, and the *GitKraken* interface will display the main Repo details. The Repo is empty to start with, with the exception of the Git meta-data files, used internally to track file changes. Excellent! We now have our first Repo.

The Git Repo interfaces

Commits and branches

The Git Repo is a folder-based database of files and changes. A Repo is effectively a chronological sequence of project Snapshots. It keeps track of the state of your project across time. A **Snapshot** simply represents the complete state of your project at a specific date and time. When you first create a Repo, the Repo consists of one Branch, called the **MasterBranch.** A Branch represents a single, complete timeline of snapshots. A timeline is a good analogy because changes to the project happen in time, one after another, and each change builds from the ones before along a continuous line or *Branch*. The GitKraken interface indicates that a Branch (named **Master**) has been created and is currently active.

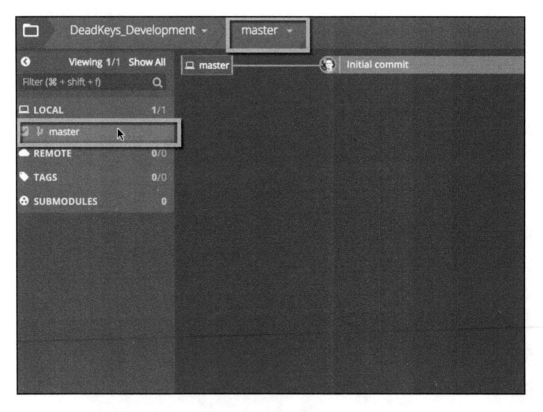

The active branch

The left-hand column lists all branches in the Repo (there can be multiple branches). The topmost breadcrumb trail indicates the currently active branch. The active branch is simply the branch that tracks all changes happening to files. Let's now make our first change to the files by copying and pasting our Dead Keys project into our Git project folder. To do this, you can use Windows Explorer or Mac Finder to transfer the files.

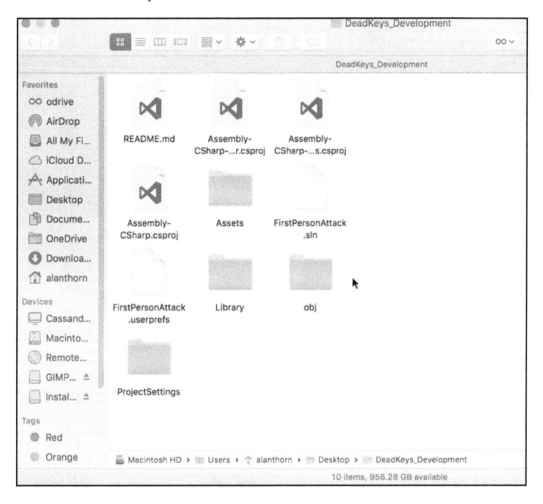

Copying files into the Git Repo

After adding the files to the `Project` folder, GitKraken detects the change and updates the interface with a new entry to the master branch. This appears at the top of the Tracked Changes list.

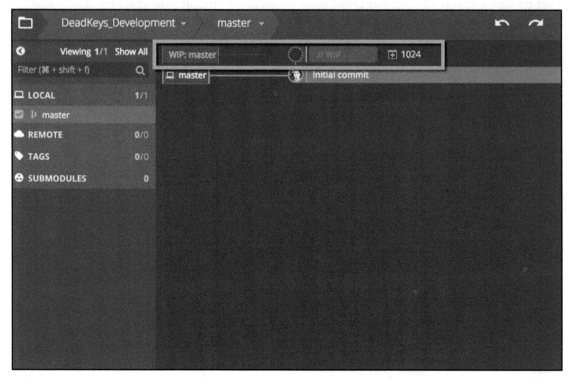

New changes tracked on the Master Branch

The tracked changes are not yet part of the Repo. Right now, Git has only detected the changes and displayed these inside the interface. The *green number* added to the list indicates the total number of files to which changes have been detected. In this case, 1,024 new files have been copied into the project folder, and these are all files included in the *Dead Keys* Unity project. For Git to accept these files and add them to the Repo as part of the Branch history, we must stage the files. This is about marking all files that Git should track and maintain as part of the Branch. For this initial change, we want to track and add all files. Select the new, topmost entry in the list to select it, and the **Properties** panel (on the right-side) displays more information.

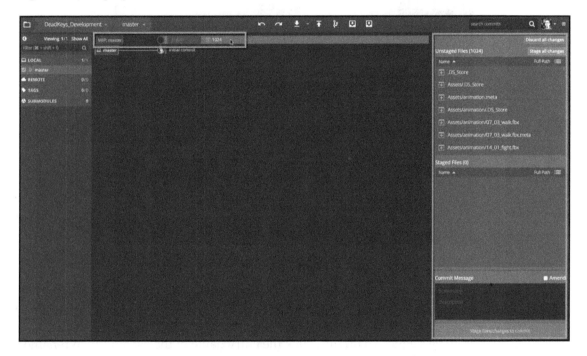

Selecting the changes

Each detected file where a new change has occurred is located by Git in one of two lists, Staged or Unstaged. All changes begin, by default, in the Unstaged list. This is a list of files where changes have occurred. Git will mostly ignore them until you specify that a specific file should be added to the Staged list. Files added to the Staged list simply remain together, in a collection, until you confirm that Git should acknowledge the change, and then add them to the activate branch as a Snapshot (called a **Commit).** Let's add all the new changes to the Staged List. To do this, click the **Stage all changes** button from the Unstaged List.

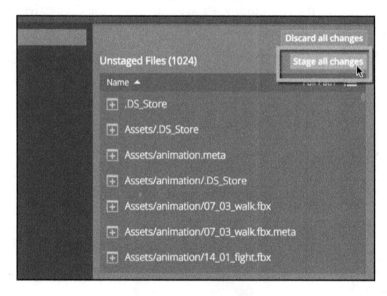

Staging changes

This adds all **Unstaged Files** to the Staged List. By doing this you are preparing to make a package (*Commit*) to the active Branch. Next, we'll need to name the Commit. A Commit represents all recently changed files to save. This should be a general summative name, describing all files to be staged. To do this, click the entry name in the list, and then rename. I've used the name **First Commit** since it represents the initial stage of our development history.

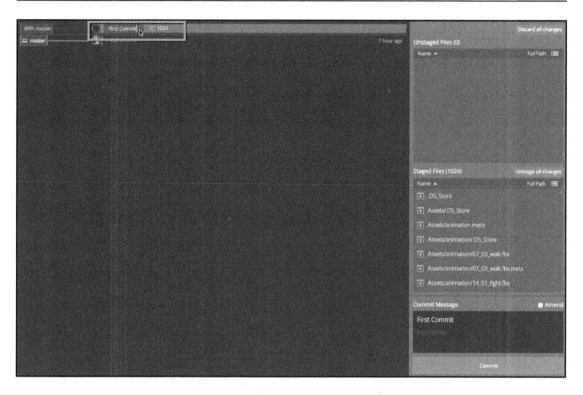

Naming the First Commit

The first commit for Git represents the starting state of a project, even if the project is actually half-finished when the first commit is made. Git only allows you to forward and rewind between actual Commits, as we'll see. We *cannot rewind* back to earlier states of the project before the first commit. For this reason, it's good practice to use Git from the outset of your project.

Now we've named the commit, let's write a comment for it. This is a user-defined message, which can be anything we want, but it should be descriptive and meaningful. In addition, the message should be written in the *Present tense* to avoid ambiguity about past work that has since changed, and future work yet to be implemented. For example: avoid writing *Added Path–finding function*, or *Will Add Path–finding function*. Instead, write: *Adds Path–finding function*. This describes what the commit actually does. For the first commit, I'll write *Initial State of Unity Project*. This is our starting point.

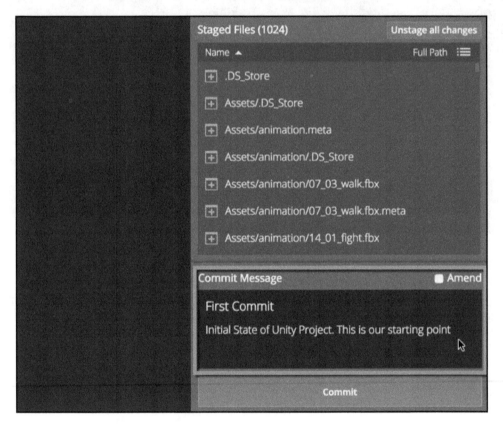

Commenting on the First Commit

Now click **Commit**, And that's it! We've now created our **First Commit**, and this is updated in the Branch History List. The topmost item in the list represents the latest *Commit*, and this features our custom name and comment.

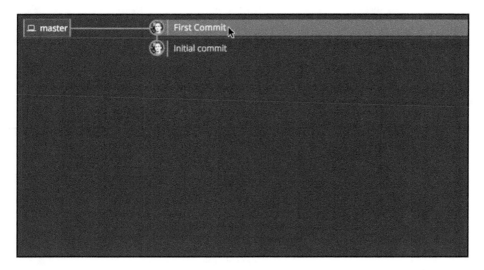

Added First Commit

You can select the commit in the Branch History list to reveal more information in the Properties panel. Each Commit has a specific time and date, author, and a commit ID, which uniquely identifies the commit within the Repo.

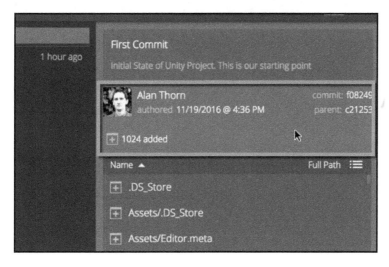

Viewing Commit Details

Great work! You've now made your first commit and have *immortalised* the initial state of your project. The Commit represents a snapshot in the project; a saved state. This means we can easily return to this state, anytime later, if we need to.

Forwards and backwards with Git

Let's test a practical case scenario for *Dead Keys* when using Git. If you open the Git project folder in either Windows Explorer or the Mac Finder, the contents will always reflect the latest commit on the active branch.

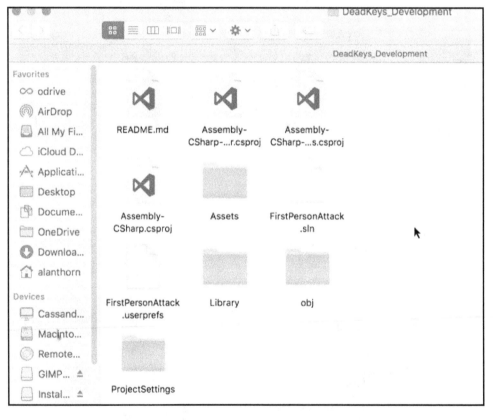

The Project folder represents the Latest Commit on the Active Branch

But, consider this, what if we made a mistake by creating the latest commit? What if we don't actually care about the latest commit (perhaps because it contains invalid files) and we want to undo it, restoring our work back to the previous commit? To achieve this, we can use the revert command. Simply right-click on the latest Commit in the **Branch History** and choose **Revert Commit** from the context menu.

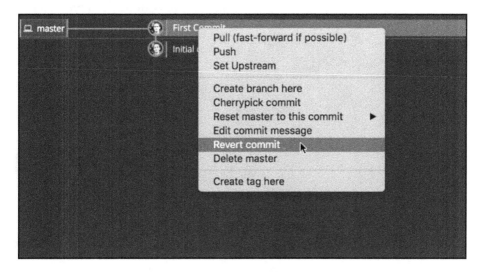

Reverting the latest commit

GitKraken then asks you **Do you want to immediately commit the reverted changes**? (to make the previous Commit the latest one). Let's choose **Yes**.

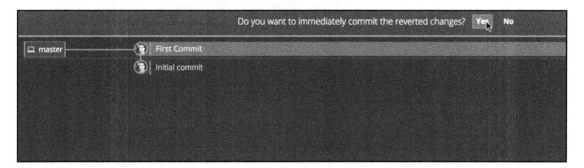

Confirming the revert

After Reverting the latest Commit Git will *undo* all changes included in it. Git does this, however, not by removing the latest Commit per se, but by creating a new Commit, reinstating the first. This highlights an important feature of Git: it never deletes anything! It always adds operations onto previous Commits. Thus, the act of undoing means deleting files or restoring earlier versions from the current state. Consequently, Git always lets you revert backwards through the history, restoring any earlier commits that you need.

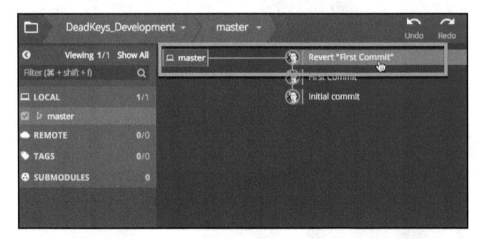

Creating a new reverted commit

Remember, you can easily revert the reverted commit too! This effectively restores the First Commit including all the *Dead Keys* files.

Restoring the dead keys project files

Excellent! We can now make Commits and revert the latest Commit. Next, we'll jump into Unity and configure it for use with GitKraken, and Git more generally.

Configuring Unity for version control

By default, Unity works nicely with Git: We don't need to change any settings for Unity to work with Git. Git is configured to work with nearly any kind of file, both text and binary (non-text). However, there are some optimization steps we can take to enhance your Git workflow inside Unity. To get started, open your Unity *Dead Keys* project, and then choose **Edit** | **Project Settings** | **Editor** from the application menu. This displays the Unity Editor preferences in the Object Inspector.

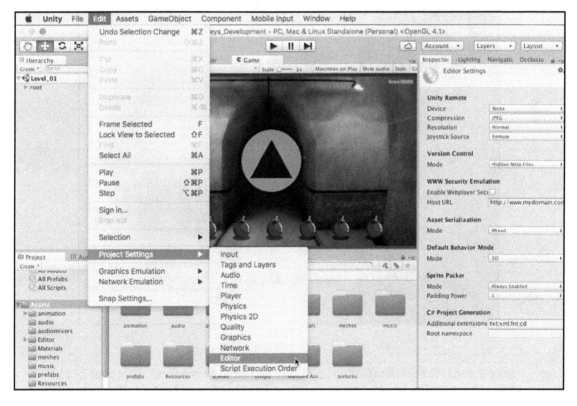

Accessing the Editor Settings

Next, change the **Version Control** mode from **Hidden Meta Files** to **Visible Meta Files**. By default, the Hidden Meta Files option applies the *hidden* tag to all meta-files, excluding them from version control. Meta-files are additional files Unity generates to accompany all assets (like *Textures*, *Meshes,* and *Sounds*) and include configuration options and preferences, like texture quality and UV Mapping. These files are named with the `.meta` extension. When meta files are hidden, Git will not include them in the Repo. This means that any other users accessing the Repo on a different computer will not have the meta-files. This causes Unity to regenerate a new set of meta-files when the project is opened. That is not necessarily problematic, but can lead to longer loading times when opening Unity projects. Thus, using *Visible Meta Files* can enhance collaborative Unity development.

Using Visible Meta Files

Now change the **Asset Serialization** mode from **Mixed** to **Force Text**. This changes how Unity saves metadata files, including scene files. By using **Force Text**, Unity saves all metadata in a human-readable text-based format. This has benefits with Git version control, as we'll see later.

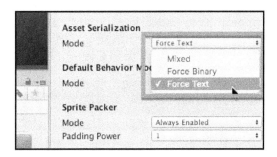

Using Force Text mode

You can confirm that Unity is using text mode for asset serialization by opening a scene file inside a text editor. The file will consist only of text instructions and definitions. This does not change how the scene appears in the viewport or during gameplay but only how the data is stored in the file.

```
                                          Level_01.unity
    serializedVersion: 4
    m_Component:
    - 4: {fileID: 4758194}
    m_Layer: 0
    m_Name: Waypoint_C
    m_TagString: Untagged
    m_Icon: {fileID: 5228209130450103505, guid: 0000000000000000c000000000000000, type: 0}
    m_NavMeshLayer: 0
    m_StaticEditorFlags: 0
    m_IsActive: 1
--- !u!4 &4758194
Transform:
    m_ObjectHideFlags: 0
    m_PrefabParentObject: {fileID: 0}
    m_PrefabInternal: {fileID: 0}
    m_GameObject: {fileID: 4758193}
    m_LocalRotation: {x: 0, y: 0, z: 0, w: 1}
    m_LocalPosition: {x: 4.53, y: 2.037, z: 12.93}          +
    m_LocalScale: {x: 1, y: 1, z: 1}
    m_LocalEulerAnglesHint: {x: 0, y: 0, z: 0}
    m_Children: []
    m_Father: {fileID: 1140567218}
    m_RootOrder: 2
--- !u!1 &6180366
GameObject:
    m_ObjectHideFlags: 0
    m_PrefabParentObject: {fileID: 139734, guid: 786ef495d3dec480094c37bd77cbd0de, type: 2}
    m_PrefabInternal: {fileID: 955551323}
    serializedVersion: 4
    m_Component:
    - 4: {fileID: 6180367}
    m_Layer: 0
    m_Name: ankle.r
    m_TagString: Untagged
    m_Icon: {fileID: 0}
    m_NavMeshLayer: 0
    m_StaticEditorFlags: 0
    m_IsActive: 1
--- !u!4 &6180367
Transform:
    m_ObjectHideFlags: 0
    m_PrefabParentObject: {fileID: 487358, guid: 786ef495d3dec480094c37bd77cbd0de, type: 2}
    m_PrefabInternal: {fileID: 955551323}
    m_GameObject: {fileID: 6180366}
    m_LocalRotation: {x: -0.061458062, y: 0.006600612, z: 0.23310521, w: 0.9704851}
    m_LocalPosition: {x: 4.307367e-11, y: 0.004532709, z: 8.657465e-12}
    m_LocalScale: {x: 1, y: 1, z: 0.99999994}
    m_LocalEulerAnglesHint: {x: 0, y: 0, z: 0}
    m_Children:
    - {fileID: 1199648754}
    m_Father: {fileID: 116805942}
    m_RootOrder: 0
```

Previewing a Scene File as a Text Asset

Finally, before making any commits to GitKraken, be sure to exit and close Unity. This is because Unity generates temporary files while running, and it can also open and edit metadata files. Consequently, close Unity and then Commit to GitKraken.

Updating Branch History

Reverting and discarding

Until now we've used **revert** to undo the latest Commit. But revert isn't limited to just that. Revert can restore a Branch back to even earlier Commits going back to the very first Commit if needed. To do this, we simply need to find the Commit we want to restore in the branch, and then revert the Commit above that. This makes sense because we're effectively reverting all commits subsequent to the chosen one. Simply right-click on the Commit above, and choose **Revert**. For this example, I am reverting to the first commit.

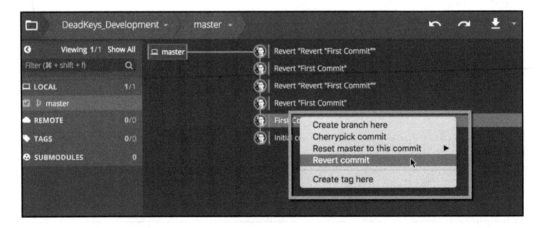

Reverting to an Earlier Commit

If you now open a Windows Explorer or Mac Finder window to your Git managed folder, you'll see the file contents updated to reflect the selected Commit on the Active Branch. In Git terminology, we are always viewing the **Head** (topmost Commit) of the **Current Branch** (Selected Branch in the Repo). The folder will not include any Unity Projects, because all commits subsequent to the first have now been undone. Note: the folder may contain some additional files. These are files *ignored* by Git, because they satisfy the GitIgnore file. Therefore, Git neither adds ignored files to Commits nor removes them from reverted Commits.

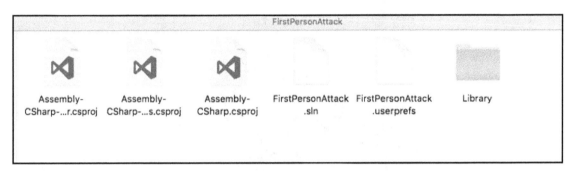

Git controls the file contents of all managed folders

We can always get back our work from any Commit, simply by using Revert again. This returns our Unity project back to the Repo folder, and this is reflected in either Windows Explorer or Mac Finder.

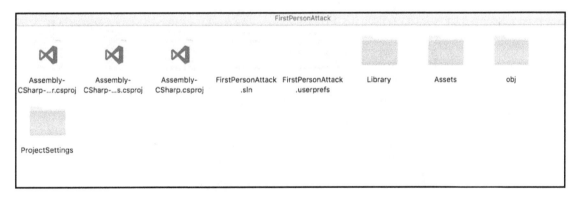

Changing the Repo folder contents by using revert

Of course, sometimes the contents of your repo folder can change unintentionally or automatically, such as when a program generates a temp file, or when Windows or Mac updates metadata for thumbnail images. Frequently, you don't need these changes. And yet, Git will still recognize them and create a new entry in the Branch History, creating Unstaged Changes ready for you to Commit.

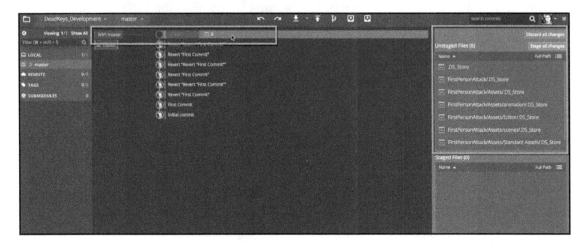

Git often detects unneeded changes

When unnecessary or superfluous changes are detected that you don't want to keep as a Commit, you can easily discard them; Tell Git to remove them and restore the folder, and all its files, back to the latest commit. To do this, click the **Discard all Changes** button from the Properties Panel. You will be asked to confirm your decision by choosing **Reset All**.

Discarding changes with Git

Great! By using a combination of Revert and Discard, you can now easily choose what should be committed, and you can undo the history back to any earlier Commit.

 For more information on Revert changes, check out the Atlassian Help documentation on using Git:
`https://www.atlassian.com/git/tutorials/resetting-checking-out-a` `nd-reverting`

Branches and branching

An impressive feature of Git is branching. There are times during development when your project enters a state that you're happy with. The work may not be completed or final, but you've reached an important milestone that should be committed and saved to the history. At this point, your project could take multiple directions, and you'd like to experiment a little, trying out new ideas or developing clever solutions for new features. On reaching this point, you effectively need to Branch your work. This instructs Git to make a *duplicate* of your work and its history to this point (a new Branch), and then you can make further commits on the new branch, without affecting the history of the original branch. That way, if you make changes that you later decide against or wish to remove, you can simply abandon the branch and return to the original, or make a new branch, and so on.

 Branching is great for team collaboration too. Different developers can each work on their own branch of the original work, taking it in their own specific direction. As we'll see soon, Git offers features for merging separate branches together, allowing developers to integrate or sew their work together into the master branch.

Let's try creating a new branch, an offshoot from the Master Branch that we already have in the Dead Keys project. First, we need to decide which Commit in the Master Branch should become the starting point for the new Branch. In this case, we can simply use the **Head** (topmost commit), but you don't have to do that. You can create a Branch from any Commit in the History. Select the bead, and then right-click with the mouse. From the context menu, choose **Create Branch here**.

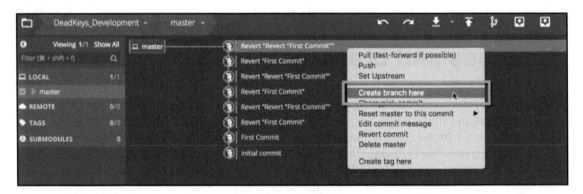

Creating a new branch from the latest commit

Next, assign the new branch a succinct but meaningful name that both justifies and describes why it was created. The name should be unique in the Repo; no two branches should ever have the same name. I'll call my Branch `IdeaPlayground_01`.

Naming a new branch

After the Branch is created, it's listed in the Branch List, shown on the left-side of the interface. In addition, the newly created Branch becomes the current Branch, and the contents of the Repo folder changes accordingly. A message also appears indicating that the new Branch is **Checked Out**. Checked Out, in Git terminology, means the Repo folder has been populated with all the files for the current branch, and these can now be edited and committed.

Viewing Repo branches from the branch list

You can easily change between *Branches* by double-clicking their names from the Branches list. Doing this checks out the selected branch. Now, by making changes to your Unity project, the updates are made to the current branch. By default, the GitKraken interface displays all changes to all branches in a single hierarchical display.

Viewing branch contents

After adding more commits to the new branch, the branch moves ahead of the original. You can easily choose whether specific branches should be shown in the list by clicking the eye icon next to the branch name. This toggles the visibility of the branch in the history.

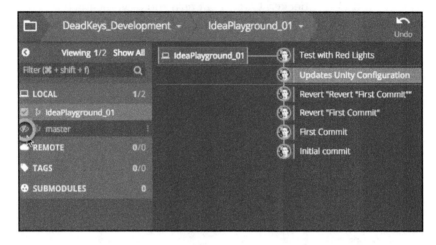

Hiding and showing branches

You may later decide that your experimentation on the ideas branch worked out well, and now you want to integrate those changes back into the original master branch. This process is called **Merging**. That is, you want to merge the Ideas Branch into the Master Branch. To do this, make sure the destination branch (the Master Branch) is active by double-clicking on it from the Branches list.

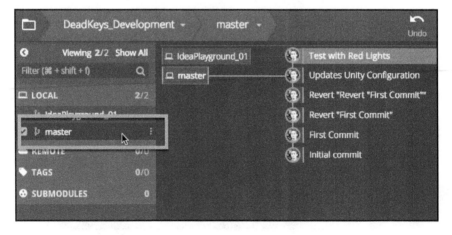

Selecting the Master Branch

Next, right-click on the Ideas branch in the Branches List and then choose **Merge into Master** from the context menu. This starts the mesh process. It leaves the merging branch intact and simply updates the destination branch with the newest changes.

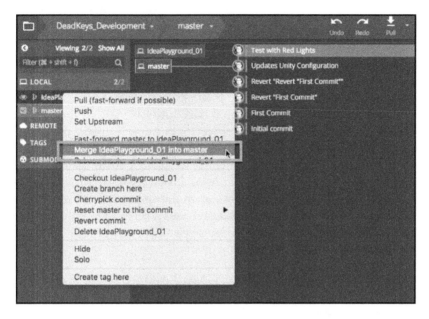

Merging into the Master branch

After the merge is completed, the Master branch is updated with the latest changes and the development history reflects this. The branch history now illustrates the Ideas Branch merging into the Master, after previously branching from there.

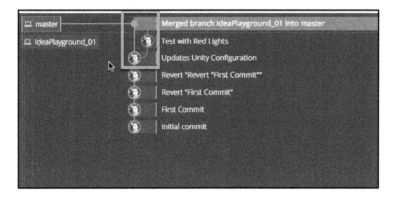

The branch history illustrates the Merge

Great! You can now create branches from specified points on the original master, and then merge back changes from other derived branches.

Conflicts and resolving

Branches in Git are especially useful whenever two coders need to work from the same *base* or *core* code but they must take the project in new directions, by adding specific features to the original work or by amending the existing work. To do this, each coder works on a separate branch, and their changes are merged back into the main branch to integrate their work together later. This workflow is very powerful because it means different coders can work in isolation on their own branch, without affecting each other. However, a problem arises with this approach logistically. Specifically, what happens if the coders take the project in different and contradictory directions and then try to merge those changes together? What happens if both programmers open the same source file and change code differently on the same line? What happens if one uses a `print` statement where another uses `Debug.Log`? What should Git do when these two divergent branches merge? In this case, a conflict happens, and we must resolve it.

Let's consider the relatively simple case of a HTML file added to the Master branch in a new Commit, as follows. The text file is as show in the following figure and in later branches the person name will be changed in a conflicting way.

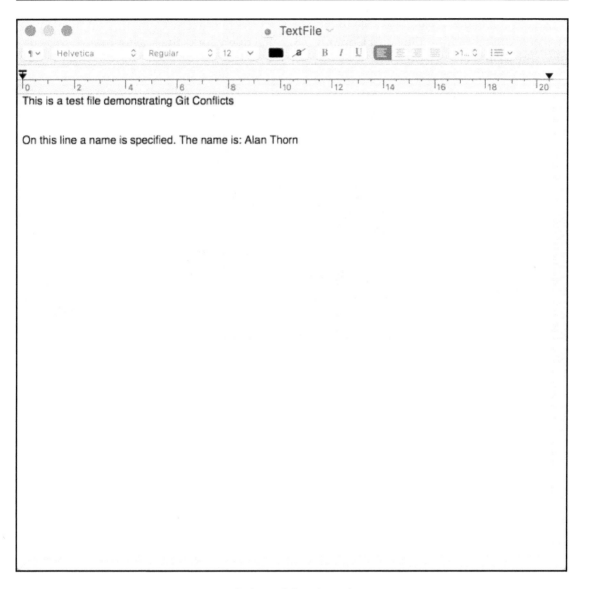

This is a test file demonstrating Git Conflicts

On this line a name is specified. The name is: Alan Thorn

Creating a text file for version control

Now add the newly created text file to the Master Branch as a new Commit, and then create two new branches from the latest Commit. This effectively forks the Master branch in two new directions.

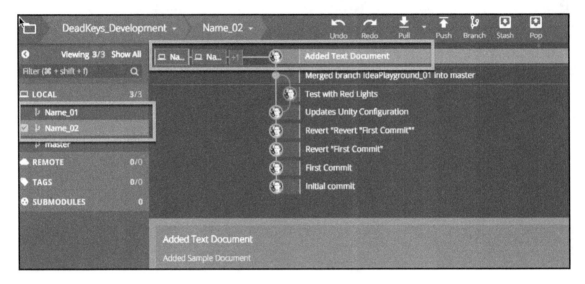

Creating new and divergent branches

Now double-click each new branch in the branches list to activate the Branch, changing the contents of the project folder to the branch files. And then, for each branch, open the text file and change its contents to create a conflict. For my example, I am changing the person name. For one branch, the name becomes John Doe, and for the other Jane Doodle. After making the change, be sure to Commit the changes to each branch.

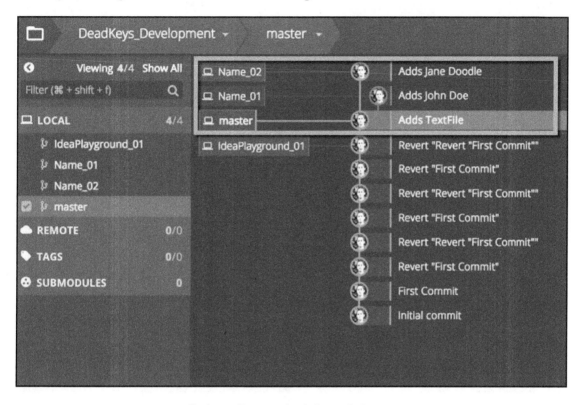

Changing a text file on separate branches in preparation for a merge

Now let's try merging these two branches (**Name_01** and **Name_02**), with contradictory changes, back into the Master Branch. Start by activating the Master Branch, double-clicking it from the Branches List.

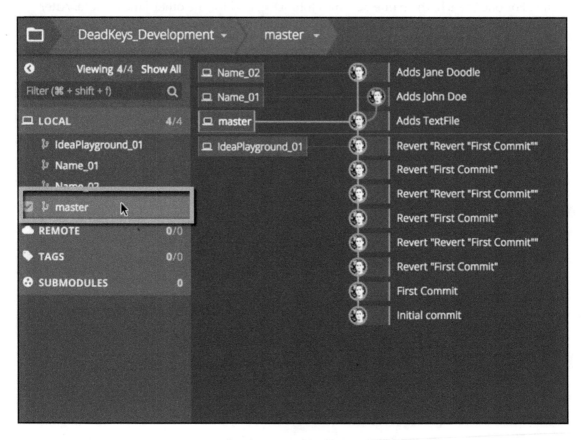

Activating the Master Branch

Right-click the first Branch, and then choose Merge to merge the selected branch into the active branch (the Master). When you do this, the Master Branch updates with the new changes. You can confirm this by opening the changed text file and viewing the new text. That's good!

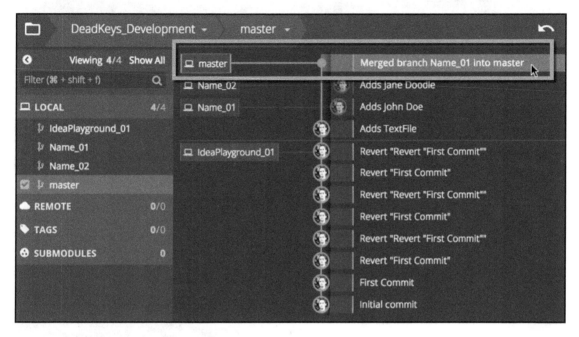

Merging

Now let's try merging the Second Branch, with conflicting changes, into the Master! Activate the Master branch, if it's not already activated, and then right-click the second branch, choosing Merge from the context menu.

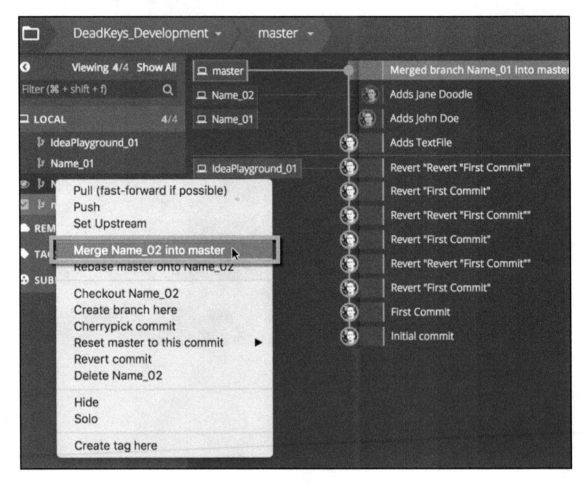

Merging the Second Branch into the Master

After merging the second branch into the Master, a conflict results. This conflict is caused by the discrepancy in the text file, where the same line differs across Commits; one uses the name John Doe, and the other Jane Doodle. A warning message is printed in orange at the top of the Branch history indicating the conflict problem. At this point, the merge is suspended until you provide input about how to resolve the Conflict.

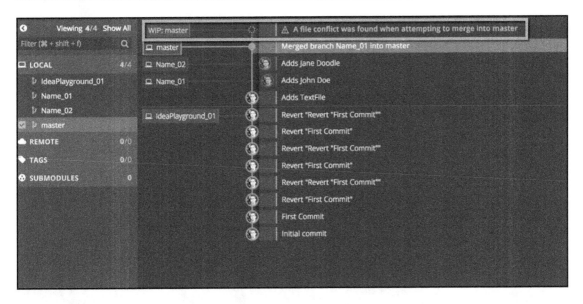

Merging the Second Branch into the Master

To resolve the conflict, select the Conflict message in the branch history. On selecting the conflict message, additional properties about the conflict are shown in the Properties Panel.

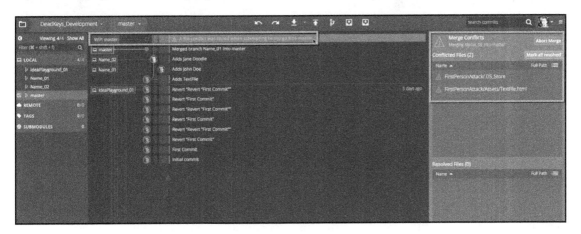

Viewing merge conflict details

From the Properties panel, two conflicts are highlighted. The first conflict is a metadata file generated for the Mac platform (DS_Store) You may not have this conflict on Windows. For me, this conflict can be resolved by selecting the file in the Properties panel. On clicking the file, a Conflict Resolution Editor is presented. The top two panels show the two conflicting files, presented side by side, and the bottom pane displays how the conflict should be resolved.

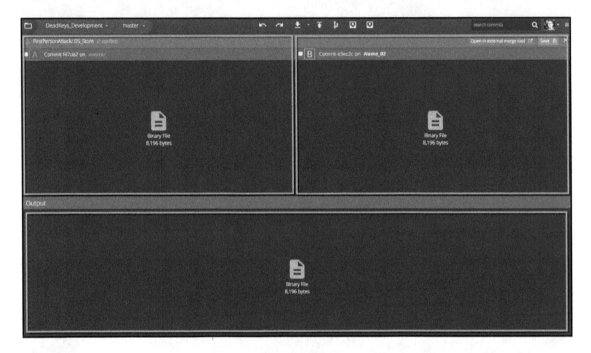

Merge Conflict Resolution Editor

Resolving a Conflict in Git is about choosing what the output should be from two divergent branches, A and B. One resolution is to choose branch A as the output; and another is to choose branch B. A third possibility is to develop a custom solution where you manually edit the resultant text file, defining what the outcome is. For the metafile DS_Store, I'll just choose option B. That is, the file included in the merging branch. This will be the output and resolution for this specific conflict. To do this, just check the option B box from the GitKraken interface.

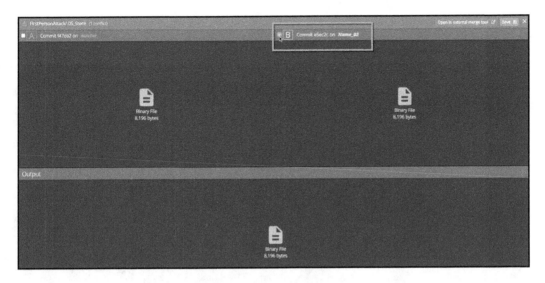

Choosing option B to resolve a Binary Conflict

After choosing option B, click the **Save** button to finalize the resolution. This returns us to the main GitKraken interface.

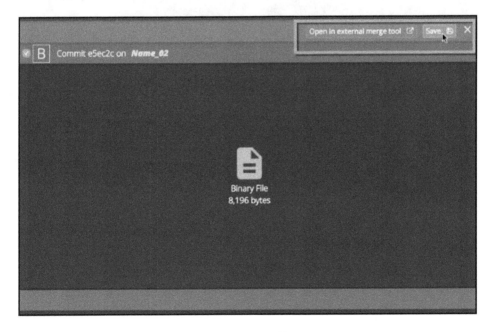

Resolving a Merge Conflict

After resolving the conflict, the file is marked as Resolved in the Commit and is also added to the Staged list, ready for Committing to the Master Branch.

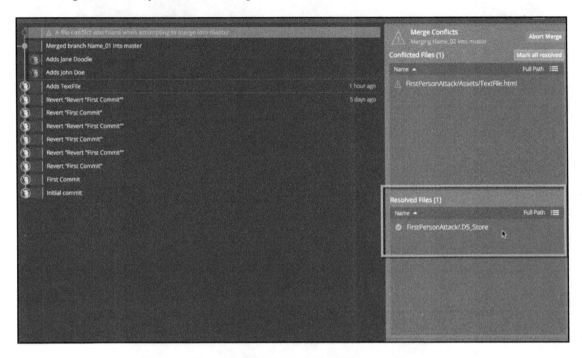

Resolved Conflicts are added to the Staged List of the Commit

Now let's resolve the outstanding text file conflict, which still remains in the Conflict list. To do this, select the conflicting file by clicking it.

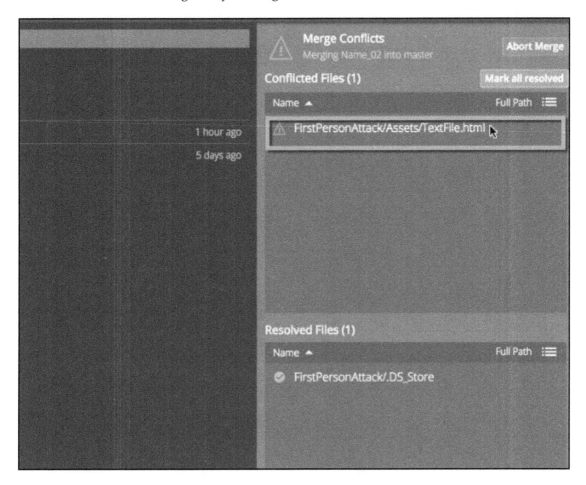

Selecting an Outstanding Text File Conflict

Again, the conflict opens inside the Conflict Resolution Editor. We can see from the top two panels, in HTML form, where the conflict occurs between the Commits. GitKraken highlights the conflict area for us.

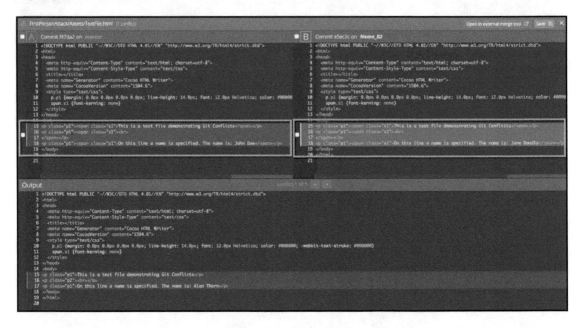

Exploring the Merge Conflict in-depth

The Output Panel displays the default solution that would be used if the Conflict was saved now. If you have GitKraken Pro, you can edit the Output solution with custom text, refining the resolution. But with the free version, you must select between conflicts: Option A or B only, or a combination of both. Here, I'll select Option B again to update the Conflict. Then choose Save to confirm the solution.

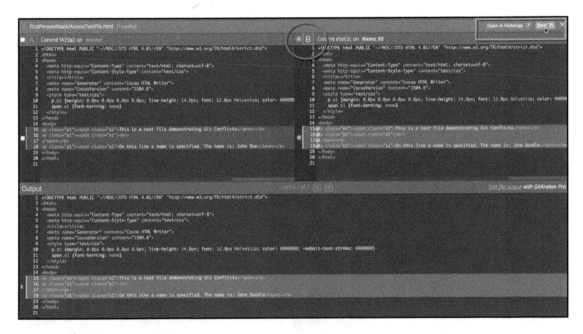

Resolving a Merge Conflict

Both conflicts have been resolved and can now be added to the Master Branch as a Commit. To do this, click the button Commit and Merge. This now updates the Master Branch with new changes integrating both Branches. In our example, the conflict mostly applied to just one text file, and the conflict existed on just one line in that file. For more complex projects there are likely to be many more conflicts both within a single file and across multiple files, and these should all be resolved carefully on an individual basis.

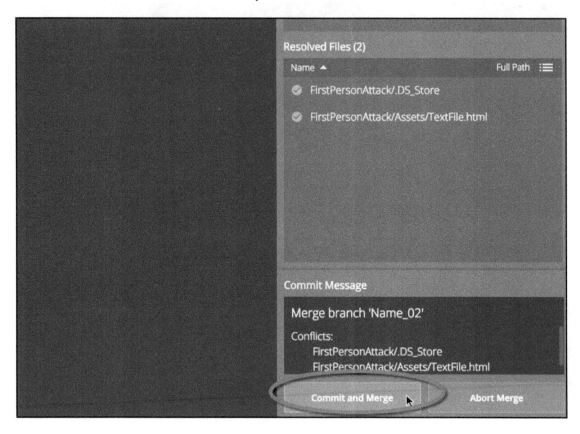

Updating the Master Branch using Commit and Merge

Voila! Great work. We've now resolved all conflicts and staged them to a new Commit added to the Master Branch. In reaching this far we've seen how to create commits on branches, how to create new branches, and how to resolve conflicts between branches during a merge process. Next, we'll see how enhance collaboration by working with Git Repos on a web server.

Git and the Web

Git is a tool that's especially useful for collaborating with other developers working on the same project. Sometimes, other developers will be working in the same room, office, or building. And, when they are, you can connect with them through an internal server or network. But often, developers will be located across the globe, working in different countries and time zones. All of them still need access to the same code and files, however; and thus, all of them need access to the same Git Repo. This allows developers to access shared files, make commits and upload branches. To achieve this, we'll need to use a Remote Repository, as opposed to a Local Repository. In Git a Repo can be either Remote or Local. A Local Repo is saved on your local hard drive, while a Remote Repo is accessed from a web server. When working with a Remote Repo, users often take a *local copy* of the Remote Repo (a Clone), and use the Clone to make changes which can be uploaded later back to the Remote Repo (the Remote).

To create a Remote Repo, you can use a freely available service, like GitHub or BitBucket. These let you host a Git Repo, with some file size and usage restrictions. This book focuses on creating a Remote Repo with Bitbucket, and then on using this Repo with GitKraken to upload and download files. So, let's get started. First, you'll need a free account at BitBucket – be sure to check the terms and conditions before joining. BitBucket can be accessed from `https://bitbucket.org/product`.

BitBucket is a free service that lets you host Git Repositories

After opening a BitBucket account you can easily link this to your GitKraken application. To do this, open *GitKraken* and, from the application menu, choose **File** | **Preferences** on Windows, or **GitKraken** | **Preferences** on Mac. This opens the User Preferences Window.

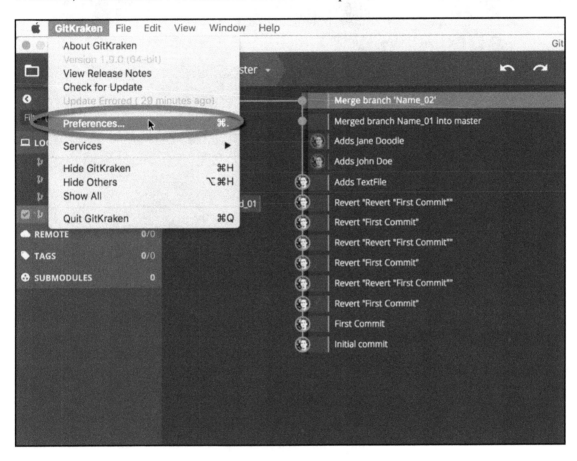

Accessing GitKraken preferences

From the **User Preferences** Window, select the **Authentication** tab and then choose the **BitBucket** tab. From here, you can enter your BitBucket credentials to link the application.

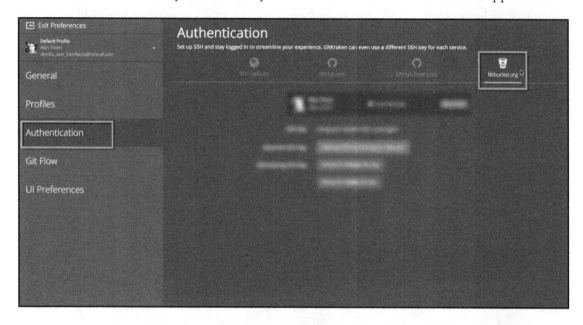

Entering your GitKraken Credentials

Having linked GitKraken to BitBucket you can now create new Repositories and clone existing ones. Let's create a new Remote Repo, and then clone it. To do this, select the **Init** option from the GitKraken start screen, and select the **BitBucket.org** tab instead of the **Local** tab (chosen previously).

Initializing a New Remote Repo on BitBucket

From the **Init** menu, select your **BitBucket** account and then enter a new name for Repo to create, along with a description and **Access** level. **Public** repositories are accessible to the public, while **Private** repos can only be accessed by approved users.

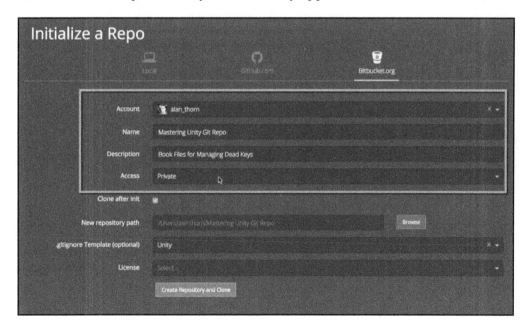

Completing the creation details for a BitBucket Repo

The **Clone after Init** option determines whether GitKraken should generate a *local copy* of the new Repo on the computer. If activated, a copy is created after the Repo is created. I'll leave this option activated.

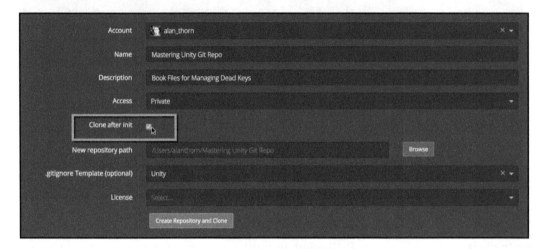

Cloning the Git Repo after creation

When you're ready, click the **Create Repository** and **Clone** button. This first generates a Remote Repo on the BitBucket serve and then generates a local copy (Clone).

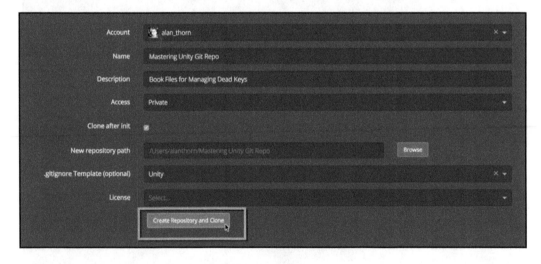

Generating a new Repo

If authentication fails for BitBucket, make sure you're logged in via the BitBucket website.

After generating the Repo, a version is created on the server, and a local clone is created on your computer too. You can confirm the remote Repo has been created via the BitBucket website. Choose **Repositories** from the top-level menu on the website to a see a list of the created Repos.

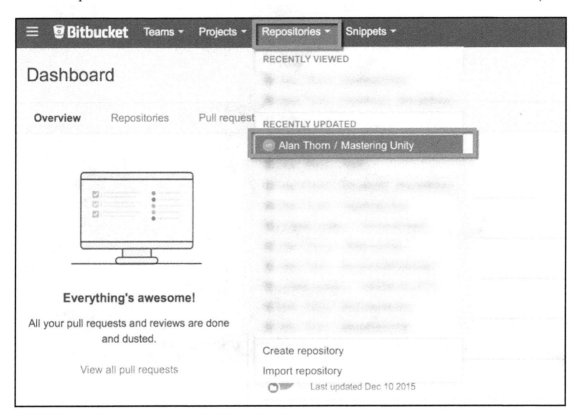

Verify that a BitBucket Repo has been created

Pushing and pulling

Now you've created a Remote Repo, it's time to see how synchronization works between the Remote Repo and the Local Repo. After making Commits on the local Repo, the changes are not automatically synchronized to the Remote. This is because changes could be undone, or because the developer doesn't have Internet access. For this reason, new Commits and Branches remain, by default, on the Local Repo only, until you explicitly **Upload** (or **Push**). To **Push** changes, you click the **Push** button.

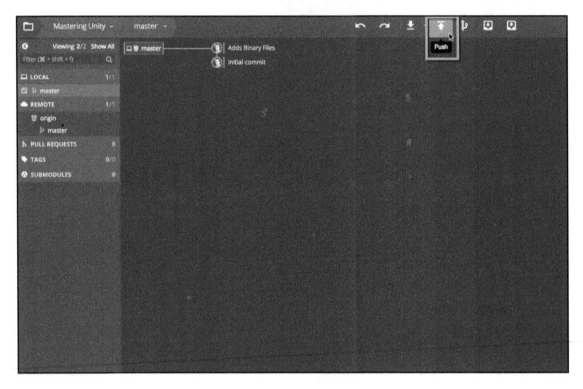

Pushing local changes to a Remote Repo

To download the latest changes from an existing Repo and merge them into the Local Repo, you click the **Pull** button. This updates the Local Repo with changes on the server. In many cases, this is the equivalent of updating the local Repo to match the Remote. But it's possible to Pull down changes into a different local Repo, merging and integrating the changes to make a completely different Repo.

A Pull operation merges the remote Repo into the local Repo

Cloning

When your remote repo is up-to-date and contains all the changes you need to preserve, then you don't need to worry if your local repo ever gets deleted or removed. This is because you can always download the complete Git Repo from the Remote, by using a Clone operation. To do this, select the **Clone** option from the GitKraken start menu.

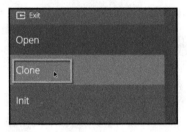

Cloning a remote Repo

From the **Clone** Menu, select the **BitBucket** tab, and then choose the **Remote Repo** to download, using the **Remotes** list. Then choose the folder where the Remote should be downloaded as a clone. Finally, click the **Clone the repo!** Button to confirm.

Cloning a selected BitBucket Repo to the computer

After *Cloning* the *remote Repo*, your *Local* version features the same files. This makes it easy for anybody to share and collaborate on the same Repo, from any location. Great work! You're now fully equipped to start using *Git* Version Control to manage your projects effectively.

Summary

Congratulations on reaching the end of this chapter. You can now use Trello and Version Control (Git) to manage your work more effectively. This helps you streamline your workflow so that you can do more with less time. Trello lets you project manage and time-block your work successfully, while Git lets you track the development of your project, both locally and remotely, and you can rewind progress to retrieve earlier states if needed. Both tools are incredibly powerful, so make them your friends!

7
Persistent Data - Load and Save Game States

This chapter focuses on **persistent data** and **Serialization** generally; specifically, this is about saving and loading information to and from files, whether human-readable text files or encrypted binary files, both online and offline. This process has two especially important functions for games: firstly, save-game states allow the player to save and resume their progress in-game; and secondly, **DDD** (**Data Driven Design**) lets developers store huge databases (such as weapon and player stats) in text files and spreadsheets for driving gameplay elements. The first use case interests us here for *Dead Keys*; allowing the player to save their progress as they move through levels. Let's get started.

Data Serialization

Data is a raw material for most games; even relatively simple games require characters to have health, damage points, shields, and others in addition to item data, such as *sword-strength*, *sword-fragility*, and so on. Thus, data is critically important for gameplay to behave as intended. When it comes to working with data, developers typically have two main needs. The need to save or export the state of a game at any time, allowing the player to save their progress and then to resume it at a later time even if the device has been powered-off between play sessions; and second, the need to import data, such as weapon-stats and character sheets (and the player's saves), from external sources created by designers, such as a spreadsheet or a database. The basic idea is that in-game objects and entities, and their relationships and states, should have a correspondence with data. We should be able to represent the state of a game in a way that can be meaningfully committed to a file or to text.

The process of saving and loading the state of a game to and from data is known as **Serialization**. For example, if the complete state of a game object could be saved to a text file such that, on the basis of the data in the file alone, it would be possible to reconstruct the game object at any later time on any computer, the game object has, effectively, been serialized. Let's take a look at some possibilities for Serialization in Unity, based on the native feature-set, as opposed to commercial third-party add-ons:

- **Player preferences**: You'll often need to store user-preferences for a game, regardless of platform: such as *screen resolution, full-screen/windowed mode, volume*, and *graphical quality*. Typically, gamers adjust these settings from an options screen to improve the experience for their computer, and they expect these settings to be retained across play sessions. An easy way to achieve this in Unity is with `PlayerPrefs`, a platform-agonistic class for persistently saving and loading *small data*– such as boolean, integer, string, and floating point values –these are characteristic of user preference data. This class is covered in-depth later in this chapter; more information can be found online (`https://docs.unity3d.com/ScriptReference/PlayerPrefs.html`). In short, it works by saving key-value data pairs (such as *HighScore=1000, Name=Joe*) to a designated location on the computer where values can later be retrieved quickly and easily by specifying the *key*.

- **INI files (Initialization files)**: They are human-readable text files containing a line-by-line database of key-value pair settings (such as *HighScore=1000, Name=Joe*). These files are commonly used in PC games, for the Windows and Mac platforms, and they're an effective method for saving user-preference data. However, Unity has no native support for INI files, and instead migrates the equivalent functionality into the `PlayerPrefs` class, as mentioned in the previous point. Nevertheless, through free add-ons and scripts, Unity can read INI files, (see `http://blog.kennyist.com/?p=864`) and we'll see examples of this later and why we'd want to do this. An example INI file is given here for storing basic game information:

```
[Player]
; Basic Player Data
Name=John Doe
Gender=Male
Level=50

  [Score]
; Score information
HighScore=8695088457694
Player=John Doe
LastScore=758596068896
```

```
[Preferences]
; Settings
Resolution=1920x1080
Volume=0.8
FullScreen=true
MouseSpeed=75
```

- **XML (Extensible Markup Language)**: XML is a dedicated, declarative language commonly used across the Web and related industries, for describing data in human-readable form. XML is, in essence, a general industry-standard for writing data (for exporting and importing data between applications). Using this standard, you can describe nearly anything, from user preferences to character sheets! XML has many advantages for encoding large quantities of game data. Firstly, it's easy to read and write; secondly, it's an established standard supported by many platforms and applications, making it easier for your game to inter-operate with third-party data sources; and thirdly, it features an intuitive hierarchical structure that matches Unity's scene hierarchy. Unity offers extensive support for XML through its mono library classes, as we'll see later. More information on XML can be found online at `https://en.wikipedia.org/wiki/XML`. An example XML file, which is content-equivalent to the INI file given previously, is shown here:

```
<root>
    <Player>
        <Name>Jon Doe</Name>
        <Gender>Male</Gender>
        <Level>50</Level>
    </Player>
    <Score>
        <HighScore>8695088457694</HighScore>
        <Player>Jon Doe</Player>
        <LastScore>758596068896</LastScore>
    </Score>
    <Preferences>
        <Resolution>1920x1080</Resolution>
        <Volume>0.8</Volume>
        <FullScreen>true</FullScreen>
        <MouseSpeed>75</MouseSpeed>
    </Preferences>
</root>
```

- **JSON**: More recently, criticism has been leveled against XML for its verbose style in which values must be surrounded by opening and closing key tags in HTML style (for example: `<FullScreen>` and `</FullScreen>`). This can make XML long, bloated, and larger in file size than needed. For this reason, **JSON** (**JavaScript Object Notation**) is often proposed as a lighter weight alternative for describing the same data. JSON is not yet as widely supported by the Web and other standards as XML, but nonetheless it is a popular standard that is increasingly adopted in games. Reflecting this popularity, Unity 5.3 onwards features native support for reading and writing JSON data: (`https://docs.unity3d.com/Manual/JSONSerialization.html`). An example JSON file is featured here:

```
{
  "root": {
    "Player": {
      "Name": "Jon Doe",
      "Gender": "Male",
      "Level": "50"
    },
    "Score": {
      "HighScore": "8695088457694",
      "Player": "Jon Doe",
      "LastScore": "758596068896"
    },
    "Preferences": {
      "Resolution": "1920x1080",
      "Volume": "0.8",
      "FullScreen": "true",
      "MouseSpeed": "75"
    }
  }
}
```

- **Binary**: One problem surrounding *INI*, *XML*, and *JSON* files when they are stored locally, is that gamers can open, read, and even change them–especially for Windows and Mac games. This opens up the possibility of cheating, as gamers can tweak files to confer benefits and advantages to themselves. For some genres and types, such open access to data files is not problematic, but often developers want to protect against cheating, and there are many reasons for why this is so.

One is to maintain a challenging and rewarding game experience. Another is to prevent cheating that could significantly impact the fun-factor in a multiplayer game. And another is to prevent the player from unlocking, modding, or circumventing monetization features and in-app purchases. The solution instead is to save and load data to and from formats that are not human-readable. One method is the binary format; and we'll consider this later too. More information can be found online here: `https://gamedevelopment.tutsplus.com/tutorials/how-to-save-and-load-your-players-progress-in-unity-cms-20934`. An example of a binary file opened and viewed in a text editor is shown here:

```
Assembly-CSharp-firstpass.dll
fihÅXZEhÑÇ[xi∆è[x9iÑ>UZDiÑÇ[Ù±iÑÇ[å,jÜú[xGjÑ™[ZdjÅº[ëÇjÑ>[Z¾jÑ´[óPÍÜ8ZXÍÅÜ[nhÍë~^Ù˜Íë´[|Oë°^aÕÜ8Z$lÕès^ó$»Ôñº^
               $0●ñf^9$Í●ëÇ^O&ÙëfX        *˛ÛÜ8Z*PÚ∆è[x*úÕÅÜ[π*ÔÜÜ8Z,àÜ∆è[x,'ÙÅUZ,˛ÚÅÜ[n,l˜Ü8Z.¿˜ës[å.˜˜ë÷^ö/˜ÅUZ0
˜Å>UZ0ó˜ÅXZ0∞˜ÅÉ]Z0˜ÅÜ[n0*,˛Ü8Z22,ÅÜ[n2D,Ü8Z4º,∆è[x4(˜ÅÜ[n4(Ü8Z6t∆è[x6¿ÅÜ[n6ÉÜ8Z8d∆è[x8ÛÉ^ô8(ÅUZ8§ÅÜ^x8ÅÜ[n8K
Û8Z:T
ës^ó:˜
ë°^
ëf^9:-
ëŒ^O<é
ëfX        @ñ
Û8Z@"
ÅÜ[n@˜
Û8ZB`∆è[xB‹ÅÜ[πB≤Û8ZDÕÅÜ[πDÛ8ZFEÅXZF\Ås
ZFÈÅ_ZF...Û8ZF‡Å>UPFÅ#_/FÚÛ8ZIhÅ>UPI·Û8ZI'Å>UZI&Åó_eI
Üë_ZJYÛ8ZJÍÅ>UZJ_Üë_ZJ;Û8ZJJÅ>UZJlÅxUZJñÛ®_ZJ˜Û8ZJÿÅxUZJñ Û8ZJ`˜Å>UZJ2!Û8ZJ:!Å>UZJh!Û8ZJà!Å>UZJó!
Å≥_"Js"Û8ZKë"Å«_ZK,#ÅŸ_¬K$Û8ZL$ÅXZL$Û8ZL[$Û8ZLD$∆P[NL`∆É_Í0<'Û8ZQD'Å>UZQT'ÅxUZQ€'Û8ZQÍ'Û8˜Q'(Ü˜_~
T(Û˜`U(Û˜Zvá(Û™˜ZV∞(Û8ZV|)Û0`˛V»)Û6˜ÇX°*Û8ZYf*ÅxUZY,Å@`*˛YD,ÅK˜vZT,Û8ZZø,Å>UZZ'.ÅxUZZÅ/Û8ZZ∆/ÅrUZZ-0Û8ZZZV0Û0`~
Zs0ÅV`~
[•0Û`_~
\∞0Üb`P]'0Ûl`P]=3Û8Z]fl3Å>UZ]4ÅxUZ]{4Û8Z]ù4Å
Z]i4Û8Z]Å4ÅxUZ],4Û8Z]5Ûx`ö]05Û`P]
7Û8Z]7Å>UZ]e7Üà`«]x7Üó`˜ ^M9Û8Z_l9Å>UP_é9Û¶`Z_Û;Û8Z_●;ÅXZ_@<ÅUZ_é<ÅxUZ_ó<Å
``Z_¿<Å≥`+_Å=Û8Z`'=AXZ`_=Ûʃ`Z`ÿ>Û8Z`ÿ>Å>UZ`Í>ÅxUZ`ÅÅÛ8Z`ÅÀÛ8Z`BÅ>UZ`BÅ
Z`SÇÛ8Z`hÇÅruZ`DÅ1Ÿ`4DÅ1Ÿ aXDÅÉ5Ÿ bzDÛ8ZcÇDÛ8ZcÔFÛ8Zc,FÅP[NcJÅÉ_Íf8JÛ8ZhRJÅrUZhfJÅ◊`ZhåJÛ8Zh¥JÜ,`ÔhŒJÅÍ˜«hÿJÜ¨˜1!
i˜JÅruZi KÜa¢jDMÅ%aV!kNÅ0aZpOÅKaZp
OÅ_ZpOÅXa+pPPÛ8ZqdPÛ8squPÛ8Zs˜PÅP[NsÉTÅÉ_Ív(ÛÜ8Zx0Üæ˜Uÿx`ÛÜ8Zz¥UÛ™aæ!zŒUÅ}a˜!zÿÜÜ¢aæ!{ÜÚÅúa˜!{_ÜÛ`aæ!|VÅΩa˜!|VÅ>UZ}
\VÛë_Z}~VÅxUZ}HYÅKaZ}CÛ8Z}LÉ~Bx}·       +_V}$·    f_V}>ÉÉBZ}NÉë_Z}àÛ8Z}1É~Bx}X·       +_V}t·   f_V}éÉÉBZ}ÛÉë_Z}Û8Z}ˉÉ~Bx}
å·        +_V}®·   f_V}~ÉÉBZ}˜Éë_Z}{,Û8Z}Ñ,É~Bx}.·  +_V}˜.· f_V}::ÉÉBZ}J.Éë_Z}˜0Û8Z}1É~Bx}2·       +_V}˜2·     f_V}:ÉÉBZ}
J2Éë_Z}Q2Û8Z}\2É~Bx}x3·      +_V}i3·  f_V}Å3ÉÉBZ}æ3Éë_Z}R5Û8Z}\5É~Bx}¿6·     +_V}‹6·    f_V}´6ÉÉBZ}7Éë_Z}˜7Û8Z}˜7É~Bx}9·
+_V}˜9ÉÉBZ}F9Éë_Z}ó9Û8Z}t9É~Bx}Å;·     +_V}ú¦·  f_V}J;ÉÉBZ}ç;Éë_Z}àÛ8Z}1DÉ~Bx}É·        +_V}$É·
f_V}>ÉÉBZ}NÉë_Z}UÉÛ8Z}˜ÉÉ~Bx}'É·       +_V}●É·   f_V}
FÉÉBZ}FÉë_Z}!FÛ8Z},FÉ~Bx}$F·   +_V}¿F·   f_V}/FÉÉBZ}ÍFÉë_Z}aÛ0Û8a8a8a8a8aæ1"9f9a80Û8§<®<'7'7'7c>≥>Ω>≥>Ω>≥1Û>Í>_?
à≥1≥1ÅX4@à4@x4@àMAMA^ApApA˜uApApApApApApApÅIApApApApApApApA≥1ñÅñÅñApApAòA≥1≥1pApAòA≥1≥1≥1MAMA●BpApApAIApApA
pApApApA≥1pApApApAIApApApApApApApA≥1¶õÜCèC≥1MAMA≥1pApA˜uApApAñÅñÅñApAIApApApApApApApA≥1-0Û-D-
0ÛDvEÅEÜEÅEÜEÅEÜEÅEÜEÅEÜEÅEÜE-0ÛDvEÅEÜEÅEÜEÅEÜE-0ÛD-09F>F-09F-0ÛD-0ÛD˜9ÍG-0ÛD:HPHZH-0ÛD-0ÛD-0ÛD-
0ÛDôH-0ÛD-HII-0ÛD-HèI-0ÛDÅEÜElôI™"ÅEÜElôI™"ÅEÜElôI™"§IÅEÜE®I≤I ÍI˜I-0JJ-0ÛD-0ÛD-0ÛD-09FÇJ≠J-0ÛDg!-0ÛD(...Ù*-09Fg!-09F
-0ÛD-09FÇJK≠J-0ÛD(K∗K(K∗K<KyK(K9Fg!-0ÛDôK-09Fg!ûK9Fg!ÔK-K"K∗K-09Fg!ŸK&K`KLŸK&K-0ÛD-0ÛDCL-0ÛD-0ÛD-0ÛD-0ÛD
0ÛDŸK&K`KLŸK&K-0ÛD-0ÛD-
0ÛDLMNMRM˜MOO¶6ÜCèCÜCèCΩ>"P/PΩ>"PΩ>ÔP'7Û5Ω>Ω>Ω>˜5`5•B>S>S>S¶6ÜCèCÜCèC≥1ôKôKÅTÇTÉTÍTÉ6ñT¶6Û6¶6ÜCèCÜCèC"9f9≥1≥1≥1
ÍMQUMQYU(M(Q(UÜÍ°!°u°¢!¢u¢£!£uÉ¶1¶u¶B!ßuß®!®u®©!©u©™!™u™`!`u`˜!¿u≠Å!≠uₓÅ!ₓuₓ8ZA
8^y#8hy08s...78xÅS8]...k8AÅÅ8Ù...¢8¢a8ZÅ8Z˜ ʃ8í    ∆8íèŸ8óÅ8íÛ8ô9íÅ8ü09§"9$9ô&9≠ö,9≠ö79≥ö;9[]yç8ç   G9íT9ø   Y9...f9h9ö!
y9●Ù9ø    å9ÿ!T9> ô9Å˜8í°º9°Ÿ9
!Å9í     19Ÿπ
:Å:|!,:ôT9[]ô2:[]!Ù9>     8:ÅÅJ:|ôS:≠     :_+   f:2)f9!|:9)"98í9Byà:h    ü:çi8Z   Å:í|:T˜:\1;_.;e1;_1-;í...
@;ˍÑ;x\;vAr;^yÅ;{...à;Å...ñ;à-;19";ô9‡;ù9Í;Í±';£-<®ʃ8ü
<...É6<s08Z˜8ʃu<\AN<ôA1<«y§<Å1
=Ÿ        =fl       #=íô;=É)8ÍAI=®QR=xaa=Ÿa=Ü-,aè=Z  Í=íQ∆=ô°=ÜQ§=ô...Ω=É9‡=íÍ=\...`=ÜÅ>|Q>"QÅ8íQ%>a+>a4>,π@>
)8í)h9ö)G>ZaQ>ZY‡;ù}>xY‡;í¢>"˜ünf>
!"9í∞>!f9!§9ö->>ñ+>>íÅ7ì"˜>‡)
```

Binary files are difficult to edit successfully

Player preferences – saving data

For *Dead Keys*, the player progresses through a sequence of levels, one after another. On reaching the end of one level, the next begins. As the player moves from level to level, their progress should be saved, so the most recent player can easily resume their progress from the highest attained level on their next play session. To achieve this, we need to use only the PlayerPrefs class for storing the highest attained level. Progress cannot be resumed within a level. That is, the player may resume play from the highest attained level, but always from the beginning of that level.

As we'll see later in this chapter, the PlayerPrefs class is all we'll need for saving and loading user data in *Dead Keys*. This makes our persistent data needs very simple. Nevertheless, we'll cover a range of data storage solutions here, for games of all sizes, both small and large.

Preparing to save data for Dead Keys

Before saving data with `PlayerPrefs`, you should specify the title and company name for your project from the **Project Settings** window, as these settings determine how and where the `PlayerPrefs` data is stored on the user's computer. To access **Project Settings**, select **Edit | Project Settings | Player** from the application menu:

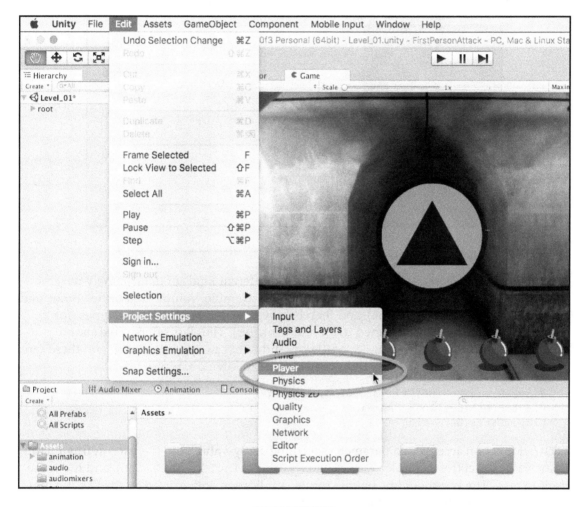

Accessing Project Settings

Next, enter a title for the project, and a **Company Name**. Here, I've used `Dead Keys` as the **Product Name**, and `Packt Publishing` as the **Company Name**:

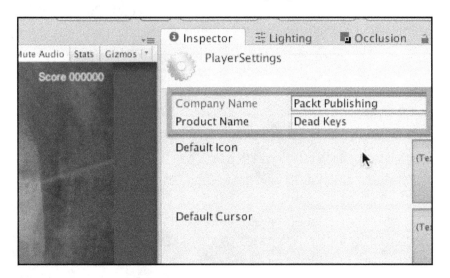

Entering a Product Name and Company Name

The `PlayerPrefs` class can ultimately save three different kinds of data, namely *integers* (for example: high score), *floating point* numbers (for example: volume and fastest time), and *strings* (for example: player name); and thereby any data derived from these types (for example, a *Boolean* can be converted to a 1 and 0 integer). The class offers three static functions to save this data; `SetInt`, `SetFloat`, and `SetString` respectively, and these can be called anywhere in your script files. Consider the following sample:

```
PlayerPrefs.SetInt("PlayerScore", 999785);
PlayerPrefs.SetFloat("RemainingTime", 5.5f);
PlayerPrefs.SetString("PlayerName", "Jon Doe");
```

Each Set function accepts two parameters forming a **key-value pair**; the **user-defined name** of the value to set (for example: `PlayerScore`, `RemainingTime`, and so on), and the value itself to save. The key should be unique for the application and, is used by the Get functions to retrieve the specified value (discussed later).

 More information on the `PlayerPrefs` class can be found online here: `htt ps://docs.unity3d.com/ScriptReference/PlayerPrefs.html`.

One important question that arises regarding the Set functions for `PlayerPrefs`, is about where on the user's computer is the, saved data stored. This varies depending on the operating system. For Windows computers, all data is stored in the Windows registry as separate keys. To access the registry, access the Start menu, and run the `RegEdit` command. Next, the Window's **Registry Editor** appears, displaying all system keys and settings. Remember; editing or changing any keys in the registry can cause your computer and software to stop working properly, so be careful!

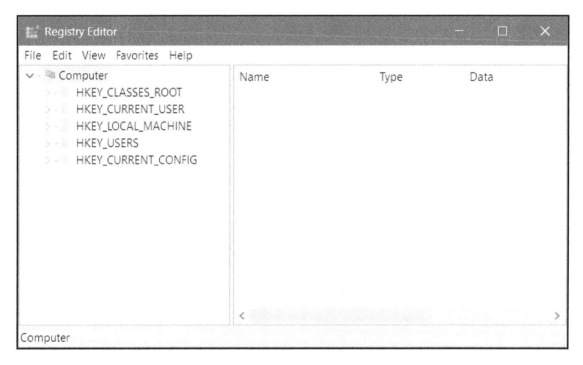

Windows Registry Editor

You can find Unity application settings under the `HKCU` l `Software` l `[company name]` l `[product name]` key. The **Company Name** and **Product Name** fields should be substituted for the values specified in the **Project Settings**, as mentioned previously. Here, all applications will save their values. These can be edited directly from the **Registry Editor**, but this is not recommended. Nevertheless, knowing how to find and access the settings can be useful for verifying and debugging your application; making sure the right values are being saved.

On a Mac computer, all settings can be accessed from Mac Finder, by navigating to `Library/Preferences/ unity.[company name].[product name].plist`.

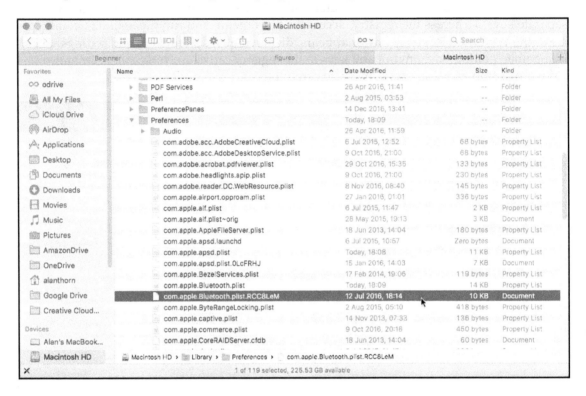

Accessing PList files

The Unity setting files contain all preferences in a human-readable, text-based XML format. Like the registry settings, this file can be edited, but this is not recommended.

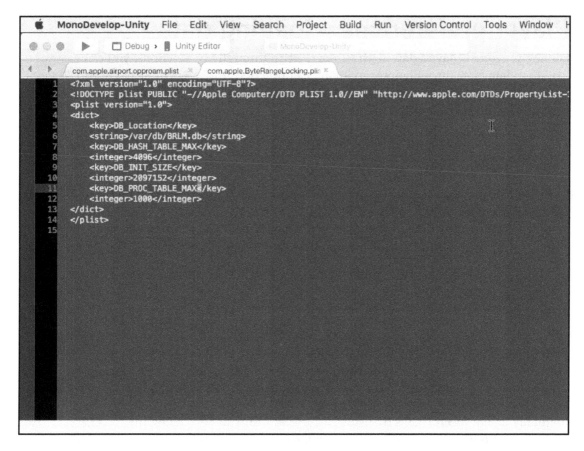

Viewing PList Files generated by PlayerPrefs

For other platforms, such as web and mobile, the storage location for `PlayerPrefs` varies widely. Further information on platform specifics can be found online at:
`https://docs.unity3d.com/ScriptReference/PlayerPrefs.html`.

The `PlayerPrefs` Set functions (`SetInt`, `SetFloat`, and `SetString`) are buffered; that is, the data is not actually committed to the computer until the application terminates. However, if you need the changes committed earlier than application exit, or to protect against a crash or failure, you should additionally call the `Save` function once after having called all Set functions. The `Save` function requires no arguments and returns no value; it simply commits all the set changes. More information on save can be found online at:
`https://docs.unity3d.com/ScriptReference/PlayerPrefs.Save.html`.

Player preferences – loading data

Having previously saved data with `PlayerPrefs` through Set functions, you can easily load that data back through accompanying Get functions (`GetInt`, `GetFloat`, and `GetString`). With these, you simply specify a unique key name, and Unity returns the respective value. Consider the following code:

```
int HighScore = PlayerPrefs.GetInt ("HighScore", 0);
float RemainingTime = PlayerPrefs.GetFloat ("RemainingTime", 0f);
string Name = PlayerPrefs.GetString ("PlayerName", "Jon Doe");
```

Each Get function requires only one essential parameter; namely, the key to retrieve. This is the first parameter. But what happens if you specify a key that doesn't exist? Which value should be returned by default in that case? To handle this, each Get function supports a second, optional parameter, which is always returned if the specified key doesn't exist.

 You can also query whether a specified key exists by using the `HasKey` function:
https://docs.unity3d.com/ScriptReference/PlayerPrefs.HasKey.html

Remember, if your game creates keys using `PlayerPrefs`, these settings normally remain even after your game is uninstalled and removed from the computer. For example, uninstalling your game on Windows will not, by default, remove all related registry keys. Likewise, uninstalling your game on Android will not remove all cached user data. You can manually delete specific keys by using `DeleteKey`, and all keys using the `DeleteAll` function, but these are only effective when the user or game takes active steps to remove keys. Sometimes, the gamer will simply delete your game without considering that user data should be uninstalled. In these cases, all user data saved with `PlayerPrefs` remains on the system, unless removed manually!

Player preferences – INI files

Now, let's consider the case of saving data using INI files instead of `PlayerPrefs`. INI files achieve a similar purpose to `PlayerPrefs`; storing key-value pairs. However, INI files contain all settings inside a single, human-readable text file. For this example, we'll work with the following INI file, which contains some basic settings for a sample game:

```
[Player]
; Basic Player Data
Name=John Doe
Gender=Male
```

```
Level=50

[Score]
; Score information
HighScore=8695088457694
Player=John Doe
LastScore=758596068896

[Preferences]
; Settings
Resolution=1920x1080
Volume=0.8
FullScreen=true
MouseSpeed=75
```

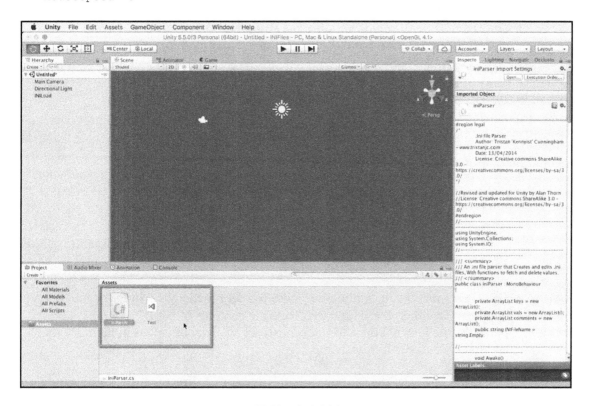

INI Unity project included

You can find a complete Unity project that works with INI files included
in this book's companion files, in the INI files folder.

Unity offers no native functionality for reading and parsing INI files. Instead, you'll need to rely on third-party add-ons or external script files to read them. One example of a free script to read INI files is featured at `http://blog.kennyist.com/?p=864`. We'll use this script as a basis, and extend upon it to quickly and easily read an INI file. This script is included in the course companion files (`iniParser.cs`). It should be added to your project, and code comments follow.

Comments on iniParser.cs

- The `iniParser` class is derived from `MonoBehaviour`. This means it can be attached to game objects as a component.
- The `iniFileName` public variable is a string representing the full name (minus path and extension) of the INI file to be saved and loaded.
- The `load` function opens an INI file, reads its contents, and parses those into an array of key-value pairs (`Keys` and `Vals`). This function is called once during `Awake`, as the level begins, to load the contents of a specified INI file.
- The Get function lets you search for an extant key by name, and then returns the associated value. This function should only be called after running `load`, to open the contents of an INI file into memory.
- The `Application.dataPath` native variable is provided by Unity and always represents a valid read-only storage location on the local computer where files can be loaded, regardless of operating system. If you need to save data permanently to the computer, the `Application.persistentDataPath` variable should be used instead. For more information on storage locations, see the online Unity documentation at: `https://docs.unity3d.com/ScriptReference/Application-dataPath.html`.
- The `load` function, in combination with the Set function, is where the magic happens. Together, these functions load the contents of the INI file into memory, parse the file line by line, and then construct an array of values in memory that are quickly and easily searchable.

The `#region` and `#endregion` directives of C# directives are used in code to group together related regions. You can further enhance your code editor and code display by using code folding.

Now drag and drop the script file onto an empty object in the scene, adding it as a component. Then use the filename field to specify an INI filename to load. This can refer to any sample INI file.

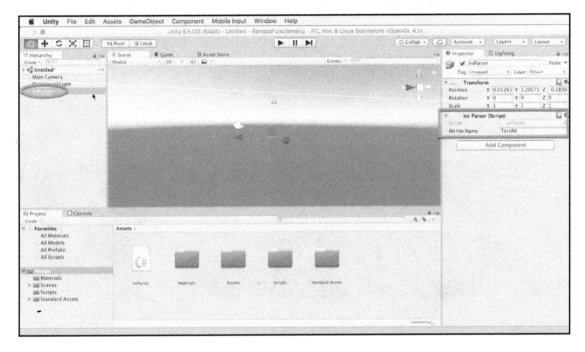

Configuring the iniParser component

When testing from the Unity editor, the `Application.dataPath` variable normally refers to the project `Asset` folder, and for compiled runtime applications, it normally refers to the accompanying `Data` folder, alongside the executable file. For this reason, add an INI file to the **Project** panel, inside the root `Asset` folder, to successfully test your project.

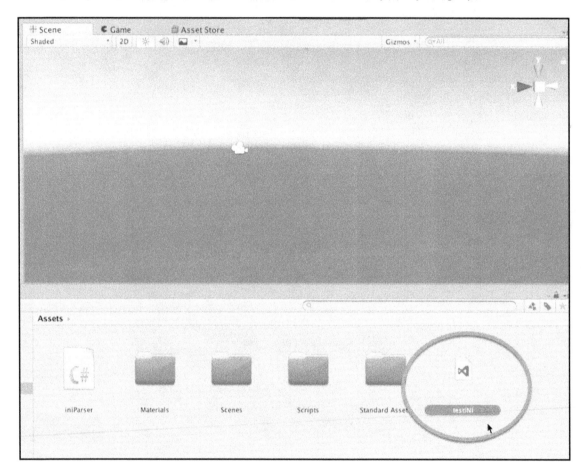

Adding a testINI file to the project

Now run the application by pressing play on the toolbar, and you'll get a success message printed on the console, indicating that the INI file was properly loaded and its contents parsed into the arrays.

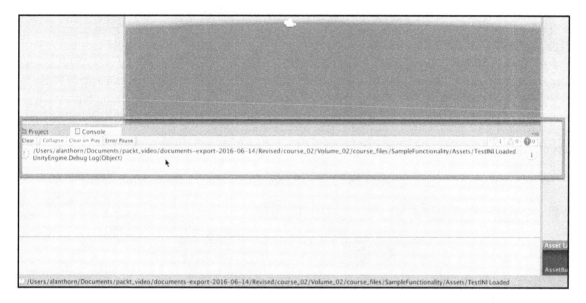

Loading an INI file

Once loaded, you can access any key-value property with a call to the Get function. Simply specify the name of the key to retrieve. This function returns all values as strings; and it is not sensitive to variable type. This means you may need to convert the string to other data types, such as integers and floats, depending on the data needed. This line can be called anywhere within the iniParser class:

```
string Resolution = Get ("Resolution");
```

Excellent! You can now import and read user data from INI files, stored locally in either the Data or PersistentData paths. Great work! INI files offer a convenient and effective alternative to the PlayerPrefs class.

Saving data – XML files

Both the `PlayerPrefs` class and third-party INI file readers are useful for saving and loading miscellaneous settings, such as high score, resolution, and volume. For complicated data, such as the state of a level, the positions of objects, or an inventory of items, both `PlayerPrefs` and INI files quickly become impractical. Instead, more robust storage solutions are needed. At this stage, we have three main options in Unity; namely XML files, binary files, and JSON files. In this section, we'll focus on XML, which refers to an HTML-like language for storing structured, hierarchical data in human-readable text. Here, we'll focus on saving and loading the position, rotation, and scale of all objects in the scene. In essence, this lets us save the complete state of a scene to a file. To start, let's begin with a scene containing some objects:

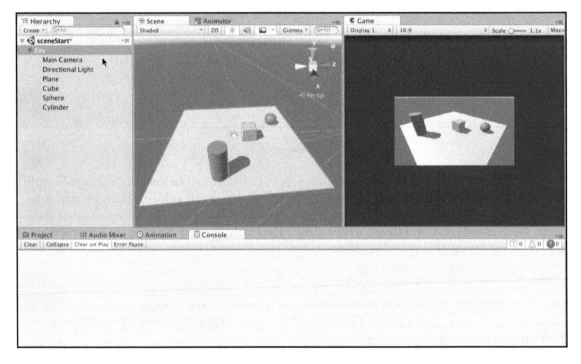

Building a scene filled with objects, ready for Serialization

You can find a copy of the XML Serialization project in this book's companion files, in the XMLSerialization folder.

Next, create a new script file, SerializeTransformXML.cs, and then attach the file to any empty object in the scene. This script will be responsible for saving all object data to an XML file. See the following sample code to do this for the script file and comments that follow:

```
using System.Collections;
using System.Collections.Generic;
using UnityEngine;
using System.IO;
using System.Xml.Serialization;
//-----------------------------------------
[System.Serializable]
public class TransformDataXML
{
    public float PosX,PosY,PosZ;
    public float EulerX,EulerY,EulerZ;
    public float ScaleX,ScaleY,ScaleZ;
    public string ObjectName = string.Empty;
}
//-----------------------------------------
[System.Serializable]
[XmlRoot("TransformCollectionXML")]
public class TransformCollectionXML
{
    [XmlArray("Items"),XmlArrayItem("TransformDataXML")]
    public TransformDataXML[] DataArray;
}
//-----------------------------------------
public class serializeTransformXML : MonoBehaviour
{
    public Transform[] TransformArray;
    public string FilePath = "/Saves/MyTransformData.json";
    public TransformCollectionXML MyData;
    //-----------------------------------------
    // Use this for initialization
    void Start () {
        //Get transform component
        TransformArray = Object.FindObjectsOfType<Transform>();
        TransformCollectionXML MyData = new TransformCollectionXML ();
    }
    //-----------------------------------------
    public void SaveData()
    {
```

```
        //Create new array
        MyData.DataArray = new TransformDataXML[TransformArray.Length];

        for(int i=0; i<MyData.DataArray.Length; i++)
        {
            MyData.DataArray[i] = new TransformDataXML ();
            MyData.DataArray[i].PosX = TransformArray[i].position.x;
            MyData.DataArray[i].PosY = TransformArray[i].position.y;
            MyData.DataArray[i].PosZ = TransformArray[i].position.z;

            MyData.DataArray[i].EulerX =
TransformArray[i].rotation.eulerAngles.x;
            MyData.DataArray[i].EulerY =
TransformArray[i].rotation.eulerAngles.y;
            MyData.DataArray[i].EulerZ =
TransformArray[i].rotation.eulerAngles.z;

            MyData.DataArray[i].ScaleX = TransformArray[i].localScale.x;
            MyData.DataArray[i].ScaleY = TransformArray[i].localScale.y;
            MyData.DataArray[i].ScaleZ = TransformArray[i].localScale.z;

            MyData.DataArray[i].ObjectName = TransformArray[i].name;
        }

    string SavePath = Application.persistentDataPath + "/" + FilePath;

        XmlSerializer serializer = new
XmlSerializer(typeof(TransformCollectionXML));
        FileStream stream = new FileStream(SavePath, FileMode.Create);
        serializer.Serialize(stream, MyData);
        stream.Close();
        Debug.Log ("Saving Data To: " + SavePath);
    }
    //-----------------------------------------
    public void LoadData()
    {
    string LoadPath = Application.persistentDataPath + "/" + FilePath;
        var serializer = new XmlSerializer(typeof(TransformCollectionXML));
        var stream = new FileStream(LoadPath, FileMode.Open);
        MyData = serializer.Deserialize(stream) as TransformCollectionXML;
        stream.Close();

        //Update objects
        for (int i = 0; i < MyData.DataArray.Length; i++)
        {
            //Find object of matching name
            GameObject Selected =
GameObject.Find(MyData.DataArray[i].ObjectName);
```

```
        //Get transform component
        Transform SelectedTransform =
Selected.GetComponent<Transform>();

        SelectedTransform.position = new Vector3 (MyData.DataArray
[i].PosX, MyData.DataArray [i].PosY, MyData.DataArray [i].PosZ);
        SelectedTransform.localScale = new Vector3 (MyData.DataArray
[i].ScaleX, MyData.DataArray [i].ScaleY, MyData.DataArray [i].ScaleZ);
        SelectedTransform.rotation = Quaternion.Euler
(MyData.DataArray[i].EulerX, MyData.DataArray[i].EulerY,
MyData.DataArray[i].EulerZ);
        }
    }
    //-------------------------------------------
    void Update()
    {
        if (Input.GetKeyDown (KeyCode.S))
        {
            SaveData();
            return;
        }

        if (Input.GetKeyDown (KeyCode.L))
        {
            LoadData();
            return;
        }
    }
    //-------------------------------------------
}
```

Comments

- For Serialization to work, you'll need to import the `System.IO` and `System.Xml.Serialization` namespaces. The former library contains classes and functions for saving data to files on the local computer, and the latter for converting data in memory to an XML string.
- The `TransformationDataXML` class is declared using the `[System.Serializable]` attribute. This means the class contains properties that can be transformed to text for Serialization, and it can also show its values in the object **Inspector**, if declared as a public object.

- The `TransformationDataXML` class contains all data needed to save a transform component to a string. The variables, **Vector3** (for position and scale) and a **Quaternion** (for rotation) do not, by default, serialize to a text stream, and thus must be converted into primitive data types, such as floats and strings. These types are more readably serialized to a file.

- The `SerializeTransformXML` class contains a `MyData` variable, which contains an array of `TransformationDataXML` objects. Each one defines an object in the scene; or more accurately, each instance describes a unique transform component in the scene.

- The `Start` function is used to retrieve an array of all transform components in the scene; one per game object. This approach only saves data for all game objects extant at level start up. It does not save objects instantiated at runtime, or particles in a particle system, even though they could be seen as separate objects.

- Each transform component is retrieved at start up from the `FindObjectsOfType` function. This function returns a static array of all instances in the scene of a matching type.

- The `SaveData` function serializes our array of transform components to an XML string that can be saved to a file.

- The `SaveData` function begins the Serialization process by converting the position, rotation, and scale transformation properties from their original data types (Vector3 and Quaternion) into primitive types; specifically floating point values. These are converted from the transform component into unique float-variables, such as `PosX`, `ScaleX`, and more.

- An object of the `XMLSerializer` type is created for converting binary data to XML, and a `Stream` object is created, which represents a file on the local computer. The `Application.persistentDataPath` variable is used to represent a platform-agnostic location for saving data.

- The `XMLSerializer.Serialize` method is called, with the `MyData` variable as an argument, to write the binary data to a file in XML format.

- To complete the process, the `Stream.Close` function is called to close the file.

- The `LoadData` function is, essentially, the opposite of the `SaveData` function. It reads data from a file, loads it into memory, and converts the data from XML into a binary version that is ready to use.

- `LoadData` begins by reading data from a specified file. To make sure each object in the scene receives the correct transform data, the object name has been saved too. Assuming each object has a unique name in the scene, the `GameObject.Find` function is used to search the scene for the named object, and then it is assigned the associated position, rotation, and scale data that was saved.
- The `Update` function is added as a temporary test measure for quickly validating and verifying the code. You can press *S* on the keyboard to save all object data, and *L* to load the saved version.

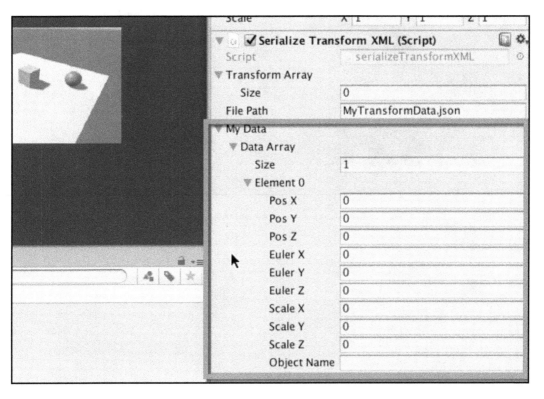

Editing serializable data from the object Inspector; from classes declared with the [System.Serializable] attribute

Great work! Let's give this code a test. Simply press play on the toolbar to run the scene, and then move some objects around inside the **Scene** view, to change the arrangement away from its default.

Moving objects away from their default arrangement

Next, press *S* on the keyboard to save the scene (ensure that the `Save` script is attached to only one object in the scene). The local is then printed as a debug message in the console, confirming that the save operation was successful and showing the full name and saved path.

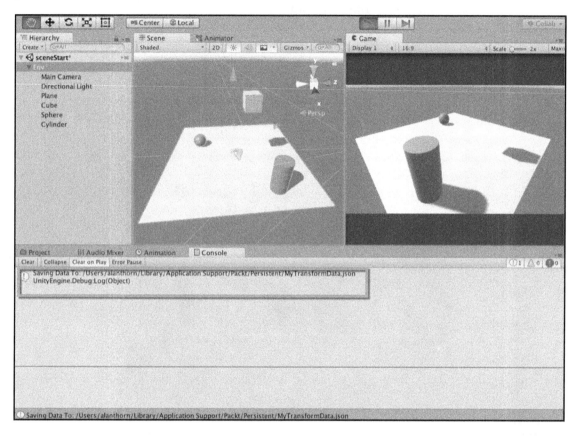

Pressing S saves data to a local XML file

Having saved the data, stop playback and check the file location for the saved XML. Depending on your operation system, version, and file structure this may be saved in a hidden folder, which is not accessible by default. To access hidden files on Windows, open an Explorer window and select the **View** tab. From there, enable the **Hidden Items** checkbox. This shows all hidden files and folders.

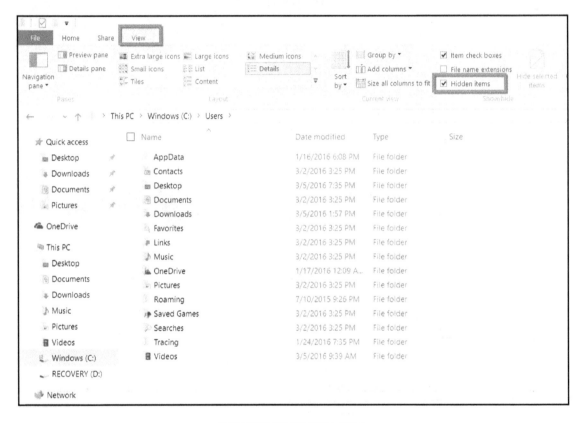

Enabling Hidden Items from Windows Explorer

On Mac, the `Application.persistentDataPath` folder usually refers to the library folder. This can be accessed by opening a Finder window, and choosing **Go** | **Go to Folder...** from the application menu.

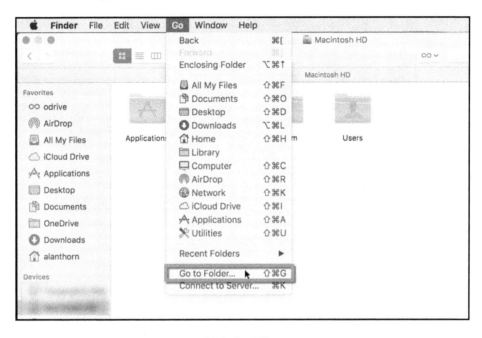

Selecting Go to Folder...

On selecting **Go To Folder...**, a pop-up dialog appears. From here, enter the command `~/Library`, and then select **Go**.

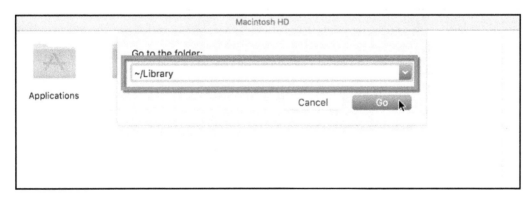

Accessing the Library folder

On running the `~/Library` command, a range of system-specific support folders are shown where many applications settings are saved. For Unity projects, data is typically saved in the `Application Support` folder.

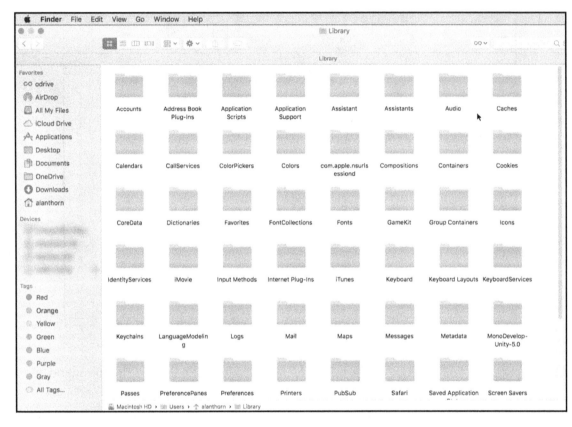

The Application.persistentDataPath normally refers to the Library/Application Support folder

Whether you're using Windows or Mac, the XML file will be the same. You can open this inside MonoDevelop, by simply dragging and dropping the file into the editor. MonoDevelop then loads and displays the file, with line numbering and complete syntax highlighting. The file should display a transform component (section) for each saved object, alongside the object name.

Viewing and editing an XML file in MonoDevelop

A newer feature added to MonoDevelop bundled with Unity 5.4 and above is a split-screen view, allowing you to view multiple source files side by side in the same editor. This is great for comparing files, copying and pasting between files, and debugging and issue tracking. To use this, simply open multiple files in MonoDevelop.

Multiple files viewed side by side

With multiple files open, just drag and drop one tab to the left or right-hand side, and then release the mouse to dock the tab as a new panel!

MonoDevelop split screen view

Here is an example of XML code saved from my scene. The great thing about Serialization, provided your game objects share the same names as mine, is that you can copy and paste my XML over to your scene and reload the same arrangement; the position, rotation, and scale of objects:

```
<?xml version="1.0" encoding="us-ascii"?>
<TransformCollectionXML
xmlns:xsi="http://www.w3.org/2001/XMLSchema-instance"
xmlns:xsd="http://www.w3.org/2001/XMLSchema">
  <Items>
    <TransformDataXML>
      <PosX>-1.54</PosX>
      <PosY>3.45</PosY>
      <PosZ>-2.84</PosZ>
      <EulerX>0</EulerX>
      <EulerY>0</EulerY>
```

```xml
    <EulerZ>0</EulerZ>
    <ScaleX>1</ScaleX>
    <ScaleY>1</ScaleY>
    <ScaleZ>1</ScaleZ>
    <ObjectName>Sphere</ObjectName>
</TransformDataXML>
<TransformDataXML>
    <PosX>3.563</PosX>
    <PosY>4.001</PosY>
    <PosZ>2.41</PosZ>
    <EulerX>0</EulerX>
    <EulerY>0</EulerY>
    <EulerZ>0</EulerZ>
    <ScaleX>1</ScaleX>
    <ScaleY>1</ScaleY>
    <ScaleZ>1</ScaleZ>
    <ObjectName>Cylinder</ObjectName>
</TransformDataXML>
<TransformDataXML>
    <PosX>0</PosX>
    <PosY>3</PosY>
    <PosZ>0</PosZ>
    <EulerX>0</EulerX>
    <EulerY>0</EulerY>
    <EulerZ>0</EulerZ>
    <ScaleX>1</ScaleX>
    <ScaleY>1</ScaleY>
    <ScaleZ>1</ScaleZ>
    <ObjectName>Plane</ObjectName>
</TransformDataXML>
<TransformDataXML>
    <PosX>0</PosX>
    <PosY>0</PosY>
    <PosZ>0</PosZ>
    <EulerX>0</EulerX>
    <EulerY>0</EulerY>
    <EulerZ>0</EulerZ>
    <ScaleX>1</ScaleX>
    <ScaleY>1</ScaleY>
    <ScaleZ>1</ScaleZ>
    <ObjectName>Env</ObjectName>
</TransformDataXML>
<TransformDataXML>
    <PosX>0.261338055</PosX>
    <PosY>7.08</PosY>
    <PosZ>1.13</PosZ>
    <EulerX>0</EulerX>
    <EulerY>0</EulerY>
```

```
        <EulerZ>0</EulerZ>
        <ScaleX>1</ScaleX>
        <ScaleY>1</ScaleY>
        <ScaleZ>1</ScaleZ>
        <ObjectName>Cube</ObjectName>
      </TransformDataXML>
      <TransformDataXML>
        <PosX>0</PosX>
        <PosY>3</PosY>
        <PosZ>0</PosZ>
        <EulerX>50</EulerX>
        <EulerY>330</EulerY>
        <EulerZ>0</EulerZ>
        <ScaleX>1</ScaleX>
        <ScaleY>1</ScaleY>
        <ScaleZ>1</ScaleZ>
        <ObjectName>Directional Light</ObjectName>
      </TransformDataXML>
      <TransformDataXML>
        <PosX>4.758632</PosX>
        <PosY>6.48045349</PosY>
        <PosZ>4.97736645</PosZ>
        <EulerX>32.1784363</EulerX>
        <EulerY>224.999954</EulerY>
        <EulerZ>4.13574853E-05</EulerZ>
        <ScaleX>1</ScaleX>
        <ScaleY>1</ScaleY>
        <ScaleZ>1</ScaleZ>
        <ObjectName>Main Camera</ObjectName>
      </TransformDataXML>
    </Items>
</TransformCollectionXML>
```

Now, let's try loading the saved XML file to the level. To do this, replay the game, and press *L* on the keyboard. This reloads the XML back, and each object is restored to their saved position.

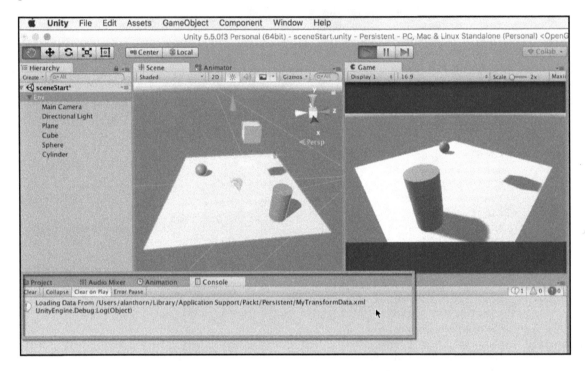

Loading data back from a file

Excellent work! You can now save and load data of practically any scale to and from XML. This is an important and powerful ability. However, XML is not the only persistent format around. Let's see another; specifically, JSON.

Saving data – JSON files

Saving data to XML is an important and powerful ability. XML is such a common data-interchange format that almost all data-driven applications must support it, both for loading and saving data. Nevertheless, XML files are often large, syntactically verbose, and inappropriate for saving small nuggets of data. XML files can be needlessly large in file size, and can be time-consuming to process. As a result, JSON has emerged as a lighter alternative, and it is commonly adopted in games. Since the release of Unity 5.3, JSON is a natively-supported format. Prior to this release, developers needed to use third-party add-ins. This section covers the latest, native JSON tools provided with Unity. However, if you want or need to use an earlier release, then take a look at the following, free third-party add-on offering JSON support, available here:

`http://wiki.unity3d.com/index.php/SimpleJSON`.

JSON parser

To get started using JSON in Unity, create a new project and add the script file, `SerializeTransformJSON.cs`. This should be attached to an empty object in the **Scene**.

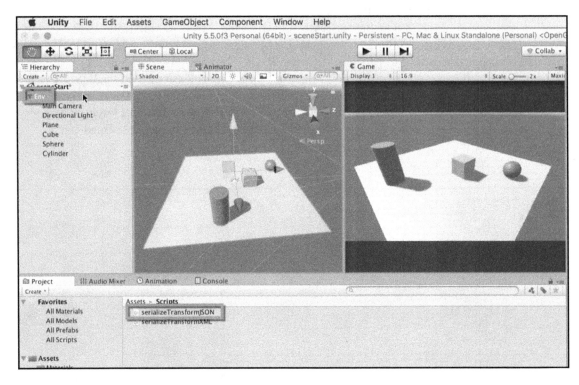

Adding a new JSON parser script to the Scene

This JSON script achieves identical results to the XML serializer; saving the transform component of each object. However, both the code and resultant JSON file are shorter, as we'll see. And have a look comments that follow:

```
using UnityEngine;
using System.Collections;
using System.IO;
//------------------------------------------
[System.Serializable]
public class TransformData
{
    public Vector3 Position;
    public Quaternion Rot;
    public Vector3 Scale;
    public string ObjectName = string.Empty;
```

```
}
//-------------------------------------------
[System.Serializable]
public class TransformCollection
{
    public TransformData[] DataArray;
}
//-------------------------------------------
public class serializeTransformJSON : MonoBehaviour
{
    //-----------------------------------------
    public Transform[] TransformArray;
    public string FilePath = "/Saves/MyTransformData.json";
    public TransformCollection MyData;
    //-----------------------------------------
    // Use this for initialization
    void Awake ()
    {
        //Get transform component
        TransformArray = Object.FindObjectsOfType<Transform>();
        TransformCollection MyData = new TransformCollection ();
    }
    //-----------------------------------------
    public void SaveData()
    {
        //Create new array
        MyData.DataArray = new TransformData[TransformArray.Length];

        for(int i=0; i<MyData.DataArray.Length; i++)
        {
            MyData.DataArray[i] = new TransformData ();
            MyData.DataArray[i].Position = TransformArray[i].position;
            MyData.DataArray[i].Rot = TransformArray[i].rotation;
            MyData.DataArray[i].Scale = TransformArray[i].localScale;
            MyData.DataArray[i].ObjectName = TransformArray[i].name;
        }

        string JSONString = JsonUtility.ToJson(MyData);
        string SavePath = Application.persistentDataPath + "/" + FilePath;

        File.WriteAllText(SavePath, JSONString);
        Debug.Log ("Saving Data To: " + SavePath);
    }
    //-----------------------------------------
    public void LoadData()
    {
        string LoadPath = Application.persistentDataPath + "/" + FilePath;
        string JSONString = File.ReadAllText (LoadPath);
```

```
        MyData = JsonUtility.FromJson<TransformCollection>(JSONString);

        //Update objects
        for (int i = 0; i < MyData.DataArray.Length; i++)
        {
                //Find object of matching name
                GameObject Selected =
GameObject.Find(MyData.DataArray[i].ObjectName);

                //Get transform component
                Transform SelectedTransform =
Selected.GetComponent<Transform>();

                SelectedTransform.position = MyData.DataArray [i].Position;
                SelectedTransform.localScale = MyData.DataArray [i].Scale;
                SelectedTransform.rotation = MyData.DataArray [i].Rot;
        }
    }
    //-------------------------------------------
    void Update()
    {
        if (Input.GetKeyDown (KeyCode.S))
        {
                SaveData();
                return;
        }

        if (Input.GetKeyDown (KeyCode.L))
        {
                LoadData();
                return;
        }
    }
    //-------------------------------------------
}
//-------------------------------------------
```

Comments

- The `TransformData` class is the serializable primitive object storing the raw transform data extracted from the transform component. However, for the JSON serializer, we'll use the `Vector3` and `Quaternion` data types, as these serialize to a file without issues.
- In the `Awake` function, all transform components are found using the `Object.FindObjectsOfType` function. This generates an array of found transform components in the class variable, `TransformArray`.
- The `SaveData` function is run to serialize all transform components in the scene to a specified JSON file in the `Application.persistentDataPath`. This method only serializes all objects currently in the scene, and it assumes each object has a unique name.
- The `SaveData` function begins by converting all position, rotation, and scale data from transform components to the `TransformData` class, ready to be serialized.
- The `JSONUtility` class features all functions for interacting with the native Unity JSON API. You can find more information on this class from the Unity documentation online here: `https://docs.unity3d.com/ScriptReference/JsonUtility.html`.
- The `JsonUtility.ToJson` function converts a serializable object in memory to a JSON compliant string, which is the function return value. This string could be written to a file, or even dispatched over an Internet connection to another computer.
- The `File.WriteAllText` function saves a string to a file, including strings with new lines and returns. This is used to save the JSON data to a file, ready for loading back at any time.
- The `LoadData` function is the reverse of the `SaveData` function. `LoadData` uses `JSONUtility.FromJSON` to convert a JSON string back into object form. This can then be loaded back into the object transform components to restore object data. Remember, this method relies on each object in the scene having a unique name, to identify associations between transform components and objects.
- The `Update` function is called once per frame and that is where *S* can be pressed on the keyboard to save a scene state, and *L* to load. This is for testing purposes only, and a production version would have this code removed.

For sending JSON data over an Internet connection, to a website or server, consider the WWW class or WWWForm class. More information on these classes can be found online here:

https://docs.unity3d.com/ScriptReference/WWW.html and

https://docs.unity3d.com/ScriptReference/WWWForm.html.

Great work! Now let's try the code. Press play on the tool bar and run the game. As with testing the XML code, move the objects around from the scene view and press *S* on the keyboard to save the scene state. When you do this, a confirmation message including the filename path is printed in the console as the JSON file is saved.

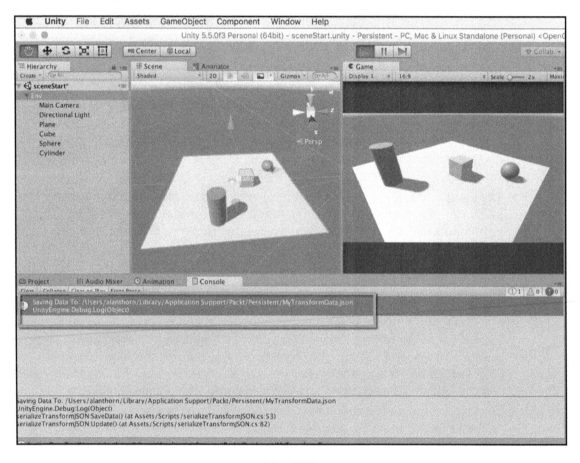

Saving a JSON file

You can open JSON files inside MonoDevelop, complete with syntax highlighting, code completion, and formatting.

Previewing JSON files in MonoDevelop

Here is an example of JSON data saved from my scene. The syntax is lightweight compared to the XML version, and if your objects have the same names, you can copy and paste this code to your scenes to reload my scene arrangement too:

```
{"DataArray":[
{"Position":{"x":-1.5399999618530274,"y":3.450000047683716,"z":3.3900001049
04Ã¥175},
    "Rot":{"x":0.0,"y":0.0,"z":0.0,"w":1.0},
    "Scale":{"x":1.0,"y":1.0,"z":1.0},
    "ObjectName":"Sphere"},
{"Position":{"x":3.562999963760376,"y":4.000999927520752,"z":-1.07899999618
53028},
    "Rot":{"x":0.0,"y":0.0,"z":0.0,"w":1.0},
    "Scale":{"x":1.0,"y":1.0,"z":1.0},
    "ObjectName":"Cylinder"},
    {"Position":{"x":0.0,"y":3.0,"z":0.0},
    "Rot":{"x":0.0,"y":0.0,"z":0.0,"w":1.0},
    "Scale":{"x":1.0,"y":1.0,"z":1.0},
    "ObjectName":"Plane"},
    {"Position":{"x":0.0,"y":0.0,"z":0.0},
    "Rot":{"x":0.0,"y":0.0,"z":0.0,"w":1.0},
    "Scale":{"x":1.0,"y":1.0,"z":1.0},
    "ObjectName":"Env"},
{"Position":{"x":0.2613380551338196,"y":3.5299999713897707,"z":1.1299999952
316285},
    "Rot":{"x":0.0,"y":0.0,"z":0.0,"w":1.0},
    "Scale":{"x":1.0,"y":1.0,"z":1.0},
    "ObjectName":"Cube"},
    {"Position":{"x":0.0,"y":3.0,"z":0.0},
"Rot":{"x":0.4082178771495819,"y":-0.23456968367099763,"z":0.10938163101673
126,"w":0.8754261136054993},
    "Scale":{"x":1.0,"y":1.0,"z":1.0},
    "ObjectName":"Directional Light"},
{"Position":{"x":4.758632183074951,"y":6.4804534912109379,"z":4.97736644744
87309},
"Rot":{"x":-0.10605409741401673,"y":0.8876926302909851,"z":-0.2560384273529
053,"w":-0.36769381165504458},
    "Scale":{"x":1.0,"y":1.0,"z":1.0},
    "ObjectName":"Main Camera"}
    ]
}
```

Now press play on the toolbar to test run JSON file loading. Simply press *L* on the keyboard to restore the scene back from the saved data.

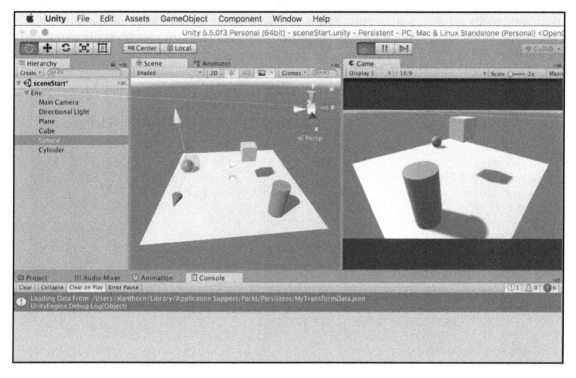

Restore data back from JSON files

Excellent work! In reaching this far you can now load data from both the XML and JSON formats into Unity for restoring games. This not only allows you to implement load and save states, but also other features such as third-party contents and assets, and user-defined levels that can be sent to others in JSON.

Saving data – binary files

If `PlayerPrefs`, INI files, XML files, or JSON files don't meet your needs, then binary files might be exactly what you're looking for. If you don't want to save data that gamers can open, read, and change, then binary is the preferred option. Binary files typically produce the smallest file size and are non-readable. Their disadvantage is difficulty of debugging (because you cannot easily verify their contents), and other applications cannot import and parse them because they conform to no other, established, standard; they don't know how your data is structured. To get started with using binary files, add the `serializeTransformBinary.cs` script file to your project; comments that follow:

```
using System.Collections;
using System.Collections.Generic;
using UnityEngine;
using System.Runtime.Serialization.Formatters.Binary;
using System.IO;
//-----------------------------------------
[System.Serializable]
public class TransformDataBinary
{
    public float PosX,PosY,PosZ;
    public float EulerX,EulerY,EulerZ;
    public float ScaleX,ScaleY,ScaleZ;
    public string ObjectName = string.Empty;
}
//-----------------------------------------
[System.Serializable]
public class TransformCollectionBinary
{
    public TransformDataBinary[] DataArray;
}
//-----------------------------------------
public class serializeTransformBinary : MonoBehaviour
{
    public Transform[] TransformArray;
    public string FilePath = "MyTransformData.bin";
    public TransformCollectionBinary MyData;
    //-----------------------------------------
    // Use this for initialization
    void Start () {
        //Get transform component
        TransformArray = Object.FindObjectsOfType<Transform>();
        TransformCollectionBinary MyData = new TransformCollectionBinary
();
    }
    //-----------------------------------------
```

```
public void SaveData()
{
        //Create new array
        MyData.DataArray = new TransformDataBinary[TransformArray.Length];

        for(int i=0; i<MyData.DataArray.Length; i++)
        {
                MyData.DataArray[i] = new TransformDataBinary ();
                MyData.DataArray[i].PosX = TransformArray[i].position.x;
                MyData.DataArray[i].PosY = TransformArray[i].position.y;
                MyData.DataArray[i].PosZ = TransformArray[i].position.z;

                MyData.DataArray[i].EulerX =
TransformArray[i].rotation.eulerAngles.x;
                MyData.DataArray[i].EulerY =
TransformArray[i].rotation.eulerAngles.y;
                MyData.DataArray[i].EulerZ =
TransformArray[i].rotation.eulerAngles.z;

                MyData.DataArray[i].ScaleX = TransformArray[i].localScale.x;
                MyData.DataArray[i].ScaleY = TransformArray[i].localScale.y;
                MyData.DataArray[i].ScaleZ = TransformArray[i].localScale.z;

                MyData.DataArray[i].ObjectName = TransformArray[i].name;
        }

        string SavePath = Application.persistentDataPath + "/" + FilePath;

        BinaryFormatter bf = new BinaryFormatter();
        FileStream file = File.Create (SavePath);
        bf.Serialize(file, MyData);
        Debug.Log ("Saving Data To: " + SavePath);
}
//-------------------------------------------
public void LoadData()
{
        string LoadPath = Application.persistentDataPath + "/" + FilePath;
        BinaryFormatter bf = new BinaryFormatter();
        FileStream file = File.Open(LoadPath, FileMode.Open);
        MyData = bf.Deserialize(file) as TransformCollectionBinary;
        file.Close();

        //Update objects
        for (int i = 0; i < MyData.DataArray.Length; i++)
        {
                //Find object of matching name
                GameObject Selected =
GameObject.Find(MyData.DataArray[i].ObjectName);
```

```
                //Get transform component
                Transform SelectedTransform =
    Selected.GetComponent<Transform>();

                SelectedTransform.position = new Vector3 (MyData.DataArray
    [i].PosX, MyData.DataArray [i].PosY, MyData.DataArray [i].PosZ);
                SelectedTransform.localScale = new Vector3 (MyData.DataArray
    [i].ScaleX, MyData.DataArray [i].ScaleY, MyData.DataArray [i].ScaleZ);
                SelectedTransform.rotation = Quaternion.Euler
    (MyData.DataArray[i].EulerX, MyData.DataArray[i].EulerY,
    MyData.DataArray[i].EulerZ);
            }
        Debug.Log ("Loading Data From " + LoadPath);
    }
    //--------------------------------------------
    void Update()
    {
        if (Input.GetKeyDown (KeyCode.S))
        {
            SaveData();
            return;
        }

        if (Input.GetKeyDown (KeyCode.L))
        {
            LoadData();
            return;
        }
    }
    //--------------------------------------------
}
```

Comments

- The `TransformDataBinary` class is the serializable primitive object storing the raw transform data extracted from the transform component. This consists of float variables, used for storing position (X, Y, and Z), as well as rotation (Euler angles) and scale.
- The two C# namespaces, `System.Runtime.Serialization.Formatters.Binary` and `System.IO` must be included to use binary files and Serialization.

- The `DataArray` member of the `TransformCollectionBinary` class represents a sequential list of `TransformDataBinary` structures, each defining the transform for a unique game object. As with the previous two methods, each object in the scene should have a unique name.
- The `Awake` function retrieves a static list of all transform component in the scene at level start up.
- The `SaveData` function converts all scene transforms into binary data. To do this, the `BinaryFormatter` class is used.
- The `BinaryFormatter.Serialize` function accepts an object instance as an argument and writes it to a specified file stream (an open file).
- By default, the file is saved to a folder in `Application.persistentDataPath`.

Excellent. Now let's give the binary code a try! Run the game by pressing play on the tool bar and then move scene objects around from the **Scene** view.

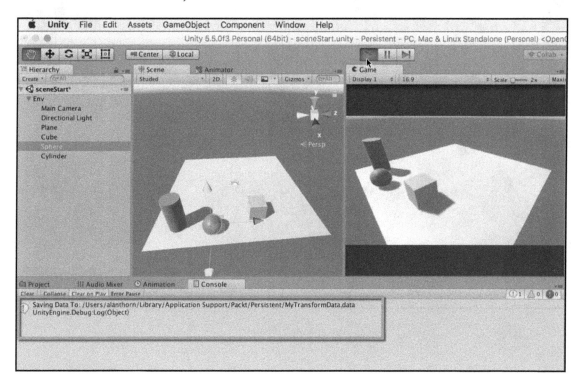

Saving data to a binary file

By default, neither Windows or Mac are configured to open and display binary files. To open these, you'll need to right-click the file inside either Windows Explorer or Mac Finder to change the file extension associations. You can configure the binary file to open MonoDevelop. To change file extension associations in Windows, see:

```
http://www.digitaltrends.com/computing/how-to-set-default-programs-and-file-typ
es-in-windows-10/.
```

For Mac, see:

```
http://osxdaily.com/2009/10/25/change-file-associations-in-mac-os-x/.
```

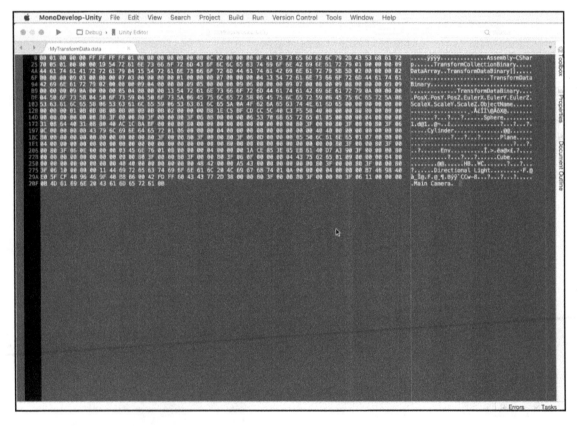

Open a binary file in MonoDevelop

Now restore the scene back from binary data by replaying the game in the **Game** tab, and press *L* on the keyboard to load back the file.

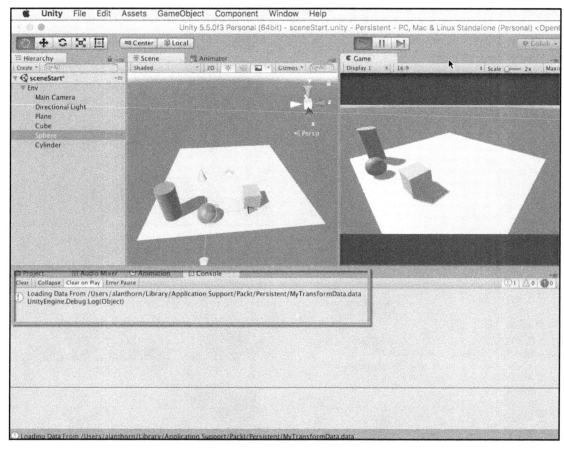

Restoring a scene from a binary file

And voila! You can now save data in Unity through many different methods (XML, JSON, and binary), each with a unique advantage.

Saving data for Dead Keys

For Dead Keys, our level loading needs are simple, technically. We simply need to save the latest level we have reached, and then restore back to the beginning of that level every time the game is started. To do this, we can use the `Player preferences` class. Create a new script, named `LevelSaveRestore.cs`.

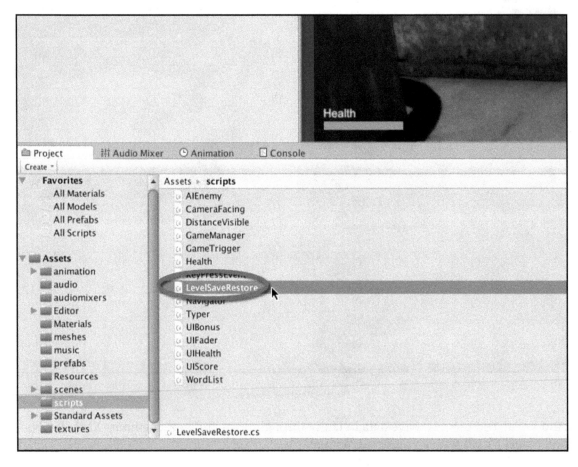

Creating a new save state script

This script file should be attached to one, and only one, empty object in the scene, which is active at level start up, and this should happen for every playable level in the game. The full code for the script file is shown as follows:

```
using System.Collections;
using System.Collections.Generic;
using UnityEngine.SceneManagement;
using UnityEngine;
//------------------------------------------------
public class LevelSaveRestore : MonoBehaviour
{
    //---------------------------------------------
    [SerializeField]
    int LastAchievedLevel = 0;    string LastAchievedLevelName =
string.Empty;    public int CurrentLevel = 0;
    //---------------------------------------------
    void Awake()
    {
        //Get latest level, if key exists
        LastAchievedLevel = PlayerPrefs.GetInt ("LatestLevel_Val",
CurrentLevel);
        LastAchievedLevelName = PlayerPrefs.GetString ("LatestLevel_Name",
SceneManager.GetActiveScene().name);

        //Should we load latest level
        if (CurrentLevel < LastAchievedLevel)
        {
            if(!SceneManager.GetActiveScene ().name.Equals
(LastAchievedLevelName))
                SceneManager.LoadScene (LastAchievedLevelName);
        }
        else
        {
            //Update latest scene
            LastAchievedLevel = CurrentLevel;
            LastAchievedLevelName = SceneManager.GetActiveScene ().name;
            PlayerPrefs.SetInt ("LatestLevel_Val", LastAchievedLevel);
            PlayerPrefs.SetString ("LatestLevel_Name",
LastAchievedLevelName);
            PlayerPrefs.Save ();
        }
    }
    //---------------------------------------------
}
//------------------------------------------------
```

Comments

- The `UnityEngine.SceneManagement` namespace should be included in every source file that changes scenes, or needs access to the current scene
- The `Awake` event is used to retrieve the last level reached, by using `PlayerPrefs` to return two values: the highest-level number, and the level name associated with that
- The `HighestLevel` is compared to `CurrentLevel`, and where `CurrentLevel` is less, a `Scene` change occurs to load the `Highest` level
- If the active level is the highest, then this value is saved to `PlayerPrefs`

Add the `LevelSaveRestore` script to an empty object in the scene, for each and every scene. For each scene, assign the script a number reflecting the level's order in progression. The first level is *0*, the next is *1*, the next is *2*, and so on.

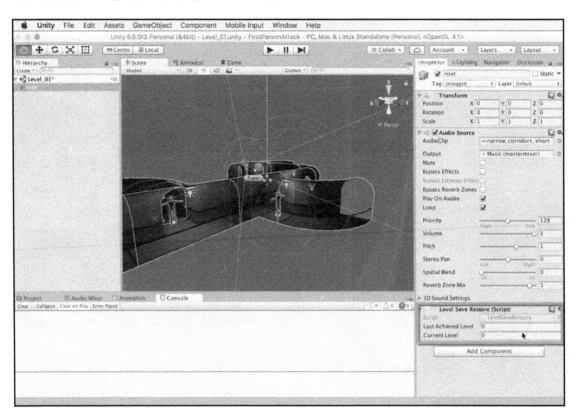

Set the level number for a level restore

Next, add all playable levels to the level list in the **Build Settings...**.

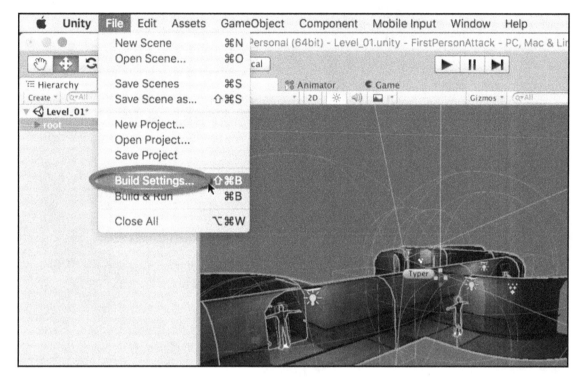

Accessing the Build Settings...

To add levels, choose **File** | **Build Settings...**, and then drag and drop every level into the list. Each level should be assigned a unique number and will be recognized by the scene manager as a separate and independent level in the build.

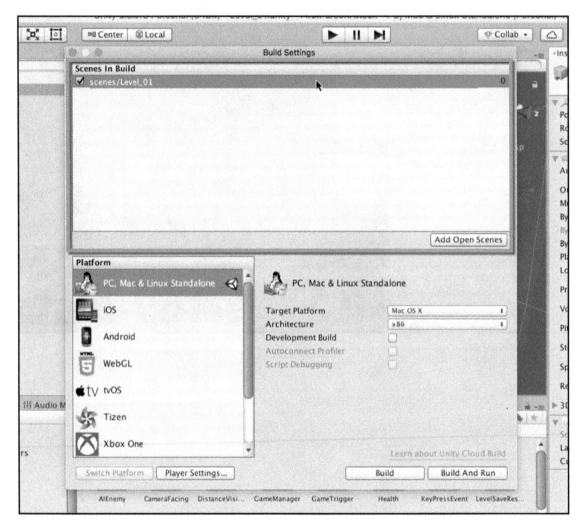

Adding scenes to the build list

Great! You're now ready to go with *Dead Keys*. Each level now has the ability to save its progress, saving the highest reached level. This will be resumed automatically, when the player enters any level.

Summary

Congratulations on reaching the end of this chapter. By reaching this point we have come a long way. We've developed Dead Keys from the ground upwards, and now the game can track user progress, from level to level. This is great, and in doing this we've seen various methods for saving persistent data. Next up, we'll complete the Dead Keys project and see a wide range of subjects along the way!

8
Performance, Optimization, Mobiles, and More

This concluding chapter completes our development journey with *Dead Keys* and Unity development. Here, we'll see tips and tricks for game optimization to improve performance across a range of systems, from desktop and consoles to mobile devices and the web. We'll explore techniques for optimizing assets for mobiles, both textures and meshes, and for configuring our scripts and software design to perform optimally. We'll also explore techniques and ideas for mobile deployment, and we'll consider VR and other platform types. In short, this chapter is a wide-ranging tour of miscellaneous topics that don't fit specifically into any single chapter previously, but are nonetheless important and should be carefully considered. So let's get started!

Stats and performance

Many people think that game optimization should be an afterthought; that is, something that comes at the end of development. This line of reasoning stresses the importance of first making the game as a complete experience, and then recommends optimizing what has been made by tweaking existing features. This approach, however, though common is not recommended.

Instead, performance and optimization should factor into the design, meaning that it should be an early consideration. From the outset of development, you should be considering ways to optimize performance and your workload. Consider the following:

- **Target Platform**: Decide early on the target hardware to be supported by your game. This should not be defined only in terms of operating system, such as Android and *Windows*, but also in terms of versions–such as *Windows 10* and *Android 4.5*. It is important to establish a minimum baseline version below which the game is not supported; that is, not tested or assumed to work properly. After establishing this, you should get access to all target hardware and software so you can test your game on the minimum systems. Do not rely on simulators or emulators, but always test on the target hardware itself.

- **Target Frame rate/performance**: Next, decide on a minimum level of runtime performance acceptable for the target hardware. Typically, this can be defined in **Frames Per Second (FPS)**. That is, the minimum FPS acceptable at any time for the target hardware, such as 40 fps or 50 fps. By deciding on a concrete minimum, you'll have a firm benchmark to make comparisons and judgments about how well your game is performing.

After deciding on target hardware and target performance, you're ready to start testing your game and assessing its performance. The best way to do this for desktop platforms is by playing your game directly from the **Unity editor**, running it from the **Game** tab with the **Stats** panel activated. You can activate the **Stats** panel by clicking on the **Stats** button from the **Game** tab. This displays an information panel in the top-right corner of the screen:

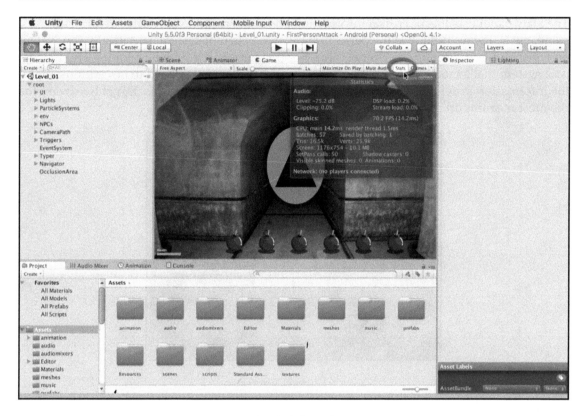

Accessing the Stats panel

The Stats panel lists lots of critical information about the runtime performance of your game, but it always describes the performance on the current system, specifically the system on which you are running the Unity editor. For this reason, if you're developing and testing on a system that's more powerful than your target hardware, you need to be cautious about the information provided by the **Stats** panel. Ideally, try testing on your target hardware for the most meaningful results:

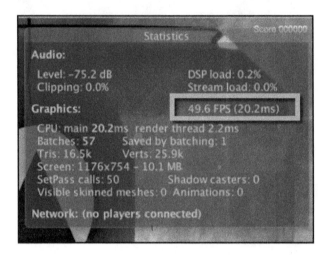

Reading the Stats panel on the target hardware

The **Tris** and **Verts** stats list the total number of triangles and vertices processed by the graphics hardware for the current frame only, specifically, all triangles (tris) and vertices (verts) within view of all active cameras. Thus, it is not a count of the total tris and verts in the scene, as this could be larger. This hints at important opportunities for optimization–on one hand, you can reduce the poly-count of models, but on the other, you can cleverly hide objects from the viewing frustum if they are not needed:

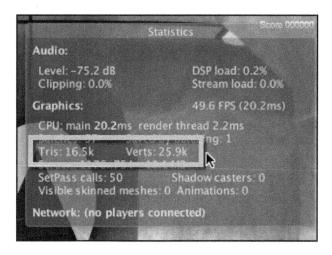

Viewing the total triangles and vertices for all active cameras

The **SetPass calls** refers to the number of distinct processing steps that the rendering engine must perform to successfully render the active frame. Fewer steps (lower **SetPass calls**) results in better performance. One quick technique to reduce **SetPass calls** is to use fewer unique materials for meshes, and to share materials among meshes where possible. Try limiting each mesh to one material (as each unique material results in an additional **SetPass calls**):

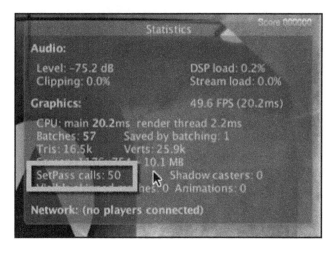

Lower SetPass calls results in faster performance

The **Stats** panel is most valuable when your Unity project is running on the target hardware and is in Play mode. More information on the statistics panel can be found online here: https://docs.unity3d.com/Manual/RenderingStatistics.html.

Profiler and performance assessment

The **Rendering Statistics Window** (**Stats** panel) can help confirm whether your game is suffering performance issues. In the first instance, your judgment about performance is normally based on whether you see a tangible problem in-game during testing. Afterwards, the **Stats** panel (such as the FPS statistic) can help confirm whether the identified problem really is related to game performance, as opposed to a scripting bug, or a software conflict. Nevertheless, the **Stats** panel can't tell you exactly what or where the problem is. To help track down the issue, you can use the **Profiler** window, which is accessible from the Unity editor menu, by navigating to **Window | Profiler**. Like the **Stats** panel, the **Profiler** measures game performance on the current hardware, that is, the system on which the editor is running:

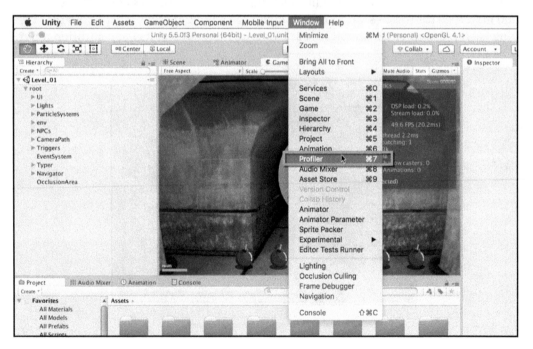

Accessing the Unity Profiler from the application menu

The **Profiler** window initially appears as a free-floating window. For best results, consider docking this window side by side with the **Game** tab, or use a separate monitor for a multi-monitor setup:

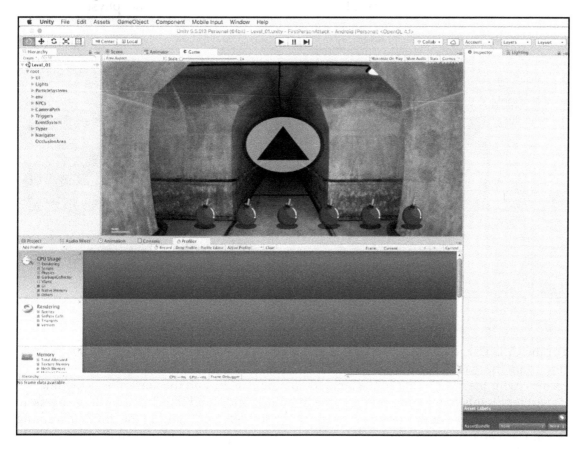

Viewing the Profiler window alongside the Game tab

Now take your game for a test run and observe the **Profiler** window, which fills instantly with performance data in a graph. The **Profiler** collects information, frame by frame, for as long as the **Record** button is active, and will add its information to the graph in real time. Data is populated on various axes: CPU usage, rendering, memory, audio, physics, and more:

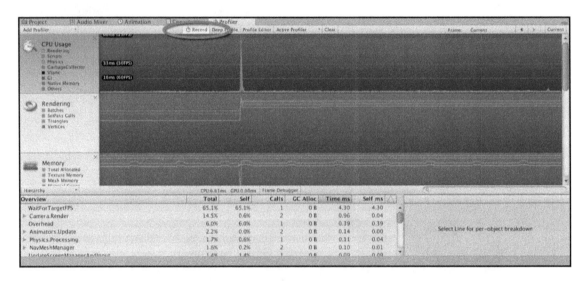

Recording frame data with the Profiler during Play mode

For the **CPU Usage** category, we learn a lot about frame computation time, which is important for overall performance and FPS. The horizontal axis (left-to-right) represents frames (with the most recent frame being on the right side), and the vertical axis (up and down) represents frame computation time in milliseconds (and thus higher values represent lower frame rates). For this reason, high peaks or sudden mountains in the graph (excepting loading screens) may represent problem areas, as they coincide with unusually high activity and performance intensity. To find out more information about a specific frame in the graph (such as a high mountain frame), simply click and drag your mouse anywhere in the graph to pick that frame:

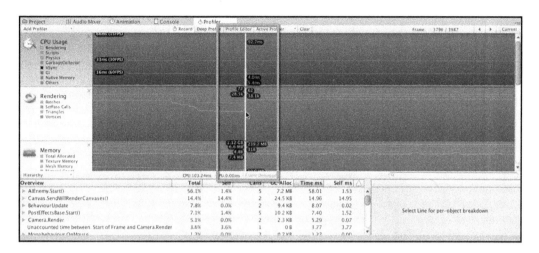

Selecting frames for investigation in the Profiler

By selecting a frame for further investigation, exploring why the FPS is as low as it is, you can view more information in the **Overview** panel. This breaks down the computational workload for the frame into distinct categories, allowing you to view the expense of each, to further narrow areas of performance intensity. Tasks are ordered by expense in the list, with the most intensive processes listed at the top. On identifying the most expensive, click the expand arrow to reveal further related processes. Unity lists the most important scripts, functions, or resources associated with the selected frame and process. This helps you trace performance spikes to specific functions in code and specific assets:

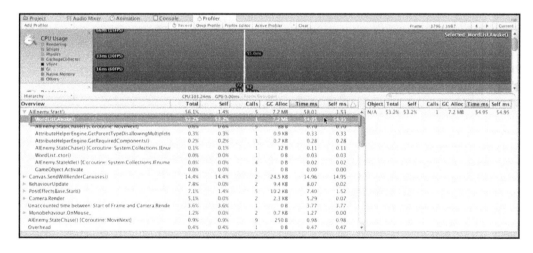

Investigating performance spikes

You can also view specific categories of performance in the graph, such as **Rendering** or **Physics**, by toggling category visibility using the visibility buttons. This doesn't affect the data recorded or collected by the **Profiler**, but only changes how the data is presented, helping you more clearly visualize the performance:

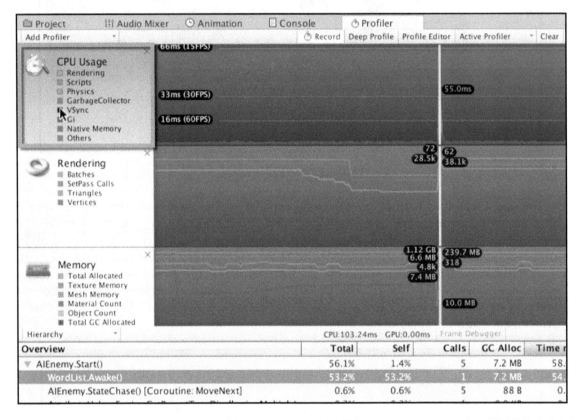

Toggling performance viewing using the graph visibility buttons

Like the **Rendering Statistics** window, the Profiler cannot always identify causes of performance problems with certainty , and even when it does identify them, it cannot propose the solution to them. But, nonetheless, the Profiler can be valuable in tracking down problems in code to specific classes and functions, which saves you time tracing the problems manually. In addition to the standard Profiler modes, you can also enable a **Deep Profile** from the **Profiler** toolbar. This mode increases the range of calls, functions, and resources in scripts that can be monitored for even greater detail, but this option is resource heavy and should only be used where essential. More information on the Profiler can be found online here: `https://docs.unity3d.com/Manual/Profiler.html`.

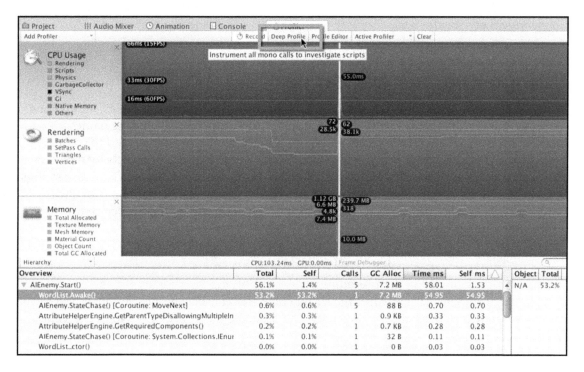

Enabling a Deep Profile

[519]

Optimization tips and tricks

The **Stats** panel and the **Profiler** are solid tools for diagnosing performance problems in your game, as well as determining where those problems are in the script, thereby suggesting how they may be corrected. However, as mentioned, optimization should begin at the design phase of development, and should persist throughout all subsequent stages. Consequently, there are some general tips, tricks, and workflows that can be followed, with proper consideration and limitations, to help optimize your game across development, minimizing problems that could emerge later. This section explores some of these tips and tricks, in addition to those already mentioned in Chapter 1, *Preparation and Asset-Configuring*. Let's see these...

Strings and comparisons

Working with strings in Unity is common. Game objects have names and tags, animations have parameters, and games feature many other string properties, including names, localization data, character dialogue, and more. Consequently, we often need to compare two strings, checking to see if two words match–such as searching for objects by name, or checking player-typed words against a dictionary. There are many ways to compare strings in code, but these vary in performance and speed–and the fastest method has not always remained constant across versions. As of Unity 5.5, the optimal method for comparing two strings for equality is as follows:

```
StringOne.Equals(StringTwo, StringComparison.Ordinal);
```

The most important part of the preceding code is supplying `StringComparison.Ordinal` as a second argument. This ensures the string comparison is based only on upper and lower case versions within the same character set, and assumes the strings are within the same language.

Beware of functions in disguise

C# properties are great language features for wrapping up access to variables through internal functions. This helps us validate values assigned to variables, and to detect when variables change. However, C# properties have a performance overhead that makes them expensive when compared to direct variable access. For this reason, to optimize script performance, always seek to cache variables. This problem is most notable in Unity when using `MonoBehaviour` class variables, or static class variables, which provide shortcut access to other components or objects. For example:

```
transform.position = new Vector3(0,0,0);
```

Here, the `transform` variable provides syntax-quick access to the `Transform` component attached to the associated game object. However, `transform` is a C# property, which as a hidden function call is equivalent to the much slower `GetComponent<Transform>()` statement. For this reason, it is better to use the `Awake` event of a script to cache the `Transform` component to a class variable for quick access later. For example:

```
void Awake ()
{
        ThisTransform = GetComponent<Transform> ();
}
```

By using this code, the `ThisTransform` variable should be used throughout to refer to the `Transform` component. Other variables that are really properties and that involve hidden function calls include:

- `Camera.main`
- `rigidbody`
- `audio`

Debug cleaning

Here's a great tip for cleaning your project and code of debug statements! We all use the `print` and `Debug.Log` functions to print debug messages to the console for validating our code and its execution. However, it's easy to add many debug statements, eventually spamming the console with many. And, furthermore, when the time comes to build our game, we normally want to remove all debug statements, to prevent our application from running code that isn't effective anymore. For example, consider the following statement:

```
Debug.Log("Hello World");
```

This code prints the following message to the console, which can be seen from the Unity editor, but not in a standalone build.

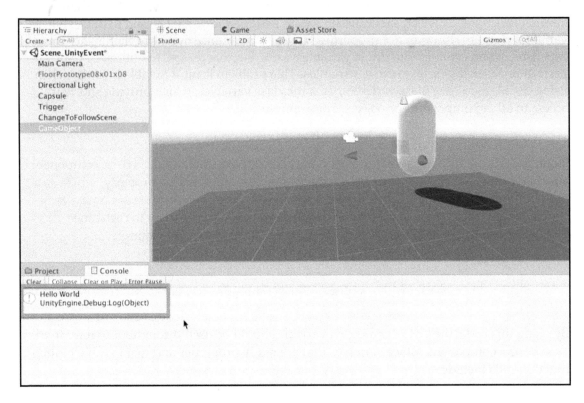

Printing debug messages

It can be tedious having to remove every `Debug.Log` or `Print` statement from a final build. So, instead, you can use the `Conditional` C# attribute. Consider the following class, which is a `DebugManager`, used for printing debug messages:

```
using System.Collections;
using System.Collections.Generic;
using UnityEngine;
using System.Diagnostics; //Namespace for conditional attribute

public class DebugManager : MonoBehaviour
{
    //This function is only valid when the DEBUG_MANAGER directive is
enabled
    [Conditional("DEBUG_MANAGER")]
    public static void PrintMessage(string Message)
```

```
    {
        //Prints a message to the console
        UnityEngine.Debug.Log (Message);
    }
}
```

This code uses the `System.Diagnostics` namespace to mark the `PrintMessage` function with the `Conditional` attribute. The function is tagged as `DEBUG_MANAGER`. This means that the `PrintMessage` function is only valid and compiled with the project when the `DEBUG_MANAGER` directive is activated in the **Player** settings window. By default, this directive is not activated, and this means that both the `PrintMessage` function and any other lines that call this function are treated by the compiler as comments. Let's see that in action. First, check the player settings to make sure that the `DEBUG_MANAGER` directive is not specified. To do that, choose **Edit** | **Project Settings** | **Player** from the application menu.

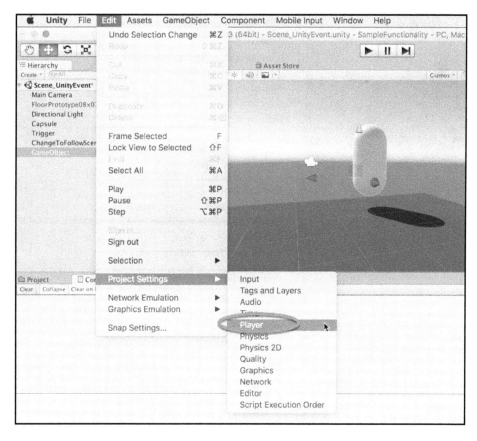

Accessing the Player settings window

The **Player** settings window displays a range of important game settings from the Object Inspector. Expand the **Other Settings** tab, and scroll down to the **Scripting Define Symbols** field. This field may be empty, or contain some symbols already defined. By default, the DEBUG_MANAGER symbol is missing.

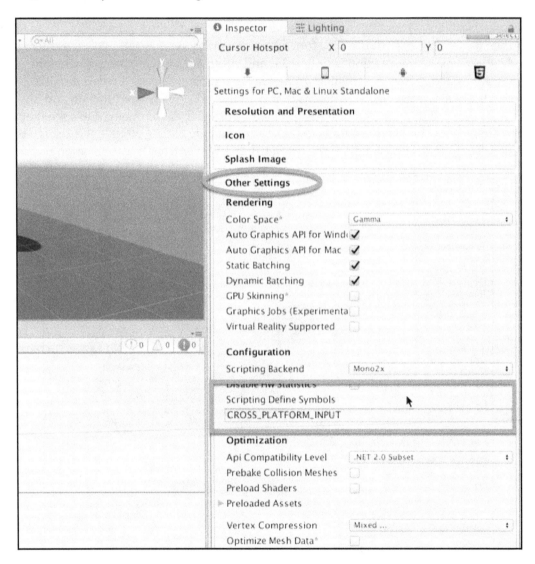

Viewing Scripting Define Symbols from the Player settings window

When the `DEBUG_MANAGER` define is missing, all lines referring to any function marked with the `Conditional` attribute will be turned into comments, effectively removing them from your script files.

```
PlayerController  ▸  □ FixedUpdate ()
 1 using System.Collections;
 2 using System.Collections.Generic;
 3 using UnityEngine;
 4
 5 public class PlayerController : MonoBehaviour
 6 {
 7     private Transform ThisTransform = null;
 8     private CharacterController ThisController = null;
 9
10     public float Speed = 2f;
11     public float RotSpeed = 90f;
12
13     // Use this for initialization
14     void Awake ()
15     {
16         ThisTransform = GetComponent<Transform> ();
17         ThisController = GetComponent<CharacterController> ();
18     }
19
20     // Update is called once per frame
21     void FixedUpdate ()
22     {
23         float Vert = Input.GetAxis ("Vertical");
24         float Horz = Input.GetAxis ("Horizontal");
25
26         ThisTransform.Rotate (0,RotSpeed * Horz * Time.deltaTime,0);
27
28         //ThisTransform.position += ThisTransform.forward * Speed * Vert * Time.deltaTime;
29         ThisController.SimpleMove(ThisTransform.forward * Speed * Vert);
30
31         if (Input.GetKeyDown (KeyCode.Space))
32         {
33             DebugManager.PrintMessage ("hello");
34         }
35     }
36 }
37
```

Debug code is turned into comments using the Conditional attribute

Now, add the DEBUG_MANAGER define into the symbols list from the **Player** settings window. Each define should be separated with the semicolon symbol (;). Thus, the DEBUG_MANAGER define can be added, as shown in the following screenshot:

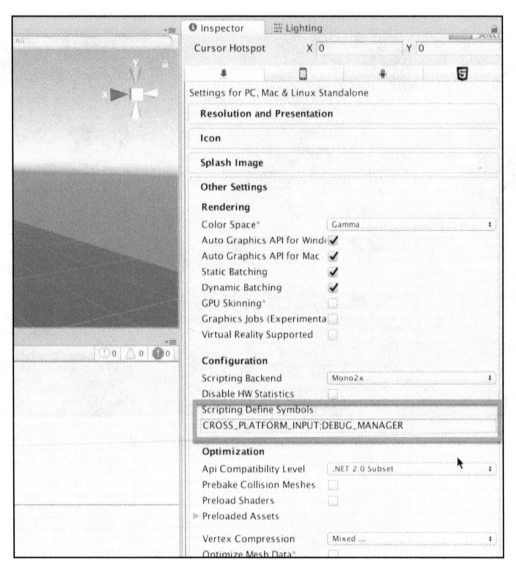

Adding the DEBUG_MANAGER define symbol

On adding the `DEBUG_MANAGER` define symbol, all code associated with the `Conditional` attribute will be activated automatically in code.

```
PlayerController  ▸  ☐ FixedUpdate ()
 1 using System.Collections;
 2 using System.Collections.Generic;
 3 using UnityEngine;
 4
 5 public class PlayerController : MonoBehaviour
 6 {
 7     private Transform ThisTransform = null;
 8     private CharacterController ThisController = null;
 9
10     public float Speed = 2f;
11     public float RotSpeed = 90f;
12
13     // Use this for initialization
14     void Awake ()
15     {
16         ThisTransform = GetComponent<Transform> ();
17         ThisController = GetComponent<CharacterController> ();
18     }
19
20     // Update is called once per frame
21     void FixedUpdate ()
22     {
23         float Vert = Input.GetAxis ("Vertical");
24         float Horz = Input.GetAxis ("Horizontal");
25
26         ThisTransform.Rotate (0,RotSpeed * Horz * Time.deltaTime,0);
27
28         //ThisTransform.position += ThisTransform.forward * Speed * Vert * Time.deltaTime;
29         ThisController.SimpleMove(ThisTransform.forward * Speed * Vert);
30
31         if (Input.GetKeyDown (KeyCode.Space))
32         {
33             DebugManager.PrintMessage ("hello");
34         }
35     }
36 }
37
```

Enabling Debug code!

And voila! You now have an easy way to activate and deactivate the debug code for your applications.

Optimizing build size

On compiling your game into a standalone executable, whether it's for PC, Mac, or mobiles, you'll always want the build to be as slimline as possible. Ideally, the final build should contain only release-relevant code (stripped of debug statements), and only assets (meshes and textures) used in the game, and these should also be formatted and compressed optimally for the target platform. This ensures that the build runs efficiently for the target hardware and is as small in file size as possible. This is especially important for mobile games and for asset store uploading, as many asset stores place limitations on acceptable file sizes for downloadable games. For this reason, we'll need a way to control the build file size.

By default, Unity removes all unused assets during a build operation. It does not remove them from the **Project** panel, but rather removes the assets from the compiled build so that they do not increase its file size. This does not apply to assets in the Resources folder. For more information on the Resources folder, see the online documentation at: https://unity3d.com/learn/tutorials/topics/best-practices/resources-folder.

To start optimizing a Build, it's good to assess how much of an impact each asset makes on the final build and where file size savings could be made. To do this, start by building your game. Select **File** | **Build Settings** from the application menu.

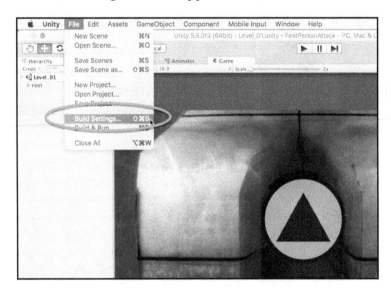

Accessing the Build Settings...

From the **Build** dialog, ensure that the correct **Build Target Platform** is selected, such as Windows or Mac. If it's not, then select the platform from the platform list, and then choose the **Switch Platform** button from the bottom-left button in the dialog.

Selecting the Build Platform

Make sure all levels are added to the **Scenes in Build** list, and then choose the **Build** button from the dialog. This prompts you for a save location for the build. Choose a location on your computer, but avoid saving your build anywhere inside the Unity project folder. Saving the build inside the Unity project folder can result in errors that prevent your project from compiling.

Building for the Target Platform

After the build completes, open the **Console** window and click the context menu icon, from the top right-hand side of the console. From the context menu that appears, choose **Open Editor Log**.

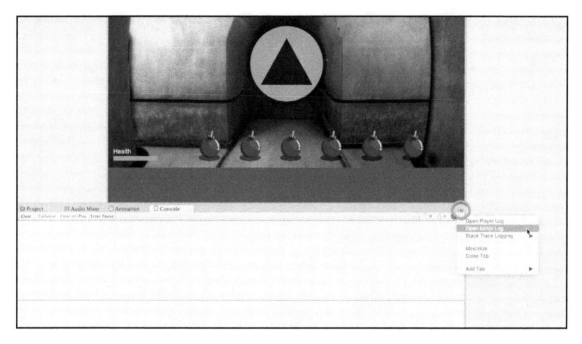

Accessing the build log

By choosing **Open Editor Log,** you can view the most recently generated build log, which is a text file produced by the compiler, indicating build statistics.

Viewing the build log

The build log lists all assets included in the compiled build, as well as their final memory consumption (in MBs). Remember, the size of the asset file in the **Project** panel (such as an imported PNG or Mesh file) is not necessarily how large the asset will be in the final build. This is because Unity uses its own internal asset storage system where the size of each imported asset is determined by its type, size, and import settings as defined in the object **Inspector**. The build log lets you determine the compiled size of each asset, and can guide you as to where improvements could be made to reduce size.

Assets sorted by size

One of the first strategies for reducing build size is to shrink textures, making them smaller in dimensions and in memory. This is especially effective for mobile platforms where textures are shown on smaller screens. To achieve this, select the texture in the **Project** panel, and change the **Max Size** setting to the smallest size consistent with your intended level of quality.

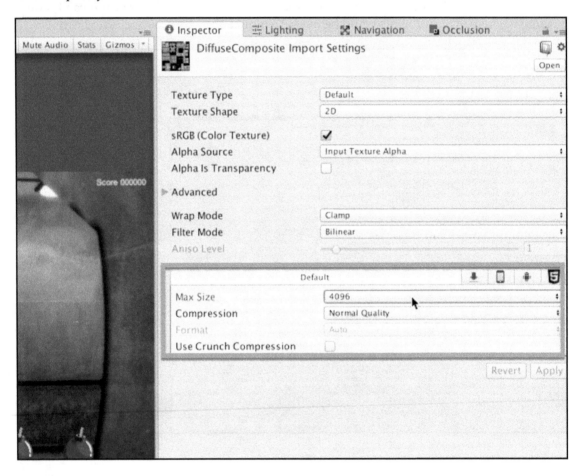

Changing texture size

Disable **Generate Mip Maps**, under the **Advanced** tab, for UI textures and other menu or HUD items, as this can result in several versions of the same texture being produced for different quality settings based on camera viewing distance.

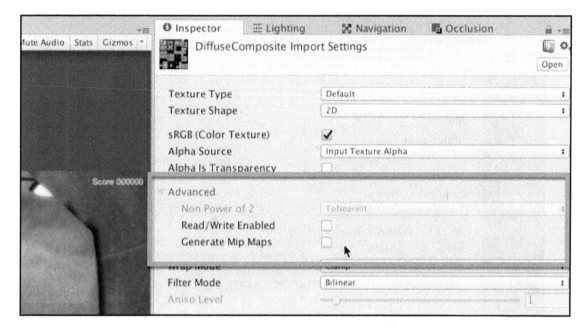

Disabling Generate Mip Maps

You can also enable **Mesh Compression** for meshes, which reduces their file size within the build, but at the expense of mesh quality. Higher compression produces lower fidelity meshes. Select the mesh in the **Project** panel, and then select the compression type.

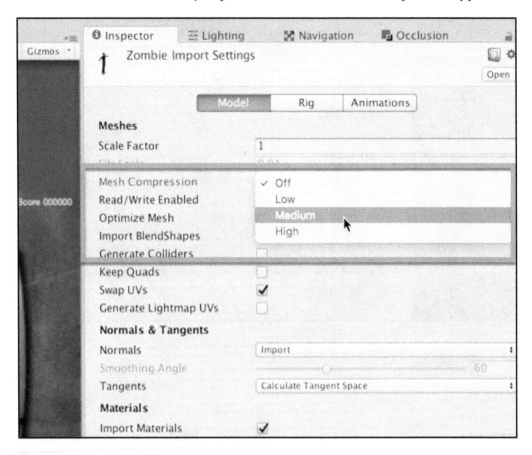

Enabling Mesh Compression

If acceptable, you can try reducing the quality of audio files. Simply select an audio file from the **Project** panel, and then reduce the **Quality** slider. Be sure to click **Apply** after adjusting the setting to confirm the change.

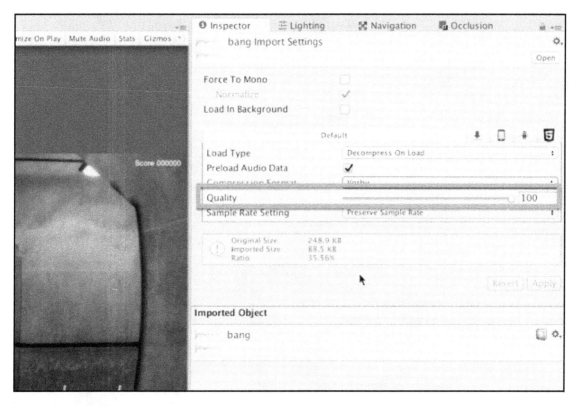

Reducing audio quality

In addition to adjusting settings for specific assets, you can change the supported API level. This defines the .NET (Mono) library of functions and classes used by your application. Most games use only a small subset of the .NET framework in their scripts and, thus, can use a lighter version of the library. By using this, your games build to a smaller size. To use the smaller version, select **Edit** | **Project Settings** | **Player** from the application menu. This displays the **Player** settings window in the object **Inspector**.

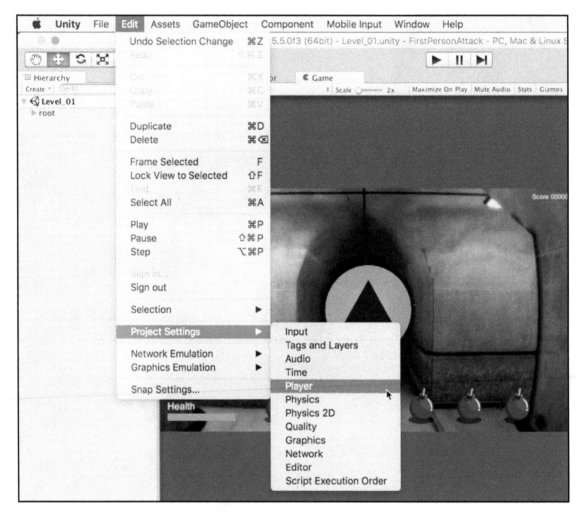

Editing Player Settings

From the **Player** settings window, expand the **Other Settings** group, and select **.NET 2.0 Subset** from the **Api Compatibility Level** dropdown menu.

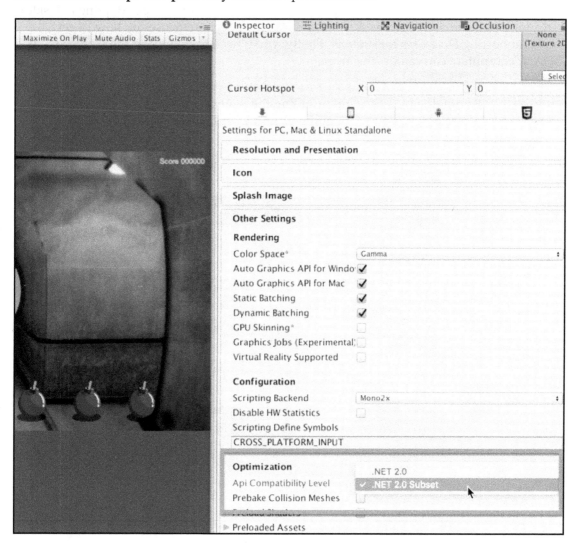

Setting the API level

Getting started with mobile development

Often you'll be developing for mobile platforms specifically, or you'll be adapting a desktop game for mobile devices, such as *Android* and *iOS*. This section focuses on how to get started at porting *Dead Keys* for *Android*. Firstly, you'll need to download the Android SDK for your computer. You can get this from:
`https://developer.android.com/studio/index.html`

 Before downloading and installing the Android SDK, or any software, please ensure you check out their **End User License Agreement** (**EULA**)!

Downloading the Android SDK

Next, run the downloaded installer application. This prompts you to select an SDK version to install. There is a unique SDK for each *Android* version, and you should choose the version that applies to your testing device. Enable the version from the list, and then click the **Apply** button. This application requires Internet access.

You can determine the Android version for your device using the following steps, listed online here:
`http://www.wikihow.com/Check-What-Android-Version-You-Have.`

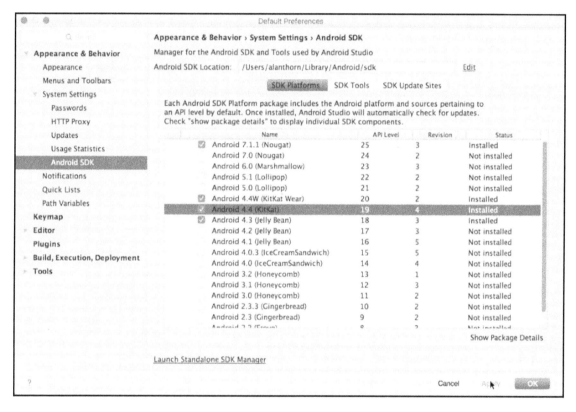

Selecting an SDK version to install

After selecting an Android version, additional files are installed to your computer. This may take a few minutes, depending on the version selected and the speed of your Internet connection.

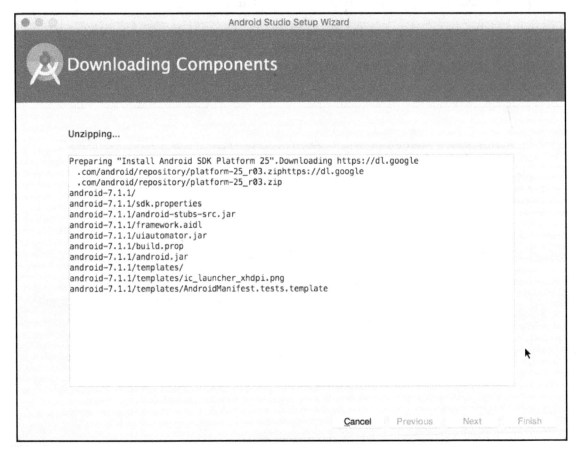

Installing the relevant Android SDK

After downloading and installing the Android SDK, copy the folder path where the SDK is located, as we'll need to paste this in Unity.

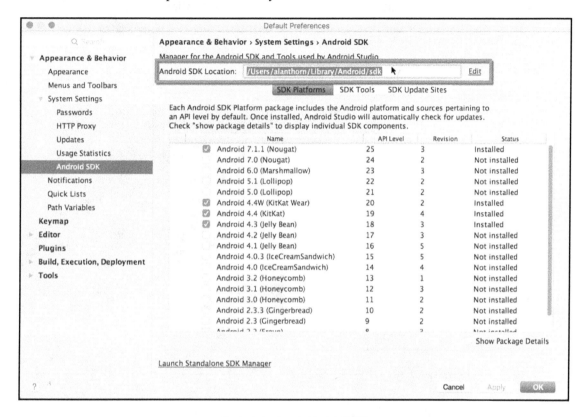

Copying the location path of the Android SDK

Now close and reopen Unity. On opening Unity, access the **User Preferences** dialog. On a Mac, this is accessed by choosing **Unity | Preferences** from the application menu. On Windows, you should select **Edit | Preferences** from the application menu.

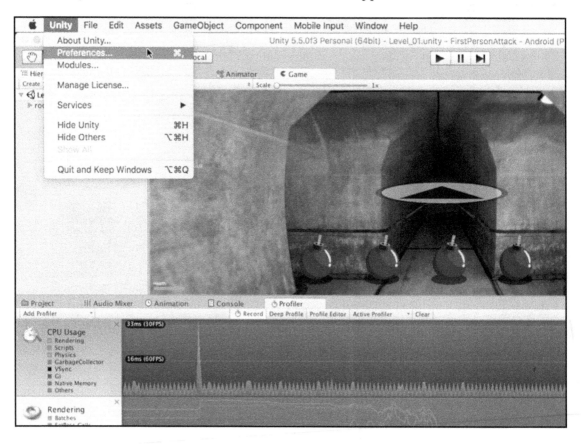

Accessing the User Preferences dialog

From the **User Preferences** dialog, select the **External Tools** tab. Then, in the Android SDK path, specify the install location for the Android SDK.

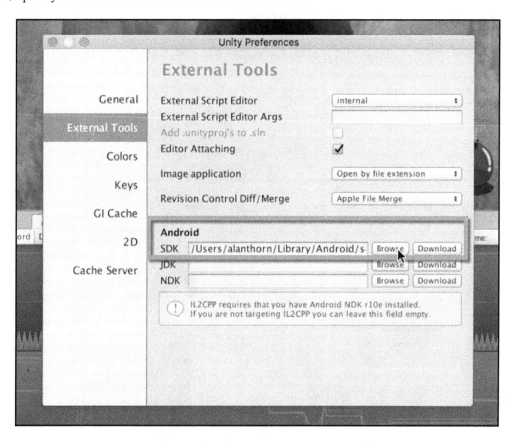

Specifying the Android SDK location from the Unity Preferences dialog

 If you don't see an *Android SDK* location field in the user Preferences window, make sure that you enabled *Android Build Support* during the Unity installation.

Next, you'll need to configure the Unity editor to work with and recognize your Android mobile. To do this, choose **Edit | Project Settings | Editor** from the application menu. This displays the **Editor** settings in the Object Inspector.

Accessing Editor settings

From the **Editor settings** menu, select **Any Android Device** from the **Unity Remote** dropdown, in the **Unity Remote** category. This configures the Unity editor to integrate with a mobile device from the Editor, as we'll see.

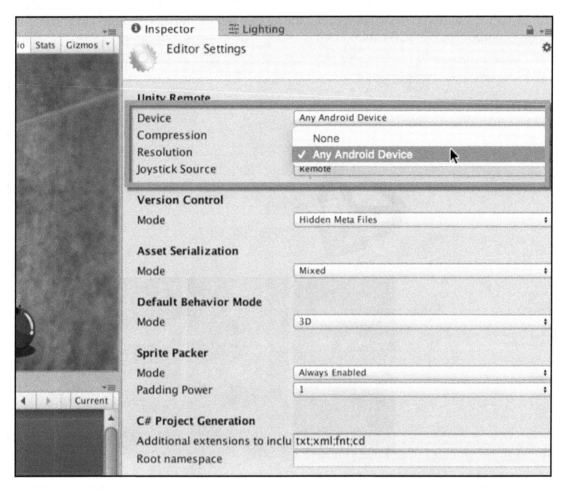

Selecting any Android Device as a remote controller

Now you'll need to download the freely available Unity Remote 5 application, which is available from the Play Store, here:
`https://play.google.com/store/apps/details?id=com.unity3d.genericremote&hl=en_G`
B. This application allows an Android mobile device, such as a phone or a tablet, to connect with the Unity editor. For Mac computers, the mobile device must be plugged in to the desktop computer via a USB cable.

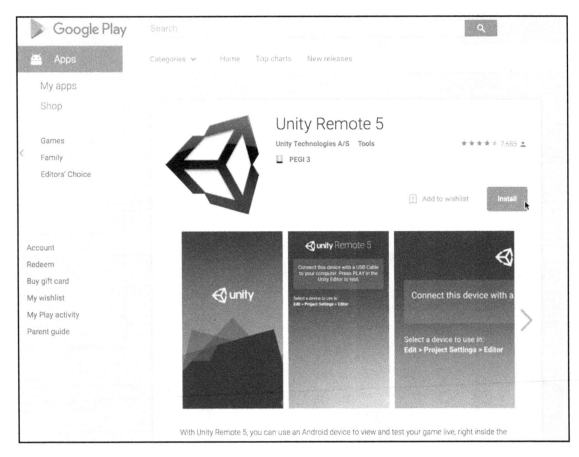

Installing the Unity Remote application on a mobile device

After installing the Unity Remote, run the application on your mobile device, with the device connected to the computer through a USB connection, and then restart Unity. Now, when you press **Play** on the toolbar, your **Game** view should also appear on the mobile device, and the mobile also allows player input through taps.

 If the Game view does not appear on the mobile device, then ensure that USB debugging is enabled on the device. To enable USB debugging, see: `https://www.recovery-android.com/enable-usb-debugging-on-android.html#part2`.

Moving forwards with mobile development

Great work! After a long configuration process, you're now ready to start developing for Android within Unity. To start, you should change the Target Development platform within the Unity editor. To do this, select **File | Build Settings...** to access the **Build Settings...** dialog.

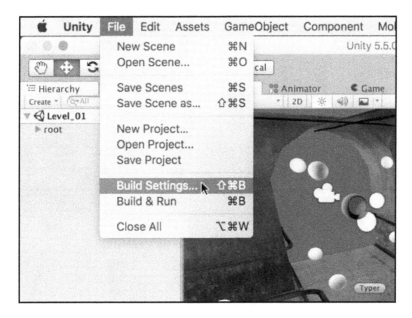

Accessing the Build Settings…

From the **Build Settings...** dialog, select the Android platform from the platform list, and then choose the **Switch Platform** button. On selecting this, Unity rebuilds, re-imports, and re-configures all assets for the Target Platform.

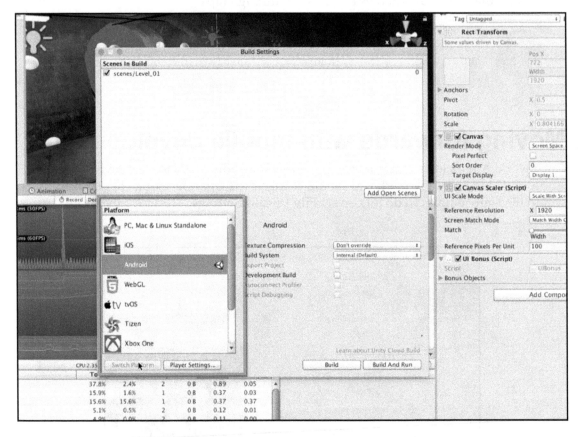

Switch platforms

You can confirm the selected platform from the application title bar. The Target OS will be listed in brackets. This should read `Android`.

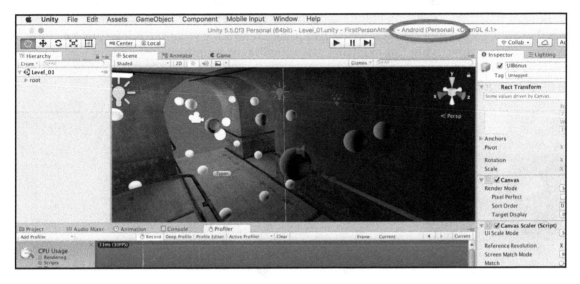

Confirming the target operating system

Depending on your application, target hardware, and **Project Settings**, your scenes may look different in the **Game** and **Scene** tab, as a result of rendering capabilities and supported rendering modes for the target hardware. In some cases, you may need to re-bake light mapping, occlusion culling data, or navigation mesh data. In addition, you may need to adjust the supported rendering API. First, determine what the minimum Android specification is, specifying this explicitly from the **Player** settings window. Aim for the highest level possible that is consistent with your target hardware and testing device, as this will give you the widest feature support possible.

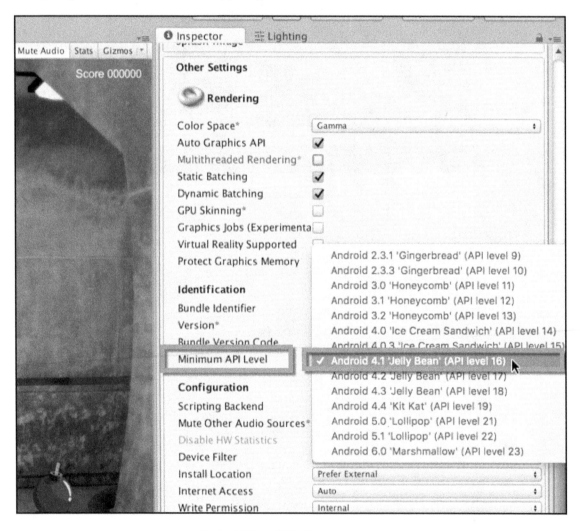

Selecting the Minimum API Level for the target hardware

After selecting the API level, choose the **Rendering API** to use. By default, this is set to **Automatic,** and when this is specified, Unity detects your graphics needs and selects the lowest API consistent with them. However, if your scene is not rendering as intended, you may need to change this. To do that, remove the check mark from the **Auto Graphics API** checkbox, and select an API from the list.

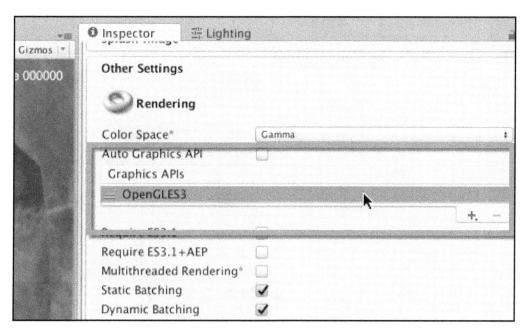

Selecting a graphics API

You should also check out which Rendering Emulation mode is being used by the editor to render your scene in the viewports. Ideally, this should match the Rendering API you are using (from the **Player** settings window), to get the highest fidelity results between what you see in the viewport and what you'll get on the device. To access the Rendering Emulation, select **Edit** | **Graphics Emulation** from the application menu, and then choose the API level needed.

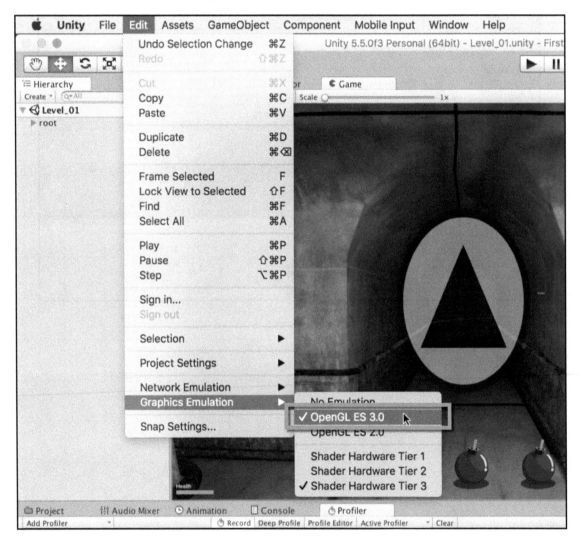

Selecting the emulation mode

Building for Android

To compile and build an executable package (APK) that runs on an Android device as a standalone application, you'll need to build your project. There are different ways to do this. Here, we'll look at a method that'll work for most Android devices, even if you cannot connect your device to Unity. Firstly, access the Player Settings by choosing **Edit | Project Settings | Player** from the application menu, and assign the application a unique *Bundle Identifier*, by entering a name in the **Bundle Identifier** field. This is used to uniquely identify the Android application, and would also be used on an App Store.

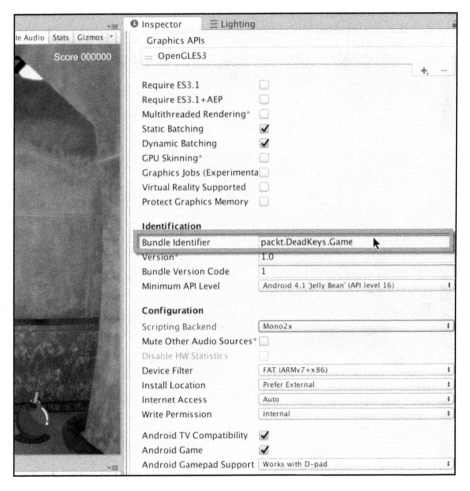

Assigning the application a Bundle Identifier

Remember, before creating your Android game, always check out the App Store submission guidelines to make sure your product will be accepted: `h ttps://developer.android.com/distribute/tools/launch-checklist .html`.

Next, to build the application, select **File** | **Build Settings** from the application menu. When the **Build Settings** dialog appears, you have the choice of **Build** or **Build and Run**. By choosing **Build and Run**, the application is compiled and then sent immediately to the connected Android device for running. By choosing **Build** only, the application is compiled to a standalone **APK** file (which is an **Android Executable Package**). Choose **Build**, and then select a destination folder on the computer outside the project folder. The **Build** method does not require an Android device to be connected.

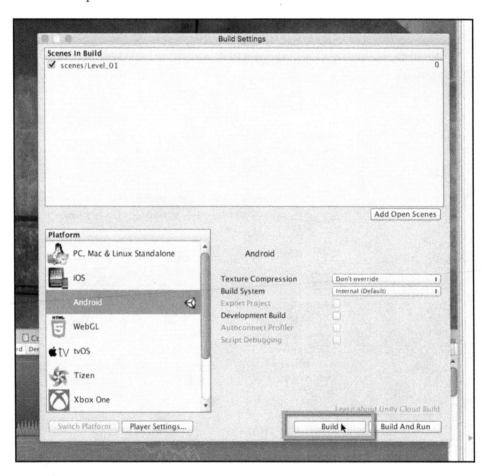

Building an APK file

If you click **Build** now you may get an error, as **Android** Compilation requires the **JDK (Java Development Kit)** to be installed. To achieve that, you can download the JDK online from: `http://www.oracle.com/technetwork/java/javase/downloads/index.html`.

 Before downloading and installing the JDK, or any software, please ensure that you check out their End User License agreements!

After installing the JDK, access the **User Preferences** dialog by choosing **Edit | Preferences** from the application menu, and select the **External Tools** tab. From here, specify the JDK location in the JDK field.

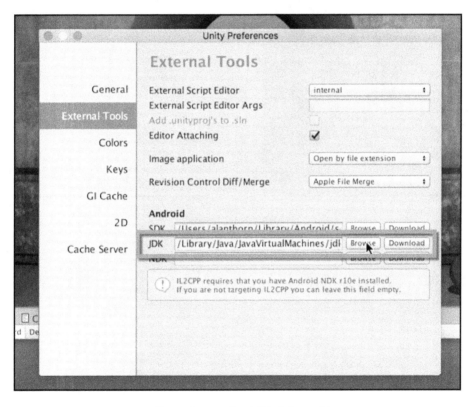

Specifying the JDK location from the Unity Preferences dialog

Now click **Build** from the **Build Settings** dialog, and this will produce an Android compliant APK file. Remember, the APK only supports Android platforms specified by the **Minimum API Level**, defined in the **Player** settings window.

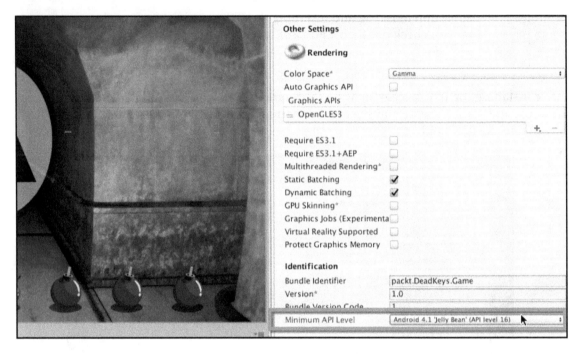

Defining APK platform support

When the build process is completed, an APK file appears, representing the compiled Android executable.

Building an APK file

You can transfer the APK to your device storage by portable media, such as an SD card, through cloud storage, or by direct transfer through a USB connection. To install and run the APK on the device, however, you must first enable a third party (or Unknown) application source, allowing custom-made applications to be installed. See the following link for instructions on this (the steps vary between OS version):

https://www.applivery.com/blog/android-unknown-sources/.

 Enabling Unknown Sources allows applications from many sources to be installed. To improve security, consider re-enabling this option after installing your Unity project.

After enabling **Unknown Sources** for application installs, you can install your APK application by using the APK Installer app, available for free from the Play Store, here: `https://play.google.com/store/apps/details?id=com.apkinstaller.ApkInstaller&hl=en_GB`.

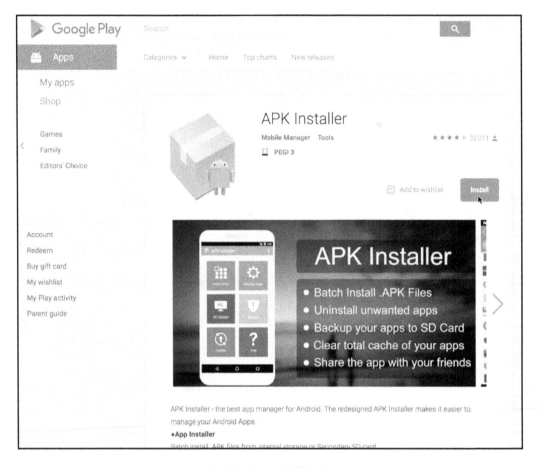

Downloading the Android APK Installer

Excellent work! You can now install and run APK applications to your Android device. This lets you build and test your Unity projects on real Android hardware, and not just through emulation in the editor. When developing for mobiles, testing in-editor is always a great first step, for visualization and convenience, but the device itself should always be the benchmark against which performance and usability is measured.

Building for VR (Virtual Reality)

Right now, there's intense interest in **Virtual Reality** (**VR**) in gaming. This is an umbrella term referring to a range of different wearable headsets that surround the eyes and immerse the player in a 3D virtual world. Head movement is tracked (that is, its rotation is monitored) and used to control what is seen through the headset. Typically, head motion controls a first-person camera in a 3D environment. Unity ships with support for selected VR platforms, including Oculus and Samsung Gear. Developing for VR in Unity is made simple in that most 3D concepts apply to VR. There are a range of interesting design considerations that apply to VR, such as interface design, player height variance, object interactivity, and 2D design.

The *Dead Keys* project is not primarily designed for VR, but this section explores a few steps that could be taken towards integrating VR support in principle. To get started with VR development in Unity, you should download the Oculus Development Kit, from here: `https://developer3.oculus.com/downloads/`.

 Currently, VR development with Oculus is supported only on Windows.

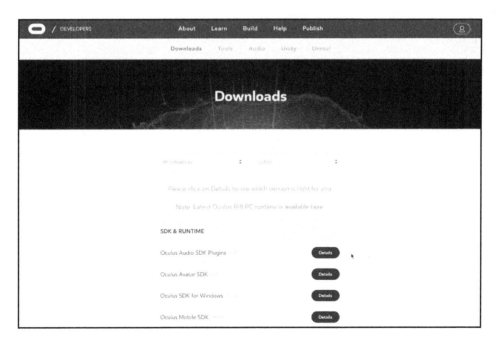

Installing the VR SDK

Next, open the **Player Settings** by choosing **Edit** | **Project Settings** | **Player** from the application menu, and from the object **Inspector** enable the **Virtual Reality Supported** option.

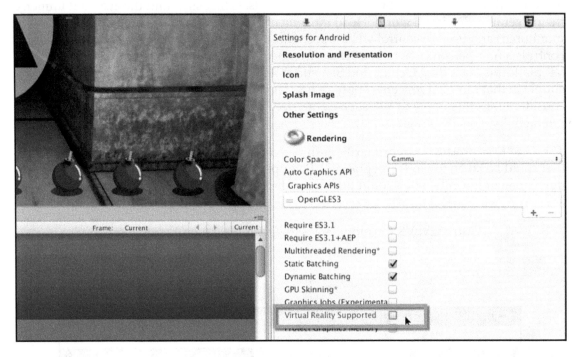

Enabling Virtual Reality Support

On enabling the **Virtual Reality Supported** option, you can select the supported SDK. By default, the only option is **Oculus**. Leave this option selected.

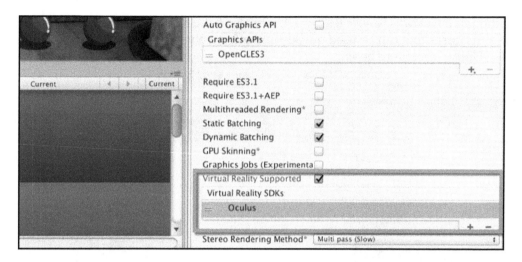

Selecting a VR SDK

Next, download the Oculus Sample Framework for Unity 5, to see a selection of projects and additional classes and libraries for use, here:
`https://developer3.oculus.com/downloads/game-engines/1.5.1/Oculus_Sample_Framework_for_Unity_5_Project/`.

Downloading Oculus Sample Packages

In addition to the *Oculus Sample Packages*, Unity also have a VR Package that features useful scripts and classes that can be used quickly and effectively in VR. This is available for free from the Unity Asset Store here:
`https://www.assetstore.unity3d.com/en/#!/content/51519`.

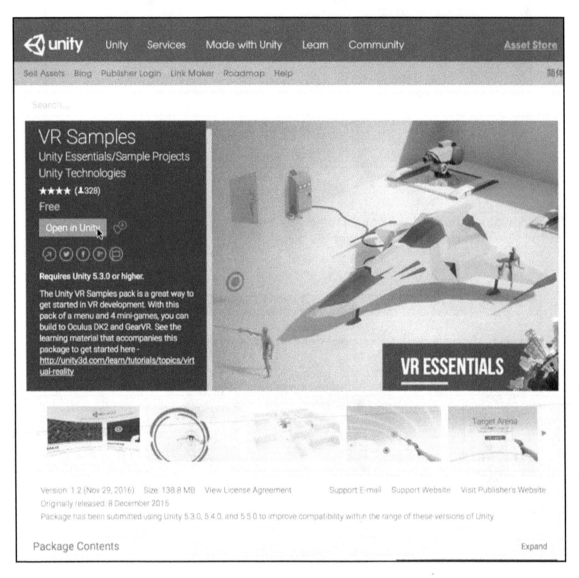

Downloading a VR Unity package

The *Unity VR* package creates two main folders, `VRStandardAssets` and `VRSampleScenes`. The `Standard Assets` folder features reusable scripts and classes for many VR projects, and the `Sample Scenes` folder contains example scenes demonstrating the use of these assets.

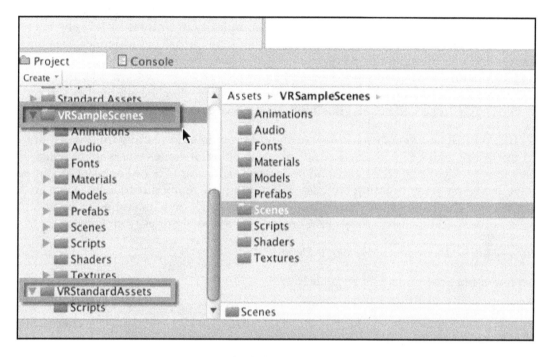

Accessing Sample VR Assets

For more information on working with assets from the `Samples VR Project`, see the online Unity documentation here:
`https://unity3d.com/learn/tutorials/topics/virtual-reality/getting-started-vr-d evelopment?playlist=22946`.

Great work! You're now ready to start working in VR. Thankfully, *Dead Keys* is a first-person project, making it easy to transition to VR. The biggest challenge is in implementing effective keyboard controls when the player cannot see the keyboard, due to wearing a VR headset. To solve this issue, you could create a world space UI for keyboard support, that is, a GUI representation of the keyboard in the world. More information on World Space User Interfaces can be found here:
`https://docs.unity3d.com/Manual/HOWTO-UIWorldSpace.html`.

Summary

Congratulations! You've now reached the end of the *Dead Keys* project, and the end of this book. In reaching this far you've seen a wide range of Unity features; but more importantly, you've seen how many of the features that you already know can be adapted and applied cleverly in an editor to get the results you need. Complexity in Unity is largely about a clever application of existing, simple features; rather than the use of hidden features or advanced tools. In reaching this point you have a Dead Keys project that supports a single player experience on desktop platforms. In the previous chapters, we saw how this experience could be deployed to mobiles, support persistent data, be adapted to VR, and how version control could be integrated into our main development workflow!

The question that now remains is how you should proceed after reading this book. On reaching this point it's a good idea to think about the kind of games you want to make professionally; identifying the genre and style, such as Horror FPS, or Fantasy RPG, or Sci-Fi RTS, and so on. After deciding on these points, there are many directions you can go. You might want to check out specific books and courses focusing on game types, or focus on specific subjects relevant to your genre. Consider the following titles from Packt:

Building an FPS Game with Unity, John P Doran

Mastering Unity Shaders and Effects, Jamie Dean

Procedural Content Generation for Unity Game Development, Ryan Watkins

Index

3

3D formats
  URL 24

A

alpha textures
  about 29
  URL 29
Android Executable Package (APK)
  about 556
  building, for Android 555
  URL 560
Android version
  URL 541
Animation Events 333
animations
  importing 53, 54, 55, 57
animator graph
  configuring 174, 175, 177, 179, 180, 182, 184, 185
App Store submission guidelines
  reference link 556
Application.persistentDataPath
  URL 466
applied Project Management
  Trello, used 380, 381, 382, 389
Artificial Intelligence (AI) 301, 307
asset preparation
  meshes, producing 14
  textures, producing 14
Attack state
  about 304, 330
  developing 331, 332, 333, 334, 335, 336, 337, 338, 339, 340, 341, 342
Audio Source 339
audio

about 147
importing 58, 59
reference link 58

B

Baked lighting 88
baking lightmaps
  details 102
  resolution 94
  size 94
believability 86
binary files
  data, saving 496, 498, 499, 500, 501
BitBucket
  about 442, 444, 445
  URL 442
Blend Swap
  URL 42
bonus items
  creating 290, 292, 293, 294, 296, 297, 298
branches
  and branching 421
Build Target Platform 529
build
  size, optimizing 528, 538
button
  about 208, 210, 212
  coding 215

C

camera
  animating 160, 163, 166, 168, 170, 172, 173
  positioning 362, 363, 364, 365, 366, 367, 369
canvas 204, 207, 346
Chase state
  developing 328
Checked Out 423